D0989346

THE KRYPTON COMPANION

A HISTORICAL EXPLORATION OF SUPERMAN COMIC BOOKS OF 1958-1986

Edited and (Mostly) Written by
Michael Eury

Special Contributions by
Daniel Best · Glen Cadigan · Mike Esposito · David Mandel · Brian K. Morris ·
Will Murray · Jerry Siegel · Curt Swan · Roy Thomas · Al Turniansky · Mark Waid ·
John Wells · Eddy Zeno

Interviews with Superman Writers and Artists
Neal Adams · Murphy Anderson · Cary Bates · Rich Buckler · Nick Cardy ·
Gerry Conway · José Luis García-López · Steve Gerber · Keith Giffen ·
Paul Kupperberg · Elliot S! Maggin · Jim Mooney · Dennis O'Neil · Martin Pasko ·
Al Plastino · Bob Rozakis · Jim Shooter · Len Wein · Marv Wolfman

A Roundtable Discussion with Curt Swan Inkers
Joe Giella · Dick Giordano · Dave Hunt · Bob Oksner · Ty Templeton

A Roundtable Discussion with Superman Writers, Artists, and Editors
Jon Bogdanove · Kurt Busiek · John Byrne · Mike Carlin · Jackson Guice · Dan Jurgens ·
Karl Kesel · Jeph Loeb · David Mandel · Jerry Ordway · Alex Ross · Gail Simone ·
Walter Simonson · Roger Stern · Roy Thomas · Mark Waid

Superman created by Jerry Siegel and Joe Shuster

TwoMorrows Publishing • Raleigh, North Carolina

TM & © DC Comics.

Dedicated to Al Plastino and Murphy Anderson, real-life supermen.

Book design by Rich J. Fowlks.
Front cover art by Dave Gibbons.
Front cover colors by Tom Ziuko.

Back cover art and colors by Curt Swan and Sheldon Moldoff.
Inside front and back cover art by Ross Andru and Mike DeCarlo.

The Krypton Companion logo designed by Robert Clark.
Proofread by John Morrow, Eric Nolen-Weathington, and Christopher Irving.

Acknowledgments

I am indebted to the Super-consultants now dubbed "the Krypton Companion Emergency Squad," whose enthusiasm for and vast knowledge of all things Superman proved invaluable to this book: Will Murray, Mark Waid, John Wells, and Eddy Zeno.

Very special thanks to designer Rich Fowlks for his patience and his talents, and to my beautiful and loving wife Rose Rummel-Eury for allowing me to crawl into the bottle (city of Kandor) for months during the research and completion of this book.

Also, my sincere gratitude to all of the following, who contributed data, art, photos, and/or their time to this book (and my apologies to anyone I might have inadvertently overlooked): Jason Adams, Neal Adams, Joe Ahearn, Jim Alexander, *Alter Ego*, Jim Amash, Jeff Amason, Murphy Anderson, Terry Austin, Mike W. Barr, Pat Bastienne, Cary Bates, Daniel Best, Jon Bogdanove, Judy Bogdanove, Brian Bolland, Chris Boyko, Rich Buckler, Gene Bundy, Mike Burkey (*www.romitaman.com*), Kurt Busiek, John Byrne, Glen Cadigan, Nick Cardy, Mike Carlin, Dewey Cassell, Russ Cochran, Gerry Conway, Ray Cuthbert, DC Comics (*www.dccomics.com*), Alan Davis, Joe Desris, Hank Domzalski, Dennis Dooley, Shelton Drum, Mike Esposito, Mark Evanier, Ron Fernandez, Tom Fleming, José Luis García-López, Gemstone Publishing, Steve Gerber, Dave Gibbons, Frank Giella, Joe Giella, Keith Giffen, Dick Giordano, Grand Comic-Book Database (*www.comics.org*), Jackson Guice, David Hamilton, Wallace Harrington, R. C. Harvey, Heritage Comics (*www.heritagecomics.com*), Ilke Hincer, Bill Howard, Adam Hughes, Bob Hughes, Dave Hunt, Carmine Infantino, Robert Ingersoll, Tony Isabella, *The Jack Kirby Collector*, Dan Jurgens, Karl Kesel, George Khoury, Thomas King, David Kirkpatrick, Paul Kupperberg, Ted Latner, Garry Leach, Paul Levitz, Steve Lipsky, Jeph Loeb, Bruce MacIntosh, Elliot S! Maggin, David Mandel, Sam Maronie, Richard Martines, Yoram Matzkin, Bob McLeod, Sheldon Moldoff, Jim Mooney, Stuart Moore, Brian K. Morris, Cookie Morris, John Morrow, Albert Moy (*www.albertmoy.com*), Edwin Murray, Terry Murray, Eric Nolen-Weathington, Martin O'Hearn, Dennis O'Neil, Bob Oksner, Jerry Ordway, Martin Pasko, John Petty, Adam Philips, Al Plastino, Joel Press, Alex Ross, Bob Rozakis, Scott Saavedra, Bill Schelly, Darrell Schweitzer, Jim Shooter, Gail Simone, Walter Simonson, John Snyder, Roger Stern, Ken Stringer, Cecilia Swan Swift, Ty Templeton, Roy Thomas, Diana Tittle, Al Turniansky, Dr. Michael J. Vassallo, J. C. Vaughn, Jeff Weigel, Steven Weill, Len Wein, Jerry Weist, Hank Weisinger, Jack Williamson, Marv Wolfman, Raul Wrona, and Paul J. Ydstie.

Published by TwoMorrows Publishing • 10407 Bedfordtown Drive • Raleigh, NC 27614
919-449-0344 • www.twomorrows.com

ISBN 1-893905-61-6
First printing, September 2006 • Printed in Canada

TABLE OF CONTENTS

CHAPTER 1

THE KEY TO FORT WEISINGER

SUPERMAN COMICS OF 1958-1964

After Jerry Siegel and Joe Shuster's Man of Tomorrow ignited comics' Golden Age, others carried the torch, illuminating Superman's flight path for the 1950s and beyond.

One such man was Robert J. Maxwell (aka Richard Fielding). A pulp writer-turned-producer, Maxwell brought Superman to the air waves in 1940 in a long-running radio program which introduced Jimmy Olsen, green kryptonite, the Superman/Batman team, and other vital Superman elements. The trailblazing Maxwell guided Superman to the silver screen in 1951 in *Superman and the Mole Men*, and a spin-off television series soon followed, *The Adventures of Superman* (1952–1958). Both starred husky actor George Reeves as the Man of Steel. Reeves made Superman a household name, and during the 1950s he popped up in everything from Kellogg's cereal commercials to a fondly remembered episode of *I Love Lucy*.

Another such man was Whitney Ellsworth. A former cartoonist, Ellsworth joined the DC (then National) Comics New York City staff in 1940 and later became the company's first editorial director. Ellsworth eventually trekked west to Hollywood to work on Maxwell's *Superman* TV series.

And Mort Weisinger was left behind.

Throughout the 1950s, DC editor Weisinger labored, under Ellsworth's editorial direction, to fine tune a well-oiled Super-"locomotive" that chugged along, adventure after adventure, through comic books, radio, TV, a newspaper strip, and a range of licensed products, with artist Wayne Boring's beefy rendition of Superman becoming the hero's signature look. When TV's *Adventures of Superman* closed shop in 1957, Ellsworth continued to work in Hollywood, leaving the Superman titles in Weisinger's hands.

And that's where our story begins.

This chapter's essays, interviews, and special features explore Superman editor Mort Weisinger's expanding "Superman mythology."

Wayne Boring's 1982 recreation of the cover to *Superboy* #1.
TM & © DC Comics. Art courtesy of Heritage Comics.

SUPERMAN COMICS TIMELINE 1958 1959 1960 1961 1962 1963 1964

While "The Super-Key to Fort Superman" in *Action Comics* #241 (June 1958, the Man of Steel's 20th anniversary issue) is now acknowledged by DC Comics as the beginning of Superman's Silver Age, elements associated with the hero's mythos of that era crept into print years earlier. This timeline records major Silver Age-connected milestones prior to "The Super-Key to Fort Superman," then regards *Action* #241 as its starting point for a comprehensive listing of all Superman-related comic-book appearances (per cover-dated years) that followed. (Regrettably, an index of story titles and creator credits is too lengthy for this volume.)

1945
More Fun Comics #101 (first Superboy)

1949
Superboy #1
Superman #58 (Superman's retreat dubbed "Fortress of Solitude")
Superman #61 (first kryptonite in comics)

1950
Superboy #8 (first Superbaby)
Superboy #10 (first Lana Lang)
Superman #65 (first Kryptonian survivors Mala, Kizo, and U-Ban)

1951
Superman and the Mole Men movie
The Adventures of Superman first season filmed

1952
Superman #76 (first Superman/Batman meeting in comics)
Superman #78 (first adult Lana Lang)
The Adventures of Superman debuts on syndicated television

1954
Superman's Pal Jimmy Olsen #1 (first Superman signal watch)
World's Finest Comics #71 (Superman/Batman team-ups begin)

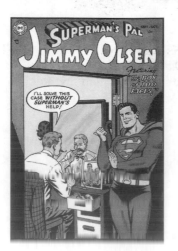

1955
Adventure Comics #210 (first Krypto the Super-Dog)

1957
Showcase #9–10 (Superman's Girl Friend Lois Lane tryout)
World's Finest Comics #88 (first Lex Luthor/Joker team-up)

1958
Mort Weisinger assumes full editorship of Superman titles.
Action Comics #241–247
  (#241: 20th anniversary issue, first Fortress key, Silver Age Superman begins)
  (#242, first Brainiac and Kandor)
Superman #122–125
  (#123: Supergirl prototype)
  (#125: first "Untold Tales of Superman")

Adventure Comics #247 (first Legion of Super-Heroes), 250–255
  (#252: first red kryptonite)
Superboy #66–69
  (#68: first Bizarro)
Superman's Girl Friend Lois Lane #1–5
Superman's Pal Jimmy Olsen #30–33
  (#30: first Krypto with Superman)
  (#31: first Elastic Lad)
World's Finest Comics #93–98

1959
Action Comics #248–259
  (#252: first Supergirl/Kara Zor-El, Argo City, anti-kryptonite; first Silver Age Metallo)
  (#254: first adult Bizarro)
Superman #126–133
  (#127: first Titano the Super-Ape)
  (#129: first Lori Lemaris)
  (#131: first Silver Age Mr. Mxyzptlk)

Adventure Comics #256–267
Superboy #70–77
  (#76: first Beppo the Super-Monkey)
Superman's Girl Friend Lois Lane #6–13
Superman's Pal Jimmy Olsen #34–41
  (#36: first Lucy Lane)
World's Finest Comics #99–106

1960
Action Comics #260–271
  (#261: first Streaky the Super-Cat, X-kryptonite)
  (#262: first yellow sun as explanation for super-powers)
  (#263: first Bizarro World)
  (#267: Supergirl tries out for Legion)
Superman #134–141
  (#127: first Titano the Super-Ape)
  (#129: first Lori Lemaris)
  (#140: first blue kryptonite)
  (#141: "Superman's Return to Krypton," origin of Lyla Lerrol)
Superman Annual #1–2

Adventure Comics #268–279
   (#271: origin of Lex Luthor)
The Brave and the Bold #28–30
   (Justice League of America tryouts;
   with Superman)
Justice League of America #1
Superboy #78–85
   (#80: first Superboy/Supergirl meeting)
   (#83: first Kryptonite Kid)
Superman's Girl Friend Lois Lane
#14–21
Superman's Pal Jimmy Olsen #42–49
   (#48: first Superman [Supermen]
   Emergency Squad)
World's Finest Comics #107–114

A GREAT 3-PART NOVEL!

1961

Action Comics #272–283
   (#279: first white kryptonite)
Superman #142–149
   (#147: first Adult Legion, Legion of
   Super-Villains)
   (#149: "The Death of Superman"
   Imaginary Story)
Superman Annual #3–4

Adventure Comics #280–291
   (#283: first Phantom Zone,
   General Zod)
   (#285: first "Tales of the Bizarro
   World" series)
   (#287: first Dev-Em)
   (#289: first Jax-Ur)
Justice League of America #2–7
Secret Origins #1
Superboy #86–93
   (#86: first Pete Ross)
   (#89: first Mon-El)
   (#90: Pete Ross discovers Superboy's
   Clark Kent identity)
Superman's Girl Friend Lois Lane
#22–29
   (#23: first Lena Thorul, Luthor's sister)

Superman's Pal Jimmy Olsen #50–57
   (#53: first Giant Turtle-Olsen)
   (#57: Imaginary Story: Jimmy Olsen
   marries Supergirl)
World's Finest Comics #115–122

1962

Action Comics #284–295
   (#284: Jor-El discovers Phantom Zone)
   (#285: Superman reveals Supergirl's
   existence to Earth)
   (#286: first Superman Revenge Squad)
   (#293: origin of Comet the
   Super-Horse)
Superman #150–157
   (#157: first gold kryptonite, Quex-Ul)
Superman Annual #5–6

Adventure Comics #292–303
   (#293: first Comet the Super-Horse,
   Legion of Super-Pets)
   (#300: first "Tales of the Legion of
   Super-Heroes")
Justice League of America #8–16
Superboy #94–101
   (#100: first Dr. Zadu and Erndine Ze-
   Da of Phantom Zone)
Superman's Girl Friend Lois Lane
#30–37
Lois Lane Annual #1
Superman's Pal Jimmy Olsen #58–65
World's Finest Comics #123–130
Mystery in Space #75 ("Adam Strange"
series guest-stars Justice League)

1963

Action Comics #296–307
   (#297: first Kru-El, Gra-Mo, and
   Professor Va-Kox)
Superman #158–165
   (#158: first Nightwing and
   Flamebird)
   (#161: death of Ma and Pa Kent)
   (#162: Imaginary Story: "Superman-
   Red and Superman-Blue")

(#164: first planet Lexor [named in
#168])
   (#165: origin of Sally Sellwyn, Clark
   Kent's forgotten girlfriend)
Superman Annual #7–8

Adventure Comics #304–315
Justice League of America #17–24
Superboy #102–109
Superman's Girl Friend Lois Lane
#38–45
Lois Lane Annual #2
Superman's Pal Jimmy Olsen #66–73
   (#70: first silver kryptonite)
   (#72: Elastic Lad becomes honorary
   Legionnaire)
World's Finest Comics #131–138

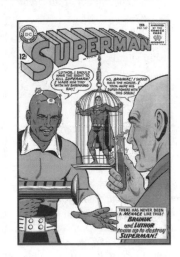

1964

Action Comics #308–319
   (#309: Superman reveals secret
   identity to President Kennedy)
   (#310: first jewel kryptonite)
Superman #166–173
   (#167: first Lex Luthor/Brainiac
   team-up)
   (#170: "Superman's Mission for
   President Kennedy!" published in
   honor of assassinated president)

80-Page Giant #1 (Superman), 2
(Jimmy Olsen), 3 (Lois Lane)
Adventure Comics #316–327
Justice League of America #25–32
Superboy #110–117
Superboy Annual #1
Superman's Girl Friend Lois Lane
#46–53
Superman's Pal Jimmy Olsen #74–81
World's Finest Comics #139–146
   (#142: first Composite Superman)

Superman's Editor Mort Weisinger

by Will Murray

A shorter version of this article was originally published in Comic Book Marketplace #58 (Apr. 1998). It was expanded by the author with additional information on March 24, 2006. Reprinted by permission of Gemstone Publishing, Inc., and the author. © 2006 Will Murray. All rights reserved.

Twenty years ago, in the summer of 1976, I squandered a wonderful opportunity when, through a mutual friend, I was privileged to spend a few hours at the Great Neck, Long Island, New York, home of the legendary Mort Weisinger, probably the most prolific and influential Superman comics editor ever. With tape recorder in hand I interviewed Mort at length, while he walked me through his photo album of the great and near great.

Unfortunately, my interest in Mort lay in his pulp career and his friendship with Lester Dent, creator of Doc Savage. We only touched upon Superman and his career at DC Comics, which lasted from 1941 to 1970.

Everybody who came into contact with Mort has a favorite story. Some like to tell of his overbearing nature, or repeat the tale of the writer who once attempted to force the 300-pound editor out a DC office window to his doom. The writer's name varies depending on who's telling the story. Weisinger was infamous for rejecting writers' plots, then offering a rejected plot as "his" idea to the next scripter writer to walk through his door.

My story is different. I met him only once, exchanged only a couple of subsequent letters with him, but

Photo courtesy of Glen Cadigan.

he treated me very kindly, despite limping around on a bandaged-up, gout-stricken foot, proudly showing me some of his earliest professional pulp sales in half-forgotten titles like *Popular Detective* and *Wonder Stories*.

It's popular these days to denigrate the Weisinger-era Superman with its reliance on formularized gimmicky plots and cookie-cutter art. Yet his Superman family enjoyed consistent sales today's editors would kill for.

The Mort Weisinger I met was prouder of his extracurricular writing than his comics editing.

"I write for the two largest magazines in America, *Readers Digest* and *Parade*," he told me proudly.

It hadn't always been that way. Weisinger started off as a science-fiction fan. While at summer camp, he borrowed a copy of the Aug. 1928 *Amazing Stories* from his counselor. It was an important issue. The seminal Buck Rogers story *Armageddon 2419* and the first installment of E. E. Smith's classic *The Skylark of Space* were both featured.

This brought Weisinger into contact with local SF fans, and a new world opened up for him.

Julius Schwartz recalled their memorable first meeting in "My Amazing Story," *Amazing Stories* (May 1993):

"Mort was a lovable kind of kid who had an easy way of making friends. I walked a couple of miles across the Bronx

because I didn't have trolley fare and showed up for the meeting in the basement of the house where Mort and his parents lived. As I started down the steps to the door, I was stampeded by a dozen or so other kids tripping over themselves to get out. It almost marked the dissolution of the Science's because of Mort's creative bookkeeping.

"'Well,' Mort explained to me, 'we pay ten cents dues each meeting, y'know, for expenses and to put out a club bulletin called *The Planet*, and when I gave the treasurer's report I announced that there was zero dollars and zero cents in the treasury. I explained that I saw some science-fiction magazines and I bought them'—Mort hesitated, looked at the ceiling—'and I went to the movies and I spent the money on a date. I told them I was going to replace it, but they got so mad they all stormed out.'"

Schwartz decided to stick around. They were 16, and became fast friends and remained so until the day death separated them.

Together, they launched the first science-fiction fanzine, *The Time Traveller*, in 1932, obtaining contributions from such future stars as Jerry Siegel and Forrest J. Ackerman.

Weisinger broke into professional print with "The Price of Peace," a short story first privately published as a fan pamphlet, and later accepted for the Nov. 1932 *Amazing Stories*. Thus began a writing career that included fiction and nonfiction done under his own name and a collection of anagrammatic pseudonyms like Ian Rectez and Tom Erwin Geris.

For Mort Weisinger, who was born on April 25, 1915, had a very specific career goal in mind. He was going be a doctor.

Truthfully, it was his father's dream. Applying to NYU, Weisinger majored in journalism, a fact he kept from his father:

"I was 19 at the time, writing my way through college grinding out pseudo-scientific stuff at 1/2 cents a word for *Amazing Stories*, Hugo Gernsback's old *Wonder Stories*, and *Secret Agent X*. I wanted to become a surgeon, and fantasy tales were a byproduct of my science courses. As a hobby, I edited *The Time Traveller*, the first SF fan magazine. Harry Bates, editor of *Astounding Stories* when Clayton owned the title, used to help me get material for this little sheet, even though he wouldn't buy my stuff. One day he phoned his star contributor, Arthur Burks, arranged for me to interview him. And that is why I never became a doctor.

"I'll never forget the impression meeting Burks made on my unprofessional soul. He had just received his mail, and slit open an envelope that contained 12 fat checks. Art let me soak up the glamour of his studio, talked shop, and invited me to call often. Months later, when I became eligible for membership in the American Fiction Guild, he signed me up, brought me to one of their luncheons. Mixing with the writers, editors, and agents there I wised up, organized a part-time agency of my own, handling science fiction only."

This was the Solar Sales Service (SSS). Weisinger's partner in the venture was Julius Schwartz, later through interesting convolutions of fate to succeed him as editor of Superman. SSS clients included H. P. Lovecraft, Henry Kuttner, Robert Bloch, Edmond Hamilton, and their most famous discovery, Stanley G. Weinbaum.

The pair had many divergent paths to follow before converging again, as Weisinger recalled:

"It was while hustling for my clients in and out of editorial offices that I met Leo Margulies, chief at Standard Magazines. A short while later one of Leo's associate editors left, leaving him in a hole. He hired me to plug the dike. I went after my degree at night, eventually decided that the only surgery I'd ever do would be cutting excess wordage on overwritten manuscripts."

Shortly thereafter, Margulies purchased *Wonder Stories*, renaming it *Thrilling Wonder Stories*. That magazine would be Weisinger's main responsibility. The year was 1935. He was 20, and already an operator. *Wonder Stories* editor Charles Hornig was supposed to continue editing the new version of *Wonder*, but Weisinger fast-talked Margulies into dumping Hornig, leaving him in full control.

Under Weisinger's guidance, *Thrilling Wonder* developed a reputation for juvenile covers and stories that Mort felt was undeserved. He laid the blame on his publisher, Ned Pines.

"Pines didn't know anything about the business. He'd call me in on the carpet about covers. He'd want a monster on every cover. That's when I created the BEM—the bug-eyed monster. I couldn't get over to him that some of these covers would be a hell of a lot more provocative *without* a monster. I would have to slip in what I'd call good science fiction, but if you didn't read it, you'd think *Thrilling Wonder Stories* was a blood-and-thunder magazine. That was just the mask it wore. Inside I had some damn good stories. I'd have stories with no action at all."

His duties weren't limited to SF. With fellow editors Jack Schiff and Bernard Breslauer, both of whom would later follow him to DC Comics, Weisinger took turns editing titles ranging from *The Phantom Detective* to *Thrilling Love Stories*. For *Thrilling Wonder Stories*, he naturally purchased tales through the Solar Sales Service, which he had left in Julie Schwartz's capable hands.

Standard had a bizarre system. In order for a story to be bought, three associate editors had to approve the purchase. Since he was the only person on staff familiar with science fiction, the other two editors soon learned to defer to his judgment. And so Mort beat the system. As he frequently would.

Just as he would later edit a flock of comics titles, Weisinger cut his teeth on pulp magazines, many of which featured heroic crime fighters.

"I edited *Thrilling Wonder Stories, Startling Stories, Captain Future, G-Men, Thrilling Detective, Phantom Detective, Black Book Detective, Popular Detective, Thrilling*

Conrad H. Ruppert, Julius Schwartz, Otto Binder, Charles D. Hornig, Jack Darrow, Mort Weisinger.

JULY, 1935

A sextet of SF luminaries, before they were stars. From Julius Schwartz's personal files; type-written caption and date by Schwartz.
Photo courtesy of Heritage Comics.

Adventures, and *Thrilling Mystery*," he recounted. "Then I read on all of them, in addition to the ones I edited and closed, did the copyediting and worked with the writers. It was a very good system, because with the training you had there, you we were proficient enough to work in any type of medium. Love stories, ghost stories, sports stories, science fiction. You were a switch hitter, so to speak. It was great experience you could never get anywhere else."

Mort Weisinger was first and foremost an idea man.

"We were constructionists," he explained. "We always studied Dumas, Jules Verne, H. G. Wells, Nick Carter, Tarzan—Edgar Rice Burroughs. We believed a story had a beginning, a

(left) Mort Weisinger with Erle Korjak, 1930s; and (right) Ray Bradbury and Leo Margulies, 1930s. Julius Schwartz collection.

middle, and an end. And with gimmicks. There was not one story sold that we did not think the gimmicks up. We invented them. And the gimmicks were very much along the lines of Sherlock Holmes. The deduction. I remember a Phantom Detective gimmick: He's in a trap, gas is coming into the room, *What is he going to do?* Well, he stands on tiptoe, gets a match, and lights the gas. They come in, expect to find him dead, and he jumps them! These are things the readers would appreciate. You think of your gimmick and write your story from that."

One of his tasks at Standard was to write stories written around covers. Out of this sometimes frustrating duty he began thinking about covers. Then rethinking them.

"In those days we weren't as much into covers as we are today," he told me. "The cover would be more or less symbolic of subtle violence. So we didn't have to sync the cover and the novel. So they could write anything more or less. We'd show a knife pointing at the hero or something like that. And later when I found out what publishing was about and I realized that sales could be hooked to covers, I started this whole evolution in the industry. Think of the cover first, and get a story written around it. Instead of waiting till it's all done and painting yourself into a corner, and ask, what is my cover going to be? That was my creative contribution to the whole field."

This pulp sales technique would later reshape how DC comic books were packaged and marketed. Weisinger later recycled some of those BEM-style covers for the Superman titles.

"It was the greatest training ground in the world," Weisinger recalled to me. "Practically all our writers made it in Hollywood. George Bruce. Steve Fisher. Frank Gruber. Richard Sale. Sale went on to do a hell of a lot of good pictures. Leigh Brackett. I was the one who introduced her to Ed Hamilton, who she married. But she did a lot of John Wayne pictures. She's done some *Rockford Files*. She did *Hatari*. She did *Rio Bravo*."

Still, it was a grind. Standard published the largest string of pulps at that time, including love, Western, and sports titles. Each editor was required to be proficient in every genre. Margulies often purchased rejects at sub-standard rates. Weisinger, Schiff, and other so-called "trained seals" were expected to revise them in-house. The pay was not wonderful.

"The only world my friends and I knew was pulp," Weisinger once lamented. "Every time I pressed a typewriter key, out rolled, 'The body fell to the floor with a dull, sickening thud.'"

Still, there were bright moments. Weisinger was allowed to start a companion to *Thrilling Wonder Stories*. He called it *Startling Stories*, after a fictitious pulp magazine mentioned in one of his own stories.

Then came Captain Future.

Weisinger convinced Margulies to attend the First World Science Fiction Convention, held in New York City in July 1939. Margulies, impressed by SF fans, blurted, "I didn't know you fans could be so damn sincere." On the spot, he promised them a new magazine built around an SF hero.

It fell to Weisinger to concoct the details. "I had the feeling that a personality character and a team—a science-fiction parallel to Doc Savage—would go," he recalled. "And we gave him some unique props, a robot, an android, and a living brain. It did well while Ed Hamilton was writing them."

Cribbing ideas from Doc Savage and elsewhere, Mort came up with a mutant superman initially dubbed Mr. Future. But Ed Hamilton modified the elements he thought were unworkable. Some of these ideas, including the hero's robot double and shape-shifting pet, would later find their way into Weisinger's Superman and Legion of Super-Heroes mythos.

Then came the offer that would lift him out of the pulp jungle. While at Standard, he had worked with a curly-haired cartoonist-turned-writer named Whitney Ellsworth on *The Phantom Detective* and *G-Men*. Ellsworth had been an early editor of *More Fun Comics*, did publicity in Hollywood, then drifted into pulp writing. Somehow, Ellsworth was lured back by the new owners of the comics house he had once quit—the renamed DC Comics—as editorial director.

"Whit came from California and knew Leo Margulies," Weisinger reminisced. "Leo said to me, 'Why don't you try Whit on *Black Bat*?' So I gave him a springboard and he wrote half of it. He brings in the half and I read it. Then he calls me up and asks, how is it? I said, 'Well, over here, this has to be changed. . .' And he didn't give me a chance to finish. He cuts me off and says, 'Well, stick it up your ass. Forget it.' I said, 'Wait a minute. I like it! Those are little things. I'm going to take care of it myself. I want you to finish it.' I gave him the advance and he started writing for me and he did all *Black Bat*s.

"Then one day we're out to lunch and he said to me, 'How much you making a week?' And I said, '35.' So he says, 'How would you like 50?' That was a lot of money then. I said, 'What was the job?' He said, 'Be editor of *Superman*.' I said, 'What's that?' And he told me. But he said, "What I want you to do is shape up *Batman* and other magazines because *Superman* is in a groove with Jerry Siegel. Try the way he recommended you.' Siegel and I were old friends. We used to work on a fan magazine together

(left to right) Robert Maxwell, National (DC) Comics President Harry Donenfeld, Mrs. Donenfeld, and Whitney Ellsworth, Selznick Studios, Culver City, July 1951

"I thought, *What do I know about comic books?* So I called up Otto Binder. He gave me a crash course in about two hours. 'It's very simple,' he said. 'You get a fight, the hero hits the villain on the head with a lamp and says, "*Lights out for you!*" Then I read it and got my own perspective. And I thought, 'What they need are more stories and plots.'"

Weisinger was hired as an associate editor. He was given a desk, a typewriter, and instructions to create three new characters. The result was Aquaman, Johnny Quick, and Green Arrow, who populated *More Fun* and enjoyed long existences in and out of other magazines. He also devised Tommy Tomorrow, Air Wave, and TNT, and scripted features like the Sandman, the Seven Soldiers of Victory, the Tarantula, and others.

Weisinger joined National (DC) Comics in the latter months of 1940. His duties were varied, and included some involvement with the *Superman* radio show that debuted the previous February.

One thing that separated him from other comics editors was to begin thinking about the field in the long term. As he explained to *The Amazing World of DC Comics* (issue #7, July–Aug. 1975), "When I took over *Superman*, a friend of mine told me that these characters, super-heroes, were cycle things that 'can't last three or four years.' So it became a challenge to me . . . to prevent Superman from being just a fad."

With the pulp magazine field dying, Mort settled into his new career. Then came Pearl Harbor.

"It was a very good job and it paid so well that I shelved all thoughts of ever doing any extracurricular writing," Weisinger recalled. "I was in a golden rut, and I would still be enjoying it if it weren't for the fact that two years later they picked a capsule with my number in it out of a fishbowl."

In "I Write From 0800 to 1800" (*Writer's Digest*, Apr. 1943), Weisinger told it this way: "One morning late last July when the mailbox disgorged a letter to me conveying greetings from the president. I taxied to my office, cleared the decks for my successor, and kissed my typewriter and secretary goodbye for the duration."

His successor was no less than Jack Schiff, whom Weisinger installed for the duration—with the tacit understanding that Schiff would relinquish the job once Weisinger was mustered out of the service. Weisinger found Army life surprisingly agreeable.

"Five-forty-five a.m. reveille at Camp Dix two weeks thereafter was a pleasure," he boasted in his 1944 *Writer's Digest* article, "A Yank at Yale." "It was the first morning in nine years that I didn't have to worry about a deadline, a caption, a missing piece of copy, or a drunken writer. A magazine to me now was merely a storage place for ammunition, and a typewriter was slang for a machine gun."

THE SUPERMAN MYTHOLOGY:
SEEING DOUBLE

Weisinger was fond of recycling pulp cover gimmicks for his Superman family titles. These noteworthy "bug-eyed monster" specimens "introduce" Jimmy Olsen's robotic "Private Monster" and his obedient giant ant Llanix:

Startling Stories (Mar. 1940)
© 1940 Better Publications, Inc.

Jimmy Olsen #43 (Mar. 1960)
TM & © DC Comics.

Jimmy Olsen #47 (Sept. 1960)
TM & © DC Comics.

Thrilling Wonder Stories (Dec. 1938)
© 1938 Better Publications, Inc.

Jimmy Olsen #54 (July 1961)
TM & © DC Comics.

At first, Weisinger was assigned to Cook and Baker School, but he sweet-talked the secretary to a high-ranking officer into getting a transfer to a more glamorous post at Yale, where his editorial skills could shine.

"One stunt I particularly enjoyed was getting Superman to come to Yale—literally. I dreamed up a rough outline for a story wherein Clark (Superman) Kent gets assigned to investigate training conditions at the AAF School at Yale for his paper. Whit Ellsworth came up here for the story conference, kicked the plot around until we had ironed out all the wrinkles. The finished product was a "Keep 'em Flying" story that has Superman proving that the job of the ground crew technician can be just as glamorous as flying a P-38 through enemy ack-ack."

"I Sustain the Wings" appeared in *Superman* #25 (Nov.–Dec. 1943). It was one of the very few times Weisinger scripted a comics story. The title came from an Air Force radio show he wrote for Glenn Miller.

It was while in the army that Staff Sergeant Weisinger met a registered nurse named Thelma Rudnick. They met on a train. Impulsively, Weisinger proposed en route. They were married on September 27, 1943.

Returning from the war, he took his place beside Jack Schiff, who was asked to stay on. They switched off editing the Superman and Batman family of magazines.

But Weisinger was not happy sharing power. He wanted his own little fiefdom, according to Schiff:

"I have a long letter of (Mort's) from when he was on vacation once, in which he laid out a detailed plan of a Red Team and a Blue Team. And then we'd switch around because we both knew all the characters. I think he broached it to the front office and they didn't like the idea. But he was determined to break away and be on his own."

The break finally came in 1953, when the National editorial arrangement was subdivided into specific groups, each with its own editor, who in turn had his own stable of writers and artists. Rarely did a member of one man's stable cross the hallway to work for another.

When Superman went to TV, Weisinger joined producer Ellsworth as story editor. "Every year the New York office would lend me Mort Weisinger for a few weeks to act as story editor," Ellsworth once reminisced. "Together we knew as much about Superman as it was possible to know. So in advance of production we'd lock ourselves in a room and work on stories. Once we did it on the train trip from New York to Los Angeles. By the time we were ready to hand out writing assignments we were able to give the writers outlines of what we wanted—not just so-called premises but complete step-by-step storylines in almost every case."

When Ellsworth stepped down as editorial director in the '50s, Weisinger took over the Superman titles, leaving Schiff with the less prestigious Batman family. DC publisher Jack Liebowitz knew that if he promoted either Weisinger or Schiff to editor-in-chief, the other would quit. Prudently, he left the spot vacant.

In the post-war period, comics sales were in decline and super-heroes were fading. With writers Ed Hamilton and Otto Binder, the former Solar Sales client who had coached him on the ins and outs of comic books back in 1940, Weisinger set about reinventing and modernizing Superman.

"I originated such characters as Bizarro, Krypto, Supergirl, Superbaby, *r* *antara*, and assigned them to various writers for scripting," Weisinger told

Mort Weisinger at the wheel of the *Albatross*, next to Doc Savage creator Lester Dent, circa 1935. Dent owned the boat from 1934–1937 and occasionally took Mort on day and weekend trips.
Photo courtesy of Will Murray.

The Legion Outpost in 1974. "I also invented the Bottle City of Kandor, the Phantom Zone, the 'LL' running gag—Lois Lane, Lana Lang, Lori Lemaris, *et al.*, the properties of the various forms of kryptonite—with the exception of Green K, which was the invention of Robert Maxwell, producer of the *Superman* radio series which featured Superman; Maxwell also introduced Jimmy Olsen there. I think the innovation I'm proudest of was the use of the imaginary story to present stories that weren't otherwise possible. And I also created the series 'Tales of Krypton.'"

One of the elements that surely came from Weisinger was Superman's Fortress of Solitude. He had earlier cribbed the idea of a North Pole laboratory-hideaway for his Captain Future and now with *Doc Savage* off the stands, cribbed it again.

"I think my greatest contribution to Superman was to give him a 'mythology' which covered all bases," Weisinger added. "All this makes Superman credible. I also went to lengths to elaborate on the 'Superman family,' and cross-pollinated these relationships by simultaneously interweaving their causes and effects in magazines appearing during one month."

This included expanding the line of Superman titles to areas previously thought unsupportable.

"I created the *Lois Lane* and *Jimmy Olsen* books over a lot of opposition as spin-offs from *Superman*," he related. "The management protested that the characters weren't strong enough and they'd never go. But I had a gut feeling . . . and I had talked to kids. I'm not taking credit for the success of those books, but I did know my Superman character and mythology, and the proof of success was in the box office."

Weisinger not only talked to kids in order to test-market ideas, they talked back through fan mail. When they complained that the invulnerable Man of Steel could not give a blood transfusion to Lois Lane, Mort explained that Superman punctured his own skin with his super-hard fingernail. Under pressure to update Lois Lane, he gave her a Jackie Kennedy-style hairdo. Jimmy Olsen was promoted from cub to full reporter.

"The kids still love this sort of stuff," he told *The New York Times* in 1962. "But in putting together the book we have to bear in mind that the kids are much more sophisticated than they were 20 years ago. There are a lot of things they just won't accept nowadays."

The Space Race of the late 1950s and '60s also forced Weisinger to stay in his toes with kids who liked fantasy, but demanded a recognizable dose of realism mixed in. Students at MIT monitored the feature for violations of the laws of physics. When hundreds of letters complained about Superman taking Lois Lane into outer space without benefit of a pressure suit, Weisinger decreed that from that point on, Superman had to place her in a NASA-style astronaut garb.

With Otto Binder, he created the most enduring Superman spin-off, the Legion of Super-Heroes.

"The first Legion story was a spontaneous idea—no thought that the readers would flip over it and demand a spate of sequels," Weisinger confessed.

Perhaps most significantly, Mort Weisinger reinvented the Man of Steel for this increasingly sophisticated audience.

"Why should Superman fly?" he once asked rhetorically. "So he came from another planet and there's a difference in gravity. Why should he be able to *fly*? Why should he have X-ray vision? It's contrary to science and to reason. I originated the concept that in a world circling a yellow sun his powers are multiplied, and that yellow sun gave him these abilities. These are things the originators of Superman didn't figure out; they gave us this fabulous character without explaining why all his fabulous attributes existed."

With the demise of the *Superman* TV series in 1958, Weisinger understood that the Man of Steel would have to keep flying unassisted by television exposure.

"I would bring out a new element every six months," he told *The Amazing World of DC Comics.* "The Phantom Zone, which would bring to life criminals from Krypton . . . the bottled city of Kandor, in which we recreated Krypton's former civilization . . . the whole mythology which made Superman different from all the other bigshot bang-crash heroic characters."

Although he was notoriously tyrannical with his writers and artists—stories abound of him browbeating, even terrorizing scripters ranging from pros like Batman co-creator Bill Finger to his discovery, teenaged Legion of Super-Heroes writer Jim Shooter—Weisinger had a soft spot for two writers in particular, Ed Hamilton, whom he read as a teenager and edited at Standard, and perhaps the most surprising of all, Jerry Siegel.

"Jerry, whom I consider the most competent of all the Superman writers," Weisinger revealed in *The Legion Outpost,* "established the foundation for the series. What his successors did was just embroidery, including my own contributions. Siegel was the best emotional writer of them all—as in the unforgettable 'Death of Luthor' (*Action Comics* #286, Mar. 1962)."

Weisinger also credited Siegel with the Legion of Super-Heroes' formative success, saying, "He revitalized the series after Binder went stale in it."

The 1960s found Mort Weisinger at career mid-point. He had edited *Superman* for a generation.

"In a sense, Superman commands greater believability now than he did two decades ago," he reflected in 1962. "Now our audience consists to a large degree of the children of former readers; the old folks now and then peek over the shoulder of their kids and get a nostalgic twinge. I think the parents help us sell the magazine."

And in a way he was himself famous—more famous than Jerry Siegel and Joe Shuster, who had dropped out of the public eye.

"The influence I had on other people's lives scares me," he once observed. "I'm astounded that people in America know such phrases as 'Up, up, and away,' 'Faster than a speeding bullet,' 'mild-mannered reporter,' and 'kryptonite.' Lois Lane and Superman are as well known as Romeo and Juliet. A lot of times I'm going to an airport and I talk to the driver. And he'll say, 'What do you do?' And I'll say, 'I'm a writer.' 'What do you write?' 'I'll tell you what, I'll make you a bet. That you would have read what I've written or seen it on television. And I'll let

The Man of Bronze's Fortress of Solitude, the prototype for the Man of Steel's headquarters.

A Wayne Boring 1973 political cartoon takes a shot at Weisinger's "hands-on" style.

Weisinger's kid-friendly Super-world ignored the violent Vietnam conflict—until *Superman* #216 (May 1969), which featured a rare Superman cover by Joe Kubert.

you be the judge. I'll rely on your honesty . . . I'm so convinced you've read or seen it that you'll have to say yes. He'll say, 'Okay.' Then I say, 'Ever heard of *Superman*?'

"I've never met anyone who *didn't*," Weisinger chuckled. "Except when I was in Russia. I told this story and they screwed it up in the fan magazine that DC puts out. I met Khrushchev. And his interpreter said, 'This is Mr. Weisinger.' 'What does he do?' 'He's a journalist.' 'What kind of journalist?' The interpreter says, 'He's the editor of *Superman*,' and explains that Superman is known as the Man of Steel, the champion of the oppressed.

"And Khrushchev said, 'The Man of Steel cannot get through the Iron Curtain!'"

Still, even that acclaim began to wear on him.

"Maybe times I'd be walking down the street and I'd say to myself, 'A guy who thinks up story ideas for Superman has to be nuts.' At least he'd have to think like a wild man," Weisinger lamented. "In all, with assists from an agile staff, I produced more than 2000 stories and plotted scores of TV films. The incessant deadline pressures sent me to a shrink, gave me an ulcer, hypertension, and insomnia."

In truth, for many years Weisinger existed on a rollercoaster of uppers and downers, which eventually led to an unpublicized nervous breakdown.

One of his last published pieces was a *Parade* article, "I Flew With Superman," October 23, 1977, in

THE MAN OF STEEL CANNOT GET THROUGH THE IRON CURTAIN!

which he reflected on his long comics career.

"Am I sorry I split from Superman after having virtually been his soulmate for 30 years?" Weisinger reflected. "I have mixed emotions. To be honest, Superman gave me a hang-up. I resented basking in his reflected glory. I was jealous of him. But then I realized Superman had the same frustrations."

Times were changing. Over at Marvel, Spider-Man was cutting into Superman's 40-year supremacy. Where before letters often challenged logical lapses or crowed over boo-boos that had gotten past Weisinger. As the '60s neared their end, the character of the letters began changing. Readers wondered why Superman wasn't solving social ills or dealing with the seemingly endless stalemate in Vietnam.

"I sweated over those Vietnam letters for a week before coming up with a halfway good answer," Weisinger told a reporter. "I finally replied that 'We figure the U.S. is powerful enough to reach a just and proud settlement of the war without Superman.' Now as I look back, I realize the answer was a cop-out. I could have done better if I had said, 'Superman doesn't believe either side is morally right in this struggle,' or 'Superman had never killed any man or animal in his entire existence, and he's not going to start now.' If you think back, the only time an enemy of Superman ever lost his life was when he self-destructed."

After 30 years, and at 55, ten years short of retirement age, Weisinger found himself something of a brontosaurus.

"Today's kids are too much for me," he observed at the time. "They're so far ahead of us in sophistication. The old villains aren't really their villains. Maybe they don't relate as much to pure fiction and diabolical plots to take over the world. Maybe they want stories that fit their experience better. Maybe they've seen so much, it's limited rather than stretched their imaginations. Anyway, I knew I'd had it. Dreaming up socially conscious plots on the kid level really turns me off."

But there were other reasons. Weisinger had sold a best-seller, *The Contest*, which in turn sold to the movies. He had hit the big-time. And made sure his coworkers knew it. The $125,000 advance check was thumbtacked to a DC wall for a solid week.

However, Weisinger, still busy at National, didn't really write the novel. He only plotted it, turning the writing over to a number of writers who

THE SUPERMAN MYTHOLOGY:
FAMOUS MONSTERS OF MORTLAND

Weisinger and his writers raided the late-night TV graveyard for not-so-threatening monsters to populate the Superman titles, as seen in this sampling of comics covers.

© 1933 RKO Pictures

TM & © DC Comics.

© 1941 Universal Pictures

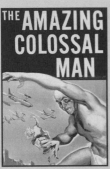
TM & © DC Comics.

© 1957 American International Pictures.

TM & © DC Comics.

© 1957 Universal International Pictures.

TM & © DC Comics.

© 1962 RKO/Toho.

TM & © DC Comics.

assembly-line fashion, but didn't share in the royalties. The true number of writers may never been known, but they include old-time pulpsters like Ryerson Johnson and Jean Francis Webb to comics hands such as David Vern and Bob Haney. Dorothy Woolfolk reportedly edited the mélange of styles into a seamless whole.

The unexpected death of an old pulp-writing friend, Frank Gruber, also played a role in Weisinger's decision to make a clean break from comic books. He told friends he had several unrealized dreams and wanted to pursue them while still relatively young.

Echoing his earlier "golden rut" comment, Weisinger told *The Amazing World of DC Comics* in 1975, "I couldn't learn from anyone up there. *They* learned from *me*! At my salary you could say it was a golden graveyard, but it was a graveyard nonetheless."

Weisinger plunged into a new book project, *The Amazing Aquarius*, about a presidential astrologer, but it would never see publication. He monitored the progress of *Superman: The Movie* when it was in its pre-production stages, offering his own take on the project.

"The way I would have done it," he said in 1975, "I would have the story involve Superman having to go back into the past to Krypton. I would have three-quarters on the thing on the planet Krypton. It would be a terrific thing, even greater than *2001: A Space Odyssey*. And the whole suspense is: can Superman prevent Krypton from blowing up?"

For years, Weisinger had warned Julie Schwartz that if anything happened to him, he was next in line to edit *Superman*. Schwartz always said he didn't want the job. But when the time came, he took it. The era of Mort Weisinger was over.

Yet in 1978, on the eve of the premiere of *Superman: The Movie*, the new, improved Superman wasn't cutting it either and DC, casting about for a solution, was on the verge of asking Mort to come back out of semi-retirement— he was doing the college circuit lecturing on the "Superman Mystique"—when Weisinger was felled by a heart attack on May 7.

At the time, his death was duly noted by a comics fandom that thought it had outgrown him. Yet nearly 20 years later there is no editor left on the scene with his credentials—or his unique ability to sell comic books to young readers.

*WILL MURRAY is the author of over 50 books and novels. A Superman reader since 1961, his novelette, "The Riddle of Superman's Mask" (*The Further Adventures of Superman, *Bantam Books, 1993) is a tribute to the Weisinger-era Man of Steel.*

Weisinger's novel *The Contest* peeked under the tiara of the beauty pageant.

A FOND REMEMBRANCE OF MORT WEISINGER BY HIS SON

by Eddy Zeno

Mort and Thelma Weisinger had two children, Hendrie ("Hank") and Joyce. Hank became a psychologist with expertise in the applications of emotional intelligence and anger management. He is also an author and a renowned public speaker. Dr. Weisinger was happy to reminisce about his dad, excerpted from a longer interview conducted on November 14, 2003 and revised by Hank on December 5, 2004.

HANK WEISINGER: I have many great memories of my dad and I love speaking about them. But first, I want to clarify two points that are often written about him in books about comics and books about Superman.

It has often been said by those who worked with him—his writers, his artists—that he was highly abrasive and critical. I remember one time a writer said that he was having terrible headaches at work and he came to realize it was because of "Mort Weisinger's criticism." I have no doubt that is true. He was very tough and at times abrasive. As an expert in anger management, I would say he had an anger-management problem. I remember one writer, Bob Bernstein, gave my father a garbage pail for Christmas with a note: "Mort, thought you could use this for my work!" And he was like this outside of work, too. My mother would often be embarrassed by the way he would treat waiters and waitresses at restaurants. One time a college friend came to visit me and he had this fiery red Brillo-like beard. When we went out for dinner, my father spent the whole night making beard jokes. My mother was embarrassed; I think my father was probably angry, but to tell you the truth, they *were* funny jokes.

So yes, he was abrasive and critical and he was a tough boss. A lot of people probably didn't like him because of this. Now, here's what is *not* said. One of the reasons my father was a difficult boss was that he thought the people working with him were "idiots." He felt very few were creative and could write well. As a result, this created much more work for him. He would give a writer a story idea, then the writer would do it. Problem was that it was so bad he would have to do it over. No wonder he was abrasive. Many times he wanted to quit, but they would offer him more stock, more money. He used to call it "the golden handcuffs." A lot of the other editors were jealous of [his] success. And yes, my father would love to gloat, which I am sure did not make him more likable. So he was abrasive and critical, but from what he used to tell me, I think it was because of his frustration from having to work with low-level creative people.

Next, it is often written that my dad would take credit for other peoples' ideas. No way; it was just the opposite. He thrived on creativity, on being original, and he despised mediocrity. The fact is, his job would have been a lot less stressful if others

Mort Weisinger, 1960s.
Photo courtesy of Hank Weisinger.

had made significant contributions. That's what he wanted. He would always give credit to others. One day, for example, he gets a letter from a kid in [Pennsylvania] whose name was Jimmy Shooter and my father said to me, "Hank, look at this. It's good." The kid had drawn out a whole story. End result, he gets a job and goes up the comic ladder. Same thing with young Cary Bates, who I believe graduated to [the] television version of *Superboy*. At my Masters graduation ceremony, Rod Serling was the speaker. Afterward, I introduced myself to him and mentioned my father. I will always remember what he said: "You should be very proud of your father. He is a very talented man." Ray Bradbury told me the same thing. Fact is, my dad didn't need to take credit for other people's ideas. To him, ideas were a dime a dozen. No doubt if he had gone to Hollywood, he would have been a major creative force, although his abrasiveness might have gotten in the way. And, there are plenty of writers he gave credit to: Ed Hamilton, Otto Binder, Alfred Bester, these are all writers whom my father respected and always acknowledged their creativity. So you can imagine that it is pretty frustrating for me to read those comments. After living in LA for many, many years, I have met many creative people in the entertainment business and as far as generating ideas, I've never met anyone who was a better "idea man" than my dad. Better writers? Absolutely. But not better ideas. FYI, he did tell me that he got the idea for the Fortress of Solitude from some earlier pulp character written by one of his favorite writers [Lester Dent, creator of Doc Savage]. Also, he once stole a *Loretta Young* [television series] story and modified it to a *Lois Lane* [comic book], but things like this were always acknowledged. The joke, though, is that a kid wrote in who had seen the *Loretta Young* repeat months later. He wanted to inform my father that *Loretta Young* ripped off *Lois Lane*.

Also, let's not forget that while your concern is comics, he was a top freelance writer: *Reader's Digest*, *Collier's*, *Saturday Evening Post*. He wrote thousands of articles on hundreds of different subjects with all different angles—many of them cover articles.

That being said, yes, I have a lot of wonderful memories of my dad. They each stir up positive emotions when I recount them.

One of my more vivid memories: We had a big house in Kings Point, Long Island. The living room was huge and had green carpet. So my friends and I turned it into a putting green. One time, I made a 25-footer and my dad just happened to be there watching the ball roll into the cup that was placed between two coffee table traps. I remember him, sort of like Jackie Gleason, dancing across the carpet to shake my hand, yelling, "What a great putt!"

Getting a Ph.D. was no big deal to my dad, especially when he was financing it. But I will always remember when I told him I sold my first book. He went nuts. That was about 8 p.m. I was living in LA doing my internship. Later that night, around 11 my time—he was in New York—he called me again just to tell me how proud he was. It really made me feel great.

I remember also when I was first driving to LA from graduate school in Kansas. That same week, my dad was giving a lecture at Utah State—my mom was with him. It was the weekend of Father's Day. Well, instead of sticking to course, I drove to Utah to be with him. My dad was so surprised and touched. He couldn't believe I drove hours out of my way to be with him. For me of course, it was my pleasure.

It was really sweet having a dad who made up all the Superman stories. Each morning, he would wake me up for school and say, "Hank, here's the cover," or, "How's this for an idea?" He would then describe the situation and I would have to guess the ending, the twist as he would call it. His rule: If I could guess the ending too quickly, he would throw it out, thinking it was too easy. But really, what a great way to wake up. Now that I think about it, I was getting a "creativity shot" every morning.

Every year my dad would let me take off from school and take a friend into his office in NYC. We would read the giant comic proofs, sit in when he would berate a writer or artist, then go to a Yankees game in the afternoon. All my friends would beg me to let them come.

I didn't [buy] books in high school. Why would I? Every night, my dad would bring home 20 comics. I would save the *Superman* stories for last 'cause they were always the best. I was his biggest fan and I believe he felt I was his greatest reader.

I remember a lot of things, too, that he told me that have helped me professionally. One of his beliefs: take a subject and be able to write about it from a million perspectives. He wrote a book on beauty pageants (*The Contest*), but he also wrote a dozen articles for magazines on beauty pageants with different angles and different audiences. So I wrote a book on criticism (*The Power of Positive Criticism*) and I learned to modify the message to

Dr. Hendrie "Hank" Weisinger.
Photo courtesy of Hank Weisinger.

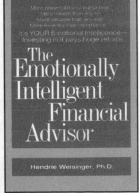

Two of Dr. Weisinger's books, *The Power of Positive Criticism* (American Management Association, 1999) and *The Emotionally Intelligent Financial Advisor* (Kaplan Business, 2004). Note the Superman-esque cover copy on ...*Advisor*.

© 2006 Hendrie Weisinger, Ph.D.

different audiences: business, parents, couples. Like father, like son in this case.

[Other] memories: playing ball together, gin (instead of studying), chess, watching TV. In fact, I am getting ready to start a book about father/son relationships. I am calling it *I Flew with Superman*, and besides the father/son psychology stuff, I will put in a lot of great inside Superman stories. There are many delightful ones to share. He was my best friend and you know, I find I am having the same type of relationship with my son, Danny, and daughter, Bri.

EDDY ZENO: Wasn't one of the reasons your dad finally left comics due to his feeling that he was working in Superman's shadow?

WEISINGER: Well, as a psychologist, I would have to say if he said it, there is probably some truth [there]. But keep this in mind: he actually got a lot of mileage saying that 'cause people/editors/writers thought it sounded interesting. I think the real reason he left was he wanted to go on to other things, like novels, perhaps try a screenplay. To a degree, he felt he wasted some of his creativity in comics, but it was also secure for him. Believe me, any time we went anywhere, it only took five minutes for him to let everybody know [*laughs*] he was the editor of Superman.

ZENO: What do you think your dad brought to the Man of Steel that was unique?

WEISINGER: The success of Superman was never greater than what it was in his tenure. That is because he was a creative genius. Remember, he was doing *Superman*, *Lois Lane*, *Action*, *Adventure* (Legion of Super-Heroes), *Jimmy Olsen*, to say nothing of back-ups like Green Arrow and Aquaman (I am surprised these are not movies). Anyway, I think what he did was he integrated all the characters into a Superman universe, and as a result, he created tremendous story flexibility, as characters from different magazines could make guest appearances, and more importantly, a consistent story mythology was created. Many times, he would get ideas from questions kids would write in, such as, "Where does Superman keep his Clark Kent clothes when he changes?" Because of that question, Superman's cape has a pocket in it and Clark's clothes are treated with a special chemical made by Superman that prevents wrinkles!

I would say he brought "newness, uniqueness, and creative development" to Superman and did it by creating gimmicks, characters, and new concepts. Remember the Six Million Dollar Man? Rip-off of Metallo.

ZENO: One final question, about Edmond Hamilton and your father. Do you remember the two of them plotting stories long distance by phone, because one lived in Ohio and the other in New York?

WEISINGER: Ed Hamilton, I think is sort of an old guy and Edith Hamilton is his wife.

ZENO: It was actually Leigh Brackett, and you're right. Hamilton was older, born in 1904.

WEISINGER: I remember they came to our house one time in the summer. That's probably where they did some plotting because we had a swimming pool in our backyard. I remember him more than I can facially remember her.

Superman artist Wayne Boring (1905–1987) got his start in the late 1930s ghosting for Joe Shuster before beginning, in 1939, a long stint on the *Superman* newspaper strip. In 1948 Boring succeeded Shuster as the principal Superman artist, his art style epitomizing the Man of Steel's comics and merchandising look throughout the 1950s. He periodically drew Superman stories throughout the 1960s — even inking Curt Swan in a one-time-pairing of Super-artists in *Superman* #150 (Jan. 1962), "When the World Forgot Superman" — before being released from DC in 1967. Boring returned to newspaper strips (doing uncredited backgrounds for *Prince Valiant* and drawing United Features Syndicate's *Davy Jones*), and briefly illustrated Marvel's *Captain Marvel* before retiring from comics. While working as a bank security guard, throughout the 1980s Boring occasionally illustrated Superman commissioned portraits and cover recreations. He died of a heart attack in 1987.

(below) Wally Wood mimicked Boring's Superman style (and the styles of other cartoonists) in "Comicland," a fashion show starring models Superman, Henry, Donald Duck, and Daisy Mae, from *MAD* #82 (1963).

Boring's Feb. 11, 1965 *Superman* daily strip, with a specialty drawing of Superman the artist added in 1985.
TM & © DC Comics. Art courtesy of Heritage Comics.

A Wayne Boring-drawn *Davy Jones* strip (dated 8-11-70).
© 2006 United Features Syndicate. Ray Cuthbert collection.

An undated concept piece for Boring's *Star Spanner* comic strip or comic book. The bespectacled "timid" hero and the Kandor-esque architecture of "Shandor" were obviously inspired by Boring's Superman tenure.
© 2006 Wayne Boring estate. Art courtesy of Heritage Comics.

THE SUPERMAN MYTHOLOGY:
ROOTS OF THE SUPERMAN CONFLUENCE

by Eddy Zeno
© 2004 Eddy Zeno.

284 Harrison Street,
Passaic, New Jersey
October 29,1931

Dear Forrest,

By way of atoning for having neglected you all summer, I will answer as speedily as possible. Even at that, it takes ten days for a round trip.

I'm glad to welcome you on our staff. We are all working hard in order to make the first issue an impressive one. Should you be inclined to, an article or a sketch on some stf. author or by some stf. author, would be enthusiastically welcomed.

Your list of items bid fair to make some of the fans open-mouthed. We plan to have about two pages alone dealing with news of that type. Have you any ideas for contests?

From Darrow comes the following: O.A.Kline has written a short for Amazing called XXXXXXXXXXXX "A Vision of Venus."

Edmond Hamilton has written "The Time Drug" for Wonder., and "The Three From the Tomb for Weird Tales.

How is the J.S.A. progressing? Or are they getting as lazy as the SCIENCEERS who haven't held a meeting for six weeks? The bulletin has gone hang for the present.

Did you know that Ghost Stories expires with this issue? Another mag. bit the dust. That makes Miracle, Visionary, Super-Science Classics, Amazing Detective Tales, and Air Wonder Stories. A flock of them And I think Wonder is going to be the fittest.

Well, I guess that ought to hold you for awhile.

Yours,
Mort Weisinger

P.S. Did you hear about SOLAR SYSTEM STORIES ?

284 Harrison Street,
Passaic, N.J.
October, 17, 1931

Dear Forrest,

Three cheers! At last the Sphinx is speaking! Really though, I'm sorry I delayed in answering your letter. You see, I was so darn busy in the past few months that I didn't have any time for any outside activities. First, I am no longer living in New York. I am living in Passaic, a rathera large city in New Jersey. We moved here for business reasons. However, I commute dai to school as we are only twelve miles from New York.

I have been completely cut off from all that's going on in the science fiction world. I was over to see Glasser and Schwartz the other day and they wised me up a bit. The only thing we have xxxx in the way of news for you is the fact that the Zagat team will soon have a yarn in Astounding called "The Dome of the Mercury". Also, Lasser's book, "The Conquest of Space"is selling strong.

However the main reason I am writing you is because we have an idea that we think can secure us pleasure and profit. The idea was somewhat inspired by your now and then issues of stf. news by "Forrie".
It consists as follows:
It is a well known fact that science-fiction fans are so enthusiastic about what's going on that they will join in any movement that's appealing to them. Now, what we intend to do is to publish a fair sized paper devoted exclusively to stf. In it we will have news of forthcoming stories, biographie of men like Miller, Zagat, Edwards, Lasser, Wesso, Paul, Bates. (This is not x far-fetched, since Glasser and myself and myself have an appointment with Wesso over at Bate's office next Tuesday)We can also have science-fiction contests, puzzles, essays. We can have a what-have-you column for the readers, not to mention a reader's department. From time to time we can publish the pictures of the readers and notes about them.

If you would like to be in with us on this, you can have the position of an associate editor along with the following.
ALLEN GLASSER - Editor-in- Chief
F.J. ACKERMAN - ASSOCIATE
LINUS HOGENMILLER-ASSOCIATE (if he wants to join us)
JACK DARROW - ASSOCIATE
JULIUS SCHWARTZ-ASSOCIATE
MORTIMER WEISINGER- ASSOCIATE

We propose to call the magazine "The Time Traveller". The price is not yet decided on. We intend to publish it every other week and later on every week. If you accept our offer, your duty will be to gather as much, news, data,and oddand ends pertaining to stf. as you can and keeping them exclusive until we release it. Keep an eye peeled for news of forthcoming stf. yarns in all newsstand publications.We will heartily welcome any suggestions you will offer. The first issue goes off the press November 14, 1931 so rush all data to me before then. We would appreciate the names and addresses of people who might subaribe or advertise. Don't worry about expenses. We'll take care of that. As for the profits, that'sy where you come in. So start hustling! Another thing. Make sure that all your data is authentic and reliable.
Please get in touch with Hogenmiller, outline the idea to him, and ask him if he's interested. I hope you will give the project some consideration.
Hoping to hear from you real soon,

These two 1931 letters from a young Mort Weisinger to Forrest Ackerman discuss plans for the soon-to-be-released *Time Traveller* fanzine.

The Big Three Superman writers of the Silver Age hobnobbed with each other and with their future editor years before any of them worked in comics. Their original ties in the early 1930s were through science fiction — Edmond Hamilton and Otto Binder were already professional authors, Mort Weisinger and Jerry Siegel were fans.

In 1932 Weisinger and Julie Schwartz produced *The Time Traveller*, the first nationally distributed SF fanzine, with help from Allen Glasser and Forrest J. Ackerman. Jerry Siegel, with aspirations of becoming a science-fiction writer, was an early subscriber and became friends with Weisinger several years before Superman began in *Action Comics* #1 (June 1938). It was Siegel who later recommended to editorial director Whitney Ellsworth that Weisinger be hired at DC. Jerry Siegel also traveled from Cleveland to Chicago, with friend and fellow SF fan Joe Shuster, to meet pros Otto and Earl Binder in the early '30s.

Ed Hamilton remembered receiving fan mail from "a lad in Cleveland who started writing to me early in 1930. He was instrumental, by his letters, in bringing together Jack Williamson and myself in a long friendship. He wrote me that he had an idea for hero stories himself, and that he and a friend were going to try to work up a new character. This youngster's name was Jerry Siegel, and the hero character he and his friend eventually created was … Superman!" In a phone conversation in June 2003, Julie Schwartz added that Hamilton had told Siegel to get in touch with Jack Williamson about how to break into the SF field. When Jerry sent Jack his story concept about a planet of super-beings, Jack said no, that it would be better to send the beings to a different world where they gain super-powers. Williamson's e-mail response in December 2003 was: "I don't recall much about the story Siegel sent me, except that his characters were geometric solids such as cubes and spheres and cones. There were no human beings and no human interest. I don't remember much of what I wrote him, except that I tried to point out the need of human interest and tried to suggest how that might be done. I don't recall the details Julie suggests, but they may be true."

Additionally Jerry Siegel published Ed Hamilton's first "book," circa 1932. It was actually an abridged mimeographed version of a 1926 story "The Metal Giants," which Siegel arranged to send as a premium with orders from the Swanson Book Company.

Ed wrote, "In 1930 in one of the earliest issues of *Astounding Stories*, the letter section carried a long, not-too-serious poem of tribute to 'Hamilton the World Saver,' written by a young reader named Mort Weisinger." Between July 1933 and October–November 1934, Weisinger and Schwartz secured the talents of many of the leading SF authors of the time to write a round-robin serial titled "Cosmos." Each installment appeared in their fanzine, by then titled *Science Fiction Digest*. Otto Binder (with his brother Earl) wrote the penultimate chapter, but it was Edmond Hamilton who was chosen to conclude the saga. Who better than "World Saver Hamilton" to wrap up the dangling plotlines and bring everyone home in one piece?

Otto Binder first met Mort Weisinger in Chicago, in August of 1934. Hamilton remembered being introduced to Binder in New York City around the same time. Whenever Ed was in the city in the late 1930s and early '40s he would meet with Mort, Otto, Julie, and other science-fiction greats of the time at Steuben's Tavern in midtown Manhattan. Other Steuben's semi-regulars who worked in comics included Manly Wade Wellman, Henry Kuttner, and Alfred Bester. Hamilton especially loved to join them in April for bock (dark) beer, "which was at that time only available for a few weeks."

When the innovative Weisinger became a professional at Standard Magazines in 1936, he changed the pulp business to meet his needs. The late Sam Moskowitz, one of the foremost authorities on SF, wrote, "Until then, editing a science-fiction magazine had consisted of reading the manuscripts that were submitted and picking the best. Weisinger switched to feeding his authors ideas and ordering a story of predetermined length built around an agreed-upon theme." Ed Hamilton was a master of accommodating this type of assignment when writing the serialized adventures of Captain Future for Mort at Standard, and again when he worked for him at DC Comics. Captain Future was a sort-of science-fiction version of Doc Savage mixed with a bit of the Shadow. The first few stories were plotted by Edmond and Julie Schwartz, occasionally with Otto Binder's input, while riding on open-air bus on Fifth Avenue in New York.

Near the end of the 1930s the fledgling comic-book market thrived and expanded, thanks mainly to Siegel and Shuster's Superman catching fire. The pulp market where Hamilton, Binder, and later Weisinger were earning a living experienced a series of downturns that, at different times, drove all three men to follow Siegel's lead into comics. Edmond was the last to take a comic-book job and the only one who continued writing simultaneously for the pulps and then afterfor the rest of his career.

THE PLOT MASTER AND THE EDITOR

by Eddy Zeno
© 2006 Eddy Zeno.

On March 8, 2003 Julius (Julie) Schwartz said of Edmond Hamilton: "He was extremely knowledgeable. He wrote all of his stories first draft; he was a complete plot master." The man's well-known wife, herself an author, once stated: "Ed always knew the last line of a story before he wrote the first one, and every line he wrote aimed straight at the target." Edmond Hamilton worked with editors Schwartz and Jack Schiff at National Periodical Publications (later DC Comics), but it was with Mort Weisinger that he achieved his comic-book zenith. For many who remember the Silver Age Superman as the noblest hero of them all, it is primarily Weisinger and Hamilton's portrayal that forged that reputation.

Edmond Hamilton

Standing on the shoulders of Edgar Allan Poe, Jules Verne, H. G. Wells, Edgar Rice Burroughs, and A. Merritt, Edmond Hamilton was an important bridge between past and modern science fiction. Born on October 21, 1904 in Youngstown, Ohio, his family soon moved to New Castle, Pennsylvania, where he finished high school at age 14. Rated tops in I.Q. in his freshman class at Westminster College, Hamilton majored in physics with plans to be an electrical engineer. Too young to feel he truly belonged, Ed was expelled for skipping chapel in his junior year. He then enjoyed working as a railroad yard clerk; cussing with the boys was much more real and enjoyable to him than listening to academics. When

Photo courtesy of Glen Cadigan.

that position ended in 1924, Hamilton began to write. His initial stories were published in 1926, the seminal year in which Hugo Gernsback began the first all-science-fiction magazine, *Amazing Stories*. The term "science fiction" did not yet exist and it would be some years before the likes of Heinlein, Clarke, Asimov, and Bradbury would enter the field. Ed believed in heroes and rousing adventure at least as much as he loved SF; that was the secret of his early success and eventual devaluing by some when the "Golden Age of Science Fiction" was born in the latter 1930s.

On a trip to Los Angeles in 1940, Hamilton met Leigh Brackett, a newly published female science-fiction author. Both were visiting their mutual literary agent, Julie Schwartz. Mort Weisinger was present, as well. Driving west again the following summer with Schwartz, Ed and Julie shared a bungalow to hold court for other SF authors, Leigh included. The three of them would occasionally visit Robert Heinlein's mountaintop home, joining other colleagues in what became known as the Mañana Literary Society. After being separated during the war years, Brackett and Hamilton finally married on December 31, 1946. Ray Bradbury was best man.

In an interview with Ray Bradbury conducted by Larry Leonard in September 2001 and later appearing in *Oregon Magazine*, the author was asked, "Can beauty be constructed from things that aren't beautiful?" "Beauty," Bradbury responded, "is often something that comes from inside. I knew Edmond

Hamilton, the science-fiction writer. When I first met him, I thought, 'What a homely man he is.' He looked like a vulture. But after an hour with him, I said, 'What a beautiful man.'" In the Jan. 1934 issue of *Fantasy Magazine*, Hamilton good-naturedly traced his appearance to the fault of his lineage: "I do have a grudge against one of them, though, who back in the 18th century got so chummy with the Indians he married one. Ever since then each generation produces one Hamilton with a pan like Sitting Bull's, and I was the goat this time."

In 1950 Edmond and Leigh bought and restored a house 130-odd years old a mile out of Kinsman, Ohio. It rested on 30 acres of land with a small lake and a good well. Ironically, these portrayers of the future became preservers of the past. With Leigh's additional success as a Hollywood screenwriter, they later lived in Santa Monica part of the year, finally buying a second home in the California High Desert.

At times his prose was awkward. Edmond never met an adverb he didn't like. "Awedly," "terrifiedly," "appalledly," "bewilderedly," and "puzzledly" are just a few examples. However, nothing could slow the forward momentum of his stories. Near the end of his life, Hamilton wrote of the early days when he dreamed of "huge and awesome suns … I well remember that, working on a big old flat-top desk on a small portable typewriter, my feverish banging on the keyboard when I came to the great space-battles made the little machine 'walk' all over the desk—and how I would get up from my chair and follow the typewriter, still banging away in my excitement." His wife, in writing of her own love of science fiction, added, "Where else can I voyage among the 'great booming suns of outer space' (now there's a phrase for you, and pure Hamilton at that … if the great suns don't boom, they damn well ought to!)?" Known as "Queen of the Space Opera," Leigh Brackett was born in 1915. She died in 1978, a month after finishing the first screenplay draft for George Lucas' *The Empire Strikes Back*.

A tremendous bibliophile, Hamilton was incredibly well read, even for a writer. Later in life, when they could afford it, he and Brackett became travelers of the world, which rounded out his education. Traveling is why Ed quit writing comics in 1966 after a 20-year foray in that medium. Though his total comic-book output was probably less than 250 stories, he made a lasting impact in that medium, especially on Superman. Hamilton died on February 1, 1977.

Weisinger's Silver Age

The beginning of the Silver Age of Comics is generally felt to have occurred with the second Flash's premiere in *Showcase* #4 (Oct. 1956). It occurred under the aegis of editor Julius Schwartz. In 1958 a different type of genesis would expand the mythos of Superman. What changed that year for the Man of Steel's by-then-longtime editor, Mort Weisinger?

Actually, a comic-book renaissance began a decade earlier with an expanded origin tale in *Superman* #53 (July–Aug. 1948). Otto Binder was still a few years away from writing for the Superman family and Jerry Siegel had been banished from DC

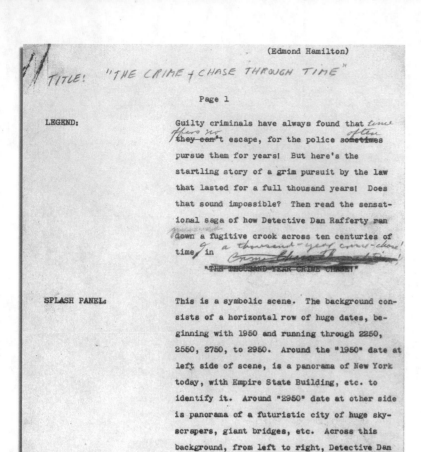

Edmond Hamilton's typewritten script for the splash page of "The Crime-Chase Through Time," from *Strange Adventures* #4 (Jan. 1951).
TM & © DC Comics.

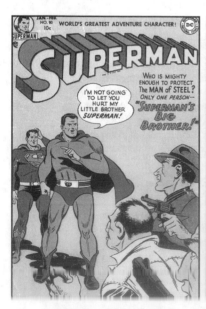

Edmond Hamilton's Halk Kar, from *Superman* #80 (Jan.–Feb. 1953), and his Earth-One counterpart Mon-El, from *Superboy* #89 (June 1961).
TM & © DC Comics.

the year before due to his and Shuster's suing to regain ownership of the character. (Jerry would return to the company in 1959.) Edmond Hamilton, however, was there as a slowly accelerating number of stories began to explore Kryptonian culture. By 1952 nearly every issue had at least one of his science-fiction tales of this type. For example, in *Superman* #74's (Jan.–Feb. 1952) "The Lost Secrets of Krypton!", Luthor attempted to dominate Earth by utilizing Kryptonian artifacts that survived the planet's destruction. It read like pure pulp-Hamilton when the villain sent "a titanic, terrifying message to millions: 'I, Luthor, possess the powers of the stars. Pay tribute to me or I will use them!'" *Superman* #80's (Jan.–Feb. 1953) "Superman's Big Brother," also by Ed, featured a burly caped man named Halk Kar who arrived on Earth suffering amnesia after his spaceship exploded. An enclosed note from Jor-El and the fact that the spaceman had limited super-powers implied that he was Superman's older sibling. Eventually, the truth was discovered, that he was not a native but had been visiting Krypton just before its doom.

For the next few years, these extraterrestrial tales slowed to a trickle. Exceptions included the 1954 reappearance (in *Action Comics* #194, July 1954) of three super-villains from Krypton, first seen four years earlier in *Superman* #65 (July–Aug. 1950). Also, there was Krypto, introduced in *Adventure Comics* #210 (Mar. 1955) with a script by Otto Binder. Another exception was the Ed Hamilton story, "Superman's First Exploit" (*Superman* #106, July 1956), in which Superbaby temporarily left his ship on the way from Krypton to Earth. Already under the influence of a yellow sun, the tyke gained super-powers and punched a crystalline space creature in the snout. Hamilton later expressed fondness for this tale: "I always remember that as the only script I ever wrote in one day, the reason being that, as a baby, he couldn't talk very well … he could just say things like 'Pretty … bright …', 'Bad mans!', and so on. This made dialogue writing a breeze."

A few months later, Edmond's tale of "The First Superman of Krypton" appeared in *Action Comics* #223 (Dec. 1956). The author gave a more active role to Jor-El when some of the deceased scientist's home movies were discovered amid cosmic wreckage. An enamored Kal-El got to watch his old man using super-powers due to gravity-distorting machines which simulated Earthlike conditions. Additionally, in that story Superman's origin was recounted as a backdrop; Hamilton elicited a new sense of irony by coinciding the planet's destruction with its people grandly celebrating their 10,000th year of civilization.

In 1958 many innovative, lasting concepts and characters exploded in the Superman family titles. Letter writer Bob Bailey surmised in *Alter Ego* vol. 3 #31 (Dec. 2003) that perhaps DC's editorial director at the time, Whitney Ellsworth, had lifted a moratorium which did not allow much variation from the generally Earthbound *Adventures of Superman* television show during its 1952–1958 run. It's also possible that Mort himself, the TV program's story editor, may have independently made that decision.

Additionally, in 1958 fan letters were introduced in Weisinger's comic book titles, allowing dialogue to flow between him and the audience. Plus, Mort's son Hank and his friends were ten years old that year. They had come of age, serving as sounding boards for the editor's thoughts and generating new ideas themselves. What would have been one-shot, castaway items before, instead became concepts which clamored to be seen again and again thanks to the readers' and neighbor kids' feedback. Consequently, the need for continuity grew much more elaborate.

About this prolific period Weisinger said, "I would bring out a new element every six months to keep the enraptured kids who were our audience involved." The best of them, like Supergirl, the Legion of Super-Heroes, and the Bottle City of Kandor had science-fictional ties and were first scripted by Otto Binder. As testament to his contribution, these innovations slowed considerably when Binder left comics in October 1960 (to return in 1964). Mort, incidentally, gave Otto sole credit for originating the space-villain Brainiac and Superman's imperfect double Bizarro, in contrast to later taking credit for the latter.

Toward Novel-Length Comics

The first *Superman* comic book to feature a full-length story was the May 1957 issue, #113. Edmond Hamilton wrote the second one in #119 (Feb. 1958) before all but leaving comics for a while. Though entertaining, his early effort was no better than the rest. The multi-parters began more as separate vignettes loosely tied together by an overlying theme. From a critical standpoint, there was repetition in each chapter with a hint of boredom as the plots couldn't sustain their lengths. Gradually, Weisinger coaxed them into something more. With Jerry Siegel's doomed Kryptonian romance in *Superman* #141's "Superman's Return to Krypton!" (Nov. 1960) and his moving death of a hero in #149's imaginary "The Death of Superman!" (Nov. 1961), the two men brought big, cohesive storylines to the full-lengthers. Ed Hamilton's ability to interweave engaging subplots around multiple supporting characters later took the genre even higher.

Where was Ed in the late 1950s, when Otto Binder and Mort Weisinger were releasing an explosion of new ideas, and the two- and three-part novels had barely begun? In 1957 Hollywood film director Howard Hawks rehired Ed's wife Leigh Brackett to write movie scripts after [Brackett's screenwriting dry spell] of more than a decade. Perhaps her newfound financial stability was a factor in Edmond greatly curtailing his comic-book activity, beginning in early 1958. Instead of just short stories, for the first time in several years he wrote new SF novels while revising and expanding a couple of older ones.

About generating ideas for his writers, Weisinger once said that he expected each of them to "be able to develop this bare skin and bones skeleton that I give him." When Hamilton returned to comics in 1962, he was eminently qualified to give Mort what he wanted. Besides his years of experience writing for Schiff, Schwartz, and Weisinger, he'd also had nearly 300 prose stories published, many of them novels and novelettes. Ed wrote that "Superman could present some knotty problems in

Splash page from the third story in *Mystery in Space* #29 (Dec. 1955–Jan. 1956). Writer Bill Finger and editor Julius Schwartz saluted Hamilton and Ray Bradbury with characters Emmet Hamilton and Ray Bradford. The artist, Carmine Infantino, had this to say about Edmond in July 2004: "He reminded me of John Broome in that there were no wasted words."
TM & © DC Comics.

plotting." And while he agreed that many of the plot threads were his editor's, he was wonderfully adept at filling out the stories from his rich imagination. Some examples:

In the 1951 book *City at World's End*, Hamilton wrote about the everyday citizens of an entire mid-twentieth century town being blasted through time to a cold, desolate Earth millions of years in the future: "And then the rolling, ocher-yellow plains were all about them, barren and drab beneath the great firelashed red eye of the Sun." This also described perfectly the landscape portrayed in *Action Comics* #300 (May 1963). Edmond stated, "In fact, my favorite of all the scripts I wrote was one entitled 'Superman Under the Red Sun.' In that story, Superman traveled into time by using his super-speed to 'burst the time barrier.' But unwittingly he went too far, into a time when Earth's sun had become old and red. The result was that he had no super-powers— and couldn't get back. Earth was dead, and he was condemned to wander alone upon it. Mort objected to the fact, that, being alone on Earth, Superman wouldn't have any companions to talk to, and the pictures, always an important element, would be dull. I got around this by having Superman, in his loneliness, constructing robots who were doubles of Lois Lane, Perry White, Jimmy Olsen, and his other pals." Both the novel and the comic book showed Hamilton's ability to use basically the same premise to challenge totally different characters in two separate literary forms—with far different resolutions. Superman was able to return to his own time while the people in *City at World's End* were not. They did, however, figure out a way to preserve what they'd enjoyed about their past lives while adapting to their new surroundings.

In both "The Infinite Evolutions of Superman and Batman!" (*World's Finest* #151, Aug. 1965) and "The Man Who Evolved" (1931), the consequence of evolution accelerator rays was to make the recipients cold-blooded and ruthless. As their skulls grew, expanding to accommodate their huge brains, they became obsessed with world domination. Ed did the same thing initially to the short story's mad scientist as he did to Batman in *World's Finest*. Only the scientist continued to evolve full-cycle until he became a helpless mass of protoplasm, while the Caped Crusader was thrown into the path of a "devolution ray" that returned him to his normal self.

Other concepts sprang from book to comic. In the 1960 science-fiction novel *The Haunted Stars*, Hamilton wrote of a Hall of Suns: "This huge, decaying monument to a once-mighty world showed glowing miniature stars, many with little worlds still attached, as a testament to the solar systems once traversed by its people." A few years later in the comics, Hamilton described a similar model solar system to denote a super-villain's arrogance and dreams of conquests ("The Composite Superman!" in *World's Finest* #142, June 1964).

The Haunted Stars also told of mighty statues, some toppled from age, outside of the Hall of Suns. Quoting Hamilton, "Others were still upright but had lost limbs. But whole or broken, they were equally impressive. In the gathering twilight the strong faces looked down at them, the faces of the men who dreamed very far and had made their dreams come true." When Ed returned to scripting Superman, he brought this imagery with him. From 1962 to the end of his run, monuments and statues were more frequently ascribed to the Man of Steel and his allies than before. In one memorable Imaginary Story, "The Superman of 2965!" in *Superman* #181 (Nov. 1965), these symbols of grandeur and solitude represented several of Kal-El's descendants.

On January 16, 2004 Stuart Moore, former Vertigo and Marvel Knights editor and 2000s *Firestorm* and SF comics writer, had this to say about Edmond Hamilton's work under Weisinger: "Jerry Siegel and Otto Binder were obviously well-versed in science fiction, but I always think of Hamilton as the one who really specialized in futuristic DC comics, both with his Legion work and in oddities like the Superman 2966 stories. The Legion stories show off Hamilton's work best. He was the first to deal with all the different planets the characters came from, and gave the book a sense of a cohesive (if somewhat daffy) universe. There's a lot of dark stuff in his run, too … Lightning Lad loses an arm, that sort of thing. Most of that was reversed later on."

Moore added, "Hamilton's stories are full of fun little details like futuristic autograph-writing machines, giant electronic brains, and planets with odd civilizations. The Superman 2966 stories, which I've been recently reading for research, are also filled with hints that the future holds some devastating times before the wonders arrive—the future-Superman's only weakness, for instance, is 'a chemical fallout left by a past atomic war, which settled in the seas of every planet.' As with the Legion stories, there's a real undercurrent of worry lurking beneath the shiny metal gadgets."

In *Adventure Comics* #333 (June 1965), "The Civil War of the Legion!", it was discovered that millions of years ago a small Kryptonian contingent settled on our planet. Hamilton's touch was apparent when he showed them bringing some of their plants and animals with them, introducing the first dinosaurs to Earth. Meanwhile, another group of colonists had also journeyed here from the stars to build the city of Atlantis. They became the enemies of the Kryptonians as two teams of Legionnaires took opposite sides in the conflict. Superboy allied himself with his comrades but became romantically involved with one of the opposing Atlanteans, a girl named

Hamilton revisited *City at World's End*'s "red eye of the Sun" in *Action* #300 (May 1963).

Dust on Hamilton's *Valley of Creation* (1948) and *Adventure Comics* #333 (June 1965)

THE SUPERMAN MYTHOLOGY:
A MINI-TRIBUTE TO EDMOND HAMILTON BY JACK WILLIAMSON

Jack Williamson, born in 1908, is the only author to have new science-fiction work published in each decade from the 1920s into the 21st century. He has sold stories to every editor of *Analog* since it began as *Astounding Stories of Super Science*. In December 2003 Jack had this to say about Edmond Hamilton:

"Ed and I were early contributors to the science-fiction magazines. I got his mail address from Jerry Siegel, co-creator of Superman. Both of us admirers of Mark Twain, we arranged to meet in Minneapolis for a cruise down the Mississippi. That was a great adventure and we were friends as long as he lived.

"About the comics, he used to say that writing the scripts was drudgery the editors wouldn't let him escape, but he did it so long and so well that he must have enjoyed it. He was good at it, well seasoned by a long career in the pulps and clever at inventing action plots.

"As a pulp writer, he began his career writing space operas for the early *Weird Tales*. His stories were well-imagined pictures of a far-off future, with bold heroes and action on a grand scale. The battles to avert cosmic catastrophe earned him the title 'World Saver Hamilton.' He may be almost forgotten now, but he pioneered the use of tropes still to be seen in books, films, and TV. I'm glad to see him remembered."

When queried about specific tropes, he added, "Hamilton's Interstellar Patrol stories in the old *Weird Tales* are the earliest space operas I know. They set a pattern for tales of far-future cultures and wars between them that we still see in the likes of *Star Trek* and *Star Wars*."

–Eddy Zeno

(right) In remembrance of the author, Superman writers Cary Bates and Paul Kupperberg introduced into comics incarnations of Ed Hamilton's Captain Future, promoting him to "Colonel" Future. Bates' version debuted in *Action* #484 (June 1978), while Kupperberg's bowed in *Superman* #378 (Dec. 1982).
TM & © DC Comics.

(above) Regarding Professor Emil Hamilton, who arrived in *The Adventures of Superman* #424 (Jan. 1987), in March 2005 writer Marv Wolfman verified that "I did indeed create him and he was named for Edmond Hamilton. I was a huge fan of his Superman comics as well as his SF work." The artist of that issue, Jerry Ordway, added, "I came up with the visual for Emil Hamilton, and I think I gave him his first name. Marv indeed did script the character, but as a loser villain, which we used in our first two *Adventures*, #424–425. I brought him back as Professor Hamilton when I was co-plotting with [John] Byrne, as Byrne wanted to give Supes a scientist-type like in the old TV show. I plugged in Hamilton because I like the idea of guys being able to redeem themselves." Hamilton is seen here in these panels from *Superman* vol. 2 #65 (Mar. 1992), written and penciled by Dan Jurgens and inked by Brett Breeding.
TM & © DC Comics.

Leta Lal. The parallels in Edmond's Legion tale to his earlier novel, *The Valley of Creation* (1948, revised in 1964), are apparent. The comic-book Atlanteans were originally from the star system of "Vruun." The people in the novel also came from space eons ago, part of them building a city on Earth named "Vruun" and becoming engaged in civil war. Likewise, as the Atlanteans had to change their physiology in order to survive, so did the people in Hamilton's *The Valley of Creation*. The reason in both cases was that in their original forms Earth's air proved deadly to breathe. Finally, as Superboy and Leta Lal of Atlantis found themselves attracted to each other across warring camps, so did the characters Eric Nelson and Nsharra in the novel.

The Plot Master and the Editor

Scripters of the Superman family during comics' Silver Age included Jerry Coleman, Bill Finger (co-creator of Batman), Robert Bernstein, and Leo Dorfman. At that time, however, the big three in terms of importance were Binder, Siegel, and Hamilton.

Part of Mort Weisinger's genius was that he placed his writers on the features to which they were best suited. For instance, with his childlike imagination and talent for whimsy, Otto Binder was perfect on titles like *Superboy* and *Jimmy Olsen*.

Weisinger called Jerry Siegel "the most competent" Superman scripter. Besides his ability to inject pathos and romance into certain tales, as in the full-length novels previously noted, Siegel also specialized in fluffy, humorous scripts involving Tales of the Bizarro World, Mxyzptlk, and even sillier premises seen in issues of *Lois Lane*.

Edmond Hamilton, while composing his share of Mxyzptlk tales and the like over the years had other preferences, which did not include writing for a certain super-hero's girlfriend. A 1965 fanzine stated that Ed "does not do the *Lois Lane* stories, although he tried one. 'I just don't have the "feel" for them,' was his comment." It was toward the end of 1962 when Mort had the foresight to make him the primary writer of the longer stories appearing in the *Superman* title. In a letter column (Smallville Mailsack, *Adventure Comics* #310, July 1963), Weisinger stated, "Author Edmond Hamilton is a highly successful science-fiction novelist and we are honored to consider him our most versatile staff writer. Ed has written some of our greatest 3-part novels, including that recent smash hit, 'The Last Days of Superman.'"

Mort was demanding a different type of story than he had a decade earlier. At the 1965 New York Comicon he summarized, "Well, we've slowed down. The stories are not as quickly written, they're not written at that white heat—they're not as glib; they're more carefully plotted. We find our readers today in a space age, advanced from the Golden Age, a lot more sophisticated than they had been."

As he developed his storytelling ability, by 1950 the protagonists in Ed Hamilton's science-fiction books had become like real people. They possessed fears and weaknesses, yet somehow found the strength of will to perform heroic deeds. Always a superior plotter, when he returned to write for Mort in 1962, Edmond finally had the space in comic books to add this brand of character development. Heroes' and villains' personalities alike sprang from actions taken and alliances made. Regarding supporting players, Jimmy Olsen was not just the goofball nor Lois Lane simply the conniver that they were in their own books. Ed made them noble and self-sacrificing while keeping intact the essence of the personalities constructed by Weisinger and the others. And to Superman, he gave a sense of honor and purpose.

Hamilton was also a realist; his fiction could be grim. This, as much as anything, helped separate his work from Mort's usual editorial slant.

Obsessions

When it first appeared in 1958, the Bottle City of Kandor was a mere story backdrop. Under Weisinger's editorial direction, Superman gradually became obsessed with returning it to normal size. Were it not for Ed Hamilton, however, we would not have cared whether that might happen. He gave us a Kandor with personality: that of a futuristic and scientific municipality surrounded by exotic Kryptonian jungle, with telepathic hounds used to hunt criminals and rarer, near-extinct animals in its zoo. To its history Edmond added the supporting character Nor Kann, an elderly scientist who'd been dear friends with Jor-El and Lara, and by extension, with their son. It was a city worthy of Kal-El's obsession. The finest Kandor story and one of the best plotted three-part Hamilton novels was "The Invasion of the Super-People!" in *Superman* #158 (Jan. 1963). (Incidentally, the character name "Nor Kann" was sometimes spelled differently in various comic-book stories; that's not surprising considering that Hamilton's original "Nor-Kan" was a man descended from birds who lived on a parallel world way back in 1931 [in the novelette called *Locked Worlds*]. And Leigh Brackett borrowed her husband's idea of telepathic hounds for three of her own novels in the 1970s.)

In a July 1975 interview with Guy H. Lillian III, Weisinger was quoted as saying, "To make him more of a likable character, the type of story I became fondest of was the one where somehow Superman lost his powers and had to survive on his natural wits. I'd do that repeatedly. You could identify with him then, an outstanding character deserving of your admiration, a real hero because of the clever things that he did when deprived of his super-powers." Ed became the dominant writer for Mort on these kinds of stories, including a series-within-a-series involving Lex Luthor. By lying, but also by doing good deeds for once in his adult life, Luthor became the hero of a people who inhabited a red sun planet; so much so that they named their world Lexor in his honor. Knowing that he was hated there and would lose his powers each time he traveled to Lexor, Superman remained undeterred in his desire to return his lifelong foe to an Earth-prison. It became his second obsession.

Edmond wrote, "I have to admit that the villains of the Batman and Superman stories interested me more than the heroes themselves. In the Superman characters, Luthor the evil scientist was a favorite … I suppose again, because he was more science-fictional." Though we'll never know the total extent of Hamilton's contribution, it was certainly within his purview to take a long-standing villain like Luthor and make him champion of an alien world. This new character development made Lex much more complex and interesting. Hamilton's finale on Lexor was a stunning two-parter in *Action Comics* #318 and 319 (Nov. and Dec. 1964).

His struggles to enlarge Kandor and to bring Luthor to justice allowed Mort and Edmond to send Superman to other worlds on epic quests. They showed us a Man of Steel who could become driven, fatigued, not always logical, and therefore more human. At times there was almost a bone-weariness in Superman that did not exist under the other writers' direction. Paradoxically, by making such a powerful hero more like us, the two men raised the level of the myth.

Add the Perfect Art Team

Curt Swan, known to many as the definitive Silver Age penciler of the Caped Kryptonian, couldn't have been more different than Hamilton. Growing up in Minneapolis during the 1920s and '30s he wrote, "you only wasn't I much interested in science fiction, I wasn't even particularly into comic books." But after surprising

AND IN THE FORTRESS OF SOLITUDE, SUPERMAN MAKES AN EARNEST VOW...

PEOPLE OF **KANDOR**, I'LL NEVER FORGET HOW YOU FREED YOUR GREAT ENEMY TO SAVE *ME*! I PROMISE THAT I WILL BRING **BRAINIAC** BACK TO JUSTICE, AND THAT **KANDOR** WILL BE NORMAL AGAIN!

FINALLY, **LUTHOR** LANDS ON THE **ONE** WORLD IN THE UNIVERSE WHERE HE'S CONSIDERED A **HERO!**

LUTHOR, THE RADIOACTIVE MATERIAL YOU NEED IS IN THIS MUSEUM OF OLD MACHINES. LET'S STEAL IT.'

LUTHOR, THE GREAT HERO WHO BROUGHT WATER TO OUR DROUGHT-STRICKEN WORLD... HE'S RETURNED! SEE, GREAT **LUTHOR**, HOW WE'VE HONORED YOU FOR YOUR GOOD DEED WITH THIS STATUE! ✻

✻ **LUTHOR** HELPED THESE PEOPLE IN **SUPERMAN** NO. 164. —EDITOR

himself in a career spent drawing hundreds of comics, including scores of Ed Hamilton SF tales, he became somewhat of a convert: "For years my favorite Superman story was the one in which Superman and Jimmy Olsen visit another world where Jimmy gets a costume, too, and superpowers. (I think his name is Flame Bird or something like that.) I got to create those costumes and those cities. I had fun with that." Hamilton's Nightwing and Flamebird was a terrific concept whereby Superman and Jimmy Olsen needed to hide their identities while visiting Kandor. They modeled their new personas after pals Batman and Robin in combination with native Kryptonian birds. Seemingly complex, Ed made all of this easy to follow in a handful of Silver Age tales.

In December 2002 Murphy Anderson remembered, "I was the first, or one of the first, to call Curt 'The Norman Rockwell of the Comics.'" This wonderful sense of Americana could be found in Swan's work especially prior to, and during, comics' Silver Age. When Ed Hamilton's expanded space sagas began to appear in the Superman family tales, art on a grander scale was required. Curt's ability to portray architecture on Kandor and on other worlds beautifully met the challenges imposed by Ed's star-spanning scripts.

In addition, the author's enlarged characterization in the longer stories was matched by the artist's ability to capture the emotions and unique body language of the primary and ancillary players. Add George Klein's brushwork, when he became Swan's main inker beginning in 1962, and the penciling was highlighted in a way that had not been demonstrated before. Mort Weisinger, too, deserves credit for matching these artistic and literary talents. In the flagship title's "The Last Days of Superman!" (*Superman* #156, Oct. 1962), "The Invasion of the Super-People!" (#158, Jan. 1963), "The Hero Who Was Greater Than Superman!" (#163, Aug. 1963), "The Showdown Between Luthor and Superman!" (#164, Oct. 1963), "The Sons of Superman!" (#166, Jan. 1964), "The Team of Luthor and Brainiac!" (#167, Feb. 1964), "Luthor—Super-Hero!" (#168, Apr. 1964), "The Tyrant Superman!" (#172, Oct. 1964), and "Clark Kent's Brother!" (#175, Feb. 1965), the attributes of four men—editor, writer, penciler, and inker—were full-borne. [*Note:* Though the Grand Comic-Book Database lists the authorship of "Lois Lane, the Super-Maid of Krypton!" in *Superman* #159 (Feb. 1963) as "unknown," the clues point to Edmond Hamilton as scripter. However, Mort Weisinger's plot guidance and use of gimmicks are so prominent that the writer's usual contributions are subsumed.]

End of an Era

Edmond Hamilton and his pulp-writing contemporaries came from a time long before man rocketed from Earth. The ideas behind their early space opera tales were newly theoretical, the stuff of dreamers. As imagined concept became scientific fact or a variation thereof, reality began to catch up to the dreamers. But it served Hamilton well on Superman, bringing a grandeur to his plots that was unmatched by his fellow scripters.

When he retired from comics at age 62 in 1966, Hamilton seemed to be running out of steam. His last story set in Kandor, "The Man from the Phantom Zone!" in *Action* #336 (Apr. 1966), while intriguing, was jumbled with too many ideas in too small a space. (Though, to be fair, according to story credit expert Martin O'Hearn, the script had to be completed by assistant editor E. Nelson Bridwell.) Likewise, Mort Weisinger, the Superman editor, never seemed to regain the 1962–1965 levels of greatness he had achieved with the plot master. For the next few years Weisinger assigned Otto Binder and artist Al Plastino to most of the comic-book-length Superman stories, but it was as if much of the enthusiasm was gone. The sagas no longer even featured the beautiful full and three-quarter splash pages announcing each chapter.

Mort's peak was over; he too would retire from comics in 1970. "Today's kids are too much for me," he observed around that time. "They're so far ahead of us in sophistication. The old villains aren't really their villains. Maybe they don't relate as much to pure fiction and diabolical plots to take over the world. Maybe they want stories that fit their experiences better. Maybe they've seen so much, it's limited rather than stretched their imaginations. Anyway, I knew I'd had it. Dreaming up socially conscious plots on the kid level really turns me off."

Triumphant Ambivalence

Leigh Brackett once wrote to friend and fellow pulp writer E. Hoffman Price about her husband: "Ed did his ball-carrying in the comics, during the falling in time of the magazine markets. And it was a man-killing business, even though he was doing it for old friends for whom he had great affection, and they for him." In his reminiscence of dear friend Hamilton, Price agreed: "Though the folding of the pulps

(top) Science-fiction author and movie screenwriter Leigh Brackett borrowed her husband's concept of telepathic hounds, only she enhanced their abilities to make them deadlier, as seen on the first two covers of Brackett's 1970s trilogy which featured the return of her recurring anti-hero Eric John Stark (art by Boris Vallejo and Jim Steranko). Also shown is the first appearance of Kandor's hounds from *Superman* #158 (Jan. 1963).

was also quoted as saying, "You know, in dealing with science fiction as a whole, the comics are just as important as the pulps," while Ed, near the end of his life, wrote a 6,000-word essay "Fifty Years of Heroes," which looked back on his prose and comic-book writing with roughly equal emphasis.

Certainly, there were limitations working in the comics medium at the time Hamilton did so. For example, no matter who wrote for Mort Weisinger, occasional plot holes and contrivances appeared in his books. Weisinger believed a story could be good in spite of the "Cinderella fallacy," that is, that Cinderella's left-behind glass slipper should have vanished at the stroke of midnight, making it impossible for the prince to find her.

Also, because kids were his primary audience, Mort felt the need to explain every abrupt change of scenery or to recap a villain like Brainiac's origin each time he appeared. Striving to keep readers well informed regarding the increasingly detailed continuity was both good and bad. A negative was the overly expository dialogue required of his writers. Big Bang Comics and children's book author/illustrator Jeff Weigel remembered Hamilton, in the early 1970s, responding to a youngster's much-enthusiastic letter about comics which appeared in a scholastic magazine. Ed wrote back that comic-book stories did not constitute great literature. From his perspective that may have been true, yet at times his and Weisinger's efforts produced great children's literature.

Postscript

The late Julie Schwartz, ever one to help us understand the histories of science fiction and of comic books, supplied a letter that Leigh Brackett wrote to Jenette Kahn and Sol Harrison at DC a few weeks after her husband's death. Dated February 25, 1977, it read:

Dear Friends:
Thank you so very much for your letter.

The comics were a very important part of Ed's life, and indirectly of mine as well, since he often used me as a sounding-board for his ideas and I have typed his scripts when he was too rushed to do the final copy himself. So I was pretty familiar with all the DC characters and their doings, and also with the high quality of Ed's work. He put just as much of himself into each script as he did into his novels, and more than once I have seen him throw away a nearly-finished job and start over again because he didn't like what he had done. He had indeed a remarkable imagination and a tremendous grasp of technique.

I also came to know and appreciate that quality of friendship and mutual respect, the feeling of family that exists among the people who work in the field. This too was a very important part of Ed's life, and of mine.

Again, my thanks.

Most sincerely,
Leigh Hamilton

drove him into the comics, a man-killing business, writing *Superman* and *Batman*, DC Comics' properties, he made it in that new, tough world, as a trendsetter and innovator whose work is still remembered, and will be." Edmond, himself, occasionally said things like, "Well, of course, the main attraction with comic books was that they paid so much more than science fiction." On the same subject Julie Schwartz added, "He was a good writer. It wasn't demanding but it didn't take much literary skill." Yet, paradoxically, Schwartz

Acknowledgments: Murphy Anderson; Chris Boyko; Gene Bundy at the Eastern New Mexico University Golden Library; Mike Carlin; Tom Fleming at Fanfare Sports and Entertainment, Inc.; Grand Comic Book Database (www.comics.org); Bob Hughes; Carmine Infantino; Sam Maronie; Stuart Moore; Martin O'Hearn; Jerry Ordway; Al Plastino; Bill Schelly, Julie Schwartz, Barton Schoonover, Ron Shogren, Jeff Weigel; Hank Weisinger; Jack Williamson; Marv Wolfman; Raul Wrona.

Callardon and Superman material © [illegible] the author in Curt Swan: A Life in Comics (Vanguard Productions 2002)

A HISTORY OF KRYPTON

by John Wells
© 2006 John Wells.

Before Clark Kent discovered his alien roots in *Superman* #61 (Nov.–Dec. 1949), Krypton seemed destined to be little more than a footnote, responsible for giving us Superman but unknown to the man himself. Once brought to light, though, Krypton could be counted on to figure into a couple stories a year, initially featuring a trio of Kryptonian villains (*Superman* #65, July–Aug. 1950) but usually revolving around some weapon or monster that had escaped the world's doom. One tale had an entire Kryptonian city (full of weapons, natch, and a kryptonite foundation) slam into an African jungle, its existence discovered by Superboy and Professor Olsen, the latter the father of a very familiar red-haired toddler (*Adventure Comics* #216, Sept. 1955).

Three developments in the latter half of the 1950s proved crucial in moving beyond the formula, beginning with the demonstration that Krypton could generate other recurring heroes. The imagery of a boy and his dog, even dressed up in capes, was an irresistible touchstone for kids and the one-shot Krypto (*Adventure Comics* #210, Mar. 1955) returned for good only four issues later. *Action Comics* #223 (Dec. 1956) and *Superman* #113 (May 1957) built on this, proving both Jor-El's ability to play a two-fisted leading man and the creative possibilities of full-length stories set on Krypton (with Superman as a virtual spectator). The capper was Superman's discovery of the bottled city of Kandor, the shrunken Kryptonian city rescued from Brainiac in *Action Comics* #242 (July 1958). In an instant, Superman (soon to be joined by Argo City's Supergirl) had been provided with the means of interacting with the culture that birthed him. And nothing would ever be the same.

Beyond nurturing new players like the Superman [Supermen] Emergency Squad (*Jimmy Olsen* #48, Oct.–Nov. 1960) and Van-Zee and his Earthling wife Sylvia (*Lois Lane* #15, Feb. 1960), Kandor made the introduction of incidental Kryptonian lore a more casual, less contrived process. In a single panel in *Lois Lane* #21 (Nov. 1960), readers saw wonders like Krypton's Scarlet Jungle (colored green, alas), Fire Falls, and Gold Volcano. If that weren't enough, a recurring series-within-a-series had Superboy using a mind-prober ray to revive his infant memories as Kal-El. "My Life On Krypton" ran only four installments (*Superboy* #79, 83, 87, 106, 1960–1963), plus a later Krypto tale (#126, Jan. 1966) and a last Superboy episode a decade later in *Superman* #286 (Apr. 1975).

For all the commercial intent involved in the Kryptonian elements of the Superman comics, there was an organic progression to them that took the stories in different directions by 1960, playing off the fact that Jor-El and Lara had become more to readers than a couple dispatched in a few panels of an origin sequence. The payoff was "Superman's Return to Krypton" in *Superman* #141 (Nov. 1960), in which the Man of Steel was thrust into the past and trapped on Krypton without his powers. Scripted by Jerry Siegel himself, the story brought cohesiveness to the piecemeal Kryptonian tidbits of recent years. It mixed the landscapes from the simultaneously published *Lois Lane* #21 with new wonders like the Jewel Mountains and Rainbow Canyon. Even Brainiac's theft of Kandor figured into the plot. In this story, more than any other, readers could actually make a personal connection with Kal-El's parents, whether it was Lara's matching the adult Kal with Lyla Lerrol or Jor-El's mounting panic in his frustrated attempts at evacuating the planet.

Krypton loomed large in the Superman titles through 1965, its culture figuring into three quarters of the issues of *Action* and *Superman* published in 1962 and 1963 and getting the reprint spotlight in 1962's *Superman Annual* #5. The Phantom Zone exploded onto the scene in 1961 (*Adventure* #283, Apr. 1961), its inhabitants proliferating across the Superman line. Kandor remained a regular presence, becoming a refuge for Supergirl's rescued parents (*Action* #310, Mar. 1964) and doling out new concepts like the Superman Lookalike Squad (*Action* #309, Feb. 1964) and Superman and Jimmy Olsen's alter egos, Nightwing and Flamebird (*Superman* #158, Jan. 1963). The latter took their names from Kryptonian birds, joining other such exotic creatures as the hippo-like Metal-Eater (*Superman* #132, Oct. 1959) and the rhino-esque Thought-Beast that had a view screen on its head that literally broadcast what it was thinking (*Superboy* #87, Mar. 1961). They'd had precursors in *Action* #242 (July 1958) and *Superboy* #53 (Dec. 1956), respectively.

Jor-El and Lara take center stage on Gray Morrow's original art to the cover of *Best of DC Digest* #40 (1983).

With the glory days of the Weisinger era fading, the latter 1960s saw dubious claims that Krypton had actually been destroyed by a super-bomb planted by the sinister Black Zero (*Superman* #205, Apr. 1968) and that Jor-El and Lara had survived Krypton's explosion in suspended animation but would have died anyway from radiation poisoning (*Superboy* #158, July 1969). These and other earlier stories, like time-travel episodes in *Jimmy Olsen* #36 (Apr. 1959) and *Lois Lane* #59 (Aug. 1965), didn't fit into the broader outline published throughout the 1960s, and that presented a problem when incoming editor Julius Schwartz slated "The Fabulous World of Krypton" as the back-up series in his revamped *Superman*. E. Nelson Bridwell, who'd done the research, explained in *Superman* #239 (June–July 1971) that "it was decided that the only thing to do was throw out part of the tales and work out the rest into a consistent whole."

Issue #239 also featured the Bridwell-designed map of Krypton, its chief surprise being the existence of Vathlo Island, "home of a highly developed black race" first glimpsed in #234. "You see blacks in the U.S. because their ancestors were brought here as slaves," he explained in #238 (June 1971). "That never happened on Krypton."

The first episodes of the Krypton series were straightforward pieces by Bridwell that starred Jor-El and expanded on 1960s flashbacks. As it progressed, other writers took over and the strip took a wider view, eschewing regular characters and running the chronological gamut from the birth of Krypton's civilization and name (#238) to the story of Green Lantern Tomar-Re's futile attempt at preventing Krypton's destruction (#257, Oct. 1972). The back-up series finally ended in early 1975 (#286) even as

This Jack Kirby/George Roussos cover to *Journey into Mystery #97* (Oct. 1963) reminds us that Thor was, more or less, Marvel's "Superman." In addition to the similar color scheme of the heroes' costumes, Thor's Asgardian heritage was rich, like Krypton's, and both Thor and Superman had powerful fathers central to their lore.

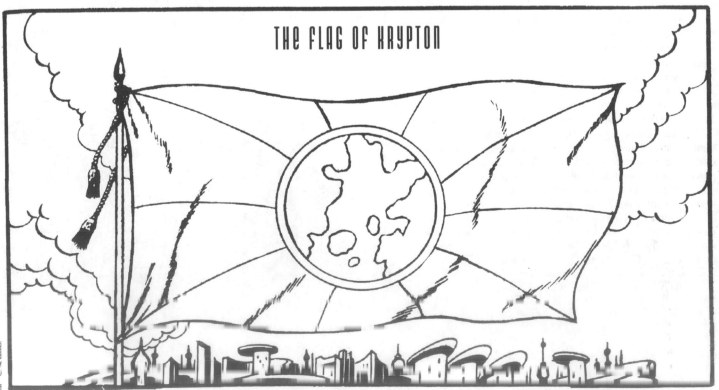

THE FLAG OF KRYPTON

Krypton-related elements in the lead stories began to proliferate again. A major new female Phantom Zoner named Faora debuted in *Action Comics* #471–473 (May–July 1977) and a Nightwing and Flamebird series ran for a time in *Superman Family* #183–194 (1977–1978), with Silver Age figures Van-Zee and Ak-Var taking over the roles. In an interesting time-travel sequence, the Justice League ran into Lyla Ler-Rol on the eve of Krypton's destruction, and she finally found out what happened to her beloved Kal-El (*Super Friends* #17, Feb. 1979).

The time seemed right to try a full-fledged Krypton series and plans were made to give it a three-issue run in *Showcase* during the summer of 1978 to capitalize on the release of *Superman: The Movie*. But the movie was pushed back to December and *Showcase* was cancelled, so *World of Krypton* finally appeared under its own title in mid-1979. And made history. The concept of a stand-alone miniseries under its own name proved more successful than anyone had expected, and both DC and Marvel were soon green-lighting all sorts of similar projects.

Just as *World of Krypton* had incorporated material from Jor-El's Silver Age appearances, so did 1981's *Krypton Chronicles* sequel miniseries utilize many more flashbacks dealing with the more distant past, among them Hatu-El's defeat of the lupine Vrangs (*Superman* #176, Apr. 1965) and the meeting of Erok and Milia that preceded the coining of the El family name (*Jimmy Olsen* #121, July 1969). Next up was a four-issue *Phantom Zone* miniseries (1982) and, finally, a digest collection of some of the 1970s short stories (*Best of DC* #40, 1983).

By this point, Kandor had been restored to full size in *Superman* #338 (Aug. 1979), its people relocated to a world they named Rokyn (literally, "God's Gift," after the Kryptonian deity Rao) and elements of Kryptonian history had become increasingly sparse. Perhaps the most interesting development of the 1980s was a trilogy in *DC Comics Presents* #37 (Sept. 1981), 51 (Nov. 1982), and 74 (Oct. 1984) involving Indian cave hieroglyphics that ultimately proved to be connected to a 19th Century visit by Superman's Kryptonian great-grandfather to Earth. That bit got a lot of mileage on the *Smallville* TV series (2001–present).

In the end, even Supergirl was dead, the kryptonite-poisoned Argo City of her birth trespassed upon by the Vrangs (*Action Comics* #548, Oct. 1983) and slammed into Metropolis by Mr. Mzyzptlk (*DC Comics Presents* #97, Sept. 1986) just to add insult to injury. Elsewhere, the Fire Falls still hung in space, their flames now a sickly green (*Action* #324, May 1965). Even statues of the El family hid pure kryptonite beneath their lead exterior (*Adventure* #313, Oct. 1963; *Superboy* #136, Mar. 1967).

And yet … somewhere beyond this galaxy, beyond Rokyn, Krypton still lived. Not the world that gave birth to Erok and Jor-El but one that honored its memory. In 1961, on the anniversary of his home world's death, Superman built perhaps the greatest monument of his career, pooling his power with that of Supergirl and Krypto to transform a dead world into New Krypton, complete with a population of androids (*Superman* #150, Jan. 1962; *Action* #299, Apr. 1963; *Jimmy Olsen* #101, Apr. 1967; *World's Finest* #190, Dec. 1969). The years passed and its Fire Falls continued to flow and its Jewel Mountains still gleamed. And once a year, at the moment of their world's doom, the survivors of the planet Krypton fell silent. And remembered.

JOHN WELLS is an authority on the history of DC Comics and its characters, contributing information to writers such as Kurt Busiek, Denny O'Neil, Roger Stern, and Mark Waid and acquiring the title of "official unofficial researcher" during the lifespan of Bob Rozakis' cyberspace Answer Man column. The creator of a massive private database of DC Comics character appearances from the past seven decades, John is also known by his online alter ego of **Mikishawm**.

THE SUPERMAN MYTHOLOGY:
UNDER THE MICROSCOPE: LITTLE PEOPLE AND SHRUNKEN CITIES

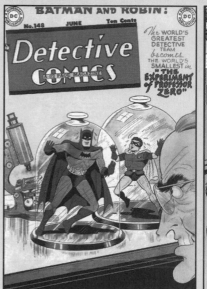

TM & © DC Comics. © 2006 Marvel Characters, Inc.

If you think Brainiac is the only super-villain to wield a shrinking ray, think again. Bad guys as diverse as Dr. Cyclops (from the self-titled 1940 motion picture) to Underdog's foe Simon Bar Sinister have miniaturized their enemies and hapless victims. Add to their roster Professor Zero, who put Batman and Robin under glass in *Detective* #148 (June 1949), and Dr. Doom, who action-figured the FF in *Fantastic Four* #16 (July 1963).

You don't need a shrinking ray to find miniature cities on Earth. The Netherlands' Madurodam, a 1:25-scale model of a Dutch village, was built in 1952 and is one of several such tourist attractions the world traveler may visit.

Copyright-free picture, from www.madurodam.nl.

THE KRYPTONESE ALPHABET
A REAL-WORLD HISTORICAL TALE

by Al Turniansky

You might be wondering where the Silver Age Kryptonese alphabet comes from.

Good question.

My name is Al Turniansky, and, as it happens, I am, by dint of, if you will, a posthumous anointing, the only living authority on the Kryptonese alphabet as presented in Superman comics from roughly the mid-1950s until 1986 (since the rebooting of Superman in that year, they've used different letters).

It happened like this:

Once upon a time, there lived a man named E. Nelson Bridwell. For many, many years, he worked in the editorial department of DC Comics, as an assistant editor, an editor, and a writer. His primary concern was the Superman comics line. But his avocation and delight was the minutiae, the trivia, the details of the fictional universe in which the characters' adventures took place. He reveled in their fictional history.

One of the things that he did was handle the letter columns for the Superman comic books. As such, every letter from fans passed through his hands.

Every so often, he'd get a letter from some reader or other proposing a "Kryptonian alphabet." Invariably, these would consist of 26 random squiggles; random squiggle (r.s.) #1 equaling "A," r.s. #2 = "B," r.s. #3 = "C," and so on (much in the same way that the current version of Kryptonese in the comic books is just enciphered English).

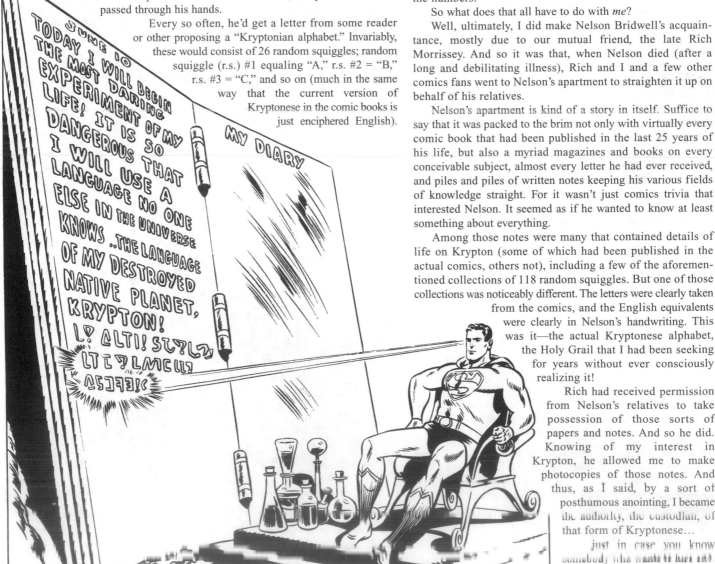

TODAY I WILL BEGIN THE MOST DARING EXPERIMENT OF MY LIFE! IT IS SO DANGEROUS THAT I WILL USE A LANGUAGE NO ONE ELSE IN THE UNIVERSE KNOWS .. THE LANGUAGE OF MY DESTROYED NATIVE PLANET, KRYPTON!

MY DIARY

Hoping to put a stop to this, he answered a letter in some letter column asking if DC could publish a Kryptonian-English dictionary by saying (more or less): "That would be difficult, since the Kryptonian alphabet has 118 letters, and most of the words are longer than 'supercalifragilisticexpialidocious'!"

But that sort of obsessive comics fan being what they are, Bridwell started getting collections of 118 random squiggles. And I know, because I was fascinated by Krypton, and I tried to develop one myself (I was about 15 at the time). Like almost everyone else, though, I hit the stumbling block of "What might the 118 *sounds* be?", and so I put aside the project without ever sending it to DC.

What I had no way of knowing at the time was that Nelson himself had begun to turn his attention to the question of the Kryptonese alphabet. But Nelson being Nelson, and very invested in the trivia and minutiae, he didn't just make up squiggles. No, he combed old Superman stories where letterers had occasion to use Kryptonese. And even though he *himself* had arbitrarily picked the "118 letters" figure, because it had been published in the comics, it was now official, and so he had no choice—he had to select 118 different symbols. And he did. He then assigned arbitrary values to them (and I know that they're arbitrary, because I tried transliterating some examples from the comics using his alphabet, and they're completely unpronounceable). He did the same for the numbers.

So what does that all have to do with *me*?

Well, ultimately, I did make Nelson Bridwell's acquaintance, mostly due to our mutual friend, the late Rich Morrissey. And so it was that, when Nelson died (after a long and debilitating illness), Rich and I and a few other comics fans went to Nelson's apartment to straighten it up on behalf of his relatives.

Nelson's apartment is kind of a story in itself. Suffice to say that it was packed to the brim not only with virtually every comic book that had been published in the last 25 years of his life, but also a myriad magazines and books on every conceivable subject, almost every letter he had ever received, and piles and piles of written notes keeping his various fields of knowledge straight. For it wasn't just comics trivia that interested Nelson. It seemed as if he wanted to know at least something about everything.

Among those notes were many that contained details of life on Krypton (some of which had been published in the actual comics, others not), including a few of the aforementioned collections of 118 random squiggles. But one of those collections was noticeably different. The letters were clearly taken from the comics, and the English equivalents were clearly in Nelson's handwriting. This was it—the actual Kryptonese alphabet, the Holy Grail that I had been seeking for years without ever consciously realizing it!

Rich had received permission from Nelson's relatives to take possession of those sorts of papers and notes. And so he did. Knowing of my interest in Krypton, he allowed me to make photocopies of those notes. And thus, as I said, by a sort of posthumous anointing, I became the authority, the custodian, of that form of Kryptonese…

just in case you know somebody who wants to hire me.

SUPERBOY AND THE
LEGION OF SUPER-HEROES

by Mark Waid
© 2006 Mark Waid.

Those of us who are dedicated fans of the Silver Age Superman speak often (and frighteningly fondly) of the "Superman mythos," which was largely an invention of editor Mort Weisinger, who was DC's hands-on caretaker of the myth from the mid-1950s to the end of the Silver Age in 1970. Up until Weisinger took control, the Man of Steel's adventures had a consistency, but not a tight, detailed continuity. Each story stood very much on its own, with little if any reference to past tales. (In fact, DC had been regularly running Superboy solo chronicles since 1945 billed as "the adventures of Superman when he was a boy!"; you can find stories published as late as 1959 that completely ignore the Boy of Steel!) As exciting and daring as Superman's exploits were, they carried with them a real sense that not much new was bound to happen in Metropolis that hadn't happened before.

Weisinger took an active hand in correcting this. He and his writers purposefully began adding new recurring characters, settings, and elements to Superman's world to make it bigger, more mythic, and more expansive. One of Weisinger's most ingenious additions to the Superman Legend was the Legion of Super-Heroes, a band of future-Earth teenagers who recruited Superboy to their ranks in *Adventure Comics* #247 (Apr. 1958). At first, the Legion was strictly a part of the Superboy storyline, but Weisinger rapidly strengthened the Legion's ties to the complete world of Superman by exporting appearances of Supergirl, Lex Luthor, the Phantom Zone, and other familiar "pieces of continuity."

And then the real fun began. Unlike most "spin-offs," which rarely contribute much of import to their source material, the Legion strip proved it could give as good as it got. Under Weisinger's direction, it not only took *from* the Superman mythos … it began adding *to* it.

It started slowly, subtly. The Legion's fourth appearance, for instance (*Superboy* #86, Jan. 1961), hinted at the possibility that Lex Luthor might someday team up with a "Legion of Super-Villains," whatever form that might take—but that prediction came true less than a year later, when the LSV (not teenagers like their heroic counterparts, but rather a trio of malevolent adults) allied with the grown-up Luthor against the Man of Steel (*Superman* #147, Aug. 1961). Thereafter, the Legion of Super-Villains became standing, if somewhat minor, members of Superman's rogues' gallery.

Siegel, Swan, and Klein in their Super-prime. From "Superboy and the Five Legion Traitors!" (*Superboy* #117, Dec. 1964).
TM & © DC Comics. Art courtesy of Heritage Comics.

When Legionnaire Brainiac 5 first appeared (*Action Comics* #276, May 1961), he was introduced as a direct descendant of the 20th-century space-pirate Brainiac. Years later, when Weisinger revealed the original villain to be a living computer, Superman's editor covered himself by establishing that Brainiac had adopted a flesh-and-blood son in order to augment his humanoid disguise. It was this "Brainiac 2" who was Brainiac 5's biological ancestor, not the great super-criminal himself—which was certainly a relief to Supergirl, who'd fallen for this young Legionnaire. Their time-tossed romance became a charming and enduring addition to Supergirl's continuity independent of the Legion.

Most of all, Weisinger enjoyed using the vantage point of the Legion's 30th century to give teasing glimpses into the future of Superman. For example, we learned in *Adventure Comics* #310 (July 1963) that the bloodline of Superman's foe Mr. Mxyzptlk would extend to the teenage Legion's time—and that one of Mxy's descendants would eventually team with one of Lex Luthor's to join the Adult Legion (*Adventure* #355, Apr. 1967). We knew, too, that the weird, cube-shaped Bizarro World and its freakish inhabitants would still exist in the Legion's time (*Adventure* #329, Feb. 1965), and that both the Batcave and Luthor's Lair would be found, virtually untouched, when the Legion was in need of refuge

(*Adventure* #341 and 360, Feb. 1966 and Sept. 1967).

"But wait," sharp readers cried. "Even with time travel a possibility, how can Superboy and Supergirl work together on Legion missions? Isn't that a paradox, if they come to the future from different points in the past? How can Superboy have met Supergirl when he was a teenager and still 'meet' her for the first time as Superman?" Weisinger was fond of explaining to fans that anything Superboy learned about his own future while with the Legion (including the existence of his super-powered cousin) would be erased from his memory via "post-hypnotic suggestion" from Legionnaire Saturn Girl. Never one to shy away from a good time paradox, however, once Weisinger had the brainstorm in *Adventure* #293 (Feb. 1962) of teaming up Krypto the Super-Dog (from Superboy's era) with Streaky the Super-Cat and Beppo the Super-Monkey (from Super*man*'s time), he couldn't resist teasing readers by reaching just a *little* further into Superman's future to pull in an all-*new* animal—a spacefaring, white-maned Super-Horse ("Yes, readers! This is a PREVIEW GLIMPSE of a superpet Supergirl will own some day in the future!"). What a way to build anticipation among young readers! They had to wait over half a year to experience that "some day in the future," when Super-Horse (aka Comet) met Supergirl in *Action Comics* #292 (Sept. 1962). (A side note: Curiously, Saturn Girl does not cause Krypto to forget this adventure, *despite* the fact that it allows him to know that Streaky and Comet, and thus Supergirl, will exist in his future, but really … who's he going to tell?)

One of the very best "reveals" ever in a Legion story came in *Adventure Comics* #356 (May 1965). For years, visitors to Superman's Fortress of Solitude had been privy to the wonder—and the tragedy—of Kandor, an entire Kryptonian city that had been shrunk to microscopic size and encased in a transparent bottle by Brainiac. Superman had vowed to one day find a way to restore Kandor to normal size and free its people from captivity, but nine years later, not much was happening on that front. And just about the time we, the readers, were prepared to surrender all hope, writer and assistant Superman editor E. Nelson Bridwell hid a nice little Easter egg for the future—*in* the future—by establishing a planet named Rokyn, "settled in the 20th Century by survivors of Krypton, when the Bottle-City of Kandor was enlarged." What a delightful surprise, to discover that the Kandorians would someday be released. When we finally saw it happen in *Superman* #338 (Aug. 1979), those only passingly familiar with the Superman mythos were stunned, but to those of us who'd been holding onto that revelation for over a decade, it was simply a moment in history—so to speak.

*Comics historian and Superman know-it-all (really! He does!) MARK "Brainiac 6" WAID is the writer of DC Comics' **Supergirl and the Legion of Super-Heroes** series.*

34

Al Plastino's 2004 recreation of the splash page from the first Legion of Super-Heroes tale.

(above) In the photo is U.S. astrochimp Ham, who "piloted" a Mercury space capsule a distance of 157 miles on Jan. 31, 1961. (below) A 1957 Romanian commemorative stamp of Russia's Laika, the first dog in space, who perished during her Nov. 3, 1957 Sputnik II Earth orbit.

During the Weisinger Superman era, animals were more than just pets—they were heroes! Dogs and chimps preceded man into space and made headlines, while animal stars like Roy Rogers' horse Trigger and America's top dog Lassie (sorry, Krypto) were television favorites. And Mort's Menagerie of Might followed in their hoof- and paw-steps.

Krypto the Super-Dog entered the Superman mythos in "The Super-Dog from Krypton" in *Adventure Comics* #210 (May 1955). Krypto, toddler Kal-El's pet, was shot into space in a test rocket made by Jor-El and landed on Earth years later, joining his long-lost master, who by that point was operating as Superboy. Krypto appeared regularly with Superboy and sometimes with Superman throughout the 1960s, serving as sidekick, obedient friend, and to-the-rescue Super-lifesaver. Fortunately Krypto was well trained, since the Dog of Steel was allowed to romp unleashed through outer space, where he built for himself a Doghouse of Solitude forged of meteors.

Beppo was another of Jor-El's test animals, arriving on Earth in "The Super-Monkey from Krypton!" in *Superboy* #76 (Oct. 1959). As Beppo the Super-Monkey, his mega-muscled mischief made him a lovable pest.

Streaky the Super-Cat was first seen in *Action Comics* #261 (Feb. 1960). The Earth-born Streaky, the pet of Linda (Supergirl) Lee, gained temporary super-powers after X-kryptonite exposure and scampered in and out of print until 1970.

Supergirl's other pet, Comet the Super-Horse, appeared—out of the blue—with Krypto, Beppo, and Streaky as the Legion of Super-Pets in *Adventure* #293 (Feb. 1962), banding together to save the Legion of Super-Heroes from the Brain-Globes of Rambat. Later that year in *Action* #293 (Oct. 1962), Comet telepathically revealed his origin to Supergirl; he was originally Biron, a centaur in Ancient Greece, who was turned into a super-powered horse by the sorceress Circe.

After their first story in *Adventure* #293, the Super-Pets reunited in *Adventure* #313 (Oct. 1963), 322 (July 1964, with protoplasmic lump Proty II joining the group), 343 (Apr. 1966), 351 (Dec. 1966), and 364 (Jan. 1968). Were Krypto not busy enough, he was also a member of the intergalactic S.C.P.A. (Space Canine Patrol Agents), whose roster included Bull Dog, Chameleon Collie, Hot Dog, Paw Pooch, Tail Terrier, and Tusky Husky (*Superboy* #131–132, July and Sept. 1966).

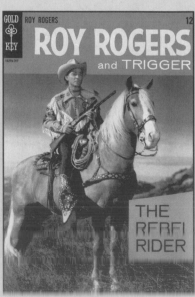

Meet Bongo, a precursor to Beppo.
Superboy #39 (Jan. 1955)

Super-Pets Poker Night, a commissioned illustration by Adam Hughes.

Characters TM & © DC Comics. Jeff Amason collection.

AL PLASTINO INTERVIEW

Editor's note: In the late 1940s Al Plastino (b. 1921) emerged from uncredited work in the Joe Shuster studio to solo-drawing Superman and Superboy stories for Mort Weisinger. Many pre-Silver and Silver Age Superman milestones were illustrated by Plastino: "The Three Supermen from Krypton" (*Superman* #65, July 1950), the first Legion of Super-Heroes tale (*Adventure* #247, Apr. 1958), Brainiac's debut (*Action* #242, July 1958), "Superboy Meets Robin the Boy Wonder" (*Adventure* #253, Oct. 1958), the original Metallo and Supergirl stories (*Action* #252, May 1959), the first Silver Age Mr. Mxyzptlk adventure (*Superman* #131, Aug. 1959), teenage Lex Luthor's origin (*Adventure* #271, Apr. 1960), "The Last Days of Ma and Pa Kent" (*Superman* #161, May 1963), "The Sweetheart that Superman Forgot" (*Superman* #165, Nov. 1963), "Superman's Mission for President Kennedy" (*Superman* #170, July 1964), the origin of the Parasite (*Action* #340, Aug. 1966), and "The Day *Candid Camera* Unmasked Clark Kent's Identity" (*Action* #345, Jan. 1967). During the 1960s and 1970s he was a regular fixture in newspapers, drawing *Batman*, *Superman*, and *Ferd'nand*, among other strips.

The following is excerpted from an interview conducted February 18, 2003 and originally published in The Legion Companion *by Glen Cadigan (TwoMorrows Publications, 2003). Reprinted with permission.*

Photo courtesy of Glen Cadigan.

GLEN CADIGAN: When did you start working for National Comics?

AL PLASTINO: Ohh … '48, '49, [something] like that. I had a studio in New York on 43rd and Lex with two other cartoonists, and I was doing other commercial art when someone suggested that they were looking for someone to do *Superman*. Of course, I thumbed my nose to it [*laughs*]. Someone told me what they were paying—at that time, Wayne Boring was getting $55.00 a page—and they talked me into doing some samples, [which] I did, and they liked them. They offered me $35.00 a page [*laughs*]. Of course, I said, "No, no. I can't do that. You're paying $55." They said, "We can't pay *you* $55. You're just a beginner." So we compromised on $50 a page.

I started out bringing the work in, and it got a little hectic. I had to bring it in for the letterer, 'cause I did my own work. No one ever penciled or inked for me. I did everything myself. In fact, if you look in the books, you'll only see one name: Al Plastino. The only thing they had was a colorist, which everybody had, so I convinced them into doing the whole thing at my studio. I left the studio [in New York] and went on my own and had a studio at home. I used to go in once or twice a week, just to go over the artwork. Then I got to a point where I said— [and] I'm not bragging now—"I don't change my artwork."

At the beginning I had to copy Wayne Boring's style, so I did that for a while, then I did my own style. I did something like 48 covers while I was doing the regular strip, and I was pretty happy there, and it was going pretty good. Then at the same time I was also offered a strip called *Ferd'nand* for United Features. [Henning Dahl] Mikkelsen needed an assistant, so I went ahead and helped him out. When he passed away, I got the strip. So I not only did *Superman* [chuckles], I did *Ferd'nand*, which were two opposites. One was a real cartoon, the other was semi-illustration. So I was pretty busy there for a while, meeting deadlines.

CADIGAN: Did you do much comic work before you got on *Superman*?

PLASTINO: I did some comic work for Funnies, Inc. I helped out with *Sub-Mariner*, I did some inking on *Captain America*—this was during the war.

CADIGAN: Who hired you to do *Superman*?

PLASTINO: I think I saw Mort Weisinger, and I think [Whitney] Ellsworth was the head of the department then. The one that wrote [the] *Batman* [newspaper strip]. I had a falling out with one of the editors [in 1970], and Ellsworth said, "Look, do you want to do *Batman*?", and I said, "I'll try *Batman*." I did that for eight or nine years. I did the dailies and the Sunday, and left *Superman*. By that time I'd been with Superman maybe 18 years, and from time to time I did special stories for them. Then eventually, just after *Batman* demised in the papers, I stuck with *Ferd'nand*. I just did *Ferd'nand* and some commercial art. Not too much. I did that for quite a while, and I finally retired in '84, '85.

CADIGAN: Did you fight with Mort?

PLASTINO: No, Mort and I had an understanding a long time ago. It was Murray Boltinoff I didn't get along with. We

NO REASON WHY **SUPERMAN** CAN'T SPARE A MINUTE TO CHASE AFTER THEM AND FIND OUT FOR SURE! MY ALIBI ON THAT HOT-FOOT WILL HAVE TO WAIT.

Early-ssssse Plastino art from Superman #79 (Feb. 1953).
TM & © DC Comics. Art courtesy of Heritage Comics.

NEXT DAY, CLARK AND JIMMY ARE RETURNING FROM AN ASSIGNMENT IN THE *PLANET* HELICOPTER, WHEN...

OH-OH! ENGINE TROUBLE! WE'RE STARTING TO FALL! I'M GOING TO PARACHUTE-JUMP. YOU DO THE SAME, CLARK!

:GULP!:

RED 'copter

AND AS THE STRICKEN CRAFT HURTLES DOWNWARD...

I SH-SHOULD JUMP, TOO, BUT I'M TOO SCARED TO MOVE! :ULP! I'M B-BLACKING OUT AGAIN...!

SECONDS LATER, CLARK REVIVES.

:AWP! -- THE GROUND IS RUSHING UP AT ME! I'M GOING TO CRASH! I'M SCARED... SCARED!

YEEOWWW!!

HE-E-ELP!

IT... HAPPENED AGAIN! I WAS PARALYZED WITH FEAR, EVEN THOUGH I HAVE THE STRENGTH OF AN ENTIRE ARMY... AND AM *INVULNERABLE!* I'LL OPEN MY PARACHUTE SO JIMMY WILL THINK I JUMPED WITH IT...

WHEN JIMMY FINDS CLARK...

THAT SURE WAS A CLOSE CALL! IF NOT FOR OUR PARACHUTES, WE'D HAVE BEEN DEAD DUCKS! WE'LL WALK TO THE NEARBY TOWN.

I STILL CAN'T BELIEVE I CAN BE SO COWARD-LY! I-I HAVE TO MAKE *ONE* FINAL TEST!

A page from the Al Plastino-drawn "The Coward of Steel!" (*Action* #322, Mar. 1965).

A comics artist sketch-off at a 1950s scouting event: from left to right, Al Plastino, Joe Simon, and (the hand of) Archie artist Bill Vigoda (brother of actor Abe Vigoda).
Courtesy of Glen Cadigan.

had a big argument! I said to Murray, "I will not work with you if you are the editor of *Superboy*!"

CADIGAN: So you got along with Mort?

PLASTINO: Only professionally, that's all! I worked on *Superboy* and *Superman* with Mort.

CADIGAN: How well did you get to know the other Superman artists?

PLASTINO: Curt [Swan] I knew pretty well. Poor Curt, he was a workhorse. All he did was pencil stories. We worked together at the beginning on a couple of things, but I didn't want to work with anybody, because then you're involved with going back and forth. I said, "I want to work at home. I don't want any of this baloney." Not that I was cocky, [but] I knew that I was good enough to do the work.

They wanted me to pencil [tight], and I can't pencil tight. I pencil very rough. I said, "You want me to pencil like Curt? Anybody can ink Curt's stuff." Everything was there—the blacks, the lines—all you hadda do was take a brush and follow his lines, put a little smaltz to it. I said, "If I'm gonna

TM & © DC Comics.

pencil that tight, I might as well finish it." I purposely didn't pencil tight, so [Mort] said, "No, no, you can't pencil," and I said, "I know. I told you I can't pencil so other artists can ink my art!"

What used to turn me off was when [Joe] Shuster and [Jerry] Siegel used to come in and Mort would talk to them like they were dirt. I could never understand that. I told Mort one time, "Mort, you're working because they created Superman." "Oh," he says, "I have other things to do." I said, "But you're still [here]." I said, "If it was me, you would never talk to me that way." They talked down to everybody. I don't understand these guys. They don't do it anymore. The fellas up at [DC] now are a different type of people. They're great people to work for!

CADIGAN: When you were working on Superman, what sense did you have of how important the Superman titles were to DC? Were they DC's most important comics?

PLASTINO: I think so. Mort was responsible for really building it up with those crazy ideas. I thought they were crazy at the time, like Bizarro and different gimmicks to get things a little different, get [things] a little interesting, so they could sell books. In those days you'd go and buy one at the stand. Now it's all by mail-order and whatnot. It's a different business.

CADIGAN: You drew the first appearance of Supergirl.

PLASTINO: Yeah, I did.

CADIGAN: Did you come up with Supergirl's costume?

PLASTINO: Well, they wanted her to look like Superman, [so] you put a skirt on her, put the red boots on her, and the red cape. The only discussion was, "Should she be blonde?", and I thought that was a good idea.

CADIGAN: Do you remember Mort telling you about it? The idea they had for it?

PLASTINO: I think they discussed it with other editors, then I would come in and they'd say, "Al, I want you to blah blah blah." I said, "Okay, I'll work on it." I don't remember specifically what he said. I got along fairly well with him, but I always kept him in his place. If you let an editor jump on your back and get you shakin' in your boots, you're dead! You're dead in the comic business. They treat you like dirt! They treat you like you're nothing. And that's when Murray just annoyed me one time. I said, "Who the hell do you think [you are]? You talk to me like a man or I don't want to even look at you."

And he went wild. He went on and on and on. I said, "Okay, let's go in your office." I got him in the office, closed the door and said, "Don't you ever talk to me that way again." 'Cause we were in the art room with a bunch of guys. And most of the guys took it. They would take it. I mean, imagine talking to Shuster like he's a piece of dirt. And the poor guy was so humble, and so afraid of Mort. I said, "What the hell is he afraid of?" And finally they consented to give the guy $20,000 a year for life. He worked at a post office. They were making millions on him. That rubbed me the wrong way.

CADIGAN: You, did the first appearance of the Legion of Super-Heroes. Do you think you designed the costumes which the characters wore in that issue?

PLASTINO: I don't know who designed those costumes. I just got something to do and I did it, I guess. I don't remember designing them.

CADIGAN: Back in those days when they would send you a script for a comic, if a character had not yet appeared, would it be up to you to design them?

PLASTINO: Yeah, I think so. I had characters I had to make up. I'm looking at [the first Legion story] now, and I probably did do it. I know the folds and the type of costume. It might have been mine, [but] it's so long ago.

CADIGAN: When you would start a feature like "Legion" or "Supergirl" and it would go on to become a success, would you keep tabs on something like that?

PLASTINO: I don't think I paid much attention to that. I don't want to sound too preoccupied, but I really didn't care. I did my job, and I never took comics that seriously. It was a job and I did it, and that was it. Some guys became really involved with their comics, which I never did. It was just a job. That's the only explanation I can give you on why I didn't follow up on most other things.

CADIGAN: **Do you remember a period in the early '70s when Jack Kirby was working for DC and you were called in to redraw some of his faces?**

PLASTINO: Yeah, I would do that once in a while. I remember bringing it in. I said, "What the hell are they bringing me this [for]?" That's another pain in the neck. You gotta redo a face over a body. You have to paste a piece of paper over it, [and] redraw it. Yeah, I would do that from time to time.

CADIGAN: **Who asked you to do that?**

PLASTINO: Carmine [Infantino] took over [DC] at that time. I was working with Carmine, and [he] started that crazy panel stuff … you know, big panel, lots of action? I worked with Carmine for a while. Maybe it was Carmine. I don't know. Carmine's a nice guy. I got along with [him]. He understood me. He would say, "Al, excuse me, but…" He would apologize first [laughs]. He'd say, "Could you do this for me?" and I'd say, "Sure."

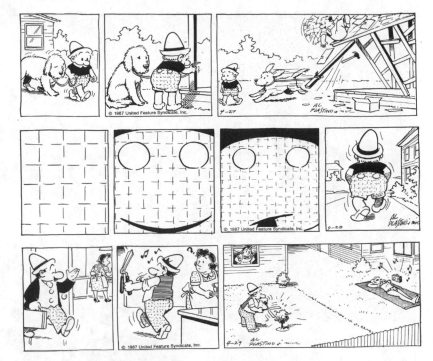

A trio of Plastino's *Ferd'nand* strips.
Ferd'nand TM & © 2006 United Features Syndicate.

Avid golfer Plastino's cartoon teams the World's Finest duo with Arnold Palmer.
Superman and Batman TM & © DC Comics.

A Nov. 2001 Superman illo of the Caped Kryptonian, by Al Plastino.

THE SUPERMAN MYTHOLOGY:
KRYPTON MEETS CAMELOT

U.S. President John F. Kennedy (1917–1963) used the then-new technology of television to win the White House in 1960, and he captured Mort Weisinger's attention, as well. JFK was an unofficial member of the Superman family, making appearances in *Jimmy Olsen* #56 (Oct. 1961), *Action* #281 (Dec. 1961), *Action* #285 (Feb. 1962), *Adventure* #294 (Mar. 1962, actually a Bizarro prankster wearing a JFK mask), and *Action* #309 (Feb. 1964, where Kennedy impersonated Clark Kent to preserve the hero's Superman identity).

The most famous of the Chief Executive's DC appearances was "Superman's Mission for President Kennedy!" in *Superman* #170 (July 1964), which has an intriguing backstory. Planned for publication in issue #168 (cover-dated Apr. 1964) as part of the president's campaign to encourage physical fitness among youths, "Superman's Mission," written by Bill Finger and E. Nelson Bridwell, was originally drawn by Curt Swan. The story was shelved immediately after Kennedy's November 22, 1963 assassination, but rescheduled for print upon the request of Kennedy's successor, President Lyndon B. Johnson. Swan's original pages were, according to conflicting reports, either lost or given to Jacqueline Kennedy, and Al Plastino quickly stepped forth to render the tale for publication. Plastino's artwork for this landmark story is displayed in the Kennedy Library.

After JFK's death, Weisinger offered him tributes in *Jimmy Olsen* #89 (Dec. 1965) and *Lois Lane* # 62 (Jan. 1966). Years later, during Julius Schwartz's editorial tenure, Kennedy was retrofitted into Super*boy*'s history in *The New Adventures of Superboy* #23 (Nov. 1981) and 27 (Mar. 1982).

A panel from the Swan-drawn version of "Superman's Mission for President Kennedy" survived via a newspaper story and a memorial in *Superman* #168.
TM & © DC Comics.

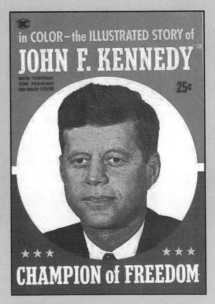

in COLOR—the ILLUSTRATED STORY of
JOHN F. KENNEDY
WITH PORTRAIT FOR FRAMING ON BACK COVER
25¢
★★★ **CHAMPION of FREEDOM** ★★★

Worden & Childs' *John F. Kennedy, Champion of Freedom* (1964) was one of two comic-book biographies of the slain president (Dell Comics produced the other).
© 1964 Worden & Childs.

Kennedy wasn't the only U.S. president to appear in Weisinger-edited tales. While trying to stop Abraham Lincoln's assassination in "The Impossible Mission!" (*Superboy* #85, Dec. 1960; art by George Papp), the Boy of Steel encountered an *adult* Luthor. Twenty-six years later, Spider-Man met Honest Abe on this unpublished Marvel Comics cover.
TM & © DC Comics.   © 2006 Marvel Characters, Inc. Art courtesy of Heritage Comics.

JIM MOONEY INTERVIEW

Supergirl and Streaky; a 1999 Mooney sketch.
Characters TM & © DC Comics. Art courtesy of Heritage Comics.

Editor's note: If anyone deserves the title of "*the* Supergirl artist," it's Jim Mooney (b. 1919). Mooney drew Supergirl's *Action Comics* back-up series starting with the Girl of Steel's second appearance in #253 (June 1959) and continued on the feature for an amazing eight years, until issue #358 (Jan. 1968). "Gentleman" Jim's other career highlights include illustrating *Batman*, Robin the Boy Wonder, Tommy Tomorrow, Dial H for Hero, Superman, Legion of Super-Heroes, *Ghost Rider*, and *Ms. Marvel* stories.

Interview conducted by Daniel Best on November 14, 2005.

DANIEL BEST: Tell me how you ended up drawing Supergirl.
JIM MOONEY: They just wanted to try me out on Supergirl. I was doing quite a few things for DC at that time. I was doing [Dial H for Hero in] *House of Mystery* and quite a few different things, and Mort thought, "Maybe we'll give Jim a shot at this."

I had suggested doing something like that a long time before they actually came up with a Supergirl script. Unfortunately, the first one they gave me was after the one that Al Plastino did, and I had to ape that at first, and I really didn't like it.

At the same time I had a studio—an art service—in Hollywood, California, and I was busy as hell at the time, but I didn't want to neglect doing it. A lot of that [early] Supergirl stuff was done by people who were working with me. It was a joint effort, and I think if you go through some of that stuff you'll notice that it's not that great. I had a girl who did a lot of the work, [so it] wasn't all mine. It was not thought out as well, and sometimes that wasn't always my inking for the first few years. [*laughter*] Later on, Supergirl became better as far as the drawing was concerned. I think it improved a lot through the years when I finally got on it myself totally.

BEST: Why did Al Plastino draw the first Supergirl story and not you?
MOONEY: Al Plastino was a [DC] house artist. He did Superman, he worked for them, and they wanted it to have that look. They never did like the way I did Superman, anyway. When I started, Mort said that I made Superman look not quite "super" enough. So occasionally they'd have somebody—Curt Swan or Al Plastino or whoever was in the bullpen at the time—work over my Superman faces.

BEST: We can't talk about Supergirl without touching on the supporting cast—Streaky the Super-Cat and Comet the Super-Horse. Who came up with those two?
MOONEY: Usually the editor came up with the ideas for any new characters, and I just designed them. So you've got a Super-Horse. You draw a pretty horse, and put a cape on him. [*laughter*]

Streaky the Super-Cat was my design. I think the writer came up with the initial idea, but I designed him so he looked a little bit more like an animated cat. I fell in love with Streaky from the very beginning. I still draw him. I love cats. But instead of the editor telling me, "Make him look like this" or "Look like that," I pretty much drew him my own way. Most of that kind of stuff was whoever it was who wrote most of the scripts. I didn't pay that much attention to it unless I liked them. [*laughter*]

BEST: Along with Supergirl, you were producing a vast amount of work during the 1960s, including Tommy Tomorrow and Dial H for Hero. Which were your favorites?
MOONEY: I liked Tommy Tomorrow about as well as anything I did. It was a strip that I enjoyed.

Dial H for Hero, which was in the *House of Mystery* book, was a chore because I had to make up new costumes for the various characters each issue. They always had one or two villains and each one had to have a new costume, so it was time consuming—it wasn't a moneymaking strip. Some of the fans who are now in their forties and fifties liked it pretty much when they were younger.

I did like Supergirl after a while. But [as far as it] being a strip of great interest, it wasn't there. It was pretty much the same thing over and over, the same plot over and over and over and over—I shouldn't say the *same* plot, but the same *plots* would be more like it.

BEST: You stayed with Supergirl for a fairly long while.

Photo courtesy of Glen Cadigan.

MOONEY: I drew Supergirl for almost nine years, and I think it changed through the years. Hopefully it changed for the better. 'Cause [later] I had the time. You see, when I came to New York I was drawing Supergirl at the time, and I gave up my studio in Hollywood. Mort's incentive was, "We'll give you more work," and that was when I did the Legion of Super-Heroes (in *Adventure Comics* #328–330, Jan.–Apr. 1965). That was the extra work that I was given. Actually, it was more of an incentive to come back to New York to work more closely with Mort. And that wasn't always a pleasure.

BEST: Where were you living at that particular time?

MOONEY: I had an art service right opposite from Grauman's Chinese Theatre, right on Hollywood Boulevard. So I handled just about everything that came in the door.

Actually, I really didn't think that I would make it last that long. But I mentioned to Mort, I said, "I'd really like to work out in Hollywood for a while. I'd like to visit my folks. Would it be all right if I took a couple of months and worked out there?" And he said, "Yeah, sure. Just send the stuff in."

And it just dragged on and on and on. I mean, week after week, month after month, year after year. I was out there ten years—no, I shouldn't say that. I was out there, I guess, eight or nine years before I made any trip to New York to make actual contact again with the others at the [DC] office. And it was just toward the very last year that I decided that I would take the offer to come to New York and work more closely with Mort,

TM & © DC Comics.

Superman artist team-up: Mooney inked Ross Andru on *Sub-Mariner* #39 (July 1971) and John Byrne on *Daredevil* #138 (Oct. 1976).

because at the time there were a lot of things going on. I was going through a divorce, so I was happy to get out of the area!

BEST: Who did you work with at DC?

MOONEY: I had to work with Jack Schiff, and Murray Boltinoff. Julie Schwartz, I never worked with, although I liked Julie a lot.

And Mort Weisinger—God forbid that anyone should have to work with him, but I did. Mort made a tremendous amount of money and was very, very successful in many ways. I think having the editorship wasn't something that he did because he liked it and had the experience, he just liked the money.

Mort made so much money that we were kidding at one time and saying, "You can't take it with you," and one guy came up to me and said, "You said Mort couldn't take it with him? I know damn well that before he died he made arrangements and took it with him!" [*laughter*]

He came out to visit me when I lived in Los Angeles and I took him around quite a bit. He was working with one of the studios there, we went night clubbing, and we got along fine socially, if you can call it getting along fine. However, he was never an attractive man personality-wise, or physically. At that time I was going to art school, and later on I had connections with Earl Carroll and his girls. [*Editor's note: Carroll, a renowned impresario during the 1920s through the late 1940s, owned two popular nightclubs, one on Broadway in New York and the other on Sunset Boulevard in Hollywood, both of which attracted entertainment luminaries. Phyllis Coates, TV's original Lois Lane, was among the actresses performing at Carroll's Hollywood club.*] But [Mort] was always trying to get me to get a date for him, and I thought, "I can't do this. I can't do it to any of my girlfriends; they'll never speak to me again." [*laughter*]

He was a very shrewd person. He was a very unusually insecure person, though. I remember one time my brother-in-law, who was a very attractive guy, I tried to get him to do comics before he made his fortune in vintage cars, and he went out to see Mort at Mort's place on Long Island. Mort's wife was there and she was obviously attracted to my brother-in-law. Everything was going fine [between Mort and my brother-in-law] until the [smitten] wife walked in, and suddenly [Mort] just said, "That's it. I've had enough, I'm busy right now. I'll talk to you another time. I'll give you a call." And he never got a damn thing from him.

BEST: What was Mort like?

MOONEY: Mort was a Jekyll-and-Hyde character. He had his ups and downs, and most of the time they were downs and you would be suffering because he was having his downs. He was vicious at times. But when he came to visit me when he was in Hollywood, when he was working with one of the studios there, we got along fine socially, if you can call it getting along fine. We didn't argue or anything like that. He wasn't objectionable. But in the office he could be a very, very difficult person. I'll give you an incident, as an example:

I had been doing Supergirl for a long, long while, and I used to come in and bring my work to Mort, and I walked into the office and Mort was busy with a writer, so he waved me out, like "I'm busy." So I walked out to the bullpen, and I was talking to Jack Schiff, and Mort came storming in, and said, "You're supposed to bring that Supergirl to me first!" His voice was cracking with anger; and I was flabbergasted, and everybody was shocked in the writers' bullpen. And he kept at it, saying, "You know, you keep at this, and you won't be drawing Supergirl," and I said, "I've got news for you, Mort, I'm not going to be drawing Supergirl anymore." [*laughter*]

That was one minor incident that was rather difficult. But he was a very talented man. He was a darn good writer. He wrote for a lot for the national magazines and did articles that were very, very well done.

BEST: You then went from DC to Marvel in 1968. What prompted you to make that move?

MOONEY: I went before they could kick me out. [DC was] getting into the illustrative type of art then, primarily Neal Adams, and they wanted to go in that direction. Towards the end there I picked up on it, and I think my later Supergirl was quite illustrative, but not quite what they wanted.

I knew the handwriting was on the wall, so I was looking around and I realized that the work was slowing up and it was going to dry up totally. I went over to Marvel and I talked to Stan Lee. The reason I hadn't worked at Marvel for all those years was because they didn't pay as well as DC.

Mooney's revamp of the first Supergirl cover, with the artist's *other* supergal, Ms. Marvel, looking a *little* overwhelmed.

Kara's rocket takes a wrong turn in this Mooney commissioned illo, courtesy of the artist.
Supergirl TM & © DC Comics.

THE SUPERMAN MYTHOLOGY:
JERRY SIEGEL'S RETURN TO KRYPTON

Public domain photo from Wikipedia.com.

The relationship between writer Jerry Siegel (1914–1996) and Superman is inarguably comics' most bittersweet story. Siegel and his Superman co-creator, artist Joe Shuster, endured decades of unsuccessful copyright litigation, humiliation, marginal employment, and medical woes, slipping into obscurity and financial destitution before 1975 negotiations with DC Comics management afforded them a pension and creator credit for their Man of Steel [see Chapter 3's Neal Adams interview for more details].

Yet none of those problems were apparent to the average Superman reader of the 1960s. After having left DC in 1948 over a rights dispute, Siegel was rehired by Mort Weisinger in the late 1950s. As one of the primary writers of Superman's early Silver Age, he contributed classics such as "How Luthor Met Superboy" (*Adventure* #271, Apr. 1960), "The Impossible Mission" (*Superboy* #85, Oct. 1960), "Superman's Return to Krypton" (*Superman* #141, Nov. 1960), "The Giant Turtle Man" (*Jimmy Olsen* #53, June 1961), "The Death of Superman" (*Superman* #149, Nov. 1961), and "The Sweetheart Superman Forgot" (*Superman* #165, Nov. 1963), plus Legion of Super-Heroes stories and a host of light-hearted Bizarro World, Supergirl, and Lois Lane adventures. Perhaps his greatest contribution to Superman's Silver Age was Siegel's transformation of Lex Luthor from a one-dimensional mad scientist into a captivating, sometimes sympathetic antagonist.

Another lawsuit over ownership of his co-creation caused Siegel to leave DC in 1963; he wrote for other comics publishers before losing his toehold in the business a few years later.

Recommended reading: *Men of Tomorrow: Geeks, Gangsters and the Birth of the Comic Book* by Gerard Jones (Basic Books, 2004).

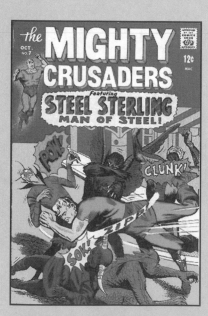

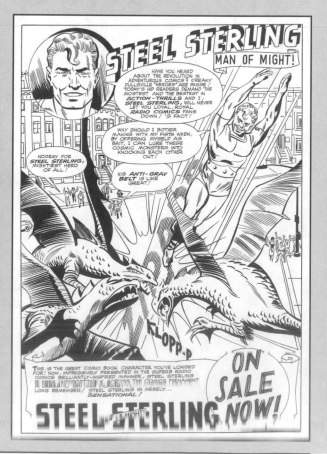

Siegel found a home at Archie Comics, scripting super-hero stories for *The Mighty Crusaders* and *Fly-Man*. Superman's co-creator was on tap to write a new title starring Steel Sterling, "the Man of Might" (aka "the Man of Steel"), but that title never materialized. One Steel Sterling story written by Siegel and illustrated by Paul Reinman, artist of the 1966 ad shown here, was produced and serialized in *Fly-Man* #39 (Sept. 1966) and *Mighty Crusaders* #7 (Nov. 1966). Siegel penned the introduction to *High Camp Super-Heroes* (Belmont, 1966), a paperback collection of his Archie stories.

© 2006 Archie Comics

Before returning to DC, Jerry Siegel wrote two issues of Charlton's own superman, *Mr. Muscles* #22 (Mar. 1956) and 23 (Aug. 1956).
© 1956 Charlton Comics.

Luthor gloats over "The Death of Superman" (*Superman* #149, Nov. 1961).
TM & © DC Comics.

In 1963 Siegel was hired by Stan Lee to write the Human Torch series in *Strange Tales*, under the pen name of "Joe Carter." After two issues (#112 and 113, Sept. and Oct. 1963) his stories were deemed too campy for Marvel, and Siegel moved on to other companies.
© 2006 Marvel Characters, Inc.

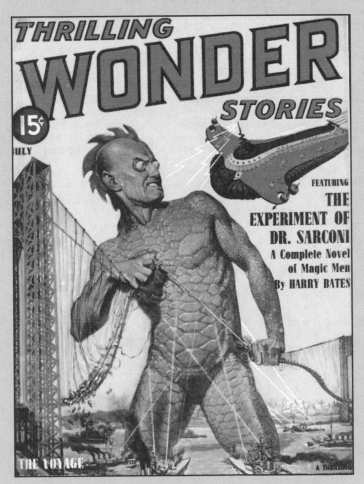

(above) The cover of the Weisinger-edited *Thrilling Wonder Stories* (July 1940) inspired the cover to the Weisinger-edited, Siegel-scripted "The Giant Turtle Man" in *Jimmy Olsen* #53 (June 1961, bottom right). In between their publication came Mort's lesser-known *Superboy* #30 (Jan. 1954).
© 1940 Better Publications, Inc   TM & © DC Comics.

"THE DEATH OF CLARK KENT" IMAGINARY STORY

Editor's note: The following is a 4-page plot for an unpublished Imaginary Story written by Jerry Siegel. Details of its origin appear at the end of the plot.

SUPERMAN Plot   Jerry Siegel

AN IMAGINARY TALE

          THE DEATH OF CLARK KENT

     Superman is being honored on a TV show which is similar to the former "This Is Your Life" program. Each guest who is interviewed is allowed to ask the Chief Guest who is being honored (who in this case is SUPERMAN) <u>one</u> question. Guest Lois/question is: "Why won't you marry me?"...Superman explains, for the zillionth time, that the life of his wife would be in danger.

     The masquerading host of the show turns out to be a diabolical alien, whose warped, cruel alien sense of humor impels him to shine a twin ray on Superman and Lois, which permanently switches Superman's super-powers to Lois. The unmasked alien easily keeps away angered now non-super Superman with one hand held against Superman's chest, and he plucks out Kent garments and glasses from the pouch of Superman's cape, forcing them on Superman and revealing Kent is Superman. Lois super-manhandles the alien with her new super-powers, in attempt to get him to return the switched powers back to Superman... but alien darts into a flight-machine which materializes and machine disappears, whiskin him away, forever.

     Lois dons super-costume from Superman's Fortress of Solitude and searches universe and other dimensions, fighting off various menaces and doing super good deeds while trying to find the perpetrator of the super-switch, but she fails.

     Meanwhile, Clark Kent is getting fed up with sympathy from well-wishers and cruel barbs from acid-tongued people who had envied Superman.

     Some gangsters try to rub out normal Clark Kent in retaliation for his having captured and jailed them, years ago, when he was Superman. They corner him in an alley. Super-Lois arrives in time to save the life of Clark, with her super-powers, and she captures the crooks.

     Lois begins a super-courtship of the non-super Clark Kent. She happily says there is no reason why he can't marry her NOW.

Super-Lois inundates Clark with super-gifts.

Super-Lois secretly helps Clark score scoops, so as to save his pride, but he isn't fooled. He complains she is undermining his manhood. She says she won't pester him anymo

Clark quits job, goes to another city, to get away from her and begins a new life. Super-Lois respects his desire to forget the past, including her. (But he can't keep Superman out of his dreams.) Clark keeps reading about Super-Lois' feats...and finds he greatly misses her. He can't eat, he can't sleep...he misses her terribly. At last, he can't take it, anymore. He goes on a campaign to make amends and win the heart of the miffed Super-Lois...he pursues her as avidly, as he had at one time avoided her.

He begs her to marry him. She accepts. The whole world is thrilled when Super-Lois marries Clark Kent in a public ceremony attended by dignitaries and friends.

The newlyweds are very happy. He resumes his job in Metropolis. But, in evenings, he frequently complains because Super-Lois is away so often on super-missions. She now benefits mankind with her super-powers, as Superman used to,

Clark finds to his dismay that he is getting jealous of his wife. He, who had once been the mighty Superman, is now...nothing, the has-been husband of the great Super-Lois

He tries to overcome his unfair jealousy, but as Lois shows him trophies she has won for great deeds, he explodes, berates her...can't she possibly imagine how he feels? She sobs she's sorry. They make up.

But Clark Kent, the man who had once been Superman, keeps brooding over his lost might. He feels he isn't worthy of Super-Lois.

Then Luthor, who Super-Lois has been almost nabbing, does some dirty work. Luthor deliberately lures a Super-Powered Man from another world into pursuing Luthor. Then Luthor lures Super-Lois into danger, and the handsome Mighty Man from another world save Lois. Luthor is captured... but he had shined a Love Ray on the Mighty Man who begins romantic super-pursuit of Super-Lois. She, a happily married woman, resents it. And though she feels an undeniable attraction for the Mighty Man, who is everything that unsuper Clark isn't, she loves Clark and demands Mighty Man cut it out. He sneers that Clark isn't worthy of her...she deserves someone equally mighty such as Mighty Man. In prison, Luthor gloats. He knows that someday he will escape prison. He exults over his vengeance. He feels he is manipulating the ruin of the marriage of Super-Lois and Clark Kent...this is his insidious revenge on the former Superman, his once great enemy

Clark leaves Lois a farewell note. He doesn't feel worthy of her, now that he hasn' got super-powers. It was a mistake to marry her. - Mighty Man sees the note, and he urge Lois to forget that weakling of a Clark and to marry Mighty Man after shedding Clark. She loses her temper, hurls Mighty Man away into stratosphere, shouting for him to get lost and stay lost. She loves Clark...she'll never love anyone but Clark... and she'll get him back!

Super-Lois self-sacrificingly tries various ways to lose her super-powers, so this barrier between her and the man she loves will be removed. All her efforts fail.

She locates, and saves life, of Clark Kent from a near-accident. Instead of being happy about it, it only makes him more conscious of his inferiority. Super-Lois begs Clark to please not let her super-powers be a barrier between them. To forget his stupid feelings of thwarted male superiority... please, please let them just be together and in love, and to blazes with his foolish pride, his thwarted male superiorit etc.

Clark realizes ...either he loves her, or he doesn't -- and he does love her. He tells her that he wants to think about it awhile. If he decides he has been wrong, he will return to their home in Metropolis. Super-Lois promises that if he does, she won't neglect him so much. Alone, she cries...she doesn't want to be super...what she really wants is the man she loves...

As Clark returns toward their home, Super-Lois brushes away her tears...and her heart leaps with happiness. She is thrilled to see him, knowing Clark's love for her has triumphed over his nagging feelings of thwarted male superiority.

But Luthor has escaped from prison. Black-hearted Luthor, who is disguised as a patrolling policeman, guns down Clark, killing him. Luthor tries to escape in a stolen police car. Super-Lois disregards jubilant Luthor as she kneels and broken-heartedly takes the dead man she loves in her arms...the man who had once been invulnerable to bullets or harm of any kind. Luthor's car, as other police-cars arrive, goes out of control, cracks up and goes up in flames together with the revenged criminal...

Later, widow Super-Lois sits in the Fortress of Solitude, numbly disregarding distress signals from scanner devices. She has decided to give up her crusade in behalf of humanity...she has no heart for it, anymore. She sobs, blaming herself for the death of Clark...

SUPERMAN had been RIGHT! SUPERMAN for years had refused to marry Lois, because he was afraid it would imperil her life. In her selfishness, her craving for the marriage, she had disregarded the danger to the life of the non-super Clark Kent and had bullheadedly married him. Now he is dead...dead...dead...and it is all her fault. If only, just as SUPERMAN had refused to marry Lois, Super-Lois had had the will-power not to marry the man she loved and endanger his existence. But now it's too late, and she will have to live with the horror of this wrong decision, forever.

But then, she numbly sights a distress-signal on a scanner device. A crying baby is lost in a woods and wild dogs are ferociously closing in on the helpless child.

SUPER-LOIS hurtles into action...no, no, she'd been wrong in her decision to abandon her super-crusading. Her beloved, slain Clark would've wanted her to continue helping humanity with her super-pwers...

SUPER-LOIS crashes into the wild dogs, sending them hurtling aside. She snatches up the baby into the safety of her arms, and flies back toward the city...the baby stops crying and falls asleep in her arms. She kisses the cheek of the sleeping babe. Yes, SUPER-LOIS will resume her super-crusade, again... because that is what her beloved, slain husband Clark, who had once been the invincible MAN OF STEEL, would want her to do...

****

Remarks Mark Waid, who graciously contributed these scans of Siegel's unpublished Imaginary Story: "The backstory, according to Julie [Schwartz], was that when Siegel showed up unexpectedly at the DC Super-Con in '76, [Mort] Weisinger created a nice photo-op moment for himself by publicly inviting Siegel to pitch a new Superman story to Julie." Siegel's effort quickly stalled over disagreements with work-for-hire contracts.

Julius Schwartz and Jerry Siegel in 1986.
Photo © 1986 DC Comics.

CHAPTER 2

UP, UP, AND AWAY!

SUPERMAN COMICS OF 1965-1970

To escape to the gravity of mid-1960s real-world headlines, from the escalating body count of the Vietnam War to civil unrest in U.S. cities, Americans ducked and covered under the warm, wacky blanket of "camp" heroes. Tongue-in-cheek champions, including gadget-loaded super-spies and Adam West's preposterously stoic Batman, invaded pop culture much like the Beatles had done a few years earlier. Super-hero comic books experienced a sales surge that paralleled the industry's original World War II boom.

In this world of farcical crime fighters, editor Mort Weisinger ruled as king. The fanciful plots that now dominated most super-hero stories had simply caught up with what Weisinger had been producing for years. The Man of Steel cemented his iconic status by becoming, quite literally, the star of stage (Broadway's *It's a Bird, It's a Plane, It's Superman*) and screen (Filmation's animated TV series *The New Adventures of Superman*).

By the mid-'60s Curt Swan was fully anointed as the prince of pencilers in Weisinger's kingdom. Having been groomed for the role after Weisinger made him the chief Superman cover artist of the late 1950s/early 1960s, Swan's naturalistic renderings now epitomized Superman's acknowledged house style, particularly when inked by George Klein.

Super-hero mania sputtered out of steam by the late 1960s, and the Weisinger formula now seemed dated. Superman was in need of a makeover, a renovation that would be left in the hands of others as Weisinger retired from DC in 1970.

This chapter examines the stories behind the stories of Superman's mid- to late-1960s' adventures, and the creative people who brought them to life.

Curt Swan's 1994 pencil recreation of his cover art to *Superman* #201 (Nov. 1967). In the inset is the cover in its original published form (inked by George Klein).

1965

Action Comics #320–331
Superman #174–181

Adventure Comics #328–339
Justice League of America #33–40
Superboy #118–125
(#124: first Lana Lang as
Insect Queen)
Superman's Girl Friend Lois Lane
#54–61
Superman's Pal Jimmy Olsen #82–89
World's Finest Comics #147–154
80-Page Giant #8 (Secret Origins),
10 (Superboy), 13 (Jimmy Olsen), 14
(Lois Lane), 15 (Superman and Batman)

1966

Action Comics #332–344
(#334: first Supergirl 80-Page Giant)
(#340: first Parasite)
Superman #182–191

Adventure Comics #340–351
(#345: Legion takes over entire title)
Justice League of America #41–49
Superboy #126–134
Superman's Girl Friend Lois Lane
#62–70
Superman's Pal Jimmy Olsen #90–98
World's Finest Comics #155–163

Aquaman #30 (Superman and
JLA appearance)
The Brave and the Bold #63 (Supergirl
and Wonder Woman team-up)
Superman Signet paperback reprint
It's a Bird, It's a Plane, It's Superman
on Broadway
The New Adventures of Superman
Filmation animated television series

1967

Action Comics #345–357
(#345: Superman on *Candid Camera*,
Allen Funt guest-stars)
Superman #192–202
(#199: first Superman/Flash race)

Adventure Comics #352–363
Justice League of America #50–59
Superboy #135–143
Superman's Girl Friend Lois Lane
#71–79
Superman's Pal Jimmy Olsen #99–107
World's Finest Comics #164–172

Blackhawk #228 (Superman and
JLA appearance)
The Flash #175 (second
Superman/Flash race)
*The Superman/Aquaman Hour of
Adventure* Filmation series expands
to one hour

1968

Action Comics #358–370
(#358–362: Virus X storyline)
Superman #203–211
(#207: 30th anniversary issue)

Adventure Comics #364–375
Justice League of America #60–68
Superboy #144–152
(#145: Ma and Pa Kent regain youth)
(#148: last Mort Weisinger-
edited issue)
(#149: first Murray Boltinoff-
edited issue)
Superman's Girl Friend Lois Lane
#80–88
Superman's Pal Jimmy Olsen
#108–116
World's Finest Comics #173–181

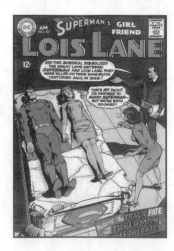

The Adventures of Jerry Lewis #105
(Jerry meets Superman)
Captain Action #1 (Superman
appearance)
DC Special #1 (Superman cover
appearance)
The Inferior Five #10 (Superman
appearance)
Not Brand Echh! #7 (Marvel Comics
"Stuporman" parody)
Wonder Woman #177 (Wonder Woman
vs. Supergirl)
The Batman/Superman Hour
Filmation series is retitled

1968

Action Comics #371–383
(#376: last Supergirl back-up)
(#377: Legion back-ups begin)
Superman #213–221
(#216: Superman in Vietnam)

Adventure Comics #376–387
(#380: last Legion story in *Adventure*)
(#381: Supergirl takes over title)
Justice League of America #69–77
Superboy #153–161
Superman's Girl Friend Lois Lane
#89–97
Superman's Pal Jimmy Olsen #117–125
World's Finest Comics #182–190

DC Special #3 (Supergirl cover
appearance), 5 (Superman cover
appearance)
Sugar and Spike #83 (Superman
uniform on cover)

1970

Action Comics #384–395
(#392: last Legion story in *Action*;
last Mort Weisinger-edited issue)
(#393: first Murray Boltinoff-
edited issue)
Superman #223–232
(#232: last Mort Weisinger-
edited issue)

Adventure Comics #388–400
(#396: last Mort Weisinger-edited
issue)
Justice League of America #78–86
Superboy #162–170
Superman's Girl Friend Lois Lane
#98–106
(#104: last Mort Weisinger-
edited issue)
(#105: first Rose and the Thorn;
first E. Nelson Bridwell-edited issue)
Superman's Pal Jimmy Olsen #126–134
(#132: last Weisinger-edited issue)
(#133: first Jack Kirby issue, first
Morgan Edge, intro of new Newsboy
Legion and Flipper-Dipper)
(#134: first Darkseid)

World's Finest Comics #191–199
(#196: last regular
Superman/Batman team-up;
last Mort Weisinger-edited issue)
(#198–199: *WFC* becomes
Superman team-up title with #198,
which is first Julius Schwartz-edited
issue; two-part Flash team-up, the
third Superman/Flash race)

Teen Titans #25 (Superman and
JLA guest-star)

DRAWING SUPERMAN

by Curt Swan

Editor's note: To several generations of fans, Curt Swan (1920–1996) was *the* Superman artist—his rendition so typified the Man of Steel that comedian Jerry Seinfeld insisted that "the Curt Swan Superman" be the version to co-star with him in a series of live action/animated American Express commercials in the early 2000s. Swan started drawing Superman-family characters in 1948, and by the mid-1960s had ascended to the top spot among Superman artists, a position he ultimately relinquished in 1986 when Superman was rebooted in *Man of Steel.* Swan occasionally drew Superman in special stories and commissioned illustrations until his death in 1996.

Recommended reading: *Curt Swan: A Life in Comics* by Eddy Zeno (Vanguard Productions, 2002).

Originally published in Superman at Fifty: The Persistence of a Legend, *edited by Dennis Dooley and Gary Engle (Octavia Press © 1987). Reprinted with permission.*

I dropped by the Smithsonian when I was in Washington one day this past June to see the new Superman exhibit. Like other Americans who will visit the museum during the exhibit's year-long run, I have a certain fondness for the Man of Steel. He and I go back a long way. For 30 years or so, from around 1955 until a couple of years ago when I more or less retired, I was the principal artist of the *Superman* comic for DC Comics.

It still surprises me sometimes when I think about it. It was never something I set out to do. It just kind of happened, the way a lot of good things do. In fact, if anybody had told me when I was a kid growing up in

Photo © 1975 DC Comics.

Minneapolis back in the '30s that I would one day be sitting on the set of something called *The Today Show* being interviewed about my work by a young woman named Jane Pauley, or that I would be a guest celebrity at a national comic-book convention, I would have thought he or she was crazy. Television was still only Science Fiction in those days, and, not only wasn't I much interested in Science Fiction, I wasn't even particularly into comic books.

My brother Stanley—I was the youngest of five children, and he was the oldest—was an avid reader of the "pulps." But I preferred curling up with magazines like *Collier's* or the *Saturday Evening Post.* I especially liked the adventure stories—I guess because of the illustrations. I was already drawing my head off every chance I got, and I was in awe of those illustrators. I admired their technique, their coloring, their composition, their honesty with the human figure. It was my dream that I would one day be an illustrator, too.

My teachers had recognized my talent early. They were always giving me projects to do, such as calling me up to the blackboard to draw a mural or illustrate some lesson. I remember a school fair we had when I was in sixth grade. Every child in the school was expected to do a project to be sold (I don't remember what they were going to do with the money). I got the idea of doing a comic book. It was a takeoff on those Big Little Books that were very popular in those days, which I discovered while babysitting for a younger child in the neighborhood. They were fat little paperback books that contained reprinted comic strips. So I got hold of a desk calendar—the kind with the big numerals on one side and nothing on the other—and I stapled together a whole year's worth of them to make a blank comic book. It was just about the right size. I wrote the story myself. It was about two young boys who ran away from home and the adventures they had. One of the other kids bought it. I was thrilled.

But it still did not occur to me that I might someday make a living drawing comic books. I had more serious ambitions.

My family were serious, hard-working folk of Swedish stock. (Our name was originally Swanson, but some ancestor of mine, my grandmother, I think, decided to shorten it.) My father, John Swan, was born on a farm just across the Canadian border, in Saskatchewan. Later, he and his family moved back to Wilmer, Minnesota, a town about 60 miles from Minneapolis where the Swansons had originally settled before moving north. My mother grew up in a nearby town called Litchfield. She was a Hanson. Leotine Hanson. She worked for a while in a local hospital; my father was a railroad man. He repaired trestles.

We were raised Presbyterians, but my father could never quite make up his mind on a religion. I guess he was looking for something—or driven by something: the fear of the unknown, perhaps. He would drag us to a Methodist church one week, a Baptist church, the next. Since I was the youngest, he latched on to me and always took me along with him. I was a very religious person up until the age of 11 or 12, when my brother Lloyd and I began to lie on the grass out under the stars on long summer evenings, just talking about everything, deciding what we thought about things. I sort of lost interest in churches around that time. My brother was once a missionary.

The Smithsonian's Superman exhibit of the 1980s may be long gone, but a permanent Superman Museum exists in Metropolis, Illinois. One of its rooms is devoted to George Reeves and is filled with promotional costumes from Clark Kent's TV attire.
Photo © 2004 Cookie Morris.

A composite of photos, all from the 1940s, of (left to right) Mort Weisinger, the rarely photographed George Klein, Curt Swan, and Edmond Hamilton.
Photos courtesy of Joe Desris, Dr. Michael J. Vassallo, Cecilia Swan Swift, and Jerry Weist.

This was during the Depression. My family was lucky. Most of us were able to get work of some kind, and we all chipped in to put food on the table and paid for our own clothes. I got a job with a small letter service doing stencils and deliveries and helping out the printer. I also worked for Sears Roebuck for a short time as a "warehouse man." I remember getting a letter in the mail—I must have been about 17—informing me that I had received a triple-A credit rating. I was proud as a peacock!

It was around this time that I signed up with the National Guard, along with some of my friends. The war in Europe was heating up, and, somewhere around the end of 1940, a bunch of us were inducted into the army—34th Division, 135th Infantry, Service Company—and moved to Camp Clayborn in Louisiana. We went from there to Fort Dix. I was made a sergeant and the following February, we boarded a ship for Belfast, Northern Ireland. I was stationed at Fintona, near Enniskillen, for about three months. It was there in Northern Ireland, with a war on, that I got my first break as an illustrator.

I met a young GI named Dick Wingert, who was a cartoonist with the army paper, *Stars and Stripes*. (He later created a strip called *Hubert*, which was one of the most successful comic strips to come out of World War II.) We became quite good friends while the two of us were doing murals for the Red Cross club in Belfast, and he suggested that I write to a Colonel Llewellyn about a position on *Stars and Stripes*. I hung back, not thinking of myself as much of a writer.

Then one day as I was dishing out grub to the headquarters staff back at camp—I was officially a mess sergeant in those days—I got this brainstorm. I went to another one of the guys on the staff who was very good with words, he was some kind of writer, and told him what I had in mind and asked him if he would script it for me. He did, and I sent Colonel Llewellyn an illustrated letter with a silhouette of him—I had no idea what he looked like—interviewing me and a caricature of myself giving him my résumé. The next thing I knew, I was being shipped to London where they made me a staff artist on *Stars and Stripes*. I did illustrations for the magazine section, war maps showing the progress of the Allies, cartoons, little spot drawings for the sports section—whatever they threw at me.

My unit, back in Belfast, was eventually shipped out to North Africa. After the war, when we got together back in Minneapolis and they talked about their experiences, I was very reticent to join in. They had gone up through Italy, through the worst of it. A lot of our friends were lost.

There was one night in London, however, when my life did flash before my eyes. I was living in a lovely, upper-middle-class neighborhood at the time on the outskirts of London, not too far from Henley Airport, which was probably the reason the Germans had us on their clipboard back across the channel where they were launching the V2s they'd started sending over after the buzz bombs. I had been up most of the night working on a war map and had finally gotten to bed about four or five in the morning, when suddenly I sat bolt upright, listening. I must have heard it deep in my sleep, the way you do with some things. A moment later the V2 came roaring in and hit very close by, rattling everything to hell. That was about the closest I came during the war to meeting my Maker some years ahead of schedule.

For a year or so I roomed with Wingert in London. We were the original Odd Couple. We originated the concept. He was Mr. Filth and I was Mr. Clean. But we had a swell time going to the neighborhood pubs and conversing with the citizenry on all manner of subjects—politics, culture, the

(above) Weissmuller in a Superman-like pose on the poster to *Tarzan's New York Adventure* (1942).
© 1942 MGM. Tarzan TM & © 2006 Edgar Rice Burroughs, Inc. Movie poster courtesy of Heritage Auctions.

George Reeves as Clark Kent, and a Curt Swan/Stan Kaye-drawn, Reeves-like Clark Kent from *World's Finest #73* (Nov.–Dec. 1954).
© 2006 Warner Bros.   TM & © DC Comics.

A Swan penciled-and-inked drawing produced in the late 1960s/early 1970s. Its contributor was told that it was an unpublished *Lois Lane* cover, which seems unlikely given its composition. It might have been produced as a magazine or newspaper article illustration.

Americans versus the English. I did a mural for an airbase somewhere in the Midlands. It was a wonderful couple of years, except for the bombs.

Wingert and I used to go down to the Red Cross Club in London, the Eagle Club I think it was called, to play ping-pong and eat doughnuts. They had comic books spread out on the coffee table, and I remember thinking, "Why would anybody want to put that much work into drawing—for a comic book?" I couldn't imagine anybody wanting to do that for a living.

One day word came through that *Stars and Stripes* needed a staff artist in Paris. Next thing I knew I was living in a little apartment near the Eiffel Tower. I would sit for hours sketching by the Seine. Once I stowed away (with the complicity of the French drivers) aboard a quarter-ton army vehicle filled with copies of *Stars and Stripes* bound for the GIs at the front—to drop in for a surprise visit on my bride-to-be, Helene Brickley, whom I'd learned was stationed just across the Belgian border with the 82nd Airborne, the paratroopers who had moved in ahead of Patton's army. We had met back at Fort Dix, New Jersey. Her family lived in a nearby town and she had come up for one of our dances. She was working for RCA in Camden at the time. Later she had signed up with the Red Cross and turned up, much to my surprise, in London. But when I walked into the dispatcher's office that day in Belgium wearing a raincoat and garrison cap, she nearly fell off her chair. The next time I dropped in, she was living with a French family in a village nearby. We were married in Paris in 1944.

After the war, we agreed that my chances of finding something in the art field were greater in New York than back in Minneapolis. Several other ex-staffers from *Stars and Stripes* were living in New York, and we all used to get together at a little place on Third Avenue called the Campus Restaurant, which is long since gone. This was 1945. One of them was a fellow named France Herron, whom I'd known as a feature writer on the Paris *Stars and Stripes*. Before the war he'd been working in the comic-book business, and now he was back at it, writing for DC Comics. He suggested I take my samples around to see Whitney Ellsworth and Mort Weisinger at DC. I shrugged and decided I'd give it a try.

They started me out on a Jack Kirby feature called *Boy Commandos*. "Well, this will be good for about two years," I told my wife I figured the comic-book business hadn't much longer to run.

I was being paid $18 a page. That didn't sound too bad at first until I discovered how much time it took me to do a single page. I was getting really discouraged until one of the guys in the inking department took me aside and gave me a few tips. In the comic-book business, I had quickly learned, almost everybody specializes. There are pencilers, and there are inkers, who turn

the pencils into finished pages, which are then turned over to the letterers and finally the colorists. Not everybody has a style of inking that is appropriate to comic books. Some people are very good at it and very fast. They have to be to make any kind of living at it. In those days the inkers were making even less than the pencilers, about $14 a page. (The writers, I would later discover, were only getting between $8 and $11 a page, depending on the quality of the writing.)

Anyway, this inker's name was Steve Brody. And he told me I was putting too much work into each panel and that he was breaking his arm inking my stuff. He showed me ways to fake things, to suggest things without putting in every last detail. After that I was able to work much faster. Soon I was turning out three to four pages a day. At the end of one year I discovered I had earned almost $10,000. That was a lot of money in those days. When a friend of mine from Minnesota heard I had made that much, his eyes bulged out and he said, "God! If I was making $10,000, I'd feel wealthy!"

We were living in the Rockaways then, out on Long Island, not far from the old Floyd Bennet Field. We lived only half a block from the beach. There was a boardwalk and we would go for long walks on the beach. We were putting away every dime we could spare to buy a little farmhouse in New Jersey.

But I was knocking myself out to make that much money— working up to 14 and 16 hours a day, seven days a week. They had me working on a variety of features: Besides doing *Boy Commandos*, I was now doing "Tommy Tomorrow" and a thing called *Gangbusters*. I even did some *Superboy* covers—whatever they pulled out of the drawer. I would come by the DC offices with my pencils and pick up a new script. (The offices were on Lexington Avenue then.) At home I had my studio set up in the bedroom or, later, when we got a big enough house, in a separate room. If the story was difficult or I got excited about it, I would work until three or four in the morning. I would usually have

Yell "help" and watch how fast your mild-mannered Continental Insurance agent turns into Superman.

A 1964 Swan/Klein-drawn ad.

THE SUPERMAN MYTHOLOGY:
UNTOLD TALES OF A SUPERMAN SCHOLAR

Editor's note: The behind-the-scenes efforts of Cleveland author Dennis Dooley, co-author and editor of *Superman at Fifty*, should not go without mention. Swan's mesmerizing essay, "Drawing Superman," was put together by Dooley, using Swan's actual words, from his taped interviews with the soft-spoken artist who, according to Dooley, "pled he was 'not a writer'" but nonetheless offered the revealing anecdotes we are honored to reprint here nearly 20 years after their original publication—and ten years after the talented Mr. Swan departed this earthly plane.

Beyond tracking down Swan and capturing his reflections for posterity, Dooley's investigative work would impress even crusty ol' Perry ("Don't call me 'Chief'!") White. "As far as I know," he says, "I was the first one ever to look into the back issues of Siegel and Shuster's high-school newspaper, *The Glenville Torch*, and make all those connections"— such as identifying the actual girl who inspired the character of Lois Lane, Lois Amster (later confirmed by Shuster), and the intriguing possibility that Jerry Siegel's shy, bespectacled high school pal Wilson Hirschfeld (who went on to become managing editor of *The Cleveland Plain Dealer*) was the inspiration for Clark Kent. The look of Superman, Dooley suggests, was influenced by the riveting images imprinted on Joe's and Jerry's brains at the neighborhood movie theater of Douglas Fairbanks, Sr. leaping from balconies and standing, head thrown back and laughing, arms akimbo, cape ruffling in the wind, in *The Mark of Zorro*, *Robin Hood*, and *The Black Pirate*.

Dooley detected Siegel's hand in several unsigned pieces in the *Torch* including a Tarzan send-up called "Goober the Mighty," parodies of S. S. Van Dine's popular sleuth Philo Vance, and a review of the 1932 novel that introduced the Scarlet Pimpernel, *A Child of the Revolution*. "All of this, unearthed without benefit of any help from Jerry or Joe, neither of whom was then giving interviews," he ruefully adds, "appeared in the original article I wrote in the spring of 1973 for *Cleveland Magazine*." Dooley tracked down several of Siegel's

high-school pals, one of whom recalled how Jerry, who liked to sleep late, often came to class with his pajamas protruding from the cuffs and collar of his school clothes.

"Siegel and Shuster gave us a mythic figure, a story, a cast of characters so compelling and so richly entangled with the yearnings and preoccupations of our time," he says, "that writers and artists and filmmakers have continued for three-quarters of a century to mine its possibilities, with no signs of letting up."

The Krypton Companion is proud to acknowledge Dennis Dooley's contributions to chronicling the Superman Legend. "It's been 70 years since Krypton exploded," says Dooley, "and we are still picking up the bits of stardust."

Curt Swan art (possibly with George Klein inks) for 1966 Superman temporary tattoos.
TM & © DC Comics.

music on or sports or maybe a talk show. I liked the Big Bands—Charlie Barnett, Benny Goodman, Glenn Miller—and occasionally I would tune in a symphony concert.

I worked three times up (that is, three times larger than the drawings would eventually appear). The script usually included a description of what was supposed to be happening in the panel, as well as the dialogue that went in the balloons. Most of the time I was free to do what I wanted insofar as the scene itself. Only occasionally would a writer suggest a "long shot" or a "closeup." The only other limitations in those days were that you shouldn't show blood or extreme violence and should keep it cool on the sex part.

So I would compose each panel as I saw it, trying to make it interesting and visually balanced. I would sketch in the balloons, too, and the lettering. Most stories in those days ran ten or 12 pages. When I was finished with a story, I would take it back into the city and lay it in front of my editor—usually Mort Weisinger in those days. He would frequently ask me to make changes. He didn't like the way I had some character's face or the way I had carried out the "stage directions" in the script. Weisinger always thought you were just goofing off. It drove me crazy. Occasionally a writer would set a scene, say, on Fifth Avenue and want you to show the crowded street and sidewalks literally, all the cars and the people. Stadium scenes were especially hard to fake convincingly.

At home I was getting more and more tense, throwing things around the room—paper, my art supplies—because I was being asked to draw things I didn't think would work. I was working too hard, anyway. I would get these terrific migraine headaches where

I would have to lie down on the bed, and heaven help anybody who dropped a pin. I figured my eyes were going. I got new eyeglasses, but it didn't seem to help. I decided I would have to give up the comic-book business and find something less strenuous.

I took a job with a small advertising studio. (This was sometime around 1951.) It was actually enjoyable. They handled a line of toys and some other things. I worked on displays and occasionally jobs for other clients. But I was making only $50 a week. My wife panicked when I brought home my first paycheck. I panicked, too. We had just bought a house in Tenafly, New Jersey, and had payments to make. So, after only one month at the agency, I went back to DC. They welcomed me with open arms.

But soon I was lying in bed at home again with a splitting headache. Suddenly it hit me. I had had no headaches during the months I had worked for the studio. It was not my eyes, after all. It was something about working for DC Comics that was causing my headaches. So I sorted it out and decided it was Mort—or, more likely, a combination of Mort Weisinger and myself, the way I was reacting to his criticisms and demands, swallowing a lot of my anger. I decided the only way to deal with it was to dig in my heels and fight him every inch of the way. It worked. My headaches stopped for good. I also think he respected me more after that, because I fought back. In time, we actually became quite close friends.

It was around this time that I started filling in occasionally for Wayne Boring, the artist who had taken over Superman from Joe Shuster. But it wasn't until around 1955 that I became the primary Superman artist. The first 3-D comics were making their appearances around that time, because of the success of 3-D movies, I guess, and DC wanted to get a 3-D *Superman* book out

(right and following page) Curt Swan/George Klein model sheets for the Man of Action
TM & © DC Comics.

in a hurry. So Boring and Al Plastino and I were all brought on to the project. We only put out one 3-D *Superman*, but Weisinger was quite happy with my work on it, and soon after that he put me on *Superman* steady. I had done *Superboy* and *Jimmy Olsen* before I did *Superman*, so I was quite familiar with the characters. I used to study Wayne Boring's work. I liked his style. I thought it suited Superman. Wayne had a real feeling for him, the way he constructed the figure, the flying, et cetera. Joe's Superman had been different. He was not trying to be realistic. His conception of the character was more cartoon-like. And my own style was different from Wayne's, just as Wayne's was from Joe's. I don't think any of this was intentional; each artist just had his own way of drawing.

Mort Weisinger told me early on that he wanted to soften the jaw line that Wayne Boring had put on Superman. I guess it had been Wayne's way of showing strength and power. Mort wanted the drawing to be more illustrative and less cartoony, maybe a little more handsome, with more emphasis on the muscles. I did speak briefly to Wayne Boring about it when I took over drawing the syndicated *Superman* strip in the late '50s or early '60s, a couple of years before they killed it. He knew how difficult Weisinger could be on the subject of Superman's looks. "Just hang in there," Wayne told me, "and don't take any sh*t."

I didn't have any conscious models for Superman. I suppose I may have been somewhat influenced by Johnny Weissmuller. I had always been kind of fascinated, as a boy, by the *Tarzan* newspaper strip and the Weissmuller movies, and I guess I may have imitated then subconsciously to a degree. Alex Raymond's strip *Rip Kirby* was probably also an influence.

At one point in the '50s, I gave some thought to making Superman look more like George Reeves, the actor who played him on television. I had seen Reeves once on the set, briefly, on one of my trips to the coast. I began to study his features on the TV show, but finally decided that it would be pointless to copy him too literally, though I think I did get his profile a little bit from time to time.

I wanted to show strength, of course, and ruggedness. And *character*. He had to be the kind of person you'd *want* to have on your side.

When I drew Clark Kent, on the other hand, I deliberately softened his features, made them less angular than Superman's. I wanted him to appear more meek. Just sort of a good Joe. I don't know if it worked, but that's what I was trying to do.

Superman's hair was different from Clark's, too, of course. That curl would come down—it was a way of showing action. I guess that had been Shuster's idea: action causing that lock of hair to fall out of place. As for Lois, I just tried to draw her pretty, but I wasn't successful enough for Mort Weisinger. From time to time, he would have Kurt Schaffenberger do Lois.

We also had arguments about showing expression. I felt it was necessary to put lines in the face to show pain or whatever. Mort and I had long discussions about this. He thought they made Superman look too old. I think I finally got through to him by pointing out that even a baby, when it's angry or crying, has lines in its face.

I also used to argue about some of the things the writers came up with. I thought it was rather ridiculous that this character could do anything the writers could dream up, like fly in space or withstand an atomic blast. "If he's that invulnerable, then where's your story?" I used to ask. But I guess they thought of me as just that stupid artist. Eventually, they had to invent things like all the different-colored kryptonite, which seemed to me a feeble way of getting out of the box they had put themselves in.

Once in the early '50s, I decided to take a course in illustration. I wanted to improve my craft. I had been more or less self-taught. So I enrolled at Pratt Institute in Brooklyn. Some of the teachers raised their eyebrows when they heard what I did for a living, but my fellow students, who were mostly attending art school on the GI Bill and still trying to break into the business, were a little bit

in awe of me. It turned out to be just a review of everything I already knew. It was a long drive in from New Jersey two nights a week at the end of a long day, and I began to find myself nodding off on the way home. So after a few months, I gave it up. So much for my formal art education.

The comics, I decided, were not a bad place for an artist to make a career, after all. Where else could you have the fun of creating an entire city in a bottle? I think Al Plastino had first drawn Kandor, the Kryptonian city that had been miniaturized by the villain Brainiac and thus escaped the destruction of Superman's native planet. But I had a lot of fun inventing all that tiny futuristic architecture, not to mention the view from inside the bottle—with the "giant" figures peering in. I've always regretted that Al Plastino and I never got to play golf together, another passion that we shared.

And it was always a special treat for me when the writers would come up with a story about Mr. Mxyzptlk. Suddenly, there in the midst of a fairly realistic comic book, was this wacky cartoon character. They excused it by explaining that he was from the fifth dimension, of course, and that suited me to a T, because they would go off the edge with some of those plots, and I knew I could have a ball. It was always like vacation time for me to get a script with Mxyzptlk.

But my favorite villain was Brainiac. I could do things with him—his expressions, et cetera—that were tough to do with some of the other villains. Lex Luthor, for example, didn't *look* evil. He was just a bald man. You could put a scowl on his face, and he still wouldn't look evil enough. But Brainiac was thin, even gaunt, you could see the bone structure of his face. And there's a lot you can do with that to make a person seem more evil. Then, of course, there were those electrodes on his head!

For years my favorite Superman *story* was the one in which Superman and Jimmy Olsen visit another dimension, another world where Jimmy gets a costume, too, and superpowers. (I think his name is Flame Bird or something like that.) I got to create their costumes and those cities. I had fun with that.

Curt Swan at work, penciling "Superman Battles the War-Horn" from *Superman #257* (Oct. 1972).
Photos © 1972 DC Comics.

But I guess the story I'm proudest of is the 1973 version I illustrated of "The Origin of Superman"—showing the last days of Krypton, the baby Kal-El rocketing to earth and being found in a cornfield by Jonathan and Martha Kent, then young Clark discovering his superpowers as a boy and going off to Metropolis to serve the world as Superman.

Carmine Infantino did the layout on that story, planning the way it was to unfold, panel by panel. It was so good. We included it in *The Amazing World of Superman*, one of those special large editions we put out for $2 a shot while Infantino was publisher. I am very fond of that one.

Nelson Bridwell did the dialogue, and Murphy Anderson inked my pencils. Murphy's inking was among the best. George Klein's was pretty good, too. But since this one's for the history books, I'll have to say that my absolute favorite among all the inkers who ever worked on my stuff was Al Williamson, with whom I collaborated just before I officially retired. He was the best. A fine draftsman in his own right, an extremely talented artist, he could render even the little mechanical parts of vehicles. He had a very special flair the others didn't have.

I've worked with some inkers over the years who did not delineate the figure of Superman the way I'd done it in the pencils. They would lose something in the face, the eyes; the features would be just a little off or the muscular structure. It used to get to me. I would have to remind myself, sometimes, that this was only, after all, a comic book and wasn't going to be hung in some gallery. I have inked my own work, of course, back when I was working on *Stars and Stripes*, but my style of inking wasn't right for comic books—a little too ornamental. It would take me too much time, and inkers, as I've said, have to work fast to make any money. Fellows like Al Williamson and Murphy Anderson are all the more amazing when you remember that.

The colorists have come a long way, too, since I was starting out in the business. By and large, they always did a nice job. But they were restricted in the old days by what the editors down the hall thought made sense. Those guys believed that a sky had to be blue, so it was blue. It was a long time before the colorists were allowed a little creativity: now, if they want to put a red sky in, they can put in a red sky and even make judgments about the overall treatment of the page. And, as a result, the coloration has improved tremendously.

I guess I was pretty far off base when I predicted, back in 1945, that comic books were only a passing fad and would never survive the '40s. As it turned out, the business was to be pretty good to me.

I've felt fortunate to be associated with *Superman* over so many years. I've met and had the opportunity of working with some wonderful people. I especially remember meeting Jerry Siegel and Joe Shuster, the creators of Superman. I used to see Jerry around the DC offices in the early '60s. This was years after their formal relationship with DC had ended, of course, but he was often there in those days, anonymously scripting stories about Superman and the other characters he and Joe had created. He was soft-spoken, a very likable person. I didn't know him socially, but I ran into him often in the offices.

Joe Shuster was a very shy, introverted person. It always struck me as kind of unusual, since most of the artists I know are extroverts. I believe Joe was living somewhere out on the Jersey shore at the time. His eyes had gotten very bad. I don't know how he supported himself. They were a couple of sweet guys.

I found myself thinking of all of these things, and of these people, after I came back from Washington and the Smithsonian's exhibition. There had been some beautiful displays—blowups of Superman, one of the costumes George Reeves wore in the TV series, a dress of Lois Lane's and lots of other artifacts and comic books, including about a dozen covers I remember having done. Nice memories.

PA KENT

MA KENT

KRYPTO

LANA LANG

A Curt Swan model sheet of some of the Superboy family, 1960s. Inks by George Klein.

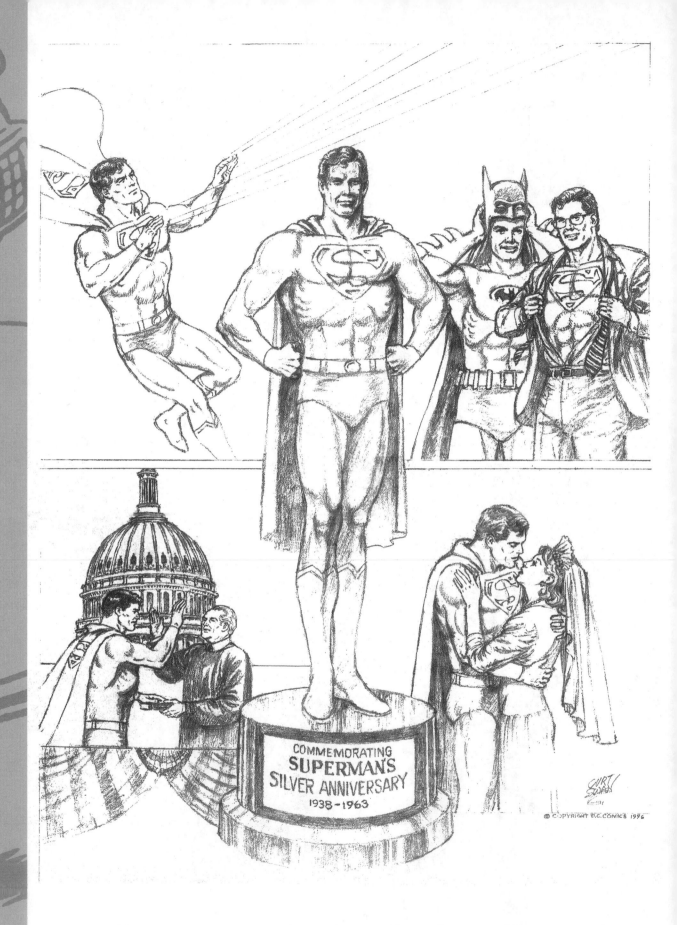

Curt Swan penciled this recreation of his cover to *Superman Annual #7* (Summer 1963) in 1996, the year of his passing, making this one of his last Superman drawings.

THE SUPERMAN MYTHOLOGY:
KURT SCHAFFENBERGER: LADIES' MAN

Lois Lane, Lana Lang, Linda Lee (Danvers) … no one drew those lovely ladies quite like Clark Kent-lookalike Kurt Schaffenberger (1920–2002). Beginning his career in the 1940s as a Captain Marvel and Bulletman artist for Fawcett Comics, the German-born Schaffenberger later illustrated various titles and covers for ACG (American Comics Group). He started working for DC in the late 1950s, most notably on *Superman's Girl Friend Lois Lane*.

Schaffenberger's accessible, lighthearted art, coupled with the girl reporter's incessant pining for the Man of Steel, often made *Lois Lane* read like a romance comic masquerading as a super-hero comic. Kurt's chirpy, impetuous Lois was a curvaceous fashion plate; for years the artist borrowed clothing styles from the Sears and Roebuck catalog, but after Lois' Jackie Kennedy-inspired pillbox hat was no longer in vogue, Schaffenberger gave her a makeover by consulting contemporary fashion magazines. His mastery of drawing feminine facial expressions became so identified with Lois Lane that Mort Weisinger sometimes directed Schaffenberger to redraw Lois and Lana heads on other artists' work, even that of Curt Swan, no slouch at rendering Superman's girlfriends himself.

When Jim Mooney departed DC for Marvel in 1968, Schaffenberger took over the Supergirl feature with *Action* #359 (Feb. 1968), staying on through the Maid of Might's last *Action* back-up in #376 (May 1969) and occasionally drawing Supergirl tales when the heroine moved to *Adventure Comics* with issue #381 (June 1969). After Weisinger's 1970 retirement, Schaffenberger continued in the Superman camp for editor Julius Schwartz, illustrating Lois, Supergirl, and Jimmy Olsen stories for *Superman Family* in the 1970s and *The New Adventures of Superboy* in the 1980s; during those decades he also returned to draw Captain Marvel in DC's *Shazam!*, and occasionally inked Swan on various Superman adventures. Yet in the hearts of most Silver Age readers, Kurt Schaffenberger is defined by his charming and unforgettable *Lois Lane* stories.

Recommended reading: *Hero Gets Girl! The Life and Art of Kurt Schaffenberger* by Mark Voger (TwoMorrows, 2003).

TM & © DC Comics.

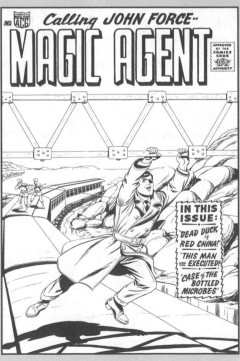

The man-hungry girl reporter makes a deal with the Devil on this Schaffenberger-drawn page from *Lois Lane* #41 (May 1963).
TM & © DC Comics. Art courtesy of Heritage Comics.

(left) Just a reminder that Kurt Schaffenberger could draw *boys*, too, as seen in this unpublished 1962 cover for ACG's offbeat Cold War series, *Magic Agent*.
© 1962 American Comics Group.
Art courtesy of Heritage Comics.

TWO WEEKS WITH MORT WEISINGER
OR, FOUR YEARS WITH AN ANGRY MOB
(TAKE YOUR PICK)

A Reminiscence by Roy Thomas

Editor's note: Missouri native Roy Thomas (b. 1940) was Stan Lee's first successor as Marvel Comics' editor in chief. Thomas has written and/or edited nearly every major Marvel and DC comic-book character. His career milestones include the introduction of the Silver Age Vision (*Avengers* #57, Oct. 1968); a lengthy run as the writer of Marvel's *Conan the Barbarian*; and his writing/editing of *All-Star Squadron* and *Infinity, Inc.*, 1980s' series starring DC's Golden Age characters. Thomas is the editor of comics' premier fanzine, *Alter Ego*, currently published by TwoMorrows.

This article saw print, in altered forms, in Comic Book Marketplace *#58 (April 1998) and in* Alter Ego *vol. 3 #50 (July 2005). Reprinted by permission of Gemstone Publishing, Inc., and the author. © 2006 Roy Thomas. All rights reserved.*

Since I was one of Mort Weisinger's "discoveries"—though maybe "fiascos" is the word he'd have used—I felt it was high time I exorcised a few demons by writing about him. Back in early-'60s comics fandom, Mort's six Superman titles, clearly aimed at a younger audience than fellow DC editor Julius Schwartz's mags, were pretty much taken for granted and rarely discussed in fanzines. *Alter Ego* [originally *Alter-Ego*], for instance, devoted a lot of space to the Justice Society and Captain Marvel, but practically none to the super-hero who'd started it all.

Because I corresponded from 1960–1965 with Julie Schwartz, I knew he and Mort had been friends since even before they'd published one of the very first science-fiction fanzines back in the '30s, but I knew little else about Mort. Still, when I wrote virtually my only fan letter to a Superman mag—one concerning Herko the Monster in a *Lois Lane* tale [issue #54, Jan. 1965], because he reminded me of old Captain Marvel creatures (and why not? the artist was Kurt Schaffenberger!)—Weisinger responded with a courteous letter. As I did with every other pro I knew of, I sent him freebie copies of *A/E* [vol. 1] #7–8 in '64 and early '65.

Then, in spring of '65, only days after accepting a graduate fellowship in foreign relations that was to be my ticket out of teaching high school, I received a second letter from Weisinger—offering me a trial position at National/DC as his assistant. My fellow teacher Albert Tindal—the guy who'd wrangled the fellowship for me and who'd go on to become a prominent attorney in Missouri—was dumbfounded that, after pacing our apartment for half an hour, I accepted Mort's offer and turned my back on an academic career. But, having sent two sample comics scripts earlier to Julie, and having just sold two scripts to Charlton, I wasn't about to turn down a chance to work in the comics industry!

Photo courtesy of Glen Cadigan.

(Besides, truth to tell, I had till summer's end to formally reject the fellowship, so I could hedge my bets.)

Mort offered me a starting salary of $110 a week (about what I was then making as a teacher) and a two-month trial period. I borrowed and read a box full of Superman comics from my friend Biljo White, bought a new suit—and waited eagerly for summer. During that time I spoke only once with Mort on the phone. One day he called me at school, out of the blue, for a reason I can't recall. All I remember of the brief conversation is his speaking of "the Superman mythology." By then I'd come to respect, at least to a certain extent, what he was doing with Bizarro, Imaginary Stories, way too many surviving Kryptonians, and all those shades of kryptonite.

At his invitation, I also wrote a *Jimmy Olsen* script in which the young reporter went undercover to join a youthful street gang. I felt it needed more pages than the usual eight, but Mort said that was impossible, so I wrote it in eight and sent it off. Mort soon advised me that he wanted a rewrite, but said that could follow when I got to New York. I was paid a $50 advance (the rate was $10 a page), to help pay for the air flight out. And so, on the last Monday in June, I arrived in Manhattan in the midst of a taxi strike, and carried my one suitcase and portable electric typewriter more than a dozen blocks to the DC offices at 575 Lexington Avenue. I was so excited that I accidentally passed right by the Standard Brands Building wherein DC was located, and had to backtrack a couple of blocks carrying my increasingly heavy load.

That day I met Mort Weisinger—and everything started to go wrong. Though Mort had known in advance when I was to arrive and had okayed the date, he now informed me he couldn't put me on the payroll until the following week. The reason: he was still paying my predecessor—who turned out to be E. Nelson Bridwell, an Oklahoma comics fan-turned-pro who had contributed an article to *Alter Ego* [vol. 1] #7 right before he'd become Mort's assistant, almost exactly a year earlier. I now learned that Mort was firing Nelson, and that I was his replacement. A bit awkward, even if I had exchanged at most a couple of letters with Nelson, who at 34 was ten years older than I. Mort had a couple of other surprises for me, as well:

(1) With no explanation, my salary had now become $100 a week instead of $110. (When I asked what had happened to the extra $10, he replied, with a contemptuous nod toward Nelson's cubicle down the hall which he assumed explained everything: "I can't pay you more than I'm paying that idiot." End quote.)

(2) Likewise with zero explanation, the two-month trial period suddenly became two weeks. Sink-or-swim time. (Right about then, I felt around surreptitiously in my hip pocket for that grad fellowship, just to make certain it was still there.)

Still, the die was cast, so I determined to make the best of it. This was DC, after all! This was the comics biz, where I'd always wanted to work, even when not consciously thinking about it!

Since I'd made no provision for a place to stay, Mort phoned the George Washington Hotel on 23rd Street to secure me a room. I appreciated that gesture, and the irony that my fellowship was to George Washington University in Washington, D.C. was not lost on me. After being shown the DC rounds, I was sent packing for the day, to begin work informally (no pay, remember?) the next morning.

Nelson was great all that week, despite the awkwardness of the situation. He showed me the ropes and never bad-mouthed Weisinger, even though it slowly became plain to me that he had doubts about how he was going to survive as a comic-book freelancer, which is what he was about to become. He shared an office with DC romance editor Jack Miller and a youngish female assistant whose name I've forgotten. Except when we were introduced, neither she nor Miller (who wasn't around much) spoke a word to me for the next fortnight. [*Note:* Jim Amash reminded me her name was Barbara Friedlander.]

But, for the most part, the people at DC were great to the new kid on the block over those two weeks, which meld into a blur in my mind:

• Joe Kubert recalled me from my fan letters and *A/E* and couldn't have been nicer, taking me into his confidence about a new independent magazine he planned which would co-star Tor, one of my favorite creations of his (the mag emerged some years later as the sadly short-lived *Sojourn*).

• When I stayed after 5:00 one day, Murphy Anderson graciously talked with me as, awed, I watched him pencil and ink several *Hawkman* panels.

• Robert Kanigher verbally assaulted me in the production room because, he asserted, some fanzine writer (Paul Gambaccini, I believe he said) had described him as wearing a bowtie, and he loudly dared anyone within earshot—which was a considerable distance—to say they had ever seen him in a bowtie.

• Production chief Ed Eisenberg showed me around the production department, and was very friendly.

• Writers Gardner Fox and Otto Binder, longtime correspondents and boosters, each invited me to their homes. (I would shortly take both of them up on it.)

• Julie Schwartz was friendly from a distance, probably because he didn't want to get in Mort's way—but Mort told me Julie had already evinced an interest in having me write for him later.

Mort even took me to lunch one day with himself and Otto Binder at the Summit, a classy restaurant nearby. I was in heaven … except for one thing:

Mort was a tyrant.

He never actually yelled at me, as he reportedly did at many others (I can guarantee I'd have been back in Missouri like a shot if he had, as I've never taken yelling from anyone), but his voice could drip scorn as if it were a venom he produced from overactive glands. And, with his looming, perhaps 300-pound frame, he was physically intimidating as well. I once described him as a "malevolent toad," and while that was unkind, it truly represented the way I felt at the time. Years later, when I saw Jabba the Hut in *Return of the Jedi*, I thought of Mort, and smiled.

When I test-proofread a Superman story at Mort's behest and missed a reversal of two letters in a long, fictitious nation-name the second time it appeared in the tale, he was scathing in his rebuke. (I was told that one reason he had fired "that idiot" Nelson was because of inadequate proofreading; still, I had missed the misspelling.) Once, when I pointed out some minor error to him, he sneered and grunted: "Chickensh*t. You know, in the Army we had a word for stuff like this: chickensh*t."

My desk in the three-person office was several doors down the hall from Mort's, so when he wanted me, a buzzer sounded and I was off like a shot. I quickly developed a Pavlovian reaction of tenseness when that buzzer went off.

THE SUPERMAN MYTHOLOGY:
KRYPTONITE: FIRST EXPOSURES

In Mort Weisinger's child-friendly Superman universe, kryptonite—radioactive fragments of the exploded planet Krypton—came in enough hues to fill a box of Crayolas. First appearances of variations of "K" can be found in:

• **K-Metal:** In August 1940 Jerry Siegel wrote the *Superman* script "The K-Metal from Krypton," featuring Superman's first encounter with a mysterious, harmful meteor. This legendary tale, which also featured Clark Kent revealing his secret identity to Lois Lane, went unpublished.
• **Green K** (lethal to Kryptonians): *Superman* radio show, June 1943; kryptonite (originally colored red) first appeared in comic books in *Superman* #61 (Dec. 1949)
• **Red K** (unpredictable, temporary transformations): *Adventure* #252 (Sept. 1958)
• **X-K** (Supergirl's unsuccessful attempt to cure kryptonite poisoning; imbues Earth-cat Streaky with temporary super-powers): *Action* #261 (Feb. 1960)
• **Blue K** (affects Bizarros only): *Superman* #140 (Oct. 1960)
• **White K** (toxic to plant life): *Adventure* #279 (Dec. 1960)
• **Yellow K** (hoax): *Action* #277 (June 1961)
• **Gold K** (permanently robs Kryptonians of super-powers): *Adventure* #299 (Aug. 1962)
• **Silver K** (hoax to commemorate Superman's silver anniversary): *Jimmy Olsen* #70 (July 1963)
• **Jewel K** (aka Kryptonite Six; magnifies mental abilities of Phantom Zone prisoners): *Action* #310 (Mar. 1964)
• **Anti-K** (harmful to non-powered Kryptonians): *Action* #317 (Oct. 1964)
• **Magno-K** (magnetically attracts anything of Kryptonian origin): *Jimmy Olsen* #92 (Apr. 1966)
• **Kryptonite-Plus** (kryptonite isotope): *Action* #350 (May 1967)
• **Slow K** (harmful to Earth beings): *The Brave and the Bold* #175 (post-Weisinger variation, June 1981; Batman/Lois Lane team-up, Metallo appearance)
• Various types of **synthetic kryptonite**, often created by Lex Luthor, appeared throughout the Silver Age.

Recommended reading (for the K-Metal story): *The Steranko History of Comics vol. 1* (Supergraphics, 1970); *Alter Ego* vol. 3 #26 (July 2003) and 37 (June 2004); and *Men of Tomorrow: Geeks, Gangsters and the Birth of the Comic Book* by Gerard Jones (Basic Books, 2004).

Modeling with Millie #44 (Dec. 1965), Roy's first Marvel scripting assignment.
© 2006 Marvel Characters, Inc.

One of Thomas' early script sales was for Charlton's Blue Beetle #54 (Feb.–Mar. 1966).
© 1966 Charlton Comics. Blue Beetle TM & © DC Comics.

My first day on staff, he flashed a four-figure check he'd received from the Sunday supplement magazine *Parade* for his "Bonanza, USA" column, to show me he was a writer of a magnitude far beyond the reach of most mortals. (I was to learn later that, during those years, he showed such a check to everyone who applied to him for a job, and to many who didn't.)

And yet, at the same time, Mort tried in his own way to be ingratiating and helpful: He introduced me to Irwin Donenfeld in the hall one day, telling DC's publisher that I "came from the fanzines," which was the only hint I ever had that he'd hired me for that reason rather than because of the letters I wrote to him and Julie.

When I suggested, upon proofreading one story script wherein supposedly "the staff of the *Daily Planet*" was gathered around the hospital bed of an ailing Perry White, that perhaps we should see more than just Clark, Lois, and Jimmy—to indicate that there were more than three reporters on the *Planet* staff—he harrumphed at me scornfully. But later he showed me he'd rewritten a balloon to have Perry explain why only those three were there. That worked just as well.

When I pointed out that, in completed artwork I was given to proof, when a big boulder on a hillside opened at a special touch, we probably shouldn't see the words "Secret Lab" written on an arrow pointing the way inside, as it had been written, drawn, and lettered he snorted again—but later he called me into his

Detail from the Swan/Klein cover to *Jimmy Olsen* #91 (Mar. 1966).
TM & © DC Comics.

office to show me that he'd had the arrow and sign removed. Now we simply caught a glimpse of the secret lab when the boulder slid to one side.

He also let me in on a little secret: in a few months, a Batman show would debut on TV, and I might want to buy some NPP stock to own a piece of DC at that time. I realize, looking back on what I've written here, that I possibly haven't really made Mort Weisinger look like the ogre that so many of us actually thought him. I believe this is partly because it was often his manner more than his words that browbeat me and others—and partly because, in spite of it all, I respected Mort, who'd had the puppeteer's skill to develop the "Superman mythology" while using several different scripters.

And yet, I can clearly recall at least one evening, sitting alone in my room at the GW Hotel, having tears well up in my eyes after a particularly bruising day with Mort, and wondering if I could take it—if my dream of working in comics was going to end with my being let go by Mort, à là Nelson, at the end of my second paid week. Let me stress that being Mort's assistant was hardly my first job. Through much of high school and college, I'd worked at a movie theatre in my hometown of Jackson, Missouri, as well as at a few other odd jobs here and there. I'd sung in a rock 'n' roll band on weekends for two years for pin money. I'd spent four years as an English teacher, at two different high schools. I was no total babe in the woods, who crumpled at the first hint of criticism from an employer. But verbal sadism was something else.

It all ended very suddenly. Suffice it to say that, without ever really quite intending to apply for a job at the much smaller Marvel Comics, I found myself on Friday, July 9th—last day of my one paid, four-day week on staff at DC—sitting in the office of Stan Lee, a ten-minute walk from Mort's office, and being asked what it would take to hire me away from National. "Just offer me what Mort promised me," I answered, meaning $110 a week. When Stan did, I accepted—and yeah, I'd have jumped for the $100 a week I was actually getting, too.

I told Stan that, in fairness to Mort, I'd have to give him time to hire a replacement, and Stan reluctantly accepted that. So I trekked back to DC, having taken an extra half hour on my lunch break. (In the elevator as I'd been leaving for that secret lunchtime meeting, I'd run into production manager Ed Eisenberg, who had said a few delicately phrased words of encouragement about "hanging in there," a clear indication that he knew what I was going through with Mort. That had given me a boost, and made me feel guilty about the fact that I was sneaking off to an appointment with Stan Lee.)

I was no sooner back at my desk at DC than the buzzer sounded and I trudged down, not eagerly, to Mort's office. To my amazement, he went into a little speech about how Eisenberg and Julie and maybe one or two others had spoken to him about his being a bit too hard on me, with vague hints of a possible change. (Later I would learn that it was suggested that he ease up on me, as I didn't seem the type to "take it" forever as Nelson had. Whoever spoke those words had sized me up pretty accurately.)

Interrupting Mort politely, I told him that I very much appreciated what he was saying, but it was all a bit academic now, as I had accepted a job offer from Stan Lee.

Mort seemed stunned. At least that's how I interpreted his glare. I suggested he re-hire Nelson, since he seemed to be able to accept the way Mort treated him, while I would not.

Mort said nothing.

I told him that I'd stay as long as he needed to find a replacement, even if that took several weeks.

Mort ordered me out of the building immediately, declaring I was "a spy for Stan Lee." I rose, said I was sorry things had turned out this way, and

Back in the romance office, I began picking up the handful of personal items in my desk. Jack Miller wasn't there, as usual; but for the first time since we'd been introduced, his female assistant looked over at me and spoke to me. She asked, "What are you doing?"

I told her I was clearing out my desk because I'd accepted a job with Stan Lee. That was the day I learned that it's not always an exaggeration when people say that someone's "jaw dropped."

A few minutes later, I was gone. I had a passing notion to say goodbye to Julie, maybe Eisenberg, but I didn't want to take the chance of encountering a glowering Weisinger in the hallway.

So I left. (Incidentally, Mort did re-hire Nelson almost immediately, not that I imagine my recommendation had much to do with it.)

Ten minutes later, I was back at Marvel's four little offices, and talking with Stan about scripting an already drawn Millie the Model story over the weekend.

That night, by coincidence, I stayed overnight at Otto Binder's home in Englewood, New Jersey—"The House That Captain Marvel Built"—as previously arranged. Otto, the soul of kindness, gave me a pep talk about how "everybody" felt more or less about Mort the way I did, even those who had known him for years—except maybe Julie, who had a special relationship with him going back so many years. Otto told me I'd done the right thing. He felt Mort was a "frustrated fiction writer," which was why he liked to brandish those big checks from *Parade* or *Reader's Digest*—to demonstrate that he, too, was a writer.

A 1973 caricature of Mort Weisinger by Wayne Boring.
© 2006 Wayne Boring estate.

I ran into Mort only twice after that. Just a couple of weeks later, at one of the first comics conventions, at the Broadway Central Hotel in lower Manhattan, Mort showed up unannounced and gave an impromptu speech after he was invited to join a panel composed of Otto, Bill Finger, and Gardner Fox. To my discomfited astonishment, he spoke of the fanzines as being the place where comics companies were going to look for future talent—quite a statement, considering how, as he'd stated that Friday, I'd "betrayed" him by taking DC's money and "using it to get to New York to go to work for Stan Lee." The two of us never let our eyes meet that day.

Some time afterward, I heard that he had told people I still owed DC repayment for that $50 advance … though I believe I placed a check to him in the mail not long after I went to work for Marvel. (Incidentally, some months later, a totally rewritten form of that teenage gang story appeared in *Jimmy Olsen* #91 (Mar. 1966), with no byline for me—and it had been expanded by 50% or more in page length, just as I'd asked Mort to do earlier.)

It was perhaps a year or so later that I encountered him again at the funeral of someone in the comics field, but once more we avoided each other. I wanted to go over and talk to him, to hold out my hand and say I respected him even though I'd felt I couldn't go on working for him—but I didn't. I wish I had, even if I still suspected that he'd have turned his back on me.

A few years later, he retired. Some time after that, I heard he had died. And I was sorry.

Though it was pros like Gardner Fox and Otto Binder and especially Julie Schwartz who had encouraged me in my half-formed hopes of entering the comics field, it was, after all, Mort Weisinger who'd actually taken the step of hiring me.

Though it was under Stan Lee at Marvel that I would find my greatest professional success, it was Mort who had brought me to New York so that, by a juxtaposition of fortunate circumstances, I would be on the spot when Stan was looking for a new writer.

The years haven't appreciably altered my view that Mort had a sadistic streak, and that he enjoyed being cruel to those who worked under him, be they assistant editors, artists, or writers. Yet, at the same time, the decades have also increased my appreciation of Mort Weisinger as an important and in many ways a positive figure in the field. Both as official editor in the 1960s and quasi-anonymously for years before as de facto editor serving under Whitney Ellsworth, Weisinger did indeed develop a "Superman mythology" which, if it perhaps owed a bit to the Marvel Family milieu of the 1940s, very definitely led in the direction that the field was destined to take for some years to come. It was around this same time, for instance, that students in college magazines began to write about Stan Lee's "Marvel mythology"—and Julie Schwartz's magazines likewise had a distinctive feel that advanced the comics industry.

Mort Weisinger, for all his human flaws (and we all have them), was a giant in the field. I honor him for what he accomplished, and I thank him posthumously (as I often wish I could have thanked him personally) for bringing me into comics. I only wish I could have liked him. Or vice versa.

Thomas introduced his Marvel surrogate for Superman, Hyperion (upper left), as one of the Squadron Sinister (later Squadron Supreme) in *The Avengers* #70 (Nov. 1969).
© 2006 Marvel Characters, Inc.

Weisinger and Bridwell, "Marble"-style.
© 2006 Marvel Characters, Inc.

Editor's note: It's common knowledge among comics collectors that Roy "a spy for Stan Lee" Thomas' tumultuous two weeks under Mort Weisinger's employ didn't permanently barricade him from the Metropolis city limits—decades later, he wrote stories featuring Superman (both the Earth-One and Earth-Two versions) in titles including *DC Comics Presents* and his own *All-Star Squadron.*

But two years after his ill-fated stint as Weisinger's assistant, "Rascally" Roy took a few good-natured jabs at Mort's Superman mythology in Marvel's *Not Brand Echh #7*'s (Apr. 1968) "The Origin of ... Stuporman!" Roy and artist "Mirthful" Marie Severin skewered every conceivable Superman convention, including the eyeglasses-and-combed-hair disguise, Clark Kent's wink to the reader, the phone booth identity change, kryptonite, and an ever-mushrooming Super-family (in this case including, but not limited to, Stuporgirl, Kreepto the Stupor-Dog, Sneaky the Stupor-Cat, Stupor-Monkey, Stupor-Snake, Stupor-Rhino, Stupor-Skunk, Stupor-Granpa, and even Stupor-Brother-in-Law!). Roy's ten-page script was laced with "DC" puns ("Don't Conceal yourself, Stupey!"), featured the high-rise headquarters of "Natural" Comics, and lampooned two DC editors, "Mr. Wienie-Burger" and his diminutive but bouncy aide "Birdwell," both of whom badger the poor "Man of Steam" with new innovation after new innovation. An exasperated Stuporman ultimately rockets his annoying Stupor-family—and Wiener-Burger and Birdwell—into oblivion, but finds his anticipated glory as the restored "sole survivor" of Kreepton usurped by the Merry "Marble" super-heroes!

The Marie Severin-drawn cover to *Not Brand Echh #7* (Apr. 1968).
© 2006 Marvel Characters, Inc.

JIM SHOOTER INTERVIEW

The Silver Age's premier child prodigy, Jim Shooter (b. 1951) began writing for Mort Weisinger at age 13, breathing new life into DC's Superman and Legion of Super-Heroes series. After creating characters such as the Parasite, Karate Kid, and Ferro Lad, Shooter vacated comics in 1970, returning in 1975. He was appointed Marvel Comics' editor in chief in 1978, a post he held until 1987, guiding the company through one of its most profitable periods. In the 1990s he spearheaded three comics companies: Valiant, Defiant, and Broadway.

Interview conducted by Michael Eury via e-mail on February 7, 2006.

MICHAEL EURY: What's your earliest memory of Superman?
JIM SHOOTER: When I was a toddler, my mother used to read comics to me, often Superman family stuff. I don't remember any particular issue or story from that time.
EURY: A lot of 13-year-olds have *wanted* to write comics, but you were the first, and probably the only, one to actually *do* it professionally. How did you break in?
SHOOTER: I think I was the one and only 13-year-old to break in. I believe Gerry Conway started when he was 14. Stan Lee started writing for Marvel—and, I think, became the editor—when he was 16. And, for the record, my good friend Joe Kubert did his first professional comics art at age 12.

Photo courtesy of Glen Cadigan.

I got the idea that I'd like to write and draw comics when I was 12. I spent a year literally analyzing and studying comics, especially Marvels, trying to figure out what made the good ones work and what made the bad ones bad.

At age 13, I thought I was ready. I wrote and drew, as best I could, a Legion of Super-Heroes story for National/DC's *Adventure Comics* and sent it off. I picked that one because I judged it to be the worst comic book published, and therefore, the place where I had the best chance to sell a story.

A couple of months later, I got an encouraging letter from Mort Weisinger, Vice President of National/DC Comics and editor of the Superman family of titles. Essentially, it said "send us another one."

I sent them two more, a two-part story that introduced several new characters, including the Karate Kid.

On February 10, 1966, I got a phone call from Mort Weisinger. He bought the second two stories I'd sent him and commissioned another story. Later, he also bought the first story I'd sent in.

After that, I was a regular writer for National, working through the mail and over the phone with Mort Weisinger on all but one of the titles he edited—for some reason, I never wrote any stories for *Lois Lane*.
EURY: Your first sales—Legion of Super-Heroes stories in *Adventure Comics* #346 and 347 (July and Aug. 1966)—led to Mort Weisinger assigning you a Supergirl script for *Action Comics* #339 (July 1966), featuring Brainiac. How involved was Weisinger with your plotting and scripting at this early stage of your career?

SHOOTER: Not at all. The first three Legion stories I wrote entirely on my own; Mort picked them out of the submissions pile and bought them as is. My first real assignment was the Supergirl story you cite, entitled, I think, "Brainiac's Blitz." Mort's entire input on that one was "Supergirl, 12 pages." Mort was never involved with the scripting, except that he would critique the scripts after they were finished. He published everything pretty much the way I wrote it with very few exceptions. During the entire time I worked for Mort I rewrote a grand total of four pages, only because Mort changed his mind about something he'd approved in the plot. I cut and pasted some of the old panels into the new pages, by the way, so it wasn't even really four pages. Probably, net, two.
EURY: In addition to your age, the other hallmark of your nascent career was your drawing your scripts in layout form. Did Curt Swan and Jim Mooney closely follow your layouts on your first Legion and Supergirl tales?
SHOOTER: Curt followed my layouts pretty closely, making improvements in the angles and composition here and there. And of course, the way he caught the sense of what I was trying to indicate with my crude scribbles and turned them into beautiful illustrations was amazing. Jim Mooney was great, and he followed my layouts for the most part, I think, but not like Curt. I don't think we communicated quite as well. If Curt changed something, it was always for the better. Sometimes, I felt that Jim had missed the point, changed something to no advantage, or had chosen an angle that was easier to draw but less effective.
EURY: Were you also drawing cover roughs?
SHOOTER: Yes. Mort required a cover sketch for every story. Mort wasn't interested in a story if it didn't have a compelling cover scene. To get a story approved, or to sell one, first and foremost, a writer had to pitch the cover idea. Cary Bates, I believe, used to send in cover sketches as submissions. Once, Mort sent me one of Cary's sketches and asked me to write a story to fit it. It was a beautiful sketch, really well drawn, with just the kind of clever "hook" Mort loved. I wrote that story, but I think after that Mort gave Cary a shot at scripting and he did well.

By the way, Mort's comics always started with a "symbolic" splash page—that is, the first page was a title page with a cover-like illustration and an intro caption, rather than being the first panel of the story. Mort called the splash page the "second cover," and insisted that it be designed like a cover. Sometimes, he would prefer the splash page idea to the cover sketch and use the splash page as the cover and vice-versa. So, in effect, he was getting two cover ideas out of me (and everyone else, I guess) for every story.
EURY: For your first Superman story, in *Action* #340 (July 1966), you created the Parasite, who would become a recurring member of Superman's rogues' gallery. What was the genesis of this villain?
SHOOTER: I was in ninth grade at the time, taking Biology I. We were studying parasites. I needed a villain….
EURY: Were you involved with the adaptation of your Parasite origin to television in the *New Adventures of Superman* cartoon?
SHOOTER: The Parasite was on the cartoon?! I didn't know that.

EURY: You introduced another Superman milestone in *Superman* **#199 (Aug. 1967) by writing the first Superman/Flash race. This** *had* **to be your idea and not the editor's, was it not? A race between DC's two fastest men alive sounds like something the fertile imagination of a teenager would concoct.**

SHOOTER: My idea, but way before I was a teenager. I think I was about six years old when Julie Schwartz and company revived the Flash. Cool. I immediately wondered who was faster. In my first-grade school tablet I used to draw pictures of the two of them racing.

EURY: You wrote another late-1960s Superman team-up, his guest spot in *Captain Action* **#1 (Oct.–Nov. 1968). For the benefit of those who haven't read my** *Captain Action* **book, what's the story behind that guest appearance?**

SHOOTER: Mort called me and asked if I'd like to create a new character. I said yes—then he said, okay, his name is Captain Action (?!). He has an Actionmobile, a kid sidekick named Action Boy (??!!), a pet Action Panther and a secret Action Headquarters (???!!!) and, by the way, he's also G.I. Joe-sized action figure. He went on: Superman must make an appearance in the first issue, because the cover was going to feature Captain Action pushing Superman aside to take on whatever menace I concocted. Sigh. Okay.

The good thing that came out of that was that one of the all-time greats, Wally Wood penciled and inked the first issue of *Captain Action*, working from my layouts. Like Curt, he followed them but made them so much better.

That issue, by the way, has my first splash page credit. In those days, DC Comics didn't run credits. Woody used to letter in his name on the splash page. Few artists got away with that—I think Mort would have had anyone else's name whited out—but, for some reason, nobody messed with Woody. Woody was generally not fond of writers—he thought they were all idiots, in fact—but because my script came with layouts, to him I was not a mere writer—I was also an artist! So when he lettered in his usual "Wood," he added "Shooter." And it got through!

EURY: How long were you working for Mort Weisinger before he discovered your age?

SHOOTER: Not long. I think that at first he thought I was a college student. Remember, I worked through the mail and by phone from 400 miles away. At some point, after I'd written several stories, he asked me to come to New York and spend some time in the office so he and his staff people could show me some things. I hesitated … then he asked me how old I was. Fourteen, at that point. I told him. Silence. Then he said, "Put your mother on the phone."

EURY: Describe your working relationship with Mort.

SHOOTER: At first, Mort had just bought stories I'd written on my own, so there wasn't much "working" relationship. His finding out how old I was roughly coincided with his starting to give me assignments. He told me right then that he wasn't going to cut me any slack because I was a kid—that he intended to treat me the same as any other writer. That seemed fine—till I found out that he

Original cover art (by Carmine Infantino, who autographed it, and Murphy Anderson) to the first Superman/Flash race in Superman #199 (Aug. 1967) written by Shooter

A rare writer's credit in a Weisinger edited story

treated all of his writers like crap. Once we were really working together, discussing plots, covers, characters and all that on a regular basis, I quickly learned that he was nasty, abusive, foul-mouthed, cruel, and vicious. If I made a spelling mistake, I was a "f*cking retard." Grammar mistake? "Illiterate moron." If something in my layouts was unclear, or I'd picked a less than perfect POV, he'd say things like, "What the f*ck is that? A gun? Or a carrot?" Or, "This is crap! Were you doing drugs when you laid this out or are you just stupid?" Mort would call me anytime he needed to, of course, but we had a regularly scheduled call every Thursday evening at a certain time—right after the *Batman* TV show—to go over the work I'd sent in that week. I came to dread that call. When you're 14 and the big, important man from New York calls to yell at you and tell you you're worthless and stupid, you tend to feel bad. Often those calls would end with him telling me that he'd give me "one more chance" because he knew my family was desperately poor and we needed the money. He used to call me his "charity case."

That sucked—but, as time passed, it finally started to occur to me that if I was so bad they wouldn't keep sending me those checks. Also, several times, Mort did things that were inexplicable if I were as lousy as he made me feel. For instance, he got me a gig writing an episode for the *Batman* TV show—an odd thing to do for your "charity case." The show was cancelled while that was still in early stages, so nothing came of it—but the fact that he apparently thought that I could cut it in that world at age 15 was a boost. He also arranged publicity for me. Because of Mort, I was featured in an article in *This Week* magazine, a newspaper insert with a national circulation in the many tens of millions. Years later, I found out from Mort's former assistant that he thought I was his best writer—the go-to guy that he could give any character, any assignment, and I'd come back with good stuff, all usable copy as delivered. The assistant, E. Nelson Bridwell, said Mort used to *brag* about me to the other editors—I was the prodigy that he, in his profound wisdom, had pulled out of the slush pile. Go figure.

I need to add one thing here—though he was very harsh in his methods, Mort knew his stuff, and when he yelled at me about something, he was almost always right. He taught me a great deal about the creative part of the craft—including writing, penciling, inking, coloring, and even production. He also taught me about the comics *business* and all related businesses, including film, TV, licensing, merchandise, and more. In retrospect, it seems clear to me that he was grooming me for a career in the entertainment business. Because of Mort, when I got the chance to be editor in chief at Marvel, I was prepared. For all he did for me, I am grateful.

EURY: Legend says that Weisinger was known for shooting down writers' plot pitches, but then assigning those plots to different writers. Did this ever happen to you?
SHOOTER: I can't think of any such incident—except once, I recall that I suggested a springboard for a story that he didn't like—and then, a couple of weeks later, he suggested the same plot idea to me. I suspect that he had enough plot conversations going at any given time with enough different writers that it's possible that he might have gotten confused. Mort was nasty, but at least to me, honorable in his way. He might rip you to shreds but he wouldn't knowingly steal from you.
EURY: Cary Bates, who was a few years older than you, started writing for Weisinger shortly after you did. Didn't Mort play the two of you off of each other?
SHOOTER: I first met Cary in DC's offices sometime long after Mort was gone. One of the first things he said to me was, "I used to hate you." Mort apparently used to say things to Cary like, "Why can't you write like Shooter? He's just a high school kid…!" Of course, Mort was also always telling me, "Bates always has good cover ideas. What's wrong with you?"

THE SUPERMAN MYTHOLOGY:
IT'S A BIRD, IT'S A PLANE, IT'S SUPERMAN

It's a Bird, It's a Plane, It's Superman, a musical comedy directed by Harold Prince with music by Charles (*Bye Bye Birdie, Annie*) Strouse, opened on Broadway at the Alvin Theater on March 29, 1966, running 129 performances and closing on July 17, 1966. Featured in the cast were Bob Holiday as Superman and Clark Kent, Patricia Marand as Lois Lane, Eric Mason as Perry White, and made-for-stage characters Max Mencken (played by Jack Cassidy) and Sydney (Linda Lavin). After its short Broadway run, *It's a Bird…* became a staple of dinner and high-school theaters and was adapted to television in a 1975 broadcast starring David Wilson (Superman/Kent), Lesley Ann Warren (Lois; Warren auditioned for the *Superman: The Movie* Lane role two years later), Allen Ludden (Perry), Kenneth Mars (Max), and Loretta Swit (Sydney).

A publicity shot from the playbill to *It's a Bird, It's a Plane, It's Superman.*
Superman TM & © DC Comics. Scan courtesy of Paul J. Ydstie.

Copycap: a *Captain America* stage show was planned in 1981 but never materialized.
© 2006 Marvel Characters, Inc.

EURY: Why didn't Weisinger credit his creative teams in print (outside of the occasional lettercol mention)?
SHOOTER: Two reasons:

(1) Mort believed that Superman was the star and the creative people were not stars. It wasn't that he didn't think that good creative people were important—he just didn't want the focus to ever be taken away from Superman. I had a chance, at age 14, to appear on the TV game show *What's My Line?* Who would have guessed that a high-school kid wrote Superman? Mort nixed it. Too much focus on me, not enough benefit to Superman….

(2) Mort actually made a great deal of his living by writing articles for magazines and the occasional book. He wrote articles about multiple sclerosis, about which he was a respected lay expert; the Miss America Pageant, which he had exhaustively researched; and many other subjects, not the least of which was Superman. No credits on the books preserved his status as the go-to authority on Superman. By the way, he wrote a novel about the Miss America Pageant entitled *The Contest*, and a book called *I Flew with Superman*.

EURY: You were fortunate to have Curt Swan illustrate so many of your early Superman and Legion stories. Your corresponded with him regularly, didn't you?

SHOOTER: I wouldn't say regularly. He wrote me several great letters on big sheets of vellum replete with useful advice, drawing tips, sketches, and very gentle criticisms—really, more just helpful hints. He was so complimentary and encouraging, and boy, I needed that. Curt was one of the nicest and most talented men I ever knew.

EURY: Did you have any personal contact with the other artists who illustrated your Superman scripts, like Al Plastino and Wayne Boring?

SHOOTER: No, but I met Wayne Boring at a convention in Florida long after he had retired and while I was EIC at Marvel. That was great. We got along famously and had a ball at that show, hanging around with all-time great and world record curmudgeon C.C. Beck, who was also there.

Kryptonians three. Page 5 of "The Fury of the Kryptonian Killer!" from *Superman* #195 (Apr. 1967), written by Jim Shooter and drawn by the 1960s' superstar squad, Curt Swan and George Klein. TM & © DC Comics. Art courtesy of Heritage Comics.

EURY: You brought a Marvel-like energy to Superman in stories like "Eterno the Immortal" and "Fight with the Fearsome Foursome." How did you approach the character and his many powers before writing each story?

SHOOTER: There are a lot of Superman stories that really make no sense, because if he had all those powers and used them logically, he would have solved the problem in two panels. I tried to think it through and make sure that the problem was such that if I had those powers and I was trying as hard as I could that the problem would still be a problem on page 20. I tried. Didn't always succeed.

EURY: Did Weisinger reject any of your proposed Superman stories? If so, do you recall their plots?

SHOOTER: I suppose there were springboards—ideas—that I tossed out in plot discussions that Mort dismissed out of hand, but by the time I sat down to write a plot, I had a pretty fair idea of what to do and no fleshed-out plots of mine were ever rejected. I can't recall a particular springboard that was rejected.

EURY: From your perspective, which of the Silver Age Superman's supporting-cast members was the most essential to the character?

SHOOTER: I guess that if I *had* to name one, it'd be Lois Lane, but to me they were all essential.

EURY: You introduced a host of new characters into the Legion, but very few additions to Superman's adventures. Why were you more vested into DC's future than its present?

SHOOTER: The "LSH" was more or less my strip. I wrote all but four stories for the Legion in the course of about five years. No other DC book was set in the future—so I owned the future! I could do continuity, set things up to pay off months down the road, and really develop characters. Most other DC titles, especially the Superman family titles, had no continuity—you could run the stories in any order—and more than one regular writer. It's hard to build momentum if the other guy might accidentally or on purpose undo everything you were trying to do. I had a unique situation with the LSH. That's not to say I didn't do my best on Superman. I did whatever Mort asked me to do, but I didn't have the freedom or enough "at bats" to get on a roll.

EURY: Your two Silver Age assignments dovetailed into the Adult Legion. How did that concept come about?

SHOOTER: There had already been stories that showed Superman and the Legionnaires as grownups. Mort kept track of the sales for each issue and "recycled" cover feature ideas that had sold well. For instance, about every two years there was a Super-Pets story. Every two years there was a Super-Babies story. What else? There was a "girls take over" story … and more I can't remember. When he deemed it time to recycle, Mort would ask for a new version of a cover that had sold well and a new story to go with it. Mort asked me to come up with a two-parter using the previously successful Adult Legion idea and gave me a great deal of flexibility to do what I wanted. I had plans…. But then I got a call from his assistant, Nelson, who had a whole list of things I *had* to do—mostly who marries whom. That was weird. Nelson *never* called me. Nelson also never went to the bathroom without Mort's okay, so at the time I had to believe that he was acting on Mort's authority. In retrospect … no way. Nelson was a big fan and he had a lot of emotional investment in the relationships between the various Legionnaires—and he didn't want me breaking up his favorite couples like Saturn Girl and Cosmic Boy. Whatever. I still had a good bit of room to play.

EURY: What do you consider to be Weisinger's greatest contribution to the Superman mythos?

SHOOTER: Mort made a lot of contributions. I don't remember, at this point, exactly which pieces of the mythos were entirely his, but I believe that a great deal of Superman's milieu—things like the Bottle City of Kandou, Supergirl, the Fortress of Solitude, the Phantom Zone, etc. (but not necessarily those particular things)—were Mort's contributions or were based upon suggestions he gave to writers.

EURY: What was Mort's reaction to your leaving DC in the late 1960s?

SHOOTER: By age 18, I had figured out Mort's ogreish-ness, and was pretty much immune to his venom. But I was also tired of it. I was going to go to NYU—I had a full scholarship—and I wanted to work part-time, preferably doing something less taxing than writing, preferably an office gig. Having worked my way through high school writing for Mort, I just wasn't ready to do another four years under that kind of pressure. Mort turned me down cold. He said he needed me as a writer (me, his charity case!). So I called Stan Lee at Marvel and ended up getting a job there as an assistant editor under Stan. Mort was furious. He called me at Marvel Comics to yell at me one last time. He felt I'd betrayed him… "after all I've done for you," etc. By the way, I left Marvel after a few weeks for personal reasons, and was out of mainstream comics all together for a few years, so my "betrayal" of Mort was short-lived.

Another by-the-way: a few years ago, at a convention, I met Alvin Schwartz, who wrote Superman during the '40s and '50s, I think. He, too, had quit because he refused to put up with Mort's abusive crap. We bonded. Great man. He wrote a wonderful book, *An Unlikely Prophet*, which was, in part, inspired by his experiences writing Superman.

EURY: In the mid-1970s you returned to DC to write Superman stories for Julie Schwartz for *Superman* #290 (Aug. 1975) and *Action* #451 and 452 (Sept. and Oct. 1975). How did your return to Superman happen?

SHOOTER: I was living in Pittsburgh, doing occasional comics format advertising work for U.S. Steel, political campaigns, and

© 2006 Marvel Characters, Inc.

other accounts, and less glamorous jobs in between those high-paying ad gigs. A fan, and now good friend, Harry Broertjes, tracked me down to interview me about the Legion of Super-Heroes. He mentioned to a friend of his who worked at Marvel that I might be available for some comics writing. The next day I got a call from an assistant editor at Marvel who invited me to come up to New York and talk about work. I did, the next day, I think. Marvel offered me a series called "Man-Wolf" [appearing in the title *Creatures on the Loose*]. Some of the folks at Marvel also recommended that I go over to DC's offices and see if they had anything to offer. I did. They offered me *Superman* and the *Legion of Super-Heroes*. I felt a lot more comfortable with Superman and the LSH, so I started writing for DC again. People at both companies told me that they'd wanted to offer me work before, but no one knew how to contact me. I guess Mort had expunged my name from the records at DC, and Marvel, well, they seemed so disorganized at that time, it wasn't surprising somehow that they couldn't locate someone who was still on their comp list....

EURY: How had the character of Superman changed from the Weisinger days?

SHOOTER: I think that in essential ways, Superman himself was about the same. Details had changed. Clark Kent was a TV newsman, I think, and there were new supporting cast members. Julie Schwartz had a more formulaic approach than Mort did. Every story *had* to have a Steve Lombard prank and a surreptitious Clark/Superman revenge, every story *had* to had a secret-identity-threatening situation and a clever escape, etc. Lots of rules.

EURY: You wrote one of the most exciting Superman stories of the early 1980s, the second team-up with Spider-Man, where you pitted Dr. Doom and the Parasite against the pair. Why Doom and not a villain more identified with Spidey?

SHOOTER: To go up against Superman, I figured I needed the heaviest-duty bad guy we had to offer—Doctor Doom. Their greatest hero against our greatest villain.

EURY: That team-up gave readers the opportunity to see Superman by drawn John Buscema. Were any other Marvel artists considered, or was John the go-to guy?

SHOOTER: John was our number one guy. Also, I think, maybe, that the folks at DC requested him.

EURY: Is there a single Superman story of yours of which you're most proud?

SHOOTER: I guess I like the Superman/Spider-Man crossover better than most….

EURY: Any chance you'll write another Superman story?

SHOOTER: I don't know. I'm pretty busy, but it would be fun. If they ever want me, they know where I am.

Story page 34 from the Shooter-scripted Superman/Spider-Man sequel, drawn by John Buscema and Terry Austin and published in *Marvel Treasury Edition #28* (1981).

(right) Titles from Shooter's three 1990s comics companies.

THE SUPERMAN MYTHOLOGY:
ALTERED STATES

Thanks to red kryptonite, magic, Imaginary Stories, or other plot devices, Silver Age readers routinely witnessed a plethora of Superman permutations, from a Super-senior citizen to a lion-headed Action Ace. Such metamorphoses were not the Man of Steel's exclusive domain — being Superman's friend frequently offered a one-story ticket to an unexpected transformation.

(left) Among Superman's pal's myriad mutations was "The Human Octopus" in *Jimmy Olsen* #41 (Dec. 1959). Marvel Comics, apparently up in arms over the cub reporter's conversion, introduced Dr. Octopus in *Amazing Spider-Man* #3 (July 1963) ... then gave Spidey himself extra limbs in 1971.
TM & © DC Comics.
© 2006 Marvel Characters, Inc.

There was no shortage of swelled noggins among Superman's cast, but the covers to Murray Boltinoff's *Challengers of the Unknown* #39 (Aug.–Sept. 1964) and Julie Schwartz's *The Flash* #177 (Mar. 1968) prove that editors *other* than Mort Weisinger had an eye for big heads.
TM & © DC Comics.

Superman (and Superboy) rarely held the title of "only super-hero in town," as Metropolis' and Smallville's mortals frequently gained temporary super powers.
TM & © DC Comics.

mike esposito on superman

by Mike Esposito

Editor's note: Native New Yorker Mike Esposito's (b. 1927) first artistic goal was to become an animator for the Walt Disney Studios, but close ties to his family kept him rooted on the East Coast. While attending art school in Manhattan he met fellow illustrator Ross Andru, with whom he formed a long-lasting partnership on a variety of Silver Age titles including *Wonder Woman*, *Metal Men*, and *The Flash*. Sometimes ghosting at Marvel as "Joe Gaudiso," Esposito inked Andru on Superman stories in *Action Comics*, *Superman*, and *World's Finest Comics* in the late 1960s, and also inked several Curt Swan Superman stories during that same period.

Excerpted from Andru and Esposito: Partners for Life *by Mike Esposito and Daniel Best (Hermes Press, 2006). Reprinted by permission.*

Carmine Infantino once said that Ross did a great Superman. I can't believe it, because Al Plastino used to re-draw the heads every time we did a book. I remember one day I was up at DC and he was reworking all of Ross' heads. He had the head down perfectly, the DC type of look. Ross had a tendency to do things differently, the three-quarters-up-the-nose shot, the behind-the-back-of-the-head shot.

So when Ross did Superman he tried to change him. On the cover of *Flash* #175 (Dec. 1967), there's Superman racing the Flash and he did the Flash great, but when you get to Superman's head, the lantern jaw, well, it's very interesting to look at because it's different. It's not what you see all the time when you see Superman. But by doing so Ross would lose sight of the crystal-clear Superman look. That's why they brought in people like Plastino to redo the faces. It wasn't the figures; it was the faces that created the problem.

Mort Weisinger had been with DC since 1939. When we were doing *Superman* and I was doing *Lois Lane* with Curt Swan I would bring the pages in and he wanted to see them. To him they were like toys. His personal fun was to look at the originals, and he'd lay them all out on the cutting table and one at a time he'd say to me, "Fix his bottom lip, it's too thick for Superman. He has a thin mouth." That's the way Plastino and Curt Swan would do; it'd be more realistic than when Ross would do it. Ross would give him a comic look with a fat bottom lip. Weisinger would take a razor blade and cut bits off at the sides, and he wasn't an artist, he was an editor. I'd think, "Jesus Christ, he's touching my artwork," but I couldn't say a word because he was the boss, he had the checkbook so we went along with it. He was very critical of faces and he didn't like the way Ross did them. The hair was not right, the mouth was too wide, and Plastino had a way of doing it that made him happy.

An early Andru/Esposito collaboration—with a red-caped muscleman, to boot: *Mister Universe* #1 (July 1951).

Andru and Esposito's cover to *Action Comics* #365 (July 1968), part of the memorable "Virus X" serial from issues #363–366 (May–Aug. 1968).

Superman by Andru and Esposito, from *World's Finest* #181 (Dec. 1968).

THE SUPERMAN MYTHOLOGY:

SUNSHINE SUPERMAN

Superman or Green Lantern ain't got a-nothin' on Donovan, the bushy-topped Scottish pop singer whose Epic Records single "Sunshine Superman" was released in the U.S. in July 1966. This trippy love song had a-nothin' to do with the Man of Steel (or Green Lantern) other than its recurring lyric parodied in this sidebar's opening line, but it illustrated Superman's pervasive cultural status—and it scored high enough on the charts to warrant the artist titling his third album (seen here in its American and French incarnations) after the hit.

© 1966 EMI International.

Andru and Esposito's version of Superman, Batman, and a bunch of Bizarros, from *World's Finest #181*.

TM & © DC Comics. Art courtesy of Heritage Comics.

When Ross would do figures he was always looking to animate them, to get the figure moving. That's not an attractive way to do things, though, because Ross would see the in-between action and sometimes the in-between action didn't look that good. I used to tell him that but he caught these things in his eye in a certain way. Gil Kane could never do it, but Ross could, and I don't think a lot of editors fully appreciated it.

Ross had one thing that no one else had, and that was depth. His camera went into the picture, like a multi-plane camera that goes down, down, down. The other guys had the figure and a background, like a wall or a garbage pail and a couple of dots on the wall. Fans like it today because they're educated. But if you go back to 1965, the young fans didn't see stuff like that. The average cartoonist didn't draw that way. Now these guys have grown up and they say, "Gee that was good" and they appreciate it more.

We didn't last all that long on *Superman* because the book didn't go anywhere sales-wise. DC kept trying different things. We had no reason to stay at DC, *The Flash* was dying, and we didn't do a good job on that book. Ross always felt that he didn't do a good job on *The Flash* compared to what Infantino was doing. It wasn't a thing he enjoyed and he wanted to go to Marvel.

Neither Ross nor I liked Superman. He was made of stone, he couldn't bleed, and, to me, he wasn't a real hero. Spider-Man could bleed. He could be beaten. In order for someone to be a real hero they have to be able to be beaten. They have to triumph over adversity, and it was impossible for any normal person to beat Superman. He was a god amongst men. The heroes have to be beaten, they have to show that they're vulnerable, and what makes them a hero is the fact that they can go into battle knowing that they can lose, yet not giving an inch. How do you beat Superman? Magic and kryptonite, but not everyone is a magician and not everyone had access to kryptonite. He was a guy who could hear a pin drop across a galaxy, and could see the atoms on the head of that pin. Spider-Man couldn't do that, he was a man, and that was the magic of Stan and Jack in creating a universe of people who weren't gods and could be beaten. They were heroes, and far more interesting to us.

THE SUPERMAN MYTHOLOGY:

THEY MIGHT BE

80 pg. GIANT

Was there any bargain bigger than DC's 80-Page Giants? Starting as "Annuals" in 1960, DC's squarebound reprint editions were cleverly themed by Mort Weisinger (and later, assistant/associate editor E. Nelson Bridwell) to recap the roots of the expanding Super-universe for the benefit of newer readers. Rising costs cut their page count from 80 to 64 pages in 1969.

Silver Age Superman Giants: A Checklist

Superman Annual #1 (1960), 2 (1960), 3 (Summer 1961), 4 (Winter 1962), 5 (Summer 1962), 6 (Winter 1963), 7 (Winter 1963), 8 (Summer 1964)
Lois Lane Annual #1 (Summer 1962), 2 (Summer 1963)
Superboy Annual #1 (Summer 1964)
80-Page Giant #1 (Superman, 1964), 2 (Jimmy Olsen, 1964), 3 (Lois Lane, 1964), 6 (Superman, 1964), 10 (Superboy, 1965), 13 (Jimmy Olsen, 1965), 14 (Lois Lane, 1965), 15 (Superman and Batman, 1965)
Action Comics (Supergirl Giants) #334 (Mar. 1966), 347 (Mar.–Apr. 1967), 360 (Mar. 1968), 373 (Mar. 1969)
Adventure Comics (Legion of Super-Heroes Giant) #403 (Mar. 1971)
Superboy #129 (May 1966), 138 (June 1967), 147 (June 1968), 156 (June 1969), 165 (June 1970), 174 (June 1971)
Super DC Giant (Supergirl Giant) #S-24 (May–June 1971)
Superman #183 (Jan. 1966), 187 (June 1966), 193 (Jan.–Feb. 1967), 202 (Dec. 1967–Jan. 1968), 207 (June 1968), 212 (Dec. 1968), 217 (June–July 1969), 222 (Dec. 1969), 227 (June–July 1970), 232 (Dec. 1970–Jan. 1971)
Superman's Girl Friend Lois Lane #68 (Sept.–Oct. 1966), 77 (Oct. 1967), 86 (Oct. 1968), 95 (Oct. 1969), 104 (Oct. 1970), 113 (Sept.–Oct. 1970)

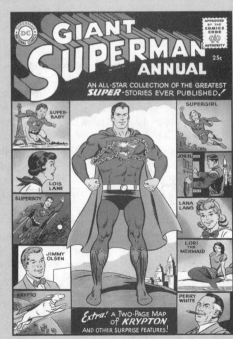

Superman's Pal Jimmy Olsen #95 (Aug.–Sept. 1966), 104 (Sept. 1967), 113 (Sept. 1968), 122 (Sept. 1969), 131 (Sept. 1970), 140 (Sept. 1971)
World's Finest Comics #161 (Oct. 1966), 170 (Oct. 1967), 179 (Oct. 1968), 188 (Oct. 1969), 197 (Oct.–Nov. 1970), 206 (Oct. 1971)

JACK ABEL (inker)

Jack Abel inking Curt Swan, from *Superman* #218 (July 1969).
TM & © DC Comics.

The crisp linework of Jack Abel (1927–1996) landed him on Mort Weisinger's radar in 1968 as an inker of Curt Swan after Swan's primary inker George Klein left DC Comics. Abel also penciled for a variety of publishers, and worked on staff at Marvel late in his career.

ROSS ANDRU (penciler)

After garnering acclaim for his runs on *Wonder Woman* and *Metal Men*, Ross Andru (1925–1993) brought his distinct storytelling style to the Superman family in the late 1960s, penciling issues of *Superman*, *Action Comics*, and *World's Finest Comics*; he was inked by his long-time collaborator Mike Esposito. The artist of Marvel's *Amazing Spider-Man* in the mid-1970s, Andru penciled the first DC/Marvel super-hero crossover, *Superman vs. The Amazing Spider-Man* (1976). He returned to DC in the early 1980s as an editor; during this period Andru was also a Superman cover and merchandising artist.

Recommended reading: *Andru and Esposito: Partners for Life* by Mike Esposito and Daniel Best (Hermes Press, 2006).

(above) From Andru's 1980s return to DC, art for a DC toy project featuring Superman (and friends). Inks by Dick Giordano.
TM & © DC Comics. Courtesy of Heritage Comics.

METALLO: THE MAN WITH THE K(IRBY)-METAL HEART?

Metallo, the Man with the Kryptonite Heart, might not have been solely created by Robert Bernstein, the writer of the character's first story in *Action* #252 (May 1959). In *The Jack Kirby Collector* #45 (Winter 2006), Mark Evanier reported that Bernstein, an anxious sort, might have picked Jack Kirby's free-flowing brain for the Metallo concept while in a panic to find an idea that would impress his boss Mort Weisinger. No matter who invented this early Silver Age super-villain, that writer wasn't the first to coin the name: Jerry Siegel introduced "Metalo" (note spelling), a scientist in a super-suit, in "The Man of Steel versus the Man of Metal" in *World's Finest* #6 (Summer 1942).

DC's second Metallo: the robot "Metallo of Krypton," from *Superboy* #49 (June 1956). And *another* connection between Jack Kirby and Metallo is the Iron Man prototype bearing that name that he drew in Marvel's *Tales of Suspense* #16 (Apr. 1961).
TM & © DC Comics.   © 2006 Marvel Characters, Inc.

ROBERT BERNSTEIN (writer)

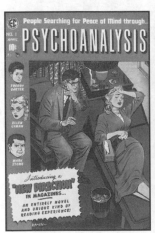

Robert Bernstein exorcised his psychological demons through his comic-book alter ego of "Mark Stone" in the four-issue EC series *Psychoanalysis*; shown here is #1 (Mar.–Apr. 1955), featuring Stone's headshot. Another of the writer's odder credits is Dell's *Movie Classics* #922 (June–Aug. 1963), starring the Wolf Man.
© 2006 EC Comics.   © 1963 Dell Comics.

Robert Bernstein's (1919–1983) first DC script was for *Green Lantern* vol. 1 #46 (June–July 1947). After penning war stories and "Congo Bill" and "Green Arrow" back-ups, he wrote his first Superman tale, "The Oldest Man in Metropolis," for *Action* #251 (Apr. 1959), then continued as a Super-scribe (mostly on *Jimmy Olsen*) throughout the early 1960s. The villain Bernstein introduced in "The Menace of Metallo!" in *Action* #252 (May 1959) might not have been his idea [see sidebar]. In the 1950s and early 1960s he scripted for a number of publishers including EC, Dell, Archie (*Adventures of the Fly*, *Jaguar*), and Marvel (early Thor, Human Torch, and Iron Man stories), using the pseudonym "R. Berns" at the latter company.

OTTO BINDER (writer)

Krypto the Super-Dog, the Legion of Super-Heroes, Braniac, Supergirl, and Elastic Lad were the brainchildren of Otto Oscar Binder (1911–1974). In collaboration with and sometimes independent of his brother Earl Andrew Binder (1904–1965), Otto authored numerous pulp and science-fiction stories under the pen name "Eando Binder" (Eando = <u>E</u>arl <u>and</u> <u>O</u>tto); perhaps the most famous of Eando's creations was robot protagonist Adam Link. Otto Binder's capricious storytelling wonderfully lent itself to Superman's imaginative landscape, especially with the eccentric tales he wrote during the early years of Jimmy Olsen's title. Binder's flair for the fantastic was honed during his 12-year stint on Fawcett's Captain Marvel franchise, where he co-created Mary Marvel and Black Adam and created the talking tiger Mr. Tawky Tawny and "the World's Wickedest Worm" Mr. Mind. Additional Superman classics penned by Binder include "The Witch of Metropolis" (*Lois Lane* #1, Mar.–Apr. 1958), the first comic-book appearances of Bizarro (*Superboy* #68, Oct. 1958 and *Action* #254, July 1959), "The Wolf Man of Metropolis" (*Jimmy Olsen* #44, Apr. 1960), and "The Story of Superman's Life" (*Superman* #146, July 1961).

Recommended reading: Words of Wonder: The Life and Times of Otto Binder by Bill Schelly (Hamster Press, 2003; out of print).

The novel *The Avengers Battle the Earth-Wrecker* (1968), written by Otto Binder.
© 2006 Marvel Characters, Inc.

E. NELSON BRIDWELL (editor/writer)

E. Nelson Bridwell in the mid-1970s.
Photo © 1975 DC Comics.

One of the original fans-turned-pro, Edward Nelson Bridwell's (1931–1987) encyclopedic memory of DC Comics' and other trivia was legendary. After scripting for *MAD* and Archie Comics, Bridwell was hired as Mort Weisinger's assistant editor in 1964. His second-in-command status on the Superman books continued after Julius Schwartz and Murray Boltinoff assumed editorship of the Man of Steel's titles in 1970. Bridwell briefly edited *Lois Lane* in the early 1970s as well as the 1979 *World of Krypton* miniseries, and wrote a variety of DC series including *The Inferior Five* and *Super Friends*. For years he was the "voice" of the Superman titles through his letters-column responses, signing his comments with his initials "E.N.B." Nelson was also DC's house historian, editing a variety of 1960s and 1970s reprint editions, including Crown Publishing's popular hardcover *Superman from the Thirties to the Seventies*. The E. Nelson Bridwell Special Collection of comics and ephemera is housed in his home state of Oklahoma, in the University of Tulsa's McFarlin Library.

BOB BROWN (penciler)

Long-time comic-book artist Bob Brown's (birthdate unknown–1977) first story for DC was *Boy Commandos* #34 (July–Aug. 1949), after which he drew *Tomahawk*, *Challengers of the Unknown*, and mystery stories for the publisher. Brown became the artist of *Superboy* with issue #150 (Sept. 1968), staying on the title until issue #197 (Sept. 1973). In the 1970s he drew stories for *Batman*, *The Avengers*, and *Daredevil*.

RAY BURNLEY (inker)

Ray Burnley (1902–1964) broke into comics in the 1940s inking backgrounds for his brother, artist Jack Burnley. He eventually went solo and became one of Curt Swan's regular inkers in the 1950s. Burnley is best known as Swan's inker on the early issues of *Jimmy Olsen*; his inks can be found in issues #1 (Sept.–Oct. 1954) through 37 (June 1959).

JERRY COLEMAN (writer)

Jerry Coleman (birth/death dates unknown) wrote nearly 100 stories for DC Comics, beginning with *Mystery in Space* #3 (Aug.–Sept. 1951). By the mid-1950s he regularly scripted for Weisinger's Superman titles. Among Coleman's best-loved Super-tales: "Superboy's Last Day in Smallville" (*Superman* #97, May 1955) and "The Girl in Superman's Past" (*Showcase* #9, June–July 1957).

PETE COSTANZA (penciler/inker)

A veteran of comics' Golden Age, with Fawcett's *Captain Marvel Adventures* among his credits, Pete Costanza (1913–1984) worked for Mort Weisinger in the mid- to late 1960s, drawing *Jimmy Olsen* and the occasional *Superman* and Legion of Super-Heroes story. Silver Age readers may recall his work on American Comics Group's super-heroes Nemesis and Magicman.

LEO DORFMAN (writer)

A prolific writer of mystery comics, Leo Dorfman (birth/death dates unknown) scripted for Weisinger's Superman titles beginning in the mid-1950s. His Superman stories continued to appear throughout the 1960s, and into the early 1970s for *Action* and *Superboy* editor Murray Boltinoff. Perhaps his most famous Super-tale was "The Amazing Story of Superman-Red and Superman-Blue" in *Superman* #162 (July 1963). Dorfman also wrote Superboy episodes for Filmation's mid-to-late 1960s *The New Adventures of Superman* TV cartoon.

BILL FINGER (writer)

Wonder Woman #177 (July–Aug. 1968) guest-starred Supergirl; written by Bill Finger, penciled by Win Mortimer, and inked by Jack Abel.

The original Batman writer, Bill Finger (1914–1974) occasionally contributed to the Superman canon, most frequently in *World's Finest* but also in other Super-titles. With co-writer E. Nelson Bridwell he penned the classic "Superman's Mission for President Kennedy" (*Superman* #170, July 1964). Other notable Super-stories by Finger: "Superman in Superman Land" (*Action* #210, May 1959), the first appearance of mermaid Lori Lemaris in "The Girl in Superman's Past" (*Superman* #129, May 1959), and "The Conquest of Superman" (*Action* #277, June 1961).

JOHN FORTE (penciler/inker)

South Sea Girl

By Thorne Stevenson

Early John Forte art on the comic strip *South Sea Girl*, circa 1953.
© 1953 Phoenix Features. Art courtesy of Heritage Comics.

To John Forte (1918–1966), the world was square. The artist of the majority of the "Tales of the Bizarro World" stories in *Adventure Comics*, Forte deftly drew the strip's kooky concepts, from the block-shaped Bizarro World to its off-kilter architecture. Forte was also the first regular Legion of Super-Heroes artist, and inked Curt Swan on several occasions in the early 1960s. Before his DC days, Forte illustrated stories for Marvel, as well as an early 1950s comic strip, *South Sea Girl*.

STAN KAYE (inker)

A panel from the *Superman* newspaper strip, August 5, 1957. Curt Swan pencils, Stan Kaye inks.
TM & © DC Comics. Art courtesy of Heritage Comics.

Stan Kaye (1916–1967) entered Superman's world in the mid-1940s as an inker of Wayne Boring. In the 1950s Kaye was frequently assigned to ink Curt Swan; their collaborations included *Superman 3-D* (1953), *World's Finest*, the daily *Superman* newspaper strip, and by the late 1950s, Swan's covers on *Superman* and *Action*.

GEORGE KLEIN (inker)

One of Mort Weisinger's smartest creative decisions was pairing inker George Klein (birthdate unknown–1969) with penciler Curt Swan. Klein's full-bodied inking line, supported by feather lines, gave Swan's pencils three-dimensional depth. Together, Swan and Klein were responsible for illustrating some of Superman's most heralded Silver Age classics, including "The Last Days of Superman" (*Superman* #156, Oct. 1962), "The Amazing Story of Superman-Red and Superman-Blue" (#162, July 1963), "The Showdown Between Luthor and Superman" (#164, Oct. 1963), and "Superman's Race with the Flash" (#199, Aug. 1967). Klein worked for Marvel Comics in the late 1960s, inking Gene Colan and John Buscema.

(right) George Klein inks over Gene Colan pencils. *Daredevil* #48 (Jan. 1969).
© 2006 Marvel Characters, Inc.

SHELDON MOLDOFF (inker)

Sheldon Moldoff (b. 1920) is best known as the artist of the Golden Age Hawkman and for drawing Batman stories (ghosting "as" Bob Kane) in the 1950s and 1960s. In 1961 he began inking Curt Swan on Superman stories and covers, and continued to do so off and on for years. He also inked John Forte on the "Legion of Super-Heroes" feature in *Adventure*.

RUBEN MOREIRA (penciler/inker)

An artist for Quality Comics and Fiction House during comics' Golden Age, Ruben Moreira (birthdate unknown–1984) illustrated covers and stories for DC's 1950s crime and mystery series. He penciled a few early Silver Age stories, inked by Al Plastino, including the first Lois Lane tryout in *Showcase* #9 (June–July 1957).

Commander Battle and the Atomic Sub, inked by Sheldon Moldoff.
© 2006 the respective copyright holder.

WIN MORTIMER (penciler/inker)

IRV NOVICK (penciler)

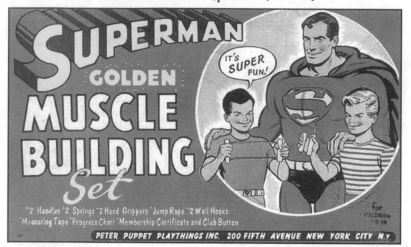

Irv Novick's splash to "Lois Lane, Convict!", from *Lois Lane* #84 (July 1968). Inks by Mike Esposito.

Win Mortimer art on the Superman Golden Muscle Building Set (mid-1950s). Also, note the similarities between Mortimer's Clark Kent (bottom headshot) and personality Steve Allen, also seen on the cover of the Nov. 1957 edition of *TV Radio Mirror*.

Winslow Mortimer (1919–1997) began illustrating Superman stories in the late 1940s, becoming DC's chief Superman and Batman cover artist during the early to mid-1950s. Mortimer's rendition of Superman was also visible in the daily *Superman* comic strip, which he penciled and inked from 1949–1955, and on merchandising. His interpretation of Clark Kent borrowed heavily from likeable TV star Steve Allen, their resemblance even being referenced in the *Superman* dailies. He left DC in 1956 to draw the syndicated strip *David Crane*, but occasionally resurfaced in comics throughout the '60s. In the late 1960s he penciled some of the last Legion of Super-Heroes tales to appear in *Adventure*, followed by Supergirl stories in that same title and Legion back-ups in *Action*. He continued to work as a comics and commercial artist throughout the 1970s and 1980s.

Irving Novick (1916–2004) may not be commonly regarded as a Superman artist, but he was assigned *Lois Lane* with #82 (Apr. 1968) and continued on the series through issue #101 (May 1970). Occasionally Novick was tapped by editor Weisinger for Superman-related covers, such as *Captain Action* #1 (Oct.–Nov. 1968) and *World's Finest* #181 (Dec. 1968). He started his comics career at MLJ in 1940, where he co-created the original star-spangled super-hero, the Shield. During the 1970s Novick illustrated long runs on *Batman* and *The Flash*.

(right) *Jackpot* #7 and *Pep* #39, cover art by Irv Novick.

GEORGE PAPP (penciler/inker)

Clark Kent's classmate Pete Ross discovered his pal's Superboy identity in "Pete Ross' Super-Secret!" (*Superboy* #90, July 1961), by Otto Binder and George Papp.
TM & © DC Comics. Art courtesy of Heritage Comics.

George Papp (1916–1990) replaced John Sikela as the artist of *Superboy* in 1958 and maintained his residence in DC's Smallville for ten years. His facility for drawing teenagers made him perfect for *Superboy*'s cast of young Clark Kent, Lana Lang, and Pete Ross, as well as for the Legion of Super-Heroes, which he also drew upon occasion. Papp illustrated the first appearances of Pete Ross, Star Boy, Mon-El, and Lana Lang as Insect Queen. His other significant contribution to DC lore is Green Arrow; Papp drew the Emerald Archer's first appearance (written by Mort Weisinger) in *More Fun Comics* #73 (Nov. 1941), and remained the Green Arrow artist until signing on to *Superboy*.

GEORGE ROUSSOS (inker)

George "Inky" Roussos (1920–2000) started his comics career in 1940 as a Batman background inker for artist Jerry Robinson. He was a regular contributor to the Superman franchise, even penciling at times; he drew uncredited Superboy stories that appeared from 1947 through 1949. Roussos was a Marvel and DC mainstay throughout the Silver Age, sometimes using the pseudonym "George Bell," and inked several Curt Swan-penciled *Superman* stories in 1969 and 1970.

ALVIN SCHWARTZ (writer)

Alvin Schwartz (b. 1919)—not to be confused with the children's book author of the same name—wrote the *Superman* and *Batman* comic strips during the 1940s and 1950s, creating Bizarro for the former in 1958. He also scripted for DC Comics during those decades, penning a number of Superman classics like the first *World's Finest* Superman/Batman team-up, "Batman—Double for Superman" (*World's Finest* #71, Jan. 1954) and "The War Between Jimmy Olsen and Superman" (*Action* #253, June 1959). He abandoned comics in the early 1960s, after nearly 20 years in the business, and in 1997 published his "metaphysical memoir," *An Unlikely Prophet*.

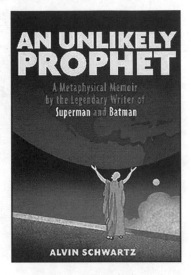

(right) Alvin Schwartz's *An Unlikely Prophet* (Destiny Books, 2006 edition).
© 2006 Alvin Schwartz.

MIKE SEKOWSKY (penciler)

Mike Sekowsky's (1928–1999) barrel-chested, Wayne Boring-like Man of Steel was widely seen in *Justice League of America*, the popular title "Big Mike" drew for most of the 1960s. Sekowsky was Supergirl's writer/penciler/editor in *Adventure* #397–409 (Sept. 1970–Aug. 1971), where he introduced a revolving wardrobe of Super-fashions for the Girl of Steel as well as a new adversary, Lex Luthor's niece Nasthalthia.

Mike Sekowsky's Superman, from *Justice League of America* #33 (Feb. 1965); inks by Bernard Sachs.
TM & © DC Comics.

DICK SPRANG (penciler/inker)

One of Batman's principal Golden Age artists, Dick Sprang (1915–2000) first tackled the Man of Steel in Superman/Batman team-ups in *World's Finest*, then was occasionally assigned to illustrate Superman stories. Notable examples: "The Girl of Steel" (the Supergirl prototype tale) in *Superman* #123 (Aug. 1958) and "Superman's Mystery Song" (guest-starring crooner Pat Boone) in *Lois Lane* #9 (May 1959).

WILLIAM WOOLFOLK (writer)

William Woolfolk (1917–2003) started his comics career in 1941, soon becoming one of the industry's highest-paid authors. At Fawcett, he coined Captain Marvel's catchphrase "Holy Moley!" One of Woolfolk's major offerings to the Superman mythos was the first tale to introduce Kryptonian survivors other than the Man of Steel, "Three Supermen from Krypton," in *Superman* #65 (July–Aug. 1950). His wife Dorothy was a DC editor, mainly for romance titles; she briefly edited *Lois Lane* and *Supergirl* during the 1970s.

CHAPTER 3

THERE'S A NEW KIND OF SUPERMAN COMING!

SUPERMAN COMICS OF 1971-1979

Mort Weisinger's shoes were so hard to fill, it took a legion of super-editors to replace him: Julius Schwartz on *Superman* and *World's Finest*, Murray Boltinoff on *Action* and *Superboy* (and *Jimmy Olsen*, although that title soon fell into the hands of its writer/penciler Jack Kirby), Mike Sekowsky on *Adventure*, and Nelson Bridwell on *Lois Lane*. Trumpeting these changes were DC house ads pledging "There's a New Kind of Superman Coming!"

That promise was only partially true. New *characters* were introduced and old ones revamped, but many of the stories simply continued the Weisinger formula, such as Boltinoff's fondness for Superbaby adventures.

But Schwartz, abetted by writer Denny O'Neil, took the "new kind of Superman" assurance to heart, weakening the Man of Steel, making Clark Kent a television newsman, eliminating kryptonite (making a new variation: *edible* K!), and toppling other conventions within the mythos. But without the other titles reflecting *Superman*'s changes, Schwartz and O'Neil's stories didn't stick.

Despite that scattershot beginning, the '70s offered exciting innovations for the Man of Tomorrow: new writers took the hero into bold directions, even questioning the reasons for Superman's existence; Curt Swan's artwork was reenergized by the rich inks of Murphy Anderson; and Neal Adams and José Luis García-López brought a fresh visual perspective to the Action Ace. Bigger-than-life super-villains threatened the hero, Lois Lane matured as a character, Spider-Man and Muhammad Ali slugged it out with the Metropolis Marvel, and Superman returned to TV (in *Super Friends*). Once all of the franchise's titles (excluding *Legion of Super-Heroes*) fell under Schwartz's watchful editorial eye, a cohesive continuity became noticeable. By decade's end, Superman was a box-office and merchandising superstar.

This chapter reviews Superman's Bronze Age, primarily through interviews with the "new kind of" writers and artists who charted the hero's course.

Neal Adams' original art to the back cover of Power Records' 1978 *Superman* Christmas album.
TM & © DC Comics. Richard Martines collection.

1971

Action Comics #396–407
Superman #233–246
  (#233: first Julius Schwartz-edited
issue; "Kryptonite Nevermore";
short-lived revamp begins; first Clark
Kent as television news anchorman)
  (#246: first S.T.A.R. Labs)

Adventure Comics #401–413
Justice League of America #87–95
Superboy #171–180
  (#172: Legion back-ups begin)
Superman's Girl Friend Lois Lane
#107–117
Superman's Pal Jimmy Olsen #135–144
  (#135: first Project Cadmus)
World's Finest Comics #200–208

100-Page Super Spectacular #DC-6
(World's Greatest Super-Heroes,
with JLA)
DC Special #14 (Superman cover
appearance; reprint)
The Forever People #1 (Superman
appearance; first Intergang)
Super DC Giant #S-24 (Supergirl)
*Superman From the Thirties to the
Seventies* hardcover reprint edition

1972

Action Comics #408–419
Superman #247–259
  (#248: first Galactic Golem)
  (#249: first Terra-Man)

Adventure Comics #414–424
  (#424: last Supergirl, spins off into
solo title)
Justice League of America #96–103
Superboy #181–192
Supergirl #1
Superman's Girl Friend Lois Lane
#118–128
Superman's Pal Jimmy Olsen #145–154
World's Finest Comics #209–214
  (#214: last non-Batman team-up)

The Brady Kids (ABC Saturday-
morning cartoon; Superman and Clark
Kent appear in episode #5, "Cindy's
Super Friends," original airdate 10-7-72)

1973

Action Comics #420–430
  (#421: first Captain Strong)
Superman #260–270
  (#264: first Steve Lombard)

Justice League of America #104–108
Superboy #193–196
  (#196: last Superboy solo issue)
*Superboy starring the Legion of
Super-Heroes* #197–199
  (#197: Legion takes over title)
Supergirl #2–8
Superman's Girl Friend Lois Lane
#129–135
Superman's Pal Jimmy Olsen #155–161
  (#155: first Jimmy Olsen as Mr. Action)
World's Finest Comics #215–220
  (#215: first '70s Super-Sons)

100-Page Super Spectacular
#DC-15 (Superboy), DC-21 (Superboy)
*The Amazing World of Superman:
Official Metropolis Edition* (tabloid)
Crazy! #3 (Marvel Comics;
"Stuporman" reprint and new cover)
Legion of Super-Heroes #1–4
(reprint series)
Secret Origins #1 (*Action* #1 Superman
origin reprint), 2 (Supergirl origin reprint)
Shazam! #1 (Superman cover
appearance)
*Wanted: The World's Most Dangerous
Super-Villains* #9 (Superman reprint)
Super Friends (long-running ABC
Saturday-morning cartoon begins, with
Superman)

1974

Action Comics #431–442
  (#432: first Toyman II)
Superman #271–282
  (#276: battle with Captain Thunder)
  (#281: first Vartox)
  (#282: first Nam-El of Phantom Zone)

Justice League of America #109–114
*Superboy starring the Legion of
Super-Heroes* #200–205
Supergirl #9–10
  (#10: last issue; Supergirl feature
continued in *The Superman Family*)
Superman's Girl Friend Lois Lane
#136–137
  (#137: last issue; Lois Lane feature
continued in *The Superman Family*)
Superman's Pal Jimmy Olsen #162–163
  (#163: last issue as *Jimmy Olsen*;
becomes *The Superman Family*
with #164)
The Superman Family #164–167
World's Finest Comics #221–226

Famous First Edition #C-26 (*Action
Comics* #1 reprint)
Limited Collectors' Edition #C-31
(Superman), C-34 (Christmas with the
Super-Heroes)
Secret Origins #6 (Superboy and
LSH reprint)
Shazam! #15 (Superman cover
appearance)
Wonder Woman #212 (Superman/JLA
appearance)
Superman and *Superboy* Aurora
Comic Scenes insert comics

1975

Action Comics #443–454
  (#447: Siegel and Shuster tribute)
Superman #283–294

Justice League of America #115–125
*Superboy starring the Legion of
Super-Heroes* #206–213
The Superman Family #168–173
World's Finest Comics #227–234

Amazing World of DC Comics #7
(All-Superman issue)
DC Special #16 (Superman cover
appearance and reprint), 18 (Superman
cover appearance and reprint)
Famous First Edition #C-26 (*Action
Comics* #1 reprint)
Kamandi, the Last Boy on Earth #29
(Superman costume on cover and in story)
Limited Collectors' Edition #C-38
(Superman), C-39 (Secret Origins of
Super-Villains), C-41 (Super Friends),
C-43 (Christmas with the Super-Heroes)
Super-Team Family #1 (Superman cover
appearance and *World's Finest* reprint)
Wonder Woman #212 (Superman/JLA
appearance)

1976

Action Comics #455–466
(#458: first Blackrock)
Superman #295–306
(#301: first Skull)

Justice League of America #126–137
Superboy starring the Legion of Super-Heroes #214–222
Super Friends #1–2
The Superman Family #174–180
World's Finest Comics #235–242

All-Star Comics #58 (first Power Girl), 64 (Earth-Two Superman appearance)
Amazing World of DC Comics #9 (All-Superboy & LSH issue)
Amazing World of DC Comics Special Edition (Super-Con)
DC Super-Stars #3 (Superboy & LSH reprint), 9, 10, 12 (new Superboy story)
Four-Star Spectacular #1–5 (Superboy reprints)
Karate Kid #1 (Superboy & LSH appearance)
Limited Collectors' Edition #C-45 (Secret Origins of Super-Villains), C-46 (JLA), C-47 (Superman Salutes the Bicentennial), C-48 (Superman/Flash races), C-49 (Superboy/LSH)
Superman vs. The Amazing Spider-Man
Super-Team Family #3, 5, 6 (Superman reprints)
Super-Heroes Battle Super-Gorillas #1 (Superman reprint)
Secret Origins of the Super DC Heroes hardcover reprint edition (Superman origin reprints)

1977

Action Comics #467–478
(#471: first Faora Hu-Ul)
Superman #307–318
(#310: first new Metallo)

Adventure Comics #453–454 (new Superboy series)
Justice League of America #138–149
Superboy starring the Legion of Super-Heroes #223–230 (title change to *Superboy and the Legion of Super-Heroes* with #231)
Superboy and the Legion of Super-Heroes #231–234
Super Friends #3–9
The Superman Family #181–186
(#183: Van-Zee and Ak-Var become new Nightwing and Flamebird)
World's Finest Comics #243–248

Batman #293 (Superman appearance)
Black Lightning #4, 5 (Superman appearances)
DC Super-Stars #14 (Brainiac's origin recounted), 17 (LSH reprint)
DC Special #27 (Superman cameo), 29 (JSA, Earth-Two Superman cover appearance)
DC Special Series #5 (Superman Spectacular), 6 (Secret Society of Super-Villains Special, Superman appearance)
Four-Star Spectacular #6 (Superboy reprint)
Limited Collectors' Edition #C-52 (The Best of DC, Superman reprint)
Pizza Hut Reprints of *Superman* #97 and 113
Secret Society of Super-Villains #7 (Superman appearance)
Super-Team Family #11 (Supergirl and Flash team-up)
The All-New Super Friends Hour (ABC-TV cartoon revamp)

1978

Action Comics #479–490
(#481: first Supermobile)
(#484: 40th anniversary issue; marriage of Earth-Two Superman and Lois Lane)
(#487: first Microwave Man)
Superman #319–330

Adventure Comics #455–458 (Superboy)
DC Comics Presents #1–4 (Superman team-up title)
Justice League of America #150–161
Superboy and the Legion of Super-Heroes #235–246
Super Friends #10–15
The Superman Family #187–192
World's Finest Comics #249–253

All-New Collectors' Edition #C-54 (Superman vs. Wonder Woman), C-55 (Superboy/LSH), C-56 (Superman vs. Muhammad Ali), C-58 (Superman vs. Shazam!)
All-Star Comics #74 (Earth-Two Superman appearance)
DC Special Series #10 (Secret Origins of Super-Heroes)
Famous First Edition #C-61 (*Superman* #1 reprint)
Karate Kid #12–13 (Superboy appearances)
Superman: Last Son of Krypton by Elliot S! Maggin (novel)
Superman: The Movie
The World's Greatest Super-Heroes (Superman featured in syndicated newspaper strip)
The Great Superman Book by Michael L. Fleisher (encyclopedia)
The Official Superman Quiz Book
Superman Tempo Books reprint
World's Finest Comics Tempo Books reprint
Challenge of the Super Friends (ABC-TV cartoon revamp; Legion of Doom, with Lex Luthor, Brainiac, and Bizarro)

1979

Action Comics #491–502
(#500: Superman's Life Story)
Superman #331–342
(#331: first Master Jailer)
(#338: Kandor enlarged)

DC Comics Presents #5–16
Justice League of America #162–173
Superboy and the Legion of Super-Heroes #247–258 (title change to *Legion of Super-Heroes* with #259)
Super Friends #16–27
The Superman Family #193–198
World of Krypton #1–3 (miniseries)
World's Finest Comics #254–259

All-New Collectors' Edition # C-62 (*Superman: The Movie*)
Best of DC Blue Ribbon Digest #1 (Superman reprints)
The Brave and the Bold #147 (Batman and Supergirl team-up), 150 (Batman and ? team-up; Superman is mystery guest-star)
The World's Greatest Super Friends (ABC-TV cartoon revamp)

THE SUPERMAN MYTHOLOGY:
JULIUS SCHWARTZ: EDITOR EVERMORE

Julius "Julie" Schwartz (1915–2004) was a man of two worlds: He co-founded science-fiction fandom and represented a stellar lineup of writers including Ray Bradbury and Robert Bloch; and he initiated the Silver Age of Comics with his revivals of Golden Age super-heroes. Hired by DC Comics in 1944, Julie spent a lifetime there. His editorial highlights include DC's 1950s sci-fi series, *Batman* (where he introduced the hero's 1964 "new look" and edited his 1970s return to "creature of the night" status), the revived *Flash* and *Green Lantern*, a 19-year stint on *Justice League of America*, and a 16-year run on *Superman*—a series he initially accepted with reluctance. After "retiring" in 1987, Julie served as DC's editor emeritus and goodwill ambassador until his 2004 death. Schwartz received Shazam, Alley, Inkpot, Jules Verne,

First Fandom Hall of Fame, Forry, and Eagle Awards, and DragonCon instituted the "Julie Award" in his honor. This two-page scrapbook spotlights Julie's impact upon the sci-fi and comics communities. **Recommended reading:** *Man of Two Worlds: My Life in Science Fiction and Comics* by Julius Schwartz with Brian M. Thomsen (HarperEntertainment, 2000).

STRANGE, BUT TRUE......

Since "Superman" was created by a couple of Jewish kids from Cleveland,that makes him Jewish. Raised in a small town by a "Goyisha" couple, he probably never knew . Also, they didn't have a Synagogue in town,so he probably wasn't Bar-Mitzvah'd. It's doubtful that he was Circumscised. The foreskin of the superbaby would've been impossible to cut ! What a mess!

Knowing that "Lois Lane" was her professional name, I checked old records and discovered that her real name was Lois Farbotnik. So a union between them would be "kosher" Let's hope we can all straighten out this mess soon.
                    yrs for Comic Fandom, I remain Sincerely,

                                                    Shel Dorf

©1981 DC Comics

Conventioneer and longtime fan Shel Dorf's 1981 speculation about Superman's heritage, from the personal files of Julie Schwartz.
Superman TM & © DC Comics. Courtesy of Heritage Comics.

Legendary horror film star Boris Karloff and Forrest J. Ackerman of *Famous Monsters of Filmland* fame, in a 1966 photo signed and dated by "Forry" to his friend Julie Schwartz.
Courtesy of Heritage Comics. J.S. collection.

Schwartz and longtime MLJ employee at a DC luncheon, mid-'70s.
Courtesy of Bob Rozakis

Courtesy of Heritage Comics. J.S. collection

(above) Dinner at a DC company retreat, circa 1986, with Bob Greenberger, Schwartz, Barbara Randall (now Kesel), and Robyn McBryde.
Courtesy of Bob Rozakis.

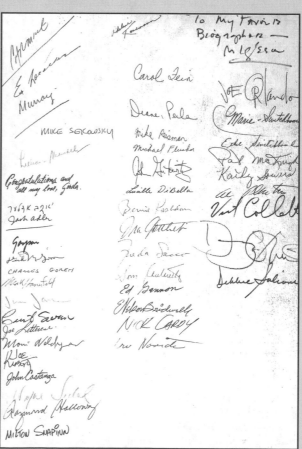

A birthday card for Julie Schwartz, drawn by John Costanza. While the card is undated, the signatures on its reverse side reveal its origin to be the early 1970s, during Carmine Infantino's tenure as DC's editorial director.
Courtesy of Heritage Comics. J.S. collection.

CARY BATES INTERVIEW

Ohio native Cary Bates (b. 1948) broke into comics as a teenager after his over-the-transom *Superman* cover ideas caught Mort Weisinger's attention. In 1967 he began a long association with DC Comics, over the years writing numerous Superman-family titles, plus *Superboy starring the Legion of Super-Heroes*, *The Flash*, *Captain Atom*, and other series. One of Superman's movers and shakers of the 1970s and early 1980s, Bates created Terra-Man, Steve Lombard, and Vartox. In the 1980s he left comics to become a screenwriter, his credits including *Superboy*, *Christopher Columbus: The Discovery*, and *W.I.T.C.H.*

Interview conducted by Michael Eury via e-mail on December 19, 2005. Special thanks to Pat Bastienne for helping arrange this interview.

William Daniels played Captain Nice in the short-lived 1967 NBC-TV series that inspired both a Gold Key spin-off comic and *Action #354* (Sept. 1967).

Captain Nice © 1967 NBC.   TM & © DC Comics.

MICHAEL EURY: What's your earliest memory of Superman?
CARY BATES: It must have been an episode(s) of the old George Reeves TV series, which led me to the comic books.

The first *Superman* comic I ever bought came out around 1957, I believe; on the cover Superman was battling a giant ant (if I had to guess, I'd say it was Mort's "homage" to *Them*, the '50s giant ant movie with Peter Graves).

EURY: You broke into comics—sort of—with *Superman* #167 (Feb. 1964), featuring a Luthor/Brainiac team-up ("The Deadly Duo!") that you suggested to Mort Weisinger via a cover idea submission. How old were you at the time?
BATES: I submitted the cover sketch sometime in '63; in the fall of that year I turned 15.

EURY: How close were the layouts of the actual Curt Swan-drawn cover to the cover you submitted?
BATES: As I recall my very crude sketch showed full figures of Luthor and Brainiac holding a tiny Superman in a birdcage. Obviously Curt's decision to depict the villains in giant close-ups greatly enhanced the visual impact of the idea. At the risk of stating the obvious, even when my general layout was followed, invariably the final cover would always be a vast improvement over what I submitted.

EURY: I've read that you weren't informed prior to *Superman* #167's publication that your idea was being used in print. Do you recall how you felt when you saw the issue on the stands?
BATES: Shocked and awed, probably … especially when I received the original cover art by Swan and Klein, which Mort sent me either shortly before or after the issue hit the stands. Awarding cover artwork for cover ideas was DC's policy back then in lieu of payment.

EURY: I understand that you visited Mort Weisinger and Julie Schwartz at DC during the summer of 1964, armed with cover proposals. Which ones saw print?
BATES: As I dimly recall, I had drawn up about 20 covers for each editor. I think Julie used maybe two or three … with Mort, he picked maybe four or five. I think one of the cover ideas he used had Mxyzptlk changing the spelling of his name so it was the same forward as backward. This was a couple of years before

Photo © 1975 DC Comics.

I was writing, so someone else (maybe Leo Dorfman or Otto Binder) ended up writing the actual story. After all these years I'd be hard-pressed to remember many of the individual covers.

EURY: Do you have copies of any of those cover roughs?
BATES: No.

EURY: By mid-1967 you were writing regularly for Weisinger, with "The Real Clark Kent" in *Superman* #198 (July 1967) and "Captain Incredible!" in *Action* #354 (Sept. 1967) being your first Superman stories. Do you recall if they were they written in that order?
BATES: That sounds about right. I believe "The Real Clark Kent" was my second sale, a spec. "Captain Incredible" was one of my first actual assignments from Mort; he asked me to write a story around a "nerdish super-hero" which was intended as a take-off on *Captain Nice* and *Mr. Terrific*, two short-lived TV series about nerdish super-heroes that were on the air that year.

EURY: Wasn't your first actual sale to Weisinger "The New Superman and Batman Team!" in *World's Finest* #167 (June 1967)?
BATES: Yes. I wrote that script on spec over Thanksgiving break my freshman year of college. It was an imaginary story that posited what would have happened if it had been Lex Luthor who became Batman (or was it the other way around?).

EURY: Luthor was Superman, and Clark Kent was Batman (don't be *too* impressed—I looked that up).

Next question: Jim Shooter, who was a few years younger than you, started writing for Mort shortly before you did. Did you know Jim at the time?

BATES: Only by name. He lived somewhere in Pennsylvania, I think, and I was going to Ohio University back in those days. As Jim has mentioned in some of his interviews, Mort used to play us off against each other, reminding that the rates I got and the I time I write

EURY: You were among the first of a new wave of young creative talent "infiltrating" the button-down editorial offices of National Periodicals. How were you received by the older writers and editors there?

BATES: It wasn't until 1971 that I moved to NY and began spending a lot of time at DC, and by then there were a bunch of us up there (Denny O'Neil, Len Wein, Marv Wolfman, Mike Friedrich, etc.). Of all the DC editors back then, Julius Schwartz was the one who was the most comfortable working with the so-called "new wave," although Dick Giordano did too during his brief stint as an editor around this same time.

In addition to Julie and Mort, I also worked with Murray Boltinoff, another veteran editor who wasn't known for using "newbies." Also, briefly, Bob Kanigher, when he was editing *Wonder Woman*.

EURY: How was your working relationship with Mort Weisinger?

BATES: Okay, I guess, all things considered. I know there are a lot of stories out there about the way he mistreated his people, and he was definitely not warm and fuzzy. But being a naïve 19-year-old college kid visiting from Ohio, I had no working experiences with other editors to compare him to, so without a frame of reference he didn't seem all that bad—at the time.

Also, I think it helped that he basically liked me (or my work), so maybe he didn't give me as hard a time as he did a lot of the older guys, some of whom apparently loathed working for him.

EURY: Legend says that Weisinger was known for shooting down writers' plot pitches, but then assigning those plots to different writers. Did this ever happen to you?

BATES: Not that I can recall offhand, although he certainly had no qualms about rejecting a pitch if it didn't grab him right away. But to be fair, while there probably was some juggling of writers' ideas, I'd bet that a large percentage of the plot ideas were no doubt his own.

EURY: Several of your earliest stories (including "The Real Clark Kent," "Clark Kent Abandons Superman," and "The Clark Kent Monster!") showed your affinity for Superman's alter ego. Which of Clark's attributes did you find most appealing?

BATES: I've always looked on him as an alien first, someone who had considerable difficulty blending in with normal human beings, which is why he often overcompensated.

I know the "meek and mild-mannered" bit fell out of favor in the comics long ago, and I'll cop to the fact that we overdid it back in the day … on the other hand, I think Chris Reeve's take on Clark still holds up remarkably well (and from what I hear Bryan Singer and Brandon Routh will be continuing the Reeve tradition). The early *Superman* films demonstrate how effective this approach to the character can be if executed well.

EURY: Writer/artist credits did not appear in Weisinger's books (although he occasionally identified talent in his lettercol responses). Do you know why Mort didn't publicly credit his creative teams?

BATES: He never discussed it with me, but there are two theories I've heard over the years, neither very flattering (or probable): (1) he wanted everyone to think he was solely responsible for all the stories in his books, or (2) he was paranoid about losing writers and artists to Marvel (as if keeping their names out of the books would render them somehow invisible).

Although I believe he was a few years behind Julie in this regard, by 1967, the year my stories started appearing, he had begun running [some] credits in his books.

EURY: What do you consider to be Weisinger's greatest contribution to the Superman mythos?

BATES: He had a tremendously inventive and ingenious mind, and used it to great advantage to embellish just about every facet

THE SUPERMAN MYTHOLOGY: IDENTITY CRISIS: CLARK KENT VS. SUPERMAN

Throughout the decades, Clark Kent has been *more* than Superman's alter ego—thanks to the imaginations of Superman's super-writers, the *Daily Planet*'s mild-mannered reporter has often been characterized as the Man of Steel's rival, replacement, teammate, and enemy!

Page 12 from *Action* #293's (Oct. 1962) "The Feud Between Superman and Clark Kent," by Edmond Hamilton and Al Plastino.
TM & © DC Comics. Art courtesy of Heritage Comics.

of the Superman myth imaginable during the so-called Silver Age. Despite various attempts over the years to chuck a lot of this stuff (kryptonite, Supergirl, Kandor, the Phantom Zone, etc.), it seems like the powers-that-be at DC always end up going back to his concepts in one form or another. Certainly the best *Superman* films (I and II) embraced many of his innovations, as well as *Smallville*, and 2006's *Superman Returns* (at least according to the last draft I read).

EURY: Of the stories you penned for Mort, do you have a favorite?

BATES: Not really, though I guess I'm still partial to his so-called "Imaginary Stories" (another Weisinger innovation that has been used over and over again through the years in various forms,

Christopher Reeve borrowed from Cary Grant's performance in *Bringing Up Baby* (1938) for his film portrayal of Clark Kent (above).

© 1938 RKO Pictures. Courtesy of Heritage Auctions.   © 2006 Warner Bros.

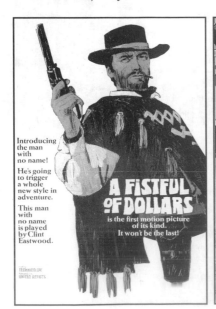

Clint Eastwood's film gunslinger and Cary Bates' super villain counterpart.

© 1964 Constantin Film Prod. Courtesy of Heritage Auctions.   TM & © DC Comics

both at DC and Marvel). I probably wrote at least a dozen Imaginary Stories for Mort.

EURY: After Weisinger left DC in 1970, you wrote Superman stories in *Action* for editor Murray Boltinoff. How did Boltinoff's style compare to and contrast with Weisinger's?

BATES: Murray was more of a "meat and potatoes" editor, not concerned so much with developing the Superman mythos as much just making sure the stories in his books were solid in terms of craft.

EURY: Meanwhile, Denny O'Neil was tapped by Julie Schwartz as the new scribe of *Superman*. Were you involved with the brainstorming of the changes implemented there, such as the eradication of kryptonite, Superman's de-powering, and Clark's new job as a television broadcaster?

BATES: Not directly. I (along with Leo Dorfman) was writing the monthly Superman stories in *Action Comics* during Denny's run on *Superman*. But Denny left (of his own accord) after a year or so; so when Elliot Maggin and I took over as Julie's primary Superman writers, we were expected to incorporate the new elements.

EURY: That "new" Superman era was short-lived, although Clark remained in front of the TV cameras for a while. Any theories on why this updated take on Superman didn't resonate with readers?

BATES: Like I mentioned earlier, most of those early attempts to get away from "classic" Superman (whether it was dropping kryptonite, dialing down the powers, etc.) never seemed to take over the long term. As you point out, the TV reporter angle was the only tweak that lasted for any significant length of time.

EURY: What was a typical Superman plotting session with Julie like?

BATES: Julie usually didn't "assign" stories the way Mort did; the storylines would most often arise out of a plotting session between the editor and writer right there in the room.

EURY: What do you consider to be Julius Schwartz's greatest contribution to Superman?

BATES: He was able to maintain an overall continuity and consistency throughout his 16-year tenure on the Superman books despite the fact he was granting lots of creative freedom to a number of writers with much disparate styles (myself, Elliot Maggin, Denny O'Neil, Marv Wolfman, Len Wein, and Marty Pasko, among others).

EURY: You introduced the first major new Superman villain of the 1970s, Terra-Man, in *Superman* #249 (Mar. 1972). What was the genesis of this character?

BATES: I had wanted to do a take-off on Clint Eastwood's Man with No Name, so then it became a challenge for Julie and I to come up with a way of transplanting a character out of the Old West and amping him up to make a worthy adversary for Superman.

EURY: Toyman got a makeover in your story in *Action* #432 (Feb. 1974), the roly-poly original version being temporarily upstaged by the jester-like Jack Nimball. Were you surprised when Marty Pasko offed Toyman II in *Superman* #305 (Nov. 1976)?

BATES: To be honest, I'm embarrassed to admit I have zero memory of what I did with Toyman.

EURY: You introduced a replacement Toyman, who appeared a few times before Marty wiped him out two-and-a-half years later. But death didn't stop Toyman II from appearing on TV in 1978 as one of the Legion of Doom on *Challenge of the Super Friends*. I'm curious, by the time this happened, were comics creators being paid royalties for their creations' TV adaptations?

BATES: Not that I'm aware of, at least not while I was at DC.

EURY: On a similar note, you wrote "It's a Bird, It's a Plane ... It's Supermobile!" in *Action* #481 (Mar. 1978), where Superman, in his first punching flying car, fought Amazo. Corgi also produced a Supermobile miniature around that time. Was this a case of the merchandising of a comic-book idea, or was the Supermobile added to the comic as a promotional tie-in?

BATES: The latter, I'm sorry to say. In my opinion, whenever merchandising needs are dictating story content, the odds of any real creativity or inspiration are severely compromised.

EURY: You introduced a number of supporting-cast members to Superman's world. Let's discuss a few of them, starting with the most (purposely) obnoxious of the batch, loud-mouthed sportscaster Steve Lombard (first seen in "The Secret of the Phantom Quarterback" in *Superman* #264, June 1973). Was he based upon someone you knew? Were you hassled by a jock during your youth?

BATES: I know saying "yes" and revealing a painful adolescent trauma would make for a more interesting answer, but sorry, adding a bully-type character to the supporting cast was just one of Julie's editorial decisions at the time, and I think I just happened to be the guy who stepped up to write the first story that introduced him.

EURY: Gregory Reed, the actor who played Superman, first appeared in *Action* #414's "Superman vs. Superstar" (July 1972). He always fascinated me, as the character was sort of a postmodern nod to Superman's cultural influence in his own fictional world. What insights into Reed can you share?

BATES: I don't recall the specifics of that story, but Reed was obviously a fictional nod to George Reeves and the classic TV series. The Reeves story has always intrigued me (including the controversy around his mysterious "suicide," the rumors that his house on Benedict Canyon was haunted for years afterward, etc). As some of your readers may know, a long-planned biopic about the end of Reeves' life is due to be filmed soon, starring (last time I heard) Ben Affleck, of all people.

EURY: Let's not forget Captain Strong, the DC Universe's answer to Popeye. I take it you're an E.C. Segar fan.

BATES: Not really. It just occurred to me one day that Popeye was another cultural icon, also super-strong, who was arguably just as famous as Superman, and so wouldn't it be interesting if our guy could meet a "Popeye-like" guy just to see what happens….

EURY: DC has often been cautious about this type of character, for legal concerns. Was there any discussion about this when you introduced Strong?

BATES: Believe it or not, it never came up. Otherwise I'm sure Julie or someone at DC's front office would've nixed the sequel we did about a year later. Just goes to show you how much simpler life was back in the '70s.

EURY: Steve Lombard aside, your best-known contribution to the Bronze Age Superman's cast was Vartox, who first muscled his way into print in *Superman* #281 (Nov. 1974). His appearance was patterned after Sean Connery, from the 1974 sci-fi movie *Zardoz*, right?

BATES: Absolutely. I remember giving Curt a bunch of *Zardoz* stills as swipes.

EURY: Speaking of Connery, in the late 1970s you were one of several writers auditioned for a new James Bond movie. What's the story there?

BATES: In 1972 I wrote an original Bond treatment using the title "Moonraker" on spec and sent it to Roald Dahl (somehow I had managed to obtain his address in Buckinghamshire). Much to my amazement he read it, liked it, and got in touch with me, offering to act as a go-between me and [producer] Cubby Broccoli. After a number of false starts and stops, Cubby finally bought the treatment two years later.

Because this was during the time they were prepping *The Spy Who Loved Me* (*TSWLM*), over the years some Bond books have incorrectly included me with the long line of writers who were somehow involved with *TSWLM*. But it should surprise no one to learn that the eventual film version of *Moonraker* had nothing to do with mine.

However, an argument could be made that a few random bits in subsequent Bond films (the killer twins in *Octopussy*, the half-car chase in *View to a Kill*) were cherry-picked from my material.

EURY: Vartox appeared occasionally for the next decade, as Superman's friend/foe and as a love interest for Lana Lang. What do you believe was the character's primary appeal?

BATES: I always saw him as a fifty-something version of Superman who managed to retain his basic nobility, even after enduring the sort of adversity and tragedy that turned many a DC character to super-villainy.

EURY: Curt Swan probably illustrated more of your stories than any other artist. Did you know Curt well?

BATES: Not really. During my 20 years on Superman we'd only see each other occasionally up at the DC offices, but he was one of the nicest guys in the business, always a gentleman, all class. I never ceased getting a little thrill every time I would first lay eyes on his penciled pages to one of my stories.

EURY: Of the other artists who drew your Superman scripts, which do you believe best understood and interpreted the Man of Steel?

BATES: Neal Adams did a fantastic job on one of my first stories for *World's Finest*, and I started with Mort just in time to see veteran artist Wayne Boring draw an early imaginary novel (if it wasn't Boring's very last Superman story it was damn close). I'm sure there are other names I'm neglecting to mention here, but let's face it, no other artist left the major imprint on the character that Curt Swan did for some three decades running.

EURY: During your long tenure on Superman, you wrote several milestones, including *Superman* #200, *Superman* #300 (with Elliot Maggin), and the 40th anniversary celebration, the marriage of the Earth-Two Superman and Lois Lane in *Action* #484 (June 1978). When surveying your Superman stint, is there a single story of which you're most proud?

BATES: I'd say there are probably a dozen or so I'm the most proud of (and yes, the ones you mentioned are among them), but I'm never able to single out one or two. One of the last stories I remember that really stood out for me was a Superman/Adam Strange team-up I wrote for *DC Comics Presents*. Klaus Janson did a great job with the art.

 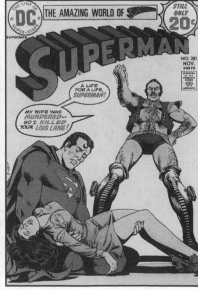

Two of pop culture's hairiest heroes, Sean Connery as Zardoz and Superman friend/foe Vartox.

© 1974 20th Century Fox. Courtesy of Heritage Auctions.   TM & © DC Comics.

THE SUPERMAN MYTHOLOGY:
CAPTAIN STRONG

For a character that appeared only five times (*Action* #421, Feb. 1973; #439, Sept. 1974; #456, Feb. 1976; *Superman* #361, July 1981; and *Action* #566, Apr. 1985), salty sailor Captain Horatio Strong permanently punched his way into the hearts of longtime Superman fans. Able to gain temporary super-strength from "sauncha" (extraterrestrial seaweed), Strong's supporting cast grew to include other Popeye analogs such as his wiry love Olivia and long-lost father Pappy Strong.

(left) Another Popeye/Superman parallel: the spinach-eater's robot twin, from Dell's *Popeye* #56 (Nov.–Dec. 1960). (right) "Sea Hag" bewitches Superman into combat with Captain Strong on the Marshall Rogers-penciled cover to *Action* #566 (Apr. 1985).

Popeye TM & © 2006 King Features.   TM & © DC Comics. Art courtesy of Jerry Ordway.

An original art page from *DC Special Series* #5, *Superman Spectacular* (1977), written by Cary Bates, penciled (and autographed) by Curt Swan, and inked by Vince Colletta.

TM & © DC Comics. Art courtesy of Heritage Comics.

EURY: Conversely, is there a story, or story element or character, of yours that you wish you hadn't come up with?

BATES: The War-Horn (from *Superman* #257, Oct. 1972). I don't remember much about the character or the story, but it was an (ill-fated) attempt to create a new recurring villain for Superman. Needless to add, there wasn't much of a clamor for a War-Horn encore.

EURY: Paul Levitz mentioned to me a few years ago that you were one of several writers considered for the 1986 Superman revamp, that ultimately fell into John Byrne's lap with *Man of Steel*. What would you have done differently, and what would you have kept the same, if you had been involved with this makeover?

BATES: As I recall, I proposed a six-issue miniseries that would revamp and "de-power" the character by having him die for real and be brought back to life—not unlike the Michael Rennie character Klaatu in *The Day The Earth Stood Still*. But defying death came at a great price, leaving the reborn Superman psychologically compromised and in terms of powers not nearly as "super" as he used to be.

Had I been more business savvy at the time, I would've realized that from DC's perspective, starting over completely with a new issue #1 and getting a "name" writer/artist (like, say, John Byrne) to do it was the approach that made the most business sense, regardless of the merits of any revamp I or any of the previous DC Superman writers could have come up with.

EURY: In 1990 you co-wrote with Mark Jones a screenplay for *Superman: The New Movie*, for producers Ilya and Alexander Salkind. I haven't read the script, but it's my understanding that it featured Brainiac. What was the story about?

BATES: It involved Kandor and not one but *two* versions of Brainiac, circa 1990: the '60s green-skinned bald guy *and* the '80s robot. More than that, I'm reluctant to say for reasons I'd rather not get into.

EURY: Why didn't the movie happen?

BATES: In 1992 Warners struck a deal with the Salkinds to buy back all the rights to the character. As often happens in situations like these, when the new owner takes over, all the material in development generated by the previous regime gets thrown out.

EURY: Any chance you'll write another Superman story?

BATES: Highly doubtful at this point... but then again, as the saying goes, never say never!

neal adams interview

Neal Adams (b. 1941) brought his photorealistic approach and non-traditional panel composition to DC Comics in 1967, after illustrating the *Ben Casey* newspaper strip. He started on lower-tier series like *The Adventures of Bob Hope* before attracting wider attention on Deadman (in *Strange Adventures*) and *The Spectre*, followed by Batman (in *World's Finest*, *The Brave and the Bold*, *Batman*, and *Detective*) and the highly acclaimed *Green Lantern/Green Arrow*. While he's rarely drawn Superman comics, Adams' interpretation of the Metropolis Marvel was widely seen throughout the 1970s on covers and merchandising. Neal Adams has inspired a generation of comic-book artists and remains influential in the contemporary comics and advertising mediums.

Recommended reading: *Neal Adams: The Sketch Book* (Vanguard Productions, 1999); *The Silver Age of Comic Book Art* by Arlen Schumer (Collectors Press, 2003).

Conducted by Michael Eury on March 3, 2006. Transcribed by Brian K. Morris.

MICHAEL EURY: When did you first meet Mort Weisinger?

NEAL ADAMS: Oh, I guess, when I went up to DC Comics to try to get work with Bob Kanigher, the war comics editor, which would have been—I guess I was in my late twenties, middle twenties, something like that. And Mort was one of those people that was shuffling around, grumpy, looking mad, that didn't seem to like anybody.

EURY: I'm guessing he didn't exactly open his arms to you on your first visit.

ADAMS: I don't think Mort opened his arms to *anybody*. [*laughter*] Mort was not an "open-your-arms" type of guy. His best relationships seemed to be with science-fiction writers and letter writers. After they worked their way into his good graces. If they came up to see him, then it was a very different thing because he had already corresponded with them for great lengths of time. But for an actual human being to meet him first time, I think he just wanted to crush them.

EURY: You didn't even make it past the door the first time you tried to show your samples.

ADAMS: No. When I came out of school, my samples were very good—and I'm only saying that as Neal Adams, the adult, grown-up artist. (I still have those samples and I would give that guy work.) I couldn't get past the door at DC Comics. A guy named Bill Perry came out and sat with me in the lobby and said, "I can't bring you inside." I said, "Well, can I just see an editor?" And he said, "They don't use anybody. You really ought to do something else." I had a hundred pages of comic-book art.

EURY: This obviously didn't discourage you, but how long did it take you before you went back again?

ADAMS: Well, I didn't really go back. I more orbited them. I did everything *but* work for DC Comics. I did Archie comics, I was an assistant on a comic strip, I did a comic strip, I did advertising comic books, I did everything. I did a syndicated strip for three-and-a-half years. It was quite successful. It was in 165 papers

around the world. I became, in effect, a world-famous syndicated strip cartoonist, and then I voluntarily ended the strip and I was going to become an illustrator. That plan kind of backfired when the portfolio that I had spent six months on, I left it at an advertising agency and when I went back to get it, it had disappeared.

EURY: And it's never turned up?

ADAMS: It's never turned up.

EURY: Who's sitting on that, I wonder?

ADAMS: I don't know. I'd like to get a hold of them in a dark room.

Anyway, I then had to face reality. I had no strip to do—I had some advertising clients, which was fine—and so I went to look for work doing comic books, which I felt was odd because I had a whole career. I had gone on above it and I really had no interest in doing comic books. They were now below me. It was comic strips and then illustration, that's where my head was at.

I realized [*chuckles*] that I was stuck for work. So instead of going to DC Comics, I went to Warren Publications and I did work for them. They were nice enough to give me work. I did work, but I discovered that it was very self-indulgent work in that I was looking to impress, by doing different styles and different concepts and different techniques and different things, and it was taking too long to do the work. I realized I could get a 12-pager, or a 24-page comic-book story over at DC Comics and take it home and crank it out. Here at Warren, I was getting six-page stories. I would put my heart and soul into them and be paid just as poorly as I would be paid at DC Comics.

So I thought, "Well, I'll try, one more time, to break into DC Comics," and I made an appointment with the war comics editor who had lost Joe Kubert to the comic strip *The Green Berets*. And he saw me, and I knew that Joe was missing from that position because I had helped Joe get that work [*chuckles*] to do *Green Berets*—it was offered to me first. So I went to speak to Bob Kanigher and I started doing war stories. And then I guess they just discovered there was a new creature in the zoo.

EURY: You spent a lot of time actually there at the DC offices, didn't you?

ADAMS: Well, a lot of it was because they wanted me to do covers. And yeah, I kind of liked the idea of being out of the house. I had worked in my house for three-and-a-half, four years, and I was used to going out, doing commercial work, and I kind of liked the idea of finding out about the company, and what's

Adams recommended Joe Kubert for the mid-'60s strip *The Green Berets*, based upon the book by Robin Moore. This daily was originally published on Sept. 26, 1967.

A trio of Neal Adams' *Ben Casey* dailies; based upon the popular TV drama, the *Casey* strip ran from Nov. 1962 through July 1966.

going on, and hanging out there during the day. So yeah, I did spend quite a bit of time at DC Comics. I took a desk in their staff room, in their Production room. They seemed to be happy to have me there until I really started to make trouble. [*laughter*]

EURY: And we'll get into some of the trouble in a minute. As far as Superman's concerned, most people regard you as a Batman artist at DC, but you actually drew Superman covers before you did Batman covers.

ADAMS: In fact, nobody in them thar days thought of me as *anything*. What really happened was that Carmine Infantino realized that here he had some new blood, maybe he could become an art director and art direct covers. And I would be the artist that would do the covers, as well as other people. But essentially, I got along pretty easy with Carmine, so in many ways that kind of pushed Carmine, who had been doing a lot of covers, into becoming an art director at DC Comics, which was a very fortuitous circumstance for him. He pushed a lot of covers my way because he could easily recognize that the tendency, the sense, was, "This guy's probably going to do a lot of good covers." And that got to be something that happened a lot.

EURY: Was Carmine heavily involved in the design of your covers, or were you flying solo?

ADAMS: He was, on and off. Sometimes he was too busy, sometimes he had an idea for a cover and we would sit and either argue it out, or I would propose something different, or I would accept his concept. I really didn't have too much trouble with Carmine's ideas because he is a good designer. My covers are all design. I would rather do situations and storytelling situations, and sometimes good design actually works against that. And design does tend to get repetitive after a while. You can only do just so many covers with the guy standing in the middle with his legs akimbo and holding a body in his arms, or standing on the side of the page and having panels go down the other side of it. There's a limit to that. You really do get bored with that. I got to change styles from mystery covers to super-hero covers and like that, so I got to play quite a bit.

EURY: What was your first Superman cover?

ADAMS: Well, I don't know. *You* probably know.

EURY: Well, I did some research. I've got it in front of me. I just want to make sure, because you can't always trust cover dates. But the two earliest ones that I found both had a Nov. 1967 cover date. One was *Lois Lane* #79, which was, if this rings a bell, "The Bride of Titan Man"; and another one was *Action* #356, "The Son of the Annihilator," which has this James Dean-type delinquent on the cover. I don't know if you recall if those were the first two you drew.

ADAMS: I really don't know. But I can tell you the circumstance behind the first cover I did for Mort Weisinger.

EURY: Please do.

ADAMS: Carmine had decided that, for whatever reason, I was worth something to the company and worth something to him. It seemed as though people were beginning to recognize my work and it made a difference in the sales. Not in the books that I drew, but in the covers that I did. The books that I drew, pretty much, the sales stayed the same. But any time I did a cover, the sales seemed to go up ten percent. So Carmine was very, very interested in having me do covers for *Superman* to see what would happen. Mort was not. [*laughter*] In fact, it's possible that you know there are people in the world whose emotions and feelings you can read on their faces, better than Mort Weisinger, but I don't know anyone like that. You pretty much know what's going on in Mort's head because he's got the look on his face … or he *had* the look on his face.

So it was very clear that Mort did not want me to do covers. After all, he had Curt Swan, to which I would agree. Hey, hey, he's got Curt Swan, that's cool. I mean, I was a fan of Curt Swan's since I was a young teenager. Anyway, Carmine seemed to be adamant that Mort would let me into his vault and allow me to do a cover. Mort, at the same time, was grumbling and bumping into doors and snarling. Anyway, knowing that this tension was there and that it was not good, [*chuckles*] I thought, "Well, we'll deal with this problem."

So I went in to see Mort and introduced myself, and apparently, I had said hello to him briefly before that, and he more or less ignored me. I introduced myself and I said, "I'd just like to talk to you for a few minutes." And he said, "All right." So we sat down and I said, "Look, Carmine wants me to do covers for you. I don't care. I have a lot of covers to do and to be perfectly honest, they get in the way of the books I'm working on. But you and he seem to be having a problem. I have a solution, if you want to try it: I'll do one cover for you. If you like it, maybe you'll have me do more covers, I don't think so. If you don't like it, tell Carmine you don't like it and that's the last cover I do for you." And I said, "As far as I'm concerned, that's fine. I'll do one cover, you tell Carmine you don't like it, I'm out, you have no problem." He said, "Good, that's a deal." And you could tell the way he said it, it was one cover and that's it.

Well, I don't know which cover, I have no idea. To be perfectly honest, it was just a cover and I handed it in and a couple of weeks later I ambled back into the office and said, "Mort wants you to do *all* his covers."

EURY: So Carmine actually broke the information to you, not Mort.

ADAMS: Mort did not. But the next time I saw Mort, he had a big grin on his face and he was very happy. Now, that was a very weird beginning to actually what I considered to be a good relationship, because my relationship with Mort after that was very comfortable. I've never really had too much problem with the editors up at DC Comics. We all got along. Each one, within their own personality, pretty much, was okay with me.

EURY: Tell me something *good* about Mort Weisinger. People relate all these horror stories, but that can't be the whole picture.

ADAMS: I'll tell you a story that will make you understand every horror story you've ever heard about Mort Weisinger and make you realize what was going on. I went into Mort's office one day because I was perturbed by sh*t that people said about [him]. I could see that he was a grumpy fellow in general, but he treated me evenly and I was fine. But it bothered me so we were talking about it. We went over a cover and whatever. We finished that conversation and I said, "Mort, I'd just like to ask you why you are so grumpy at people? You know, everybody thinks you hate them and you just seem grumpy." And I could see his face change in front of me, and he said, "I'll tell you … I don't tell people this. Try to imagine that you get up in the morning and you go into the bathroom to shave, and you look into the mirror, and you see *this* face."

Now, for everybody out there who thinks he was grumpy, I say to you, the man had a soft side, dealing with his reality as best he could. Underneath he was a good, sensitive man.

EURY: So you developed a good working relationship with him.

ADAMS: Oh, sure.

EURY: Was he chummy or friendly with anybody at all, to your knowledge?

ADAMS: He loved Cary Bates. Cary Bates, the sun rose out of Cary Bates' ass. Because Cary had ideas that were *his* kind of ideas. I believe that there was a cover that I did—I hope I don't say that it was Cary's and it was really somebody else's, it might be Mike Friedrich's—but [Mort] was deliriously happy about this cover. I don't know if it was for *Adventure* or *World's Finest*, maybe *World's Finest*, and what it had was two heads of two super-heroes on the left and two heads of two super-heroes on the right, I think. And in the middle, was a guy sitting in a chair with some kind of a gun or something and he was in silhouette, and on him was this question mark, "Who is it?" Do you remember that cover?

EURY: I do.

"This face" of Mort Weisinger.
Photo © 1975 DC Comics.

ADAMS: In his mind, that was the greatest cover because it asked a question and made you buy the book. A very intelligent editorial approach. And you know, it was a boring cover to draw. I hated it. It was simple and essentially boring and it was sloppy, but it sold comic books.

EURY: It was *World's Finest* #176 (June 1968)—and it *was* a Cary Bates story, "The Superman-Batman Split!"

ADAMS: I think it was. All it was, from his point of view, was the idea and that idea came from one of his fan guys.

EURY: Cary, as you know, broke in by suggesting cover concepts and then finally got his chance to write for Mort.

ADAMS: And from Mort's point of view, with Cary Bates he [had] found a guy who thought like him—ask questions, make the reader read the comic book. One of his favorite covers was one that actually was one of my favorite covers, was Superman is sitting in the witness chair in the courtroom and there's a little girl on the floor below him, very small with a little polka-dotted dress. And she's pointing at Superman in the witness chair, which is an odd place to be for this to be happening, and she says, "That man killed my father."

EURY: That's "The Case of the People vs. Superman," *Action* #359 (Feb. 1968). Very dynamic.

ADAMS: Well, more than dynamic, it was a great idea. How can you *not* buy that book?

"He's the man who killed my father!" … "My *daddy*," I think she said. My goodness.

EURY: Those covers were definitely good points of entry to pique the fans' curiosity. Every now and then, you see—or you *did* see—misleading comics covers that proposed something you didn't find inside.

ADAMS: And that's one of the most popular female heroes in comics, Miss Leading Comics.

EURY: I have an entire run of her adventures. [*laughter*]

It was in *World's Finest* that you actually did your first interior Superman and Batman story (issue #175, May 1968).

ADAMS: Oh, yeah. Wasn't that sad?

EURY: [*laughs*] And Dick Giordano inked you, and you weren't that happy with the results.

ADAMS: No, and I wasn't very happy with the pencils. I was not ready for it, psychologically. First of all, it was a complicated story and had lots of stuff going on. But when you read a synopsis or when you read a script that has Batman, Superman, and a squad of guys dressed like them, so you go, "Oh, God. Every panel, I have to do like fifteen people." It's a daunting thing, you just don't want to do it. It's like somebody's telling you to draw up a picture of the floor of the Stock Exchange. "Oh, thank you. That's what I want to do. I want to draw 400 people on the floor of the Stock Market today." An aircraft carrier with planes taking off and all the officers are all lined up on the deck and there's a fly on the nose of the Admiral. [*laughter*]

It wasn't like it didn't heat my cookies. And because of that—no, not because of that. What I was about to say was bullsh*t. I take it back even before I say it. I just did a sloppy job. You know, I really wasn't doing the characters well, and I really wasn't enthusiastic about it, and I would have to say at that point, I was still in the throes of wanting to go off and become an illustrator, and I really wasn't enjoying comic books that much. I was doing my job, I was like getting off on the experience of doing it like, "Oh, God. I finally get to do regular comics after doing everything

TM & © DC Comics.

TM & © DC Comics.

An unpublished version of Adams' cover to *Lois Lane* #87, 1968, plus its published version.

TM & © DC Comics. Art courtesy of Heritage Comics.

around it, and I really can't do this very long because they don't pay enough money, and it's comic books, after all. I want to do this, that, and the other thing." So there was a transition point there where I wanted to get out and I didn't think I was going to do this.

So that first book was just done like that. On the other hand, I wasn't willing to give up certain ideas that I had while I was doing it. So within that story, you will find different approaches to ideas scattered throughout the book and nothing really great, but it was fun.

EURY: When you did the very next issue of *World's Finest*, were you more comfortable with it at that point?

ADAMS: No, not really. I mean I was doing the yeoman's job. Anybody could have done it. Curt probably could have done a better job.

EURY: So what was the first story that you did for DC where you really felt that you were vested into the interiors?

ADAMS: I don't think that happens. You know, everybody likes to know themselves, but nobody does, so I can't tell you where the transition point was. But if you'll look at those first two books that I did, the *World's Finest* books, and then you look at *Superman/Muhammad Ali*, you'll see a person who has decided that he's a comic-book artist and he was going to do the best comic books he can do in *Superman/Muhammad Ali*. In those first two books, it was very indecisive. Anybody could have done them.

EURY: Well, they still stood out. They were very unique, and at least for the readers, exciting.

ADAMS: Yeah, it seemed to be that way. They became attracted to certain things—faces—and there's a part of me that says, "See, it would have been fun continuing doing that." But other trumpets called.

EURY: A lot of people have commented that your style was very photorealistic for DC. But you also brought with you a new energy that the medium didn't have at the time. I was on the threshold of puberty back then, and when a lot of my contemporaries were "outgrowing" funnybooks, your art encouraged me to stick around and look deeper into comics.

ADAMS: The truth is, many people have a limited point of view about what the potential of comic books are, and part of it was engendered by the terrible rates that people were paid, the publishers' attitudes, and the Comics Code. Before the Comics Code, you had EC Comics, you had guys who were doing tremendously incredible comic books, but then that all went away so comic books in America were held back. We just had little sparks here and there that went off and those of us who were outside of it, we kept on looking for those sparks.

EURY: What were some of those sparks for you, as a younger reader?

ADAMS: Jack Kirby being inked by Wally Wood on *Challengers of the Unknown*, Joe Kubert doing *Brave and the Bold* stories, Russ Heath doing "Golden Gladiator", just Mort Drucker showing up out of nowhere and doing war stories that look like real, gritty war stories, we *lived* for those things, and they were few and far between. So when I got to do comic books from my point of view, all those really wonderful things came back to me and I thought, "God, I have whole pages here that I can design. I can just go crazy." And I had fun, you know?

In all honesty, if you were to look at me, you'd say, "fireman," [*chuckles*] but I'm a fireman who likes to have fun. I really, really, really, really enjoyed doing comic books.

EURY: You're not wearing a red hat, are you? [*laughs*]

Let's talk about Curt Swan. You said that you were a fan of his when you were a teenager. You inked him on a handful of covers. Did you lobby for that?

ADAMS: I didn't necessarily lobby for it, but I was delighted to

Curt Swan pencils and Neal Adams inks on the covers of *Action Comics* #371 (Dec. 1968) and 378 (July 1969).
TM & © DC Comics. Art courtesy of Heritage Comics.

do it and I didn't really think other people did him justice. You know, Curt used to make Superman chunky, but he made him chunky with muscle. When people inked him, they'd sometimes leave out the muscle and they'd leave in the chunky. So I thought, "If I'm going to ink him, I'm going to leave out the chunky and put in the muscle." So if you look at the stuff I did, whatever stylistic things you can spot and say, "Ah, that's Neal." One of the things you see in Superman is you see a ten-pounds-leaner body and a more muscular Superman, a more powerful Superman.

EURY: That's very obvious. Wayne Boring also had a tendency of making Superman very, very thick through the middle.

ADAMS: Barrel-chested, beer-bellied.

EURY: Let's go to *Superman* #233 (Jan. 1971), which might be an issue number which will trigger a memory with you. That was "Kryptonite Nevermore," the big, iconic cover with Superman bursting from the chains.

ADAMS: Yeah.

EURY: You've recreated that cover a few times, too. Is that your favorite Superman cover, or among your favorites?

ADAMS: Oddly enough, no.

EURY: Really?

ADAMS: When, in fact, I was asked to do it, I thought, "Well, here's cutting my Achilles' tendon. I'm a storyteller." All they wanted was Superman just standing there, because they found that the character standing there, the feet spread out wide, sold comic books. So I said, "Well, why don't I have him break chains, and since it's 'Kryptonite Nevermore,' we'll do the chains out of kryptonite and we'll make that a scene I remember from my youth, but never quite looked like this." You know, bursting chains, when you think about it, that's an unrealistic picture. It doesn't make any sense. You know, when you put the chains on him, maybe he'll stretch the metal a little bit, but you're not going to burst them because the chest doesn't become that big. It has nothing to do with that. It just has to do with a symbol. So breaking chains on the chest are symbol, not really a real thing. So I thought, "Well, okay, I'm just going to do the symbol, forget the rest of it. Don't get real," and I did it. And to be perfectly honest, I did it very fast and very sloppy. I didn't really put my heart and soul into it. It was just another instruction. You know, do just the figure with chains bursting and that's good, that's it. So that's what I did. And I've heard about that cover ever since then for ages—"Oh, that cover, oh, that wonderful cover." And I've looked at it and it's like, "Geez, what a sloppy job."

EURY: Interesting, because I had a totally different perspective as a reader and as a fan. Maybe some of my reaction was shaped by the momentum behind this change with Superman.

ADAMS: You know, there's many things that you look at when you look at a piece of art—and I hate to call it "art" because, of course, that's a little too pompous—but you have to look at the artist, you have to look at the character, you have to look at the idea, and then you have to look at the iconography. In this case, the iconography overcame the artist, and all I did was fill in the lines. I had people say to me, "Wow, how did you know that would be a great cover?", and I, like, look around for help because I don't know if I thought it was going to be a great cover. Why didn't I do that every time I did a cover? I mean, there's no way to know ahead of time what people will view as a good or important or a terrific or a wonderful cover. You can put your heart and soul into a cover and it'd be forgotten the next day. You can put the kind of effort I put into *that* cover and it's remembered for years. You don't know. As the artist, your job is to do the art. It's the audience's job to respond, and so you do what you can.

I just recently did a *Superman* cover for DC Comics. It's an alternate cover where he's kind of moving away from the sun, and something goes on and explodes from his body.

EURY: I've seen it—don't *own* it, but have seen it. The *All Star Superman* #1 variant [see opposite page].

ADAMS: Now, I was just going to do a Superman cover. [But] that cover has already become an icon. People spent $25.00 to get it because it's an alternate cover, but people now talk about that cover and my suspicion is that it will keep rising like foam at the top of a wave because it's one of those covers where all you see is Superman suffering and something terrible happening to him. And you go, "Yeah, yeah, right."

EURY: The background colors on that cover are similar to the "Kryptonite Nevermore" cover's—very warm oranges and reds behind Superman.

ADAMS: That certainly is a scientific analysis. It is, in fact, true, because yellow and red tends to leap to your eye because of the light spectrum. The light wave or red at that end of the spectrum is faster than the light wave at the back end of the spectrum. So what happens is if you look at something that's blue or blue-gray, it tends to fall back—actually, it does take longer to get to your eyes so it seems further back, whereas red and yellow leap towards your eyes. You can take a blue-gray field and put an orange-red dot somewhere, and that's the thing that will leap to your eye. You can't similarly do an orange-red field and put a blue dot there and expect anybody to just notice the blue dot because you're looking at the field.

EURY: Both covers definitely attract the eye, so you were very successful there.

ADAMS: But, you see, that was not intentional, in either case.

EURY: Really?

ADAMS: They didn't ask me to do a cover for *Superman* and I did something beyond doing the cover, just turns out "coinkidinkily" [*laughter*] that turned out to be a cover where everybody goes, "Whoa, wow, this is so cool."

EURY: A lot of us are just glad to see you do a Superman cover, or *anything* Superman, again. Were you, by chance, offered the interiors of *Superman* back during that 1970 revamp?

ADAMS: I think that it wasn't so much that I was either offered or not offered, I think that I was so busy doing other stuff that there was no opening for me to do it. There were enough people that wanted to do Superman. There certainly weren't a lot of people that could really high-style Batman, know what I mean? And "Deadman" was like way off the wall for anybody, and *Green Lantern/Green Arrow* was my idea to do it ... not so much to do it differently, but to do it because Gil Kane had left and they were handing it out to anybody who walked in the office, and they were going to cancel the book. So I thought, "Before they cancel the book, I want to be able to do *Green Lantern* because I love Gil Kane's work so much." So the subject of doing *Superman* never really came up. They already had people.

EURY: Alex Ross remarked [in the Superman roundtable later in this book] that DC, after *Superman vs. Muhammad Ali* and at the time of the first *Superman* movie, should

TM & © DC Comics.

have offered you a ton of money to draw *Superman* for a year and really pump up the character.

ADAMS: Mmm.

EURY: So your doing *Superman* interiors was never discussed?

ADAMS: Well, DC wasn't paying anyone a ton of money back then. Let me tell you a story.

EURY: Please do.

ADAMS: It concerns Curt Swan and the Academy of Comic Book Arts. I was the Vice President of the Academy at the time, and I didn't really want to be anything more because I was already doing all the work. And we had meetings at the Illustrators' Club, and the idea was you want to bring comic-book artists together to talk because they never got to see each other. You know, everybody worked 15 hours a day, locked in a closet somewhere so they would never get together—Jack Kirby never met Joe Sinnott. So meeting at the Illustrators' Club was very nifty because pencilers got to meet their inkers, inkers got to meet their pencilers, something that hadn't happened in comic books. Things like that happen all the time now, but in them thar days, that kind of stuff wasn't going on.

Anyway, I had plans, little devious plans, in the back of my head about certain things that were happening in comic books and different ways to approach undoing them. But one of the plans was getting people to talk about their rates and trying to get rates up because rates were in an awful state.

So I tried this as an experiment: I met Curt Swan, I praised him and told him how much I loved his work and blah, blah, blah. And once all that fannish stuff was over—of course, I was an adult and he treated me like an adult—I said, "Do you mind if I ask you a question? What are your rates? What are your pencil rates?" And Curt went all just blushy, and kind of stepped back a half a step. He said, "Well, I don't think it's right to talk about your rates." And I said, "Well, okay, if you don't want to. But I get $50 a page." [*laughs*] And he said, "*What?* You get $50 a page for pencils?" He said, "I get $45 a page." I said, "You shouldn't be paid $45 and me

TM & © DC Comics.

be paid $50 a page. You're Curt Swan." He said, "Well, it won't be that way on Monday." Now, I went around the room and had similar conversations with other people. But when I checked up on this on Monday, Curt's rate was raised. Not bad. And if you think about it, at $50 a page from $45 a page, how much of a raise is that? That's a pretty good raise, a ten percent raise! A ten percent raise because of a conversation at the Illustrators' Club. That raise happened because we had a short conversation.

It's one of the things I tried to teach the guys at the Illustrators' Club when we had our meetings: "Guys, it doesn't pay to keep information to yourself. It pays to talk to other people, because that's how you learn. That's how you discover somebody's taking advantage of you."

EURY: Curt's attitude to your question was very polite and very professional, and gentlemanly—you just didn't talk about that type of thing.

ADAMS: And wrong, so wrong. I mean, I carry that through in any area I'm at. There were people doing animatics, which is something we do [at the Continuity studio]. The clients would say, "Well, so-and-so doesn't charge that. He'd charge practically *half* of what you charge." I'd say, "Oh, yeah?" I'd pick up the phone and call him. Because I knew everybody. "What's your rate?" "Well, we charge $300 a frame." "Oh, okay. Just checking, thanks a lot." Hang up the phone, "No, he charges exactly what I charge."

I guess I'm not so much a union man, although God knows part of me is, but I do believe in union principles. I believe in communicating and sharing information. If you're a freelancer you should not work at one company all the time, it's stupid to do that. Go back and forth to see where the flexibility is, relative to how much your income can be, and don't allow them to oppress you. I mean, they used to make people change their names. I don't think anybody was "forced" to change their name, but somehow, guys like "Mickey Demeo" [pseudonym for Mike Esposito] would show up and you'd wonder, "Who the hell is this guy?"

EURY: Don't forget "Frankie Ray" [Frank Giacoia's pseudonym].

ADAMS: Yeah, Frankie Ray. And it was because of fear, you know? "Maybe they'll take work away from me," or whatever. So I put an end to that.

EURY: This is a perfect segue to a discussion about Jerry Siegel and Joe Shuster. Some people would say that your biggest contribution to Superman was your role in getting them a pension and creator acknowledgement for Superman.

ADAMS: Yeah, I'm thinking *Superman/Muhammad Ali*. [*laughter*]

EURY: Did you have a personal connection with Siegel and Shuster?

ADAMS: No, nobody did.

EURY: Where were they at the time when you decided to rally on their behalf?

ADAMS: Okay, well, we didn't know. What happened was that Jerry wrote a letter to various news media and to the Academy of Comic Book Arts, of which, at that point, I was president, and I got the letter and I let folks see the letter. But it was one of these letters you just can't believe because, first of all, Jerry was very bitter toward DC Comics and Jack Liebowitz. Joe didn't seem to have anything to say. He was the super-nice-guy partner. Joe was legally blind at that point and was living in his brother's apartment, sleeping on a cot next to a window that had a broken window pane.

EURY: This was in 1975, when the news about the Superman movie being in development was breaking.

ADAMS: Yeah, it was breaking and that was part of the impetus of this letter. And the letter was volatile and vociferous and any other "V" words you want. [*Michael laughs*] Vehement, vascular—

EURY: Venomous.

ADAMS: Venomous, yeah. And if he was a company, I would bet that DC Comics would have sued him.

But he made $7,500 a year being a clerk. He also had a heart condition. A heart condition and $7,500 a year, for the guy who wrote Superman. Joe had no income and was living off his brother in Queens, for the artist who created Superman. Not very good. And they had kept silent for *15 years* on the advice of their lawyers who told them that, when [they] get to be 60, they will go, if they have to, to the Supreme Court and get the rights to Superman back into their hands. And then, when the time rolled around—the lawyers didn't answer their mail or phone.

These people—I call these particular lawyers "people" because we're forced to call all lawyers "people" [*Michael laughs*]—of course, they *do* work from the level of humanity down to the slugs, in my opinion, and many of them are at slug level, and there are some that are human.

So anyway, they essentially deserted the boys, these 60-year-old boys. And so Jerry, in frustration, wrote this very, very powerful nine-page letter. And it got to *The Washington Post*, and it got to *The New York Times*, and it got to various people; and even *The Washington Post* wrote an article about it and it was carried on the news wires and it was carried to other newspapers.

I read it and then I saw the article in *The Post* and I sat back, and I thought about it, and I thought, "Well, you know what? This is, sort of, what will happen: They'll get the article in *The Post*, which they did, then it will be run in a smaller article in *The New York Times*, then some other newspapers around the country, and then it will slowly go away. [*pause*] And that's not going to fix things. What has to happen is somebody has to stand up and say, 'Okay, starting today, we're going to decide that this is going to

end, that these guys are going to get some kind of a pension from DC Comics, the people that are making all of this money, and we are not going to stop working on it until this happens.'"

So I told the guys in the studio, "Look, you know I'm going to be spending an awful lot of time doing this. Anybody that wants to help voluntarily, I appreciate the effort. But I'm letting you know now that my studio is going to be dedicated to this until it changes, no matter when that is." Anyway, so I called up Jerry and Joe and told them I'd like to represent them, and Jerry said, "But we can't go to court anymore. We've run out the time." I said, "No, you basically lost the court thing, you know that. That's what it says in your letter and I believe you. But that's not what I'm talking about. I'm not a lawyer, I can't represent you in court. But I can represent you to the *people*. That's all I can do, and maybe not well, but I'd like to take the job." He said, "Well, what will you do?" I said, "Well, I don't know what I'll do. But if you let me do it, I will do it. I will get publicity, I will get attention, and I will try to turn this around." He said, "Okay," and then he wrote a note, and Joe wrote a note, that said they'd let me do this for them.

And so, from that point on, I worked on the media. We did interviews, we did television interviews, newspaper interviews. By the time the thing was coming to an end, which was three-and-a-half months later, reporters were calling me just about every day to find out if anything had changed. We got a fair amount of attention and DC Comics, or Warners, assigned a person—a vice president of the company, because Steve Ross didn't want to talk to me—assigned Jay Emmett, the nephew of Jack Liebowitz, to be the liaison to communicate and to talk me out of this.

EURY: "Talk you out of it"?

ADAMS: Well, you know, it's a big company, you want to pay out the least you can. Of course, *something* would be good. And so his goal was "nothing," my goal was "something," so we had to find a meeting of the minds. I don't think we ever found a meeting of the minds, exactly, but we were back-and-forth and it was a fairly friendly discussion. It got a little bit unfriendly now and then, but I can't even imagine why anybody'd be angry at me. You know, I don't do anything to get angry at!

And the conversation would be, "Why are you doing this? We are going to sell DC Comics. We're not even sure we're going to keep it because it's not making any money, so it's ridiculous and you're looking for money for these guys." I would say, "First of all, I'm not looking for a lot of money. I'm looking for you guys to pay them what you'd pay a glorified secretary. That's not a lot of money. These guys created Superman." And I'd say, "Jay, you're the nephew of the man who basically was the accountant and held on to DC Comics. You came back from the Korean War and your uncle gave you the right to do the licensing for DC Comics. And you created, and live within, Licensing Corporation of America and you made millions of dollars. And you're going to tell me that DC Comics or Warners is going to give up DC Comics with all that licensing? You know how much that is." He said, "Well, let's change the subject."

EURY: So you did this negotiation without any—if I could use the "L" word—legal power at all?

ADAMS: I wasn't trying to do anything legal.

EURY: You were just nudging them along into doing what was right.

ADAMS: Yeah. Well, you know, I don't really think the law and ethics and justice really belong in the same room. To me, the law is in the anteroom, screwing everybody. [*Michael laughs*] And ethics and justice and doing the right thing, they're in a room by themselves where people talk to one another and act real, and that's a totally

"To the Rescue," Adams' illustration produced as part of his media campaign behind Jerry Siegel and Joe Shuster.
Superman TM & © DC Comics

different thing and I think people will listen to that. And I wasn't talking to a judge. I was saying to people, whoever would listen, "Listen, is this right? These guys created Superman. There's going to be a movie, a multimillion dollar movie. My understanding from the rare publicity that they've put out is that DC Comics—not Warners, DC Comics—is immediately going to get an initial payment of three million dollars. And the guys that created Superman, one of them lives in an apartment by a broken window on a cot; the other one has a heart problem and he makes $7,500 a year as a clerk. Does anybody think this is right? I mean, you'd have to be insane, so why are people arguing with me? I know that Warners recognized this immediately. Warners was not responsible for oppressing Jerry Siegel and Joe Shuster. But they *could* be responsible for fixing it. So wouldn't that be nice?" Well, it took me three-and-a-half months to convince people that that *would* be nice, but we managed.

EURY: Well, we appreciate what you did, too. I'm actually surprised that it was accomplished in such a short amount of time. It probably didn't *seem* like a short amount of time when you were going through it.

ADAMS: Well, we had some high points. [But] I got very frustrated because Joe would come into town from Queens and we'd do TV spots, and then Jerry would come in from California, and the problem was, Jerry had to go back to California because he couldn't afford to stay in New York because he couldn't afford to pay the hotel bill. So I would call the news reporters who were interested. I'd say, "Are you interested in interviewing Jerry Siegel and Joe Shuster, the creators of Superman, before they get away?" And they'd say, "Oh, yeah." I'd say, "Well, when can you do it?" They'd say, "How about like early next week?" And I'd say, "Well, no, we can't do it because Jerry has to go back to California. He can't afford to stay in New York *unless* you pay his rent at the hotel." And they'd say, "Well, we can't do that because we're a news medium. That's like buying news. You can't do that." And I'd say, "Well, not exactly. Don't you guys have what they call 'petty cash'? I mean, petty cash for you guys is the hotel bill for two days or three days for Jerry and his wife. How about you just pull some money out of petty cash and pay a couple of days of hotel?" "Well, I guess we can do that." [*Michael chuckles*] "Okay, good. Let's do that."

So I got Jerry to stay in town quite a bit of time. Joe [couldn't afford] to come in from Queens, and I gave him taxi money. He'd come in, but because he was legally blind, he kept on bashing his head on the edge of the cab. So I'd have to put my hand up there any time he got in or out of a cab because he'd smack his head on the doorway.

EURY: The poor guy!

ADAMS: And we would sit and they'd tell stories to me about what it was like, horror stories. (I'm leaving out the worst stuff here.) On a less dramatic note, DC's officers would donate hundreds of thousands of dollars to the war effort while Jerry and Joe were sitting in the cheap seats up in the balcony and could barely see who was on the stage.

And I asked Joe one time, "Joe, there was a Superman musical on Broadway, right? Did you ever see the musical?" And Joe said, "Oh, you know that musical was so popular that everybody came there. I used to go down there and I would watch the famous people that would go in like the President of the United States, famous movie stars, Frank Sinatra, and all these people would go in and they were going to see *my* character." And I said, "Joe, that's interesting—*wow*. But what I really wanted to know was what you thought of the show." Joe said, "Oh, well, I couldn't afford to go to the show. Much too expensive."

EURY: How tragic. There's a similar story from Jerry Siegel where he couldn't bear to say hello to George Reeves. His wife knew George Reeves, but Jerry was so frustrated over this horrible situation, he couldn't even say hello to the man who played Superman.

Superman meets "Best Cop," from the original art to 1976's *Superman* Power Records BR-514.
TM & © DC Comics. Art courtesy of Heritage Comics.

ADAMS: The turning point really sort of came in frustration, when I'd gotten a lot of notice from some certain TV shows, [like] *The Tomorrow Show*, the old Tom Snyder show—the tape of which, by the way, is missing. I heard it's the only tape in their library that went missing. It's interesting because I asked him one time, "So, Tom, you ever think of replaying that show?" He said, "Neal, I was going to replay it just a couple months afterwards, especially when the whole thing got cleared up. We went to the library, it wasn't there."

EURY: [*mock gasp*] Where … could … it … be?

ADAMS: I wonder where it could be, hm, hm, hm. Anyway, Jerry was going to have to go home the next week, and I wasn't making enough of an impact and was frustrated. So I called the National Cartoonists Society, of which Jerry Robinson was the president at that time, and I said, "Look, I'd like to have a meeting to see if you guys can do anything."

So we went to what was then called the Allied Chemical Building—I believe that's what it was, it was that building on Times Square—and they apparently were doing their meetings there. They had this meeting in a room that was like a cartoon. It was gigantic and there was one table and there were lights hanging over the table like an old pool table from a black-and-white movie. And the cartoonists' board, or whoever they were, were sitting around the table and they were talking with me about what they could do—you know, "What's going on, how'd we get so far, blah, blah, blah." So I described the whole thing and told them about the shows that we were on and I said, "We can continue doing shows and stuff, but I'd like to get some help from professionals. And to be perfectly honest, DC Comics isn't going to help me and Marvel Comics isn't going to help me, and told me so. But maybe *you* guys can do something."

So they talked about it for a while. Most of these guys were syndicated strip cartoonists. Some of them used to work for DC Comics, but then they went on to do their syndicated strips. And they said, finally, "Why don't we do a letter, an official letter, from the National Cartoonists Society?" [Their idea was,] they'll do a letter, and then they'll send it up to the gag cartoonists who were at another floor and *they* were having a meeting, so they would get a letter from them, too.

I'd just been through a ragged couple of months. And so they turned to me and they said, "So what do you think, Neal?" I was quiet for a while. And I got up and said, "These two guys, Jerry Siegel and Joe Shuster, created the comic-book business. Half the people in this room owe their income and their livelihood, their ability to put their kids in school, to these two men. They created the comic-book business … and you're going to tell me you're going to write a letter … and then you're going to ask me if I'm happy. No, I'm *not* happy. Goodbye."

Well, the speech was a little bit longer than that. It took about five or six minutes. It was very eloquent because I was feeling eloquent that day. [*Michael chuckles*]

So I'm on my way out and there's this long walk across the floor and to this cloakroom, and there's a guy standing by the cloakroom, kind of an Irish-looking guy—a little bit short, but not too short—and he'd just gotten his coat and he was just kind of standing there under another light—it's like movies, you know? I walk over and I'm going to get my overcoat and go. And he says, "Excuse me." I said, "Yeah?" He says, "You know, that was a pretty good speech." I said, "Thank you. I wish I could do more with it than just talk." He says, "You know what you ought to do?" I said, "Well, I don't know. I'm trying whatever I can." He said, "You ought to have a press conference." [chuckles] I said, "I wouldn't know the first thing about a press conference. I would have no idea what I would do." He said, "You know what building this is?" And I said, "The Allied Chemical Building, or something like that?" He said, "This is the home of the International Press Corps." [Michael laughs] I said, "Really? Wow."

EURY: "Right place at the right time…"

ADAMS: And he said, "You know who I am? I'm the president of the International Press Corps. If you want to have a press conference any day on this subject, any day that you want, you got it." I said, "Come with me." [laughter] And I hurried over to the [cartoonists'] table and I said, "Gentlemen, this is the president of the International Press Corps and he says we can have a press conference any time we want it, and he's going to see to it that it gets done. We can do it tomorrow, but probably not a good idea."

So the guy was *great*. He set up a press conference, we had many artists, creators of comic strips, that were in the New York area come up. Irwin Hasen came up, he did a drawing of Dondi with a tear in his eye, [and we got] letters from Milton Caniff and all these other guys getting behind Jerry Siegel and Joe Shuster. It was so impressive that after I made my personal statement, I got the hell out of there. But enter all the cartoonists, and it just totally torpedoed Warners. They were like, "Whoa, step back! We gotta do something about settling this. This can't go on."

EURY: What was Jerry and Joe's emotional reaction to this out-pouring?

Adams' 1970s Superman merchandising art. [illegible] a registered trademark of Corgi Toys.

ADAMS: Well, their eyes, at a certain point, they started to open up. First of all, they're going on these shows and doing interviews and being spoken to by some famous interviewers and people, so they're very impressed by that. But when the Cartoonists Society got behind them, they were totally blown away that anybody would, that *everybody* would want to stand up for them. They were in awe.

EURY: Cue the weepy soundtrack—this is a classic Hollywood moment.

ADAMS: Yeah, totally. The problem was, right after the press conference, when Warners was feeling good, Jerry finally had to go back to California. He got together with me at my studio and he said, "Neal, whatever they offer, now take it." I said, [disbelieving] "Oh-kay. You know, the last conversation I had, they were like at $**,000 a year. I'd really like to bring it up to ** at least, minimum, with benefits and other things." [Editor's note: Exact figures are confidential.]

In those days, that was not too bad. It's way more now—Warners is treating the [Siegel and Shuster] families very nicely. Anyway, they said, "Neal, we just can't do this anymore. We're gone, we're exhausted. Take whatever they offer. It's ** now. If they add a couple more thousand, that'll be fine." I said, "Okay," and I put them on a plane and sent them to California.

So I get the call from Warners and I say, "Okay, what's it going to be? What have you got?" And they said, "Well, $**,000 a year [three thousand more], and that's our last offer." I said, "Well, I'll ask them, see if it's okay." So I held the phone and I didn't do anything. [Michael chuckles] At the end of the day I called them back and I said, "Well, I guess I'm just not good at this." They said, "What do you mean?" "Well, you were at $**,000 and then you go to $**,000, it's insulting. So they said they can't do it. They were just pissed off." They said, "How much would they need?" I said, "A minimum of $**,000 [five thousand more]." [pause] "So okay, they got it." *Whew!* Oh, boy. Oh, boy.

EURY: What a fabulous story.

ADAMS: What happened in the end, we sealed it up before the Christmas holidays. And so when the reporters called and we're finally able to accomplish just a couple of more little things, I said to the reporters, "Look at this. You know, Warners was never involved in this to begin with. Now they've solved the problem and we have a Jerry Siegel and Joe Shuster that can go to see their character in the movies. Everybody's happy, they're happy, Warners is happy—Merry Christmas, guys." Hurray, great story. So Warners came out looking good. In the end, they look like the rescuers.

EURY: The Christmas timing too was just perfect. [Editor's note: The agreement was announced on Friday, December 19, 1975.]

ADAMS: It worked out great. So it all turned out great and it's exactly what I told them when I was talking to them. I said, "Look, you guys can end up easily being the good guys here. Question what it would cost you to hire a couple of secretaries and you're the good guys. You're the heroes. Why wouldn't you do that? You're gonna, you know, save this and it'll never show up again. You're good." And that's exactly the way it turned out. It's good for Warners, it's good for Jerry and Joe, it's good for the comic-book business to get this stupid sh*t settled—everybody benefits. It worked out great.

You know, I went through a bad time. It was a tough time. I mean, It wasn't "tough" tough, not like being trapped in an alley with three guys with knives, but it was tough—but when it was finished, it was *great!*

EURY: It had to be exhilarating. Did anybody try to professionally pressure you against getting involved like this?

ADAMS: You know, I have never said anything to anybody in the comic-book business that didn't make more sense than the way it was before. I have never tried to get DC or Marvel to do anything that's against their best interests. I have never given bad advice. It's all been good advice and I've never done it without thinking about it long and hard, and discussing it with people, and saying, "Okay, finally, why don't we do this? Isn't this better? What if you give royalties to the people who do the work, aren't they going to make a better comic book to earn that royalty? So what you can do is you can figure out how much money you have to make before you'd ever give a royalty, and then from that point on, you give a royalty? Let's say you're not going to do well until you sell 75,000 copies of a comic book. At that point, start the royalty. What is your problem with that? If that's what you want, and they do more, then you give them a little piece, doesn't that make sense? Why are you arguing with me? I don't understand. [laughter] You're not making any sense. What are you doing with your original art? You're destroying it! [chuckles] Think about it. It's stupid! Give it back to the artists."

EURY: With all the original art that was destroyed back then, I'm surprised to find as much of it surfacing today in the marketplace.

ADAMS: Because a lot of it was taken illegally, and that's just too bad. I tried to deal with it, but you can't because it's gone generations down. You know, it's with the fifth guy or the third guy, and he bought it in all honesty. He didn't steal it, he just *bought* it because he's a fan. He kept it, he loves it, but now if he sells it, he'll probably get ten times as much as he paid for it and somehow he thinks he deserves it because he made a smart investment. Well, although that's not true, that's just the way it is with folks.

EURY: Let's talk about your other big Superman moment of the late '70s, the *Ali* book.

ADAMS: Okay.

EURY: How did that wind up with you? Originally, Joe Kubert was attached to it.

ADAMS: Yeah, exactly right. And I thought he was doing a great job, but apparently the Muslims that were representing Muhammad Ali did not think that Joe was doing likenesses properly. That really came down to likenesses and Joe's style is a little bit of a rough style. So even if he did a likeness, for somebody who's untutored in art style, they would still find that, "No, that's not going to do it. That's too rough, too hard to deal with."

So I was asked because, of course, I'm more realistic and I draw more photorealistic stuff. If I would do it, that would be the right answer. I've done likenesses so it really came down to doing likenesses. So as a tribute to Joe, I kept the composition of the cover that Joe made, only I replaced it, replaced it with the art that would be satisfactory to the people. So the one thing that's remaining of that book that's Joe Kubert is the layout and composition of that cover.

EURY: Did he do any interior pages?

ADAMS: He just did the cover, and that's what the judgment was based on. The Honorable Elijah Muhammad decided it did not look enough like Muhammad Ali. In fact, it was even [chuckles] more interesting than that. Denny O'Neil, who was going to write it, and myself had to be approved of by the Honorable Elijah Muhammad.

EURY: And what kind of approval was required?

ADAMS: Denny and I had to fly to Chicago, be taken by limousine out to the house of the Honorable Elijah Muhammad, and to be approved. It wasn't exactly a ceremony. We went out to Chicago and there's this gated mansion. The house looked like it was about ten blocks from the gate, with armed guards, and they designed the living room area like a Turkish living room where you have columns around the outside

and you sit around the outside and the center is empty, I guess for the dancing girls or whatever. Anyway, they served us anything we wanted, a coffee, Tab, or whatever. In those days, it was Tab, not Diet Coke. [chuckling] And we sat there like bumps on a log. Across the room, the Honorable Elijah Muhammad came out with two women, and he sat there, nodded at us, picked up the phone, had a phone conversation, looked at us, somebody came in and had him sign something. [He] sort of waved, left the room, and we're back to New York.

EURY: So it was you and Denny, not your work, that had to be approved. What an experience *that* had to be.

ADAMS: Right. Well, we didn't know what to expect. We definitely got what we deserved. We were both approved, whatever that means.

EURY: [laughs] And Denny didn't finish the project.

ADAMS: No, I don't think that Denny was thrilled doing the project to begin with because, essentially, his outlines were rejected at the beginning and then I took his outlines and moved them into a slightly different direction, and that made the editor happy, and everybody was happy with the outline, and Denny seemed to be okay with it. He started to write it and then basically he lost enthusiasm for it. And he decided for whatever reason that he wasn't going to finish it. He was

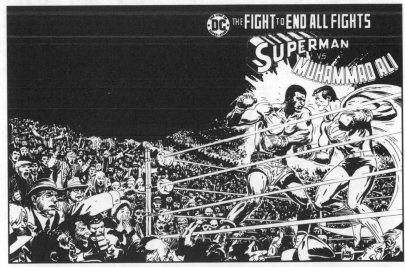

Joe Kubert's original, unpublished cover for *Superman vs. Muhammad Ali*, and Neal Adams' celebrity-packed published version, recreating Kubert's composition.

THE SUPERMAN MYTHOLOGY:
STAR-CROSSED SUPER-STORIES

Superman vs. Muhammad Ali continued a long-standing tradition of the Man of Steel meeting real-life celebrities. Mort Weisinger and Whitney Ellsworth were fond of such crossovers, guest-starring *Truth or Consequences'* Ralph Edwards, late-night TV star Steve Allen, and singer Pat Boone in 1950s' Superman tales. Other notable examples from later years:

(left) Clark Kent, punk'd by Allen Funt, in *Action #345* (Jan. 1967). (right) Before he met Jerry Seinfeld, Superman met another funny Jerry in *Adventures of Jerry Lewis #105* (Mar.–Apr. 1968).
TM & © DC Comics.

Guest-star Don Rickles in *Jimmy Olsen #139* (July 1971) and 141 (Sept. 1971).
TM & © DC Comics.

 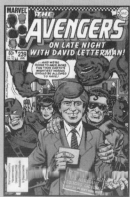 

Other publishers have produced reality-bending comics, such as *Marvel Team-Up #74* (Oct. 1978), *Avengers #239* (Jan. 1984), and *Godzilla vs. Barkley* (Dec. 1993).

exhausted at the time. He actually needed a vacation so he took some time off. It was, I think, coincidental, the burden of the thing and his overwork—he was called upon to do so much work at the time that he basically just had to go take a rest. I think it just got to be too much for him.

EURY: Denny has said many, many times that he just never really could get his hands around Superman. At least he doesn't feel that he could.

ADAMS: You have to remember that Denny is a reporter and he likes "real." One of the reasons that he's good for Batman is because Batman isn't a super-hero. He is the antithesis of Superman. Superman is the ultimate super-hero, Batman is the *non*-super-hero super-hero. He has no super-powers, everything is *him*. Even his gadgets are exaggerated too much by a lot of people. He is Sherlock Holmes and some powerful gladiator wrapped in one body, so Denny could more easily deal with that. Look at Ra's al Ghul, look at the work that he did. He stuck more to the real stuff. There was no Penguin. Later on, yes, you know you get pushed into doing these things.

But when I worked with Denny, I saw more of the reporter there than I saw of the super-hero writer. So I think that made a big difference—to do Superman, you know, Superman was just too much. What are his powers? What can he do? *I* like it as an exercise. I enjoy it, you know. I like to create limits and then work within the limits, even though those limits can be grand—so I was way more comfortable writing *Superman/Muhammad Ali* than Denny was. He was not comfortable, clearly not comfortable.

For me, at the time, he was the perfect writer because my stuff was more realistic so if you take somebody who's very realistic and you have him do too much fantasy, it just ruins the realism—I mean, humans *bleed*. We have this sequence in *Green Lantern/Green Arrow* where Green Arrow gets a quarrel shot into his shoulder from a crossbow. Well, you can see a ton of action in lots of other comics where stuff ought to happen and the consequences should be so great. Well, Green Arrow gets a quarrel in his shoulder and you go through two or three pages of him just crawling along the street, not being able to get it out of his shoulder, asking for help from people, going into a hospital, fainting across the desk of a nurse, and you realize, yeah, he may just have a thing in his shoulder, there's *definitely* consequences. In comics, people are [routinely] getting blown up and shot up, and I think Wolverine just got clove in half the other day.

EURY: Ouch! No kidding?

ADAMS: Yeah. It has aspects of unreality, and yet you're putting realistic illustrators to do this. It's just a little crazy and Denny, for me at that time, was very, very good. It was a terrific partnership.

EURY: Despite the outer-space setting of *Ali/Superman*, there was a lot of realism there, too. You have Superman bleed, which is something you don't see every day.

ADAMS: And he gets the sh*t kicked out of him.

EURY: Which was groundbreaking at the time. Bone-breaking, too.

ADAMS: I did so many things in that comic book. I got to get Superman beat up, *really* beat up nice and slow. Then you got to *see* him beaten up.

EURY: That great downshot on the stretcher, yeah.

ADAMS: Then he essentially recreated himself. His super-powers came back, and you saw him using his super-powers in space where you can't hear—but suddenly, you can hear his cry. Using this [artistic] idea of a small, little body, you can do all these things. He would fly through a spaceship, he would look like a needle punching through a piece of cloth. So I had him grab the hatch of a ship and drive the hatch through the ship, so the relationship between Superman and the hatch and then the hatch and the ship blasted this big hole through it, dealing with what do you do with a Superman? How do you make him effective flying through stuff? It was lots of fun.

EURY: We had a lot of fun reading it. What a great book. But you took some heat for it being late. It was 72 pages. How long did it take you to draw it?

ADAMS: Oh, it didn't take me that long to draw it. The truth is that when Joe turned it down and it came to me, I said, "Look, you know, I'm really not working for DC any more. Maybe *you* guys know that, okay? But this is, to me, an important project. I cannot accept this project if you give me a deadline, because I'm starting a studio. I mean, I'm out of here and I have my own studio and doing lots of advertising work. I'm supporting a family and I'm supporting my studio. I can't just sit down and do this book. If I can do it on an open-ended deadline, that's fine." They said, "Fine, it's in the contract. There's no deadline."

"No deadline" to me means "no deadline." [*Michael laughs*] I don't know what it means to anybody else, but to me, it means "no deadline." After a while, they start hokking me and they were really worried because in the middle of the thing, Ali lost the championship, which was going to hurt it. And I'm going, "Guys, he lost it twice before and got it back. What are you worried about? He's going to get it back, right?" And he did just before we came out.

EURY: Great timing.

ADAMS: So I don't mind the criticism, but I think when people criticize people, they ought to check the facts and find out if it's really a criticism. You're talking to a guy who did consecutive issues of "Deadman", consecutive issues of *Green Lantern/Green Arrow*. Consecutive, that means every month or every two months, whenever they came out; consecutive issues of *X-Men*. People used to bitch at me because they'd see me doing covers, and you'd have editors going up and down the hallways at DC: "He's supposed to be working on this and he's doing covers," and I want to stop time and go, "Okay, we'll stop it right here. I'm doing the covers *why?* Because you want me to, okay? I've been just assigned five covers for you guys; one for you, the one who's bitching, Julie; two for Murray and two for Joe Orlando, okay? Five covers. I shouldn't do *any* of your work this week. Five covers should take me five days, why should I be doing your work? But I'm *going* to be doing your work or Carmine, take the covers away, have somebody else do the covers. Or you go to Carmine, Julie, and you tell him that you don't want Neal to do your cover." "I'm not going to do that." "Then stop bitching, you know? If I fail to get a book out, then you have a right to complain, fine. But if I don't, what are you complaining about?" "Well, you shouldn't be doing covers for those other editors." "Okay. All right, fine. I can't have this conversation. I really can't." All you've got to do is on my site, there's a list of all the stuff I did in those few years at DC Comics. Figure out how much I did in a given year, [*laughs*] figure out how many days there are in that year, and then add in the covers and see how much work I did. See if there's anybody in the business that turned out as much work in a short time.

EURY: You were definitely all over the place.

ADAMS: Maybe Steve Dillon, maybe it's possible. And Jack Kirby, Jack Kirby beats everybody. And Joe Kubert. Okay, I'll give it to Joe Kubert, [*Michael laughs*] Jack Kirby, and Steve Dillon. That's it.

EURY: I want to ask you a question about when Kirby was doing *Jimmy Olsen* and the Fourth World. Years later, a whole generation reveres those characters and Kirby himself, but at that time, what was the reaction in the artist community?

ADAMS: You're going, "So, what did you think about Jack Kirby coming over to DC Comics?" Oh, there's way more to the story than that and there's, of course, the relationship between Jack Kirby and Stan Lee and Marvel Comics, which

could have been settled, but Jack is a hothead so Jack didn't want to settle it. Exactly. So he came over to DC and he demanded certain things. One of the things he demanded was to write his own stuff without really having stuff edited. But you know, when you say something like that, and you say it in words, it doesn't necessarily happen in fact. That's one on the side of the creator. On the side of the company, it's a stupid deal to make. I wouldn't have somebody come to my company and say, "I get to write everything that I do." "No, because if I give you the right to write everything you do, you can just voluntarily write sh*t. I've made an agreement to let you write everything that you do. Now there has to be some kind of control. How about this? I'll give you the right to write everything *if* we approve it? If I don't approve it, we rewrite it, or restructure, or whatever it is we have to do to make it fit the standards of our company, but we'll pay you for the writing. In other words, you can do the writing." Well, if you start giving away too many freedoms to people, people abuse them. Have a conversation about Jack's work, okay? At DC Comics, you sort of have to. If you look at the writing, you have to say, "Let's call it 'brief,' okay? Sort of as a flow, unedited."

EURY: That's fair.

ADAMS: If a writer had come back and said, "Well, okay, this is a rough thing. Now I'm going to rewrite it so that things are clear, there's an evolution of the dialogue, then we throw in little anecdotal things, other things to make it flow like a book or a movie or a comic book." It wasn't done that way. Because he was cranking out so much stuff, he never went back over the stuff, but he was given the right *not* to because he was foolishly given the right to have total autonomy. It should not have been done. Everybody needs somebody. You could be a Stephen King, you could be anybody—well, I don't know what autonomy Stephen

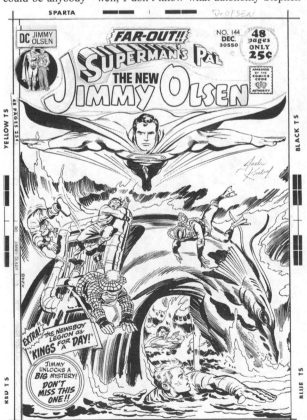

A "far-out" collaboration of Jack Kirby and Neal Adams on the cover of *Jimmy Olsen* #144 (Dec. 1971). Original artwork signed by Kirby.

TM & © DC Comics. Art courtesy of Heritage Comics.

King has—but you write a novel, right? And you hand it in to your editor, everybody has an editor, and the editor sits back, takes it home, and reads it, and calls you in and says, "Look, chapter seven here, can you just read this over? You don't actually need chapter seven. And I just marked up this other stuff over here, but this is redundant dialogue, isn't it? Take a look at it. And the writer takes it home and goes, "Oh, sh*t. I don't really need chapter seven, take it out. Redundant dialogue, blah, blah, blah, blah, blah." *That's* what you need an editor for, a wall to bounce ideas and to bounce your skills off of.

Well, Jack hadn't written stuff in a long time. He was writing notes in the sides of the pages for Stan Lee. Why would people, why would *anybody*, assume that he could really dialogue a story? It doesn't make any sense, not to say that he didn't *tell* a story. That is not to say that he didn't put melodrama in the story, but it's brief and unedited. That's not the way it ought to be.

Well, DC did it to themselves, okay? I don't know that Carmine recognized it, but I think everybody recognized it. I don't think I'm telling stories out of school, either. I think everybody knows it, okay? And it's a tragedy of what happened. You give

Page 3 of Len Wein and Neal Adams' unfinished Superman anti-pollution tale, from *The Amazing World of DC Comics Special Edition #1 (Feb. 1976).*
TM & © DC Comics.

somebody too much freedom, very often, they screw themselves, and that's what Jack did. And yet nobody came to Jack and said, "Jack, we gotta redo this thing. Let's sit and talk here. I really have to give this to some professional writers and have them flesh it out because we're not getting whole stories here, too much of it is being left out, it's just not working."

It should have been done early on, but wasn't done. Well, what happens is then animosity builds up, you know, [then they do] whatever they can—"Well, if you do Superman, we'll *change* Superman if we don't like it. You know, we'll change the stuff that belongs to us." So they started to do that. They had nothing else that they could do. Now there was also a certain amount of freedom that Jack Kirby had that other people didn't have, so people actually were happy to make these little changes, to do this stuff. People without being happy, you know, they didn't dance down the hallways, but the King was given too big a kingdom. People resented it. I'm not going to say who resented it, but I know people resented it and I found myself in a very weird situation. People were being asked to change his artwork. Al Plastino was being given figures to redo.

EURY: Murphy Anderson, as well.

ADAMS: A definite schism in style. So I went to Carmine, I said, "Carmine, if you're going to make these changes, let me do it. Then if Jack gets upset, he gets upset at me and then it's okay. But really, this stuff is bad. You've got Jack Kirby, hard with all these angles, and then you've got these soft, mushy characters. They don't go together. So I'd rather take a hit on this than just to go on." He said, "Well, if you're willing to do it." I said, "I'm willing to do it. Just let me—anything you want to do and screw around with this stuff, I'll fix it, whatever it takes." So I plugged myself into that place and those things that I did, yes, they didn't look like Jack Kirby. They looked like I was working for DC Comics and doing my job. On the other hand, they didn't look that bad and they were action, and they didn't really conflict that much with the hard edge because my stuff is kind of hard. So I did what I could to soften the blows that were coming and there were lots of blows, so it shouldn't have happened that way, but there you go.

EURY: What about that Superman story you did that was in *The Amazing World of DC Comics*, the convention booklet. The five-pager that Len Wein wrote? Do you remember this?

ADAMS: I sort of remember it.

EURY: It's a curiosity for a lot of us who saw it years ago. Len didn't remember it. I sent him jpegs of the pages and it still didn't trigger a memory for him.

ADAMS: Every once in a while, DC Comics does things that are socially activist to show that they're on the side of the good guys. And this had to do with some kind of a direction, that they were promoting goodwill in some area or something, and they would pick people at various times to go ahead and do this. Sometimes, it would be strips to help sell comic books through the distributors, sometimes it would be to help homeless kids, sometimes it would be this, that, or the other. Well, it was some kind of project that they wanted to do and nine times out of ten, these things would go to bust. You know, we'd do the work, show the work, and then the enthusiasm for it would dribble away, and then it would be gone. Sometimes it would happen, sometimes they wouldn't, and this was one of those things, but because it didn't happen, you kind of go, "Well, who gives a crap? I was a good scout and I did the work, but nobody cares so the hell with it." And you could tell from the creators that we were disappointed in the people who wanted this to happen. The people who did it, did it with all honesty and straightforwardness. But the people who were supposedly behind it really didn't do much of anything. DC is not known for going out of their way to do stuff.

EURY: I bring this up because that particular story and the "Secret Origins of the Justice League" that you did are some of

the rare instances where you drew Superman beyond covers and merchandising—and *Muhammad Ali*, of course.

As far as *Ali* is concerned, is there a chance it will ever be reprinted?

ADAMS: My mom used to say to me, "You know, time only works one way, forward. It never goes backwards." And you never know what to expect.

EURY: It would be nice to see some type of collection of your Superman work.

ADAMS: You know what I'd like to see—I understand that this is about Superman, but I'd love to see a *Muhammad Ali* book, even if it's not extra thick or anything, just by itself, maybe a few extra pieces in it to decorate it. And I think that would make a great book.

EURY: It would.

ADAMS: What I'd like to see is a book that collects the extra stuff, the other stuff that I did for DC, perhaps re-colored and turned into an "all-the-extra-stuff" or something book. I did some *Spectre* stories that were pretty nifty.

EURY: Package all the other odds and ends in one nice volume.

ADAMS: *Superman/Muhammad Ali* did better in the world than it did in America. In other words, every country in the world bought licenses for DC Comics, paid extra money to get that book, and they had great sales.

EURY: Two of the most recognizable figures in the world there together.

ADAMS: Well, one of them more respected out in the world than respected in his home.

EURY: That is very true.

Signed original artwork to one of Adams' "Justice for All Includes Children" comic-book public-service announcements.

ADAMS: Something that I have to say that I resent my home country for. But there you go. I think of Muhammad Ali as a man who stands up for what he believes in.

EURY: Well, as Cassius Clay, he was sort of like the Siegel and Shuster Superman, the champion for the oppressed.

ADAMS: Yeah. I did a cover for *ESPN Magazine* at the turn of the century. The art director of *ESPN Magazine* said, "We're going to have on the Hundred Greatest Athletes of the Century and we have to do a wraparound cover. I'm stuck with doing a hundred photographs, or pictures, of these people just smeared all over the cover with some kind of designs. Or … do you remember that *Superman/Muhammad Ali* comic book you did?" I said, "Yeah." She said, "You think you can do it again and do Muhammad Ali and Michael Jordan boxing and then have the hundred greatest athletes, or the [remaining] 98 greatest athletes as the audience around them?" I said, "You're kidding." She said, "No, I think that would be great." And I thought, "God, that was a horror, doing that cover." But I thought, "When's the next time this kind of job is gonna come around? A hundred years from now. I don't think I'm going to be doing *that* one." [*Michael laughs*]

So I did Ali and Jordan boxing—actually, that's very interesting, but there's one more thing that's interesting. It's a nifty cover. The thing about the cover is that it went out to three million people, subscribers to *ESPN Magazine*. Among those, I figure about five of them are comic-book fans. It didn't go to the comic-book fans so they didn't get to see it. It went to ESPN subscribers. At any rate, it was it was sort of a poll, and each one of the sports networks and the sports groups had the same thing, the Hundred Greatest Athletes. The people voted, or the staff voted, or whatever. And *ESPN Magazine* decided, in their great wisdom, that the number-one athlete was going to be Michael Jordan. I thought, "You know, Michael Jordan is a great athlete, I agree. And Michael Jordan may even be a great man. But Muhammad Ali changed people's views about black people in America and no greater thing could be done by an athlete."

EURY: Absolutely.

ADAMS: "But to take his athleticism and to channel it for good, and you're going to vote for Michael Jordan? I don't get it. It doesn't make any sense."

EURY: I guess that Jordan was, from their perspective, more recognizable as a brand name.

ADAMS: Hey, that sounds like that bullsh*t, too.

EURY: [*laughs*] I'm just parroting it. I don't believe it.

ADAMS: Right. [*chuckles*]

EURY: I do agree, though, about what he did as a human being as being very, very important.

ADAMS: He put it on the line. He lost the championship for it. He was—oh, man. It was tough. I mean, they were threatening to put him away for a *long* time, a long time.

EURY: Oh, yeah. Yeah, did you see the Will Smith biopic of him?

ADAMS: Yeah.

EURY: What did you think about that?

ADAMS: I thought it was okay, I thought it was okay. I saw it just to see Will Smith doing Ali. You know, they hung around too much about the relationships and stuff, and that's not the public image that we saw. We saw him going through this process. We didn't see the process of women. I never saw the women. I didn't know what the hell was going on with that and I didn't, to be perfectly honest, give a sh*t. I was interested in his involvement with going through the process with the boxers and going through the political process.

EURY: So, who's going to play you in the Neal Adams movie?

ADAMS: He hasn't been born yet.

THE SUPERMAN MYTHOLOGY:
KIRBY IS HERE!

DE SAAD OF THE NEW GODS

JACK KIRBY

TM & © DC Comics.

When Jack "King" Kirby, the co-creator of the Fantastic Four, the Incredible Hulk, and the X-Men, jumped ship from Marvel to DC Comics in 1970, his heart was set on experimenting with new formats and concepts, an itch he was barely able to scratch through his short-lived black-and-white comics magazines *In the Days of the Mob* and *Spirit World*. Always the visionary, Kirby was, perhaps, a bit ahead of his time, as well as ahead of what DC was looking for *at* the time—the Kirby "magic" applied to its super-hero titles. Jack could have had his choice of any DC series, but between his disinterest and his refusal to unseat current creative teams, he responded to pressure to take on one mainstream DC series by agreeing to produce *Superman's Pal Jimmy Olsen*, a book that was without a writer and artist after Mort Weisinger's retirement.

Initially, Kirby on *Jimmy Olsen* seemed like pure folly—the man who ushered readers to the Negative Zone now drawing an Archie Andrews doppelganger with a signal watch??!—but, in retrospect, Kirby's *Olsen* (along with his companion "Fourth World" titles *Forever People*, *New Gods*, and *Mister Miracle*) was a gateway to concepts that have become integral to DC's contemporary Superman comics, as well as the publisher's entire Universe—Darkseid, DeSaad (seen above in a rare Kirby sketch), Morgan Edge, the Boom Tube, Mother Box, and the Anti-Life Equation, to name but a few.

"Be careful what you wish for," the saying goes, and DC executives were given pause upon seeing Kirby's renditions, in pencil form, of Superman and Jimmy Olsen from the King's first two issues (*Jimmy Olsen* #133 and 134, Oct. and Dec. 1970). Kirby's energetic figures looked nothing like the house (and licensing) style for these highly visible characters. Enter Al Plastino, and later Murphy Anderson, who redrew Superman heads (and sometimes bodies) and Olsen heads over Kirby's art. This was a long-standing procedure at DC, however, and artists as versatile and talented as Nick Cardy, Mike Sekowsky, Alex Toth, Art Saaf, and even Curt Swan and Kurt Schaffenberger had, at least once, seen their Superman-related art altered with facial paste-ups or redrawings.

Kirby's *Jimmy Olsen* ran from issue #133 through #148 (Apr. 1972), with the exception of #140 (Sept. 1971), a reprint Giant. Superman guest-starred in Kirby's *The Forever People* #1 (Feb.–Mar. 1971), and the Man of Steel's (possible) legacy was explored in his *Kamandi, the Last Boy on Earth* #29 (May 1975).

Recommended reading: *The Jack Kirby Collector* (quarterly magazine from TwoMorrows) and Mark Evanier's "News from ME" online column (*www.newsfromme.com*). [Editor's note: Jack Kirby coverage in *The Krypton Companion* is limited due to the wealth of Kirby-related material found elsewhere.]

From *Jimmy Olsen* #145 (Jan. 1972). Kirby's pencils (top), and the published version, inked by Vince Colletta with Murphy Anderson redrawn Superman faces.

TM & © DC Comics. Special thanks to Murphy Anderson.

Dennis O'Neil Interview

Dennis "Denny" O'Neil (b. 1939) was at the forefront of a youth movement of creators unbound by tradition and inspired by the human portrayals of super-heroes seen in Stan Lee's Marvel Comics titles. Starting his comics career at Charlton in the mid-1960s, O'Neil was lured to DC in 1968 by Dick Giordano, recently hired from Charlton. O'Neil's infusion of social relevance into his stories made him one of the medium's hottest writers, known for his revamps of *Wonder Woman*, *Superman*, *Green Lantern/Green Arrow*, *Batman*, and Captain Marvel (in *Shazam!*). He later spent a few years editing at Marvel, where Frank Miller's *Daredevil* series was among his accomplishments. O'Neil was back at DC later in the 1980s, where he editorially steered the Batman line for years before returning to his freelance-writing roots, where he remains today, occasionally penning comics scripts and novels based upon super-heroes.

Conducted by Michael Eury on January 11, 2006.

MICHAEL EURY: Dick Giordano recruited you to DC, and you soon began writing for Julie Schwartz. Did you do any work for Mort Weisinger before his retirement?
DENNIS O'NEIL: No. I only had one conversation with Mort, and that was at a magazine writers' dinner or meeting. Mort was active in that organization and I was there as a guest of someone. We chatted for ten minutes or so, but I had no professional dealings with Mort at all.
EURY: At the time you were coming into DC, it was almost a revolving door between you and Mort, with you entering the company and him leaving it.
O'NEIL: Yes, but he was very financially successful at the time. It wasn't the sad story of a comic-book guy finding himself broke with no prospects in his golden years. Mort did very well for himself.

From what I've heard about working for Mort, we would not have been a good match.
EURY: Yeah, his reputation was that of a taskmaster. Some people responded okay to that, but many didn't.
O'NEIL: Jim Shooter, who lives not far from me here, seemed to admire Mort's way of doing things.
EURY: Mort was Jim's mentor.
O'NEIL: Yeah, he took this 13-year-old kid from Pittsburgh and gave him a career.
EURY: But working for Weisinger was no bed of roses for Jim. So, you and Shooter live in the same neighborhood?
O'NEIL: Well, we live in the same town. It's a relatively small town. It's pretty amazing that I actually haven't seen him, because he lives behind the post office and I do a lot of business with the post office. [*laughter*]
EURY: When Julie tapped you to revitalize Superman in 1970 (for *Superman* #233, Jan. 1971), were you gung ho to take on the Man of Steel?
O'NEIL: I don't think I was gung ho—it was an assignment. I did not realize then that there was a pecking order ... in some

Photo © 1973 DC Comics.

ways I was really obtuse. And I now know that the guy who wrote Superman was probably higher in professional esteem than the guy who wrote the Atom, or one of the minor-league characters. But I never thought about that at all. If anything, I think I'd wanted to avoid the high-profile characters, because I thought they'd come with too many strings attached.
EURY: That's interesting, because Superman came on the heels of your revitalizing Wonder Woman and Batman—and those are high-profile characters.
O'NEIL: Well, the assignments were, "Do something new with it." With Batman, it was, "We're not going to do this camp thing anymore." And likewise with Wonder Woman, who had been very spotty in terms of commercial success ever since the '40s. I had a crack at her, as did a lot of other people. But with Superman, he was still the flagship character, and I don't remember the guys in the corner office thinking that he was particularly broken.
EURY: The first thing you did was make "kryptonite nevermore." Was that your idea or Julie's?
O'NEIL: It was mine.
EURY: It was yours. Granted, kryptonite had become overexploited, but what was the motivation behind stripping DC's mightiest hero of his one actual Achilles' heel?
O'NEIL: A couple of things. Mainly, as you said, it had become overdone and was an all-purpose crutch. I wanted to deny myself that easy way out. The problem with Superman will always be that he's too powerful, that he's a god. It seemed that there had been enough kryptonite managing to get to our solar system to fill the planet. [*laughter*] So it was a way of taking away that overused, too-easy gimmick. Also, it was a signal to readers that a new day is dawning.
EURY: That was indeed the signal. The cover that Neal Adams did for your first issue has become legendary.

De-powering the Man of Steel was another of your innovations. With all of the character's super-powers, how did you and Julie decide which powers to keep, and which ones to diminish?
O'NEIL: Oh, I don't think we ever sat down and said, "We're going to take away this, we're going to take away that, and we're going to keep this." The general agreement was, we would take him *almost* back to where he started—not quite, because the original 1938 Superman couldn't fly. I've heard two versions of how Superman came to fly, but in any case, the character had been in existence for at least a year before he became officially airborne.
EURY: "Able to leap buildings…"
O'NEIL: "…in a single bound," yeah. "Nothing short of an exploding shell could penetrate his steel-hard skin." Well, I didn't want to make him *that* weak, but I wanted to get rid of things like Superman being able to see into the past, or into the future. One example I like to use in lectures is, in one story Superman blew out a sun, a star. [*laughter*] With a guy that powerful, where's your conflict going to come from? By the way, I thank Michael Fleisher for making me aware of that sun story in one of his books.

I didn't know much about dramatic construction in writing back then, but I knew enough to realize that it's essential to put conflict into a story. And if you're talking about quality, it's essential to get that [conflict] without violating the premise. Well, a guy who makes the entire Greek pantheon look like a bunch of first-graders, as Superman eventually did … what are you going to put against him? It was established at one time that he could search every room in Metropolis within a second—how are you going to hide from that guy? His X-ray vision won't penetrate lead, but he's smart enough to know that if he's flying over something, and there's a lead roof [laughs], he probably figures out that's where the bad guy's hiding.

EURY: Or he could tune in with his super-hearing.

O'NEIL: Yeah. I used to get laughs at lectures by saying he could break through walls by his listening to them. [laughter]

So you had a lot of stories that I thought weren't terribly dramatic and violated the essential appeal of the character. To give myself the possibility of giving Superman stories with real conflict I decided to scale him back to a *reasonable* scale of super-powers.

EURY: Do you think that since Superman inspired so many different super-heroes, that his powers had to be routinely amplified simply to keep him ahead of the pack?

O'NEIL: I have a couple of theories about that. One is the old conventional wisdom that said, "Nobody's really paying attention to this stuff, and that the readership turns over every few years." I think that was the conventional wisdom that was still around when I started in the mid-'60s, although it was probably waning by then. So I don't think these [writers] were ever worried about being stuck with something. It was probably like, "Gee, I've got a plot problem. I could really solve this if Superman could see into the past. Hey, let's do that … besides, that's pretty cool." So it was just guys making up stories as they went along, without any consideration of how this would play out next year, or how logical this was.

EURY: The tool that you used to de-power Superman was, of course, the Sand-Superman, an entity from the antimatter realm of Quarrm, who slowly siphoned Superman's powers away—or at least diminished them—and ultimately set its mind upon becoming the only Superman in town. Was any discussion given to using the Parasite, who had drained Superman's energy in previous stories, in this capacity?

O'NEIL: No, if I was aware of the Parasite, I certainly didn't consider using him. I guess I didn't want to look to the past—and Julie didn't want to look to the past, either.

EURY: It wasn't until recently, when analyzing all things Superman for this book, that I made the connection between the similar abilities of the Parasite and the Sand-Superman. I've read your stories several times over the course of a few decades, and I never thought, when reading the stories earlier, "Oh, wait a minute—why didn't they use the Parasite to weaken Superman?" The fact is, you didn't use *any* of Superman's traditional rogues' gallery, which shows, as you said, you were committed to looking forward, not back.

O'NEIL: Yeah. The fact that I was never a fan has been both a strength and a weakness. [O'Neil's wife] Marifran makes me aware of fans' considerations—she'll say, "It'll really please the

This late-1970 DC house ad previewed the post-Weisinger Superman era.
TM & © DC Comics.

fans if you'd do *this*." But even now, trying to honor the past is not anything that I think about naturally. I think that once you establish a continuity, it's very important to adhere to that, and to make it consistent. You can change the continuity, but that does not violate the enjoyment of those earlier stories. It's sort of like if you're reading Henry James and on page 140 it turns into Mickey Spillane. [laughter] There's an emotional investment in a version of a character, and then suddenly, that's pulled out from under you.

EURY: As you note, when things change, that should not negate your appreciation of the previous stories. Superman today is not the same Superman from the era we're speaking of. But those old stories keep getting reprinted in different forms, so they remain alive.

O'NEIL: Yeah, if you look at them as stories. I think with a lot of people, it becomes something *more* than stories for them. There's a very smart guy I met at M.I.T. about three years ago. I had just lectured and was at a party afterwards, and I realized, "I'm in a room with probably 20 of the smartest young people in the country." Because M.I.T. had started this media studies program, they were all knowledgeable about comic books, so I thought, "Maybe *they* can answer the question that nobody's ever answered for me: Does anybody know what it is fans want?" Speaking not as himself but in the persona of a fan, this fellow said, "I want you to recreate a part of my childhood for me." And I thought, "Yeah, that's probably pretty much dead-on." But it's impossible—I can't recreate your childhood, because I'm working for a broad audience, and we all had different childhoods. And the characters that don't evolve, die: The Shadow. Doc Savage.

EURY: True. That's an interesting observation about recreating one's childhood. I believe that almost everyone has something from their childhood that they, as an adult, dearly hold on to: music, which can be very nostalgic … and that's one reason why so many people are rabid sports fans—it takes them back to when they were playing, as a kid, in a sandlot or in Little League—

O'NEIL: —or going to games with Dad.

EURY: Exactly! So for some of us, we have that connection to these characters. That's why some very, very dedicated fans have had … *adjustment problems* to changes in continuity.

O'NEIL: And I think that's a career-killer, the need to keep harkening back to the past. People forget that what you're being paid for is to tell stories.

EURY: When you were telling these stories of Superman, you chipped away at much of what readers expected from a Superman adventure: you weakened his powers, Superman became a threat to Earthlings by carrying a plague (#237, May 1971), he operated undercover (#238, June 1971), he failed on a mission and was rejected by the public (#240, July 1971), and he ultimately had to rely upon others for his survival, particularly I-Ching [O'Neil's Asian sage from Wonder Woman, seen in Superman #240–242, July–Sept. 1971].

O'NEIL: That I refer to as my passport to hell, the name I-Ching. Big mistake.

EURY: [*laughs*] Maybe the name, but the character himself, and his philosophy, added a perspective, color, and mindset to comics that had not been previously seen.

O'NEIL: But it was all in the interest of what I'd hoped would be an interesting story. These dimensions were just sources of conflict. Jim Shooter would be the first to tell you that. One of the things I always quote when I'm teaching comics writing is Shooter's dictum that a conflict has to be introduced as early as possible in the story. And then you add to that, but the conflict has to be logical. There's no point in putting Superman up against a pickpocket, no point at putting Superman against a bank robber. They didn't much do that after the early '40s.

EURY: When you were putting Superman through the wringer like this, what did Superman discover about himself?

O'NEIL: Nothing. Superman doesn't really exist. That's a kind of school of literary criticism that I don't understand. Characters don't discover things about themselves unless it's part of the writer's intention to make that a part of the story.

EURY: Fair enough. Then what did *you* discover about Superman?

O'NEIL: I discovered I couldn't handle it very well. I've only really walked away from two assignments in my life, and they both involved Superman, come to think of it: *Superman* and *Justice League*.

EURY: I talked to you about *Justice League* last year [for the book *Justice League Companion*], and now *Superman*, so I'm highlighting sore spots in your career….

O'NEIL: But they're not sore spots. I re-read some of those *Justice League* stories awhile back when DC reprinted them and thought, "I have nothing to be ashamed of. These are okay. For the time, they were probably pretty good."

But I was just having a hellish time doing *Superman*. After about a year, I asked off of the assignment. I don't know how I had guts enough to do that, because I had mouths to feed and no other source of income, but I did it. And within one month, Julie had commissioned that cover from Neal Adams where Superman was pulling that planet around (*World's Finest* #208, Dec. 1971), and I think that was Julie's signal to the reader that "the experiment's over."

Who took over *Superman* after me? I don't even know.

EURY: Len Wein. Then Elliot Maggin. And Cary Bates, who'd previously written *Superman* and had been writing for *Action* for Murray Boltinoff during your stint—which leads me to another question. You called your *Superman* revamp an "experiment." Was this Julie's perception, too? *Superman* was the only title in the franchise edited by Julie Schwartz. Were you content with being in a universe all your own, or do you think the revamp would have been better received if it had been coordinated throughout the other titles?

O'NEIL: I think that was a problem that DC had. There really was no attempt to reconcile this version of the character with the other books'. Julie's Superman was different from Murray's. It was a very compartmentalized company. I was one of the first guys who crossed over to be both a Julie writer and a Murray writer.

This is secondhand, something I'd heard before, but in the '50s each editor staked out his turf and protected it, and that included creative people. So there was no attempt for any other editor to pay attention to what we were doing, and I don't think that Julie expected that there would be. Nobody paid any attention to what the Batman character was doing, either, or any character that crossed over [into other titles]—everybody was doing their own version.

EURY: But Julie eventually took over all of the Superman titles, so if he had that level of control from the beginning, do you think your changes might've had permanence?

O'NEIL: Yeah, I think so. But when I later talked to Julie about the end of the "experiment," as we will call it, he said it wasn't selling. Back then, sales figures were this great enigma because nobody ever saw them. But I think he looked upon it as an interesting thing that ultimately didn't work.

Don't tell Mr. Kryptonite that Denny O'Neil turned K into iron! During the hiatus from filming *The Adventures of Superman*, George Reeves, playing the upright bass, would tour county fairs with a small band and Noel Neill as his vocalist. Between numbers, "Clark Kent" would wrestle one of his musicians who was dressed in this outfit that now hangs in the Metropolis, Illinois, Superman Museum.
Photo © 2004 Cookie Morris.

Before Clark Kent's TV newsman stint (left), the *future* Superman's (aka the Superman of 2965–2966) alter ego, Klar Ken T-5477 (right), broadcast live "Ultra-News" reports, beginning in *Superman* #181 (Nov. 1965). Klar Ken's editor was a computer, PW (Perry White)-5598.
TM & © DC Comics.

EURY: It *did* create some fan buzz during an era when there wasn't a mechanism to do such a thing. I've read that you were interviewed on NBC's *Today* about the Superman revamp. Is this true?

O'NEIL: I've been interviewed on *Today*, but I don't remember being interviewed about Superman.

My first wife pointed out that my timing is always lousy. If we'd done it 20 years later, we'd have actually made some money off of it. [*laughter*] I know that there was some media buzz, but now, it'd make page 3 of *The Daily News*. And all of the fan publications, and the cable news sources, and probably *The New York Times* would have paid attention to it. But at the time, I wasn't being paid any more to write *Superman* than I was to write *Super Friends*. A lot of what I was doing was an interesting job. There was no way to profit from it. There were no royalties. If they paid you for reprints, they did so out of the goodness of their hearts. There were no legal or particularly moral obligations to do that.

A friend of mine in California said he'd just come across those paperback reprints of the first *Green Lantern/Green Arrow* stories. He was thinning out his library because he's living in a trailer, and had asked if I'd like those back, and I was reminded that Neal [Adams] and I had gotten 250 bucks for that, and they didn't have to give us anything.

Danny Fingeroth's [*Write Now!*] magazine interviewed a bunch of us about career management, and there was no such thing back then. Nobody who was thinking about managing their career got into comics. There was no career path—there really was no expectation of any serious profit, at least not by me. I was a freelance writer, and this was a medium that was available to me, and it was a medium I liked. I was also writing magazine stories. I wrote a book on presidential elections. It was *work*. I was probably a better comic-book writer than a journalist. But I wasn't thinking, "Well, in 20 years I will have obtained this position in the comic-book world." There was no reason to believe that the comic-book world would exist in 20 years, much less that we would have hundreds of websites, and magazines—and that the *New York Times*, which had generally ignored this type of popular culture, would begin reporting on what DC and Marvel Comics were doing.

EURY: I think it's interesting that it's the mass-media interpretations of comic-book characters that have made the comic books themselves a subject of interest within the media.

O'NEIL: Exactly. Money always does that. [*laughter*] Those movies have made, probably at this point, billions, and *that* makes it respectable. Also, there's this kind of *delay* that happens with American popular culture where once it's recognized abroad, then it becomes respectable at home—jazz and movies are the two best examples. When I was a kid, jazz was disreputable music. Kay Kyser, Guy Lombardo, Mantovani—*those* were "real" musicians. God forbid, you should have heard what people were saying when the first rock 'n' roll music happened. Movies, when I was in college, were not a valid art form to most people. And comics—I'm totally blown away with how respectable we've become. I never expected this, and I'm not sure I like it.

EURY: For decades, comics were something a boy was supposed to read with a flashlight under the bed sheets, in hopes that Mom wouldn't catch him.

O'NEIL: Yeah. Comics people back then were just about half a step above pornographers. [*laughter*] I thought that Gerry Jones did a wonderful job with his book [*Men of Tomorrow: Geeks, Gangsters and the Birth of the Comic Book*, Basic Books, 2004], which I belatedly read. Actually, just a few years earlier, they *were* in trouble at what became DC Comics for publishing smut. It was certainly not considered an art form.

EURY: Your updating of Clark Kent from newspaper man to television reporter, and contemporizing his wardrobe, got you some news buzz with *GQ*, didn't it?

O'NEIL: [*laughs*] Yeah, I, who have lived my life in blue jeans and T-shirts—

EURY: —you made it into *Gentleman's Quarterly*! [*laughter*]

O'NEIL: We were hired to do a semi-tongue-in-cheek piece on Superman's makeover. I mean, how was I going to *not* accept that assignment?

EURY: Just imagine, with all of the makeover TV shows on the air, what kind of buzz something like that would get today?

O'NEIL: But that, too—none of that really lasted: Clark Kent, the TV reporter, which was Julie's idea, I think. There was a good logic behind it. Television had become more glamorous than print, but somehow the idea of Superman as a print reporter has persisted to this day.

Written by O'Neil and drawn by Murphy Anderson, this fumetti feature appeared in the Nov. 1971 edition of *Gentleman's Quarterly*. Characters TM & © DC Comics. GQ is a trademark of Condé Nast Publications. Courtesy of Murphy Anderson.

EURY: Clark Kent the TV newsman was the one thing from your revamp—or "experiment," as you call it—that lasted the longest, though, because after you left the title, he was still in front of the camera for years.

O'NEIL: Maybe other writers found that easier to work with, or Julie—who was not a very dictatorial guy most of the time—maybe he made that part of the assignment.

EURY: You were able to add dramatic elements by having Clark Kent needing to change into Superman while on the air. It was easier when he could sneak away to a *Daily Planet* storeroom to change….

O'NEIL: Yeah. You could read more into that, if you wanted, and ask if it really made sense for Superman to have a double identity. That is a convention that I, for one, would not want to mess with, but it does raise that question.

EURY: John Byrne played with that during his first year on Superman, with Lex Luthor not believing that Superman would even entertain the notion of a secret identity—he's a god, why would he want to fraternize with the rest of us "guys"?

O'NEIL: That's part of Alan Moore's character closest to Superman in *Watchmen*, that excellent series—

EURY: Ozymandius?

O'NEIL: —yeah. After a while, he couldn't really relate to people. And that was a good writer not ignoring the elephant sitting in the corner, but making a story out of it. The big elephant is, of course, Lois Lane would recognize that Superman is Clark Kent—it's almost not worth joking about. With Batman, the elephant became, "We have a character who refuses to kill, but suddenly movie screens are full of characters who not only kill, but make jokes about it." I just ignored that for years, and finally confronted it with "Knightfall" [the early 1990s Batman storyline where Batman is critically injured and temporarily replaced by a violent surrogate].

EURY: From your perspective, which was Superman's true personality—the Man of Steel, Clark Kent, or the last son of Krypton Kal-El?

O'NEIL: If I would've had to answer that question back then, I would've said Superman is the real person and Clark is the fabrication, but I'm not sure I would answer it that way now. Writers after me, who did a much better job of it than I did, began to explore the psychology of it all—okay, he's an alien, but he was raised in Kansas. Where would his values come from?

EURY: Do you recall any Superman storylines you'd planned on doing but didn't get around to?

O'NEIL: No. I found it very hard to get a Superman story out of myself. When I would do Batman, a script would take me three days, maybe, but with Superman it was pulling teeth.

EURY: With the "super-power" of hindsight, if you could relive the 1970 *Superman* revamp, what would you have done differently?

O'NEIL: I think I did as much as it was possible to do then. As Jack Kirby later found out, there was not that much freedom, and the medium was nowhere near as sophisticated as it is today. I think the readers [then] were smarter and more sophisticated than they were being given credit for. I don't think that anybody was really writing down to them, but the tacit line was, "Yeah, we're writing this stuff for kids, and not the brightest kids in the sixth grade."

But there were people like Will Eisner who, from the very first second, thought that this was a valid art form and that it should be treated as such. But I don't think that the guys who ran the companies thought that. Like when the whole big Estes Kefauver/*Seduction on the Innocent* thing happened in the '50s, most comic-book guys caved in: "We're sorry, we're bad." They didn't know that these kids, the oldest of whom were in their early twenties, had created an art form, had created a mythos. And had even created a language. They were made to feel ashamed of this extraordinary achievement.

EURY: If you hired to revamp Superman today, how would you approach the character?

O'NEIL: I've done Superman in two novels, and found, to my surprise, that I made those scenes longer than I had originally anticipated, because I was enjoying writing him.

I would be more logical. I would lean a lot harder on characterization—the basic trick in writing "realistic" super-heroes is always, knowing what I know about human nature, "If this guy existed, what would he be like?" I would ask myself that question a lot longer and a lot harder now than I ever did back in the '70s.

I don't think it's wrong to scale down the physical powers to a reasonable level. My perception back then was, the more powerful the character is, the more you have to contrive in order to create conflict. And contrivances aren't desirable in stories.

EURY: One thing that has happened in more recent continuity is, instead of Superman's powers being lowered to make him a more believable hero, the villains' powers have been amplified. You now have more cosmic, larger-than-life threats. Darkseid was probably the first at DC, but a number of other characters, including Mongul, Doomsday, and Imperiex—omnipotent, butt-kicking killers and dominators—often come in and make it a job for Superman.

O'NEIL: Obviously, whoever's writing it is addressing the problem, but in a different way.

I may be wrong in thinking this, but there's only so far into that direction that you can go. One of the ways that Mort Weisinger solved the problem was to have a *lot* of stories with Lois trying to figure out if Clark was Superman. Almost sitcom-y situations, meaning, he's got these powers, but that doesn't mean we have to bring them on stage. And I wonder back then if anybody other than Nelson Bridwell really kept track of what Superman could and could not do. Now, I can't imagine a comic-book company that wouldn't pay a *lot* of attention to that sort of thing.

EURY: Absolutely. One of my guilty pleasures, my favorite totally absurd Superman super-power from the Silver Age, was super-ventriloquism, which he used on several occasions.

O'NEIL: [*laughs*] You know, one of the things we haven't talked about is the old *Superman* radio show. During the last year of my office job, I had a collection of tapes of the *Superman* radio show which I would listen to … for a month or two, that was my commuter entertainment. And I think maybe that was a bigger influence upon me than the *Superman* comic books. That was everyday [during my childhood], Monday through Friday, 5:15, St. Louis radio. Comic books were maybe once a week, until I got older and into the habit of trading them with my friends. But we all listened to those radio shows. And when hearing them, not as a six-year-old, but as a 60-year-old, I admired the craft that went into them—how they established everything, every day, without slowing the story down; how many of them, like the very earliest comic books, dealt with social issues, such as the war, and anti-Semitism. I can remember as a kid hearing Superman talk about melatonin, and I think that was the first thing I ever heard about why some people have different skin colors. I couldn't have been more than six, and that was 60 years ago. Listening to those shows was good training for comic-book writing, because it forced me to visualize—you participate in it, through your own visualization.

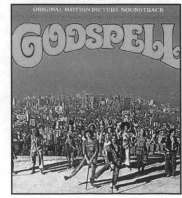

Julius wasn't the only Schwartz making Super-headlines in 1971: Stephen Schwartz's off-Broadway musical *Godspell*, an updating of the Gospel of St. Matthew, debuted that year, featuring Jesus in a Superman shirt.
© 1973 Columbia Pictures.

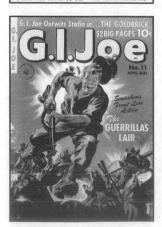

A sampling of Ziff-Davis' comic-book titles.
© 1950-1953 Ziff-Davis.

MURPHY ANDERSON INTERVIEW

Murphy Anderson's (b. 1926) polished illustration style typified the look of DC Comics' Silver Age super-heroes. Influenced by artistic masters Will Eisner and Lou Fine, Anderson began his career in the 1940s drawing comics for Fiction House, and in 1947 became the illustrator of the syndicated newspaper strip *Buck Rogers in the 25th Century*. He was a DC regular in the 1950s as a penciler/inker and inker, making his mark on science-fiction features like "Captain Comet" and the "Atomic Knights." Anderson worked closely with editor Julius Schwartz throughout the 1960s, frequently inking Carmine Infantino on "Adam Strange" (in *Strange Adventures*) and *Batman* and Gil Kane on *Green Lantern* and *The Atom*. He was also the solo illustrator of DC's *Hawkman* and *Spectre* (beginning with the Ghostly Guardian's *Showcase* revival), and drew a wealth of DC merchandising art during that decade. Anderson was tapped to ink Curt Swan with the early '70s revamp of Superman, and their perfectly meshed styles earned the team the nickname "Swanderson."
Recommended reading: *The Life and Art of Murphy Anderson* by Murphy Anderson with R.C. Harvey (TwoMorrows Publishing, 2003).

Conducted by Michael Eury on March 6, 2006. Transcribed by Brian K. Morris.

MICHAEL EURY: Wasn't your first professional connection to Superman an indirect one, through Jerry Siegel?
MURPHY ANDERSON: Yeah, I guess you could say that, because I met Jerry and worked for him at Ziff-Davis before I had any connection to DC.
EURY: This would have been late 1949 or early 1950, right?
ANDERSON: Right. It was my first work for Ziff-Davis' *comics*. I'd been illustrating stories for their pulp mags since 1945 or so. I was contacted by Herman Bollin, a long-time acquaintance and then the art director, I think, of Ziff-Davis, for all their publications. That included *Popular Photography*. I don't know if you're familiar with that magazine.
EURY: I am.
ANDERSON: They were technical publishers, you might say: popular newsstand-type things such as *Radio News* and *Flying Magazine*. They also published hardcover books. They were into many things. They're still around, as far as I know, publishing that type of material — mostly of a technical nature.

Photo © 1997 Heroes Aren't Hard to Find.

EURY: Had you met, or did you know, Jerry Siegel before this?
ANDERSON: No. Herman Bollin, as I say, called me. I was working freelance for him. I'd moved to North Carolina to manage my dad's cabs at that point in time; that was after I gave up on [the syndicated newspaper strip] *Buck Rogers* the first go-round.

Anyway, he contacted me and said that [Ziff-Davis was] starting up a comic-book division, and that they'd hired Jerry Siegel to be their Editorial Director, and would I be interested in doing some work for them? And I said, "Well, I think so," and he got me in touch with Jerry, and Jerry sent me a script. I worked on the script and when I finished it, I decided it was a good time to visit New York and to talk to him at length. He wanted me to come aboard and do a lot of work for him. My work was in the first issue of *Amazing Adventures* (#1, Nov. 1950). I think it was a 32-page book.

[With] the first issue, I learned later, they had tried a little ... oh, I guess you'd call it an "ashcan" version, and sent it out through the mail, and had a good enough response from the people that they'd contacted, so they decided to go ahead with the book.
EURY: According to the *Overstreet Comic Book Price Guide*, the ashcan was an eight-page test-market edition of *Amazing Adventures* #1, sent to subscribers of Ziff-Davis' sci-fi magazines.
ANDERSON: That's right. In that first book, they had something they'd already commissioned from Alex Schomburg, and they asked me to do the one that they called "The Asteroid Witch." That was the name of the story I was assigned, and I believe Jerry wrote it, to accompany a cover done already by Robert Gibson Jones. Does that artist's name ring a bell with you?
EURY: Sure does. Wonderful painter.
ANDERSON: The best! So I did the cover story, Ogden Whitney did a story for them, Alex Schomburg had already done a story, and guess who else did? Wally Wood did one.
EURY: Wow, that *is* an amazing line-up. An aptly titled comic, wasn't it? [*chuckles*]

So, how much work did you do with Jerry Siegel at Ziff-Davis?
ANDERSON: I did quite a bit for him. He asked me to come to New York, if I was interested, and he would assure me of plenty of work. So my wife and I decided to take another stab at me being an artist. We moved to New York, got an apartment—we were married for about a year-and-a-half, two years by that time. So we relocated to Bayside, New York, and I started working for Jerry. He flooded me with all the work I could handle. I did romance, I did weird—you know, kind of weird fantasy, you might say. They had one title they called *Weird Comics*, I think, or *Weird* something or other. [*Editor's note: Ziff-Davis published Weird Thrillers.*] And then later they had others, *Space Rangers* ... *Space Busters*, something like that. I loved *Space Busters*. And they started getting artists from the field and they were at a premium. They were paying maybe, I would say, 30 percent more than most of the other publishers were paying.

EURY: Ziff-Davis must have been serious about its comics line, investing that type of capital.

ANDERSON: That's right. From the story I heard, they put two or three million dollars aside just to gamble, to see what they could do with it, and Jerry got the line started for them. He had a book called *G.I. Joe*. And he had a number of top artists: Dan Barry, Joe Kubert, and others … though I'm not so sure about Joe, whether he was aboard a little later or what. If memory serves, I think Irving Novick was doing work for them, and so was one of my favorite artists, and favorite people—I knew him quite well—Henry Sharp.

EURY: Did you develop a personal relationship outside of the office with Jerry?

ANDERSON: Not outside of the office, but we had a lot of talks.

EURY: I'm curious about Jerry and Superman at this stage of his life.

ANDERSON: He was totally divorced from [DC]. He'd had the lawsuit and lost, you know.

EURY: Understood. But over the years, he grew increasingly bitter as Superman blossomed into a multi-media sensation. Did he show any signs of that during this time?

ANDERSON: No, other than just that he was obviously upset about the whole thing. Anyhow, he came up with an idea of a strip that we would do together and he launched it. It was *Lars of Mars*. Eclipse Comics picked it up some years back [in 1987] and reprinted some of it, and I did a new story for them. I was to have inked it, but I was so busy with [the U.S. military publication] *P.S. Magazine* that I was really starting to get antsy because I wouldn't get it finished on time. So Jim Mooney wound up inking that.

But Jerry wrote *Lars of Mars* and we did two issues of it (#10, May 1951, and 11, Aug. 1951). Evidently, it didn't find a market. The idea of Lars of Mars was that he was a Martian who had come to Earth, and he looked just like an ordinary human, but he had all of his scientific gear with him. And there's a little bit of a corny story of how he got involved with television and played a character that was from Mars. [*chuckles*] And of course, he had a girl, kind of a Lois Lane girlfriend.

EURY: Of course.

ANDERSON: A lot of it had elements of Superman [mixed] with Buck Rogers-type stuff. And essentially, the character was a Buck Rogers guy. He had a flying belt and he looked a great deal like Buck.

EURY: So *Lars of Mars* only ran two issues?

ANDERSON: It never got a fair shot, really. A lot of people seemed to have liked it, but Ziff-Davis had a full line out and they were starting to get pretty bad sales reports, I guess. It was about the time, also, that the Wertham situation started.

EURY: Bad timing for the release of new comic-book titles.

ANDERSON: Ultimately, Ziff-Davis decided they didn't want to stay in comics, so they sold the inventory to St. John's. St. John's did [new] stuff and reprinted stuff. That's when Kubert was involved with Ziff-Davis. Norman Maurer [and Joe Kubert] were partners and they were producing a lot of work for St. John. I think *Tor* came out of that.

EURY: How did you shift from Ziff-Davis to DC?

ANDERSON: I came in one day, delivering a story for Jerry. He always had scripts ready for me, but this time, he didn't. He said he was embarrassed and said the writers hadn't brought the scripts around. He was counting on them and they hadn't brought them in. He said, "I'll get back to you as soon as I can." He couldn't promise me just when, and I panicked. You know, you move to New York and I had an apartment and all the obligations of rent, and I had picked a studio space … I think at that time, with Dan and Seymour Barry. And one thing led to another, so I decided I'd better go looking for work.

So I went home and mid-afternoon, I called on two or three publishers, and I got a job from one whose name I don't want to bring up. That's the only job I ever did for them. And I called on Avon. Sol Cohen was interested, but he had no work. In fact, he just wanted to see what I was doing for Ziff-Davis. Of course, I was reluctant to show any of my work that had yet to be published.

EURY: Understandably so.

ANDERSON: And I contacted DC Comics, and Murray Boltinoff interviewed me and we talked. He said, "You know, I think you're just the man that Julie Schwartz would like to meet, but Julie's not in today. Can you come in tomorrow?" And I said, "Sure," and I came in the next day. That's when I got started with Julie. We got to comparing notes, and learned that we both knew [sci-fi pulp editor] Ray Palmer. Ray Palmer was a good friend of his—

EURY: A good enough friend that Julie borrowed Palmer's name as the alter ego of the Atom!

ANDERSON: —and so we had that in common, and Julie knew all about the Ziff-Davis line, of course. Anyhow, he gave me a script and the first thing you know, I had three or four scripts on hand. Then Jerry called me up and said that the scripts had come in. [*chuckles*]

EURY: And you were already committed at that point.

ANDERSON: Yeah. I had even called on [EC Comics' Bill] Gaines at the time, and they were publishing all their science-fiction line and they wanted me to do work … at least Al Feldstein *said* he did. And I kind of thought it was a polite brush-off. He said, "I don't know how quickly, but we'll get back to you soon." They did call me later, but I had to turn them down because their page rate was considerably less than Ziff-Davis', while DC's was close. In any event, it didn't make sense for me to work for them. I knew that if I got in with that crowd of perfectionists—you know how good they were: Wally Wood, Reed Crandall once worked for them, and Jack Davis—if you get involved with people who work like that, you've got to do your best to stay up with them. But as slow as I was, I had to let that one go by the boards when they called me up. I really hated to turn that down, but economically, I had to.

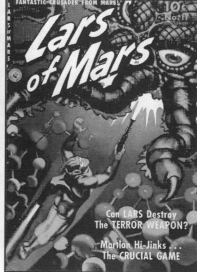

Writer Jerry Siegel and artist Murphy Anderson collaborated on Ziff-Davis' two-issue series *Lars of Mars*. Issue #10 (#1, May 1951) and 11 (#2, Aug. 1951) included the back-up feature "Captain Ken Brady, Rocket Pilot," illustrated by Gene Colan.
© 1951 Ziff-Davis.

EURY: Let's fast forward a few years to the '60s. At this point you had been working with Julie Schwartz for some time. Jerry Siegel wrote for Mort Weisinger back then, but I don't think you were paired with him again … or *were* you?

ANDERSON: Not really, no. I *might* have done a few things that he might have written. DC, for a while, published a little tabloid paper. It was more or less for John Lindsay, the mayor of New York, and I did a pseudo-Superman strip and a couple of other things for them. Jerry might have written those.

Whether Jerry wrote those or not, Mort Weisinger was handling them. That was really my first immediate contact with Mort.

EURY: You illustrated a great deal of Superman and other DC-related merchandising art in the mid-1960s, such as Aurora model media ads and various toy packages for Ideal.

ANDERSON: Yeah, I did a lot of that, through referrals from Jay Emmett and Sol Harrison. As a matter of fact, when DC went public, they had a seat on the New York Stock Exchange, and Irwin Donenfeld had the seat—they had to

advertise in *The Wall Street Journal*, so they had me design an ad for it that appeared in *The Wall Street Journal*.

EURY: I wasn't aware of that … when did that happen in relation to something we've discussed in the past (for the 2002 book *Captain Action: The Original Super-Hero Action Figure*, from TwoMorrows), your drawing box art for the Captain Action line in 1966 and '67?

ANDERSON: Well, that was a little later. See, I had been, for some time, quite friendly with Jay Emmett. I don't know if that name rings a bell with you or not. He was Jack Leibowitz's nephew, and he had started the Licensing Corporation of America (LCA). And when that was absorbed by all the mergers a little later on, he became Steve Ross' right-hand man. But Jay, sometimes through Sol Harrison, would recommend me to his LCA clients. As a result, I did a lot of stuff. When a licensee would have to use a qualified artist, they would send me directly to a client or to his ad agency … that's how Captain Action came about.

EURY: With LCA's supervision of the wealth of Superman, Batman, and other DC merchandise during the '60s, how involved was Jay Emmett with the comics division of DC?

ANDERSON: Jay was still very much a part of DC, on the board up there and all, even though he had LCA going. There were many anecdotes about him. If you remember at about that time, there were a lot of bomb scares … you know … hijacked planes?

EURY: A frightening time, I'm sure.

ANDERSON: It was, and there were some speculations in the general public media about how an explosive might be placed in elevators, and so forth. Jay was a guy with an *outrageous* sense of humor. He was a very nice guy, you know, but he … how to put it … he wasn't impressed with the bigwigs there [*laughter*]. During the height of that bomb scare, they were having a board meeting, and the story is, he came in, late for the meeting, and he cracked the door a little bit and rolled a cherry bomb under the table. [*laughter*] They were ready to kill him. [*laughs*]

EURY: I'll bet! [*laughs*] Today, with the Department of Homeland Security and the NSA, somebody would have carried him off in shackles, wouldn't they?

ANDERSON: No doubt. [*laughs*]

EURY: By the late 1960s you were doing covers for Mort— and as you know, it was Mort Weisinger who first paired you with Curt Swan, inking Curt on some Superman family covers.

ANDERSON: Yeah, I was inking those covers for Mort when he was having problems getting them done, or that was the story, anyhow. Julie would lend me out to do a cover. Maybe Curt would come in the morning and pencil it. He'd get a cover okayed, and pencil it, and two or three hours later, he was done with it. He'd hand it over to me and I could get it inked before the end of the day. That way, they could get a cover out right away.

EURY: There's a misconception among many fans that Julie Schwartz was the editor who first combined the "Swanderson" team, but Mort Weisinger, and later Murray Boltinoff, teamed you two before you worked together with Julie.

ANDERSON: Curt was doing a little bit of work for other editors, when necessary. But of course, mainly, he was doing the *Superman* daily strip; or perhaps, also, the Sunday if it was still being produced at that time. When Curt was doing the daily, two or three different inkers were usually available to ink them, so I never had anything to do with those.

EURY: The earliest covers I found with your inks over Swan pencils on Superman-related material were cover-dated

Murphy Anderson produced much of the super-hero box art for Ideal Toys' Captain Action action-figure line; note that the Superman uniform included Krypto, a Phantom Zone projector, and a piece of kryptonite.
Superman TM & © DC Comics. Captain Action TM & © Joseph Ahearn.

Sept. 1969. There were three published that month: *Action #380,* "The Confessions of Superman," with Superman typing his crimes on a confession sheet; *Jimmy Olsen #123,* with Jimmy's dad on the cover; and *World's Finest #187,* with Superman using his heat vision to burn Batman at the stake.

ANDERSON: That sounds accurate.

EURY: When Mort Weisinger left, Julie Schwartz, as you know, inherited *Superman,* but Murray Boltinoff got *Action.*

ANDERSON: I think that was Julie's election, basically. He wasn't too interested in doing Superman.

EURY: And why was that?

ANDERSON: You know, I think that Julie and Mort were still friends, even though they seemed to not be friendly.

EURY: So you surmise that their relationship made Julie reluctant to edit *Superman*—to avoid competing with what Mort had done, perhaps?

ANDERSON: Yeah. Julie and Mort had started out together as [sci-fi] fans. They had a fan club, and after that opened a business together, a literary agency that represented mostly mainstream writers in science fiction. Julie, I guess, was the chief worker because Mort, about that time, got the editorship of some pulp magazines.

EURY: That's an interesting theory, Murphy.

Before you became Curt Swan's primary inker, that distinction was probably George Klein's.

ANDERSON: No, no, George Klein did a lot of work on Curt's pencils, and John Forte did, too, I think. Also, I believe Shelly Moldoff was involved in inking Curt's work during the period we're talking about.

EURY: I didn't mean to suggest that he was Swan's *only* inker, but Swan and Klein had the most definable Superman style of the 1960s, the Silver Age of Superman.

ANDERSON: There's another guy, I'm trying to think of his name…

EURY: Stan Kaye?

ANDERSON: Exactly. And Stan Kaye as well, because Stan did an awful lot of work on him. But he and George were both inking Curt and, I guess, Wayne Boring's stuff before that.

EURY: Wayne Boring's art did occasionally appear in Superman stories throughout the '60s, although the '50s were more his era.

ANDERSON: I'm lumping that all in with the [*Superman*] strip, too, you know.

EURY: Did you know Stan Kaye and George Klein?

ANDERSON: Sure did … and I liked both Stan Kaye and George Klein very much. They were both regular gentlemen and really nice friends.

EURY: Any impressions of how their particular styles meshed with Curt's?

ANDERSON: No. I mean, Curt's pencils were very clear

Original artwork to two early Swan/Anderson covers, *Action #384* (Jan. 1970) and *Lois Lane #105* (Oct. 1970).

TM & © DC Comics. Art courtesy of Heritage Comics.

A Swanderson page from *Superman* #238 (June 1971).

and very direct, and they didn't need any real input or creative input from the inker other than just a good line—doing their own thing, of course, with blacks, folds, and things like that, in their particular style. But the basic structure was always there. Curt was such a completist, you know. He left no questions in your mind as to what something was or how it should be done.

EURY: Murray Boltinoff considered you and Curt to be the perfect match, too, because he ran your bios together on a text page in *Action* #394 (Nov. 1970).

ANDERSON: Perhaps. Murray, of course, was the brother of the well-known cartoonist Henry Boltinoff, who was also a good friend and, incidentally, one of my sponsors when I joined the National Cartoonists Society.

EURY: I wasn't aware of your connection to him.

ANDERSON: Murray served in the Army during World War II. He really loved the Army and was a great military buff. And if you remember, Murray edited a lot of the DC war books and did an excellent job on them.

As much as I liked Murray, personally, and as an editor, he was really, essentially, a pulp-oriented editor/admirer. And I've often felt that the guys working in [Murray's and editor] Jack Schiff's department were all very much oriented toward the pulp-type of story. I don't think their imaginations ranged quite as far as Julie's.

EURY: Most readers took notice of you and Curt Swan as a team on the "Kryptonite Nevermore" issue of *Superman*, #233 (Jan. 1971), which is today considered a major milestone.

ANDERSON: Was that Denny O'Neil's story?

EURY: You're absolutely correct—Denny's first issue. Kryptonite was destroyed and Superman's powers started to diminish over the storyline. Did this get a lot of media coverage, to your recollection?

ANDERSON: I'm not sure about that. I know Julie was trying to do things to perk the readers' interest up in Superman, to make Superman more human … kinda funny to say that about Superman.

EURY: You teamed with Denny on a Clark Kent fashion story for *Gentleman's Quarterly* around this time.

ANDERSON: It was during those years.

EURY: That was an interesting venue for you and for the character. Also, Clark Kent was a TV newscaster. How did that idea sit with you?

ANDERSON: [*chuckles*] Oh, it was fine with me. I wasn't penciling it, so I didn't have to worry. Curt did all the research and stuff, I just had to roll with the flow, you know.

EURY: Concurrently, Jack Kirby came on board to do *Jimmy Olsen*. Since Jack was based in southern California, his appearances in the New York offices must have been rare.

ANDERSON: Right.

EURY: Did you know Kirby? How did you feel about redrawing his Superman and Jimmy Olsen faces?

ANDERSON: I met him during that period for the first time (at a convention, actually), and I was able to apologize to him for having to change the faces. The order came down, you know. [The Kirby-drawn faces] weren't looking enough like Curt's Superman.

EURY: Was that order directly from Carmine Infantino?

ANDERSON: I guess. I'm not really sure. Sol Harrison was involved in it, too, probably.

EURY: I hope I don't make you feel awkward about this, because I know you were doing what they asked you to do, but I suspect you were apprehensive about changing Jack Kirby's art.

Murphy Anderson's inking hand in action, in 1973.
Photo © 1973 DC Comics.

ANDERSON: Yeah, well, I didn't like to do that because I knew Jack's work from the time when I was a kid. It was never my cup of tea to try to work like that. You know, that "Bigfoot" kind of stuff. Not Bigfoot, exactly, but greatly exaggerated action, contorting figures as he did, the foreshortening and stuff, didn't turn me on. But I admired his work. I especially like what he did on *Blue Bolt*.

See, what a lot of the people copying Kirby didn't understand or just wanted to overlook, was the fact that he was a master draftsman. Even though he exaggerated, he really knew how to draw. Young guys came along, trying to copy [him], but the trouble is, they didn't have that underpinning. They didn't know how to draw well enough to really bring off that stuff. [Jack Kirby] was a master draftsman, just no question about it.

EURY: In the late '60s/early '70s, you were also also inking Bob Brown on *Superboy*.

ANDERSON: Yeah, I did that regularly.

EURY: I consider Bob Brown an unsung hero—solid work, but underappreciated.

ANDERSON: Yeah, he was one of DC's most effective adventure/super-hero artists, with great drawing abilities, no question about it. But I always felt there was a certain influence of Kirby on *his* work, too. I don't know how to describe that, but he was another guy who really drew well, and he was a very dependable aritst, a very good artist.

EURY: Absolutely true.

Let's go back to Curt Swan. You and he were friends.

ANDERSON: Right.

EURY: Was Curt a fast penciler?

ANDERSON: He was fast for the type of work he was doing. But I think more than anything else, he just put the time into it. He'd get a cover knocked out in a couple of hours, so you can't say that's not fast. That *is*, you know?

EURY: Oh, yeah. Are there any particular stories, issues, or covers that you recall that you did over him that just resonate with you?

ANDERSON: No, not really. You know, if you wanted to take a particular one and put it under my nose, I might be able to comment. [*laughter*] When you're inking, you're not as involved in the storyline as you would be if you were doing the entire job. So mostly, it was just a job, but it was a pleasure to work on his stuff as opposed to some others that I had [to ink] from time to time.

EURY: When you came on board to ink his stories, there seemed to be a synergy between the two of you, and Curt was revitalized—that's not to suggest that his work had suffered prior to your inking him, but he *had* been drawing Superman for a long time.

ANDERSON: Well, I'm not sure what Curt's reaction was to my work. Having worked both sides of the street, I can also understand things as a penciler. When I was penciling stuff, I never cared much for what any inker did to my work, to be honest with you. It wasn't that there was anything *wrong* with it, it's just that they couldn't interpret it and carry it on like I felt it should be carried on.

And so I'm sure Curt had those feelings. But sadly, [DC] would never let him ink and he was a good enough inker to have inked his own stuff, no question about it. But they were looking for a certain attitude and flair, I guess. I think, perhaps, that my work reflects my love of the medium, my love of the characters and the comics. A lot of artists never really had a great interest in comic books. They were interested in making [a living] at it, but they all had aspirations to go on to do something better. We all had that, but I was satisfied working in comics.

EURY: And readers are satisfied with, and appreciative of, that fact.

So, Murphy, you were a hard person to replace when you left DC in 1973 to go back to *P.S. Magazine*, because Julie brought on a succession of inkers over Curt: Bob Oksner, Dan Adkins, Tex Blaisdell, Frank Chiaramonte, Al Williamson, even.

ANDERSON: I think, actually, Curt liked Al's work about the best of anybody. I can see that because with a lot of Curt's stuff, I'm sure he was trying to get—oh, how to put this—sort of a *Rip Kirby/Mandrake* look to his work.

EURY: You did return to ink Curt a few times— and one of my favorite instances was *Superman* #411 (Sept. 1985), the Julie Schwartz birthday issue. [*Murphy chuckles*] Do you have any stories about how tough it was to produce that comic behind Julie's back?

ANDERSON: Well, it wasn't really *that* difficult. I just had to squeeze in the time to ink it, since I was fully engaged with *P.S. Magazine*.

I guess you know Todd Klein, the letterer.

EURY: Of course.

ANDERSON: Todd lived close by and he also worked in the Production Department at DC, and he would often act as courier, carrying rush stuff out to our company (Visual Concepts). I'd meet him in the morning to give him a ride down to the train station, a matter of five or six blocks he didn't have to walk, and repay him a little bit for couriering Visual Concepts' work. He snuck those pages out of the Production Department. Curt would get them done, managing somehow to hide them from Julie. Bob Rozakis was masterminding this.

EURY: This sounds like a spy movie. Did Bob Rozakis issue trench coats, hats, and sunglasses to you guys?

ANDERSON: No. [*chuckles*] Curt manufactured reasons for coming in … or maybe he would mail his stuff in, I don't recall.

EURY: Having known Julie, I'll bet he was a difficult person to trick.

ANDERSON: Oh, yeah. Julie would encounter me then, and I'd probably be bringing some stuff in for Bob. I'd say, "I'm delivering color separations to Bob." [*laughter*] And Julie would see that I wasn't able to do work for him if he wanted me to.

EURY: I presume that from your perspective, Curt Swan is the number-one Superman artist.

ANDERSON: Yeah, I always felt that. The only possible exception to that, is to go back to Joe Shuster himself, you know. I loved his approach to Superman. I really thought that Shuster was great on that stuff, and that's partly because he was such a big fan of Roy Crane's, and I was, also. Something a lot of people never really noticed—and I once asked Jerry Siegel about it, and he confirmed what I suspected— is that he also was a big fan of Hal Foster's. His Superman figure was largely his version of Foster's Tarzan figure. You look at the head of Tarzan and compare him to Superman, or better still, to the Roy Crane Captain Easy head. You can see how it all kind of melded together to make Shuster's version of Superman.

EURY: What do you recall about Shuster and Siegel getting their pension and their creator credit with Superman?

ANDERSON: I don't believe it would have been possible without the guy I was talking to you about before, Jay Emmett.

EURY: Oh, really?

ANDERSON: Yes! Because Jay masterminded, on the Warner Bros. side, that whole thing. It came from Warners more than you know. I'm sure that if not for him, it wouldn't have happened. He was Jack Liebowitz's nephew, and he and Steve Ross were really good friends.

EURY: When Neal Adams told me of his role in this process, he said that he was very supportive of Warners, remarking that he tried to keep this a win-win situation.

ANDERSON: I'm not trying to downplay what Neal did. He and Jerry Robinson were instrumental in getting the whole thing to work, but it took Jay Emmett, who was more or less in Jerry's corner, [to make it happen]. Even though he was related to Liebowitz, there was no question in my mind that Jay was very instrumental in that whole deal. At least that's my conviction. I can't back it up with anything other than that I know he was involved in it.

EURY: Is there anything else you'd like to add about Superman?

ANDERSON: Have you seen the book by Gerard Jones [*Men of Tomorrow: Geeks, Gangsters and the Birth of the Comic Book*, Basic Books, 2004]?

EURY: It's on my bed stand, but I haven't read it. It's funny you should mention that … I'm actually going to start reading it tonight. [*Murphy laughs*]

ANDERSON: It's quite good.

EURY: It's a history of comics, from the perspective of Jerry Siegel's plight, correct?

ANDERSON: Yes. Jones gets in a lot of things in there that I haven't heard about, but they make good sense. And then, of course, I think there are some gaps in what he tells where I might be able to bridge up a few holes. My knowledge is not firsthand in every case, of course, but I was privileged to information from people, like Julie and others, behind quite a bit of stuff that went on.

EURY: I'm about to start reading it tonight, and I'm looking forward to it.

ANDERSON: You may find that you won't be able to put it down until you have read it … start to finish!!

Foster's Tarzan, Crane's Captain Easy, and Shuster's Superman
Tarzan © Edgar Rice Burroughs.   Captain Easy © NEA   Superman TM & © DC Comics

NICK CARDY INTERVIEW

Born Nicholas Viscardi, Nick Cardy (b. 1920) honed his craft during the Golden Age on series like *Jungle Comics* and *Fight Comics* for the Eisner-Iger Studio, and illustrated the newspaper comic strips "Lady Luck" (for Will Eisner's *The Spirit*) and *Tarzan*. He gravitated back to comic books in the 1950s, working for a variety of publishers including DC (*Congo Bill* and *The Legends of Daniel Boone*). His star rose at DC in the 1960s during his long and lauded stints on *Aquaman* and *Teen Titans*, as well as shorter but highly regarded runs on the offbeat Western *Bat Lash* and the Batman team-up title *The Brave and the Bold*. In the early 1970s Cardy was selected by publisher Carmine Infantino as DC's principal cover artist, his skillfully composed covers gracing numerous titles for much of the first half of the decade.

Recommended reading: *The Art of Nick Cardy* by John Coates with Nick Cardy (Vanguard Productions, 1999).

Conducted by Michael Eury on February 10, 2006. All original artwork accompanying this interview is courtesy of Nick Cardy.

Courtesy of Glen Cadigan.

MICHAEL EURY: For the first half of the 1970s, you were *the* cover artist at DC Comics. Do you have any idea of how many covers you drew during this time?

NICK CARDY: John Coates, who wrote my biography [*The Art of Nick Cardy*], is a fan of my art, and when he was doing my book he sent me these three thick volumes, each one about three inches deep, with all of the covers I did. I think I must have done four or five hundred.

EURY: I can tell you how many *Superman* and *Action* covers you did—because I counted!

CARDY: Oh, you did?

EURY: I did. From 1972 through early 1975, you did 36 *Action* covers, 32 *Superman* covers, plus various *Jimmy Olsen*s, *Superboy*s, *Legion*s, *Superman Family*s, *World's Finest*s, *Justice League*s, and other random titles thrown in for good measure—and those are just the Superman-related ones! Of course, you did lots of *Batman* covers, plus horror....

CARDY: You know, whenever they write something about the first issue of *The Witching Hour*, they say it has Neal Adams and Alex Toth—but nobody mentions that I did the first cover! [*laughter*]

When [Jim] Steranko came to town, my publisher printed something to promote an appearance of different artists. He had Carmine Infantino, Joe Kubert, Steranko, and a few of the others. There was a dash line under those names, and then they had Murphy Anderson, Nick Cardy, and a few of the other guys. I told my writer, "I must be in the grade-B movies." [*laughs*]

EURY: Oh, I don't know about that! A lot of people think you're A-list. Murphy Anderson, too!

CARDY: My publisher *idolized* Steranko. So my writer went up there to the show and said, "You know, Nick Cardy said you put him in the grade-B category!" And Steranko, who was present, blew his stack. He turned to the publisher and said, "What's the *matter* with you? This is Nick Cardy," and he was heaping praises on me, which were nice to hear. But I don't care if I'm at the top or the bottom of the page, so long as people enjoyed my work.

EURY: Maybe because you were so prolific with these covers during the '70s, some people might have taken your art for granted. I certainly don't mean that in a negative way. Some artists didn't produce as much work as you, so when they *did*, it was out of the ordinary. But you were there, month in and month out, with these wonderful covers all over the place. Now, years later, we look back at these pieces and realize, "Wow, Nick Cardy produced some *amazing* work."

CARDY: The reason people don't relate to me as much is, before I started to do all those covers, I never did the big super-hero-type things. I never did *Superman* or *Batman* or *Fantastic Four* or *Captain America*—I just did *Teen Titans* and *Aquaman* and *Bat Lash*, and a few others. I think that's why people don't remember me as well, because I did the secondary characters, the ones DC weren't promoting, you see.

A 2006 Nick Cardy Superman pencil drawing.
Superman TM & © DC Comics.

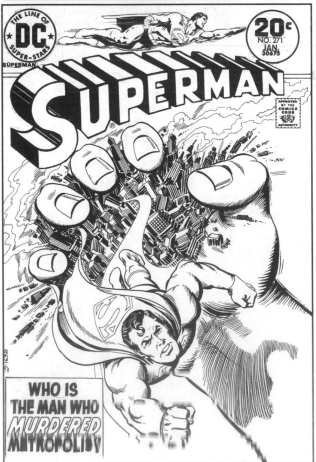

EURY: Didn't you enjoy some publicity in the mid-'60s when *Aquaman* was a TV cartoon?

CARDY: Well, when *Aquaman* was first started, DC's publisher at the time was Jack Liebowitz. And he said, "We're going to have animation that's done in Australia." They talked about sending me there [to work with the animators], but someone decided, "No, we can do it here." So there went my trip to Australia! [*laughs*]

EURY: But they obviously were working from your rendition of Aquaman, because the cartoons look like you had your hand in them.

CARDY: It was *so* long ago—if you asked me what I had for breakfast, I wouldn't know [*laughter*]—but what I did was, with each character, draw a profile, a three-quarter view, and a full-face view, and the animators would carry it on from that, you see. And I did all the animals, from different views, so [the animators] could move them on from there. But the animators didn't do the cartoons the way I'd wanted, though.

EURY: So, you did all those covers in the '70s, many of which featured Superman, but how many Superman *stories* have you drawn?

CARDY: I never drew a Superman story.

EURY: I knew that. I just wanted to hear *you* say it.

CARDY: I could've done it, but I just never did. Carmine Infantino used to say, "Of all my artists, Nick Cardy can draw anything."

EURY: I agree. And I'm sure you remember, you *did* draw a couple of Superman *guest-star* appearances—he was with the Justice League in *Aquaman* #30 (Nov.–Dec. 1966) and *Teen Titans* #25 (Jan.–Feb. 1970), both of which you drew—but his "on-screen" time was brief. Do you feel like you've missed out, not getting to do any Superman continuity?

CARDY: I just never had much interest, you know.

EURY: Were you ever offered a Superman story by Mort Weisinger or Julie Schwartz?

CARDY: No. Mort Weisinger and I would exchange greetings when he passed each other in the hall, but that was it. I never worked for Weisinger.

Mort Weisinger reminded me [*chuckles*] of the rabbit in *Alice in Wonderland*. You'd see him and he'd go, "I'm late, I'm late. Oh! There's the phone!" And he was always running back and forth. I think it was just his way of saying, "I don't want to talk to you." And there were a lot of people that didn't care for him.

EURY: He had a style that rubbed some people the wrong way.

CARDY: Now, with Murray Boltinoff, *he* was a nice guy. Julie Schwartz—I never worked with him until the end [of my DC career], on some of the covers. When I'd do covers for the books that Julie was handling, like *Batman* or *Superman*, we'd do them in Carmine Infantino's office. When Carmine Infantino would do a layout, he'd say, "This is the layout for the cover," and I'd say, "Okay, let me work it up. I think I have an idea from that." We'd work together. Carmine always told me, and he told other people, that he respected my work. He very seldom gave me criticism. He'd more or less let me run wild. So when he edited the covers, sometimes I'd say, "Well, I like the design, but can we just add this here, or move this around, for more composition?" Things like that. And he'd say, "Sure," and we'd work it that way.

But in my book, Julie Schwartz wrote this tribute to me, and he wrote, "I remember once, Nick Cardy came in with a cover and showed it to Carmine. And Carmine said, 'This isn't the layout I gave you.' And I said, 'No, this is better.' And so Carmine said, 'You're *fired*!' So I turned, and I left. So Julie Schwartz turned to him and said, 'You know, Carmine, that *is* a beautiful cover.' And Carmine said, 'Okay, call him back.'"

Well, it turns out that at one of the conventions, Carmine and I were there and I told him what Julie wrote. And Carmine said, "That's crazy. You know I always loved your work. I never gave you any criticism. I never said anything like that." So Julie Schwartz was in a different booth at the con where he was selling his book, his biography—he was sitting next to Irwin Hasen. So I said, "Look, let's walk over to Julie." And I said, "You know, Julie, that article you wrote about me…" And Carmine said, "Yeah, *that* never happened." Well, Julie looked up, very nonchalant—he always had to have the last word—and he said, "Ahhh, you know, it was a good story anyway!" He'd just made it up! [*laughter*]

EURY: That *is* a good story. [*laughs*]

Nick, you mentioned Murray Boltinoff. You worked with him for years—you also did a lot of Superman covers for him, for *Action*, *Superboy*, and *Superman Family*. You really liked working with him, didn't you?

CARDY: Yeah. You know, I was at a convention, on a panel, along with Arnold Drake, who's a good writer. And Arnold said, "The best editor up there was Murray Boltinoff. He was really good, but they just sort of overlooked him. Whenever a new artist had to be interviewed, they always passed this job to Murray Boltinoff." He wasn't in the social circle, I guess.

EURY: What do you remember about when Jack Kirby was at DC, on *Jimmy Olsen* and his *New Gods* books?

CARDY: Now, Kirby—Kirby was a very dynamic artist. He went "slam-bang" and did some things that were very effective. But I don't know where the hell he found these muscles he put on these characters! They were never in the right place. [*laughs*] But Kirby had his own style.

EURY: Do you think he was too "Marvel" to fit in at DC?

CARDY: DC was a lot different from Marvel, you know. Kirby was an artist with a certain aura, and they accepted him at DC because [his style] was very effective. DC wanted all their characters to be drawn in the same way, from the model sheets. But each artist has his own style.

As a freelance artist, I never met Kirby or knew what was going on with him at DC … everything I knew was hearsay. What I was told was that Carmine asked Kirby to come up there to DC. I don't know how long he was there, or what the ins and outs were, but I have a feeling that some people think that Kirby was slighted up there.

EURY: Jack Kirby was reportedly unhappy over Al Plastino or Murphy Anderson redrawing his Superman and Jimmy Olsen faces. You know, that happened to *you* when Murphy Anderson redrew the Superman face on your cover to *Superman* #264 (June 1973, "The Secret of the Phantom Quarterback").

CARDY: Well, I've told Murphy Anderson this, but …you *know* how many covers I've done. I could draw Superman's face while standing on my head! [*laughs*] But there was one time when I drew Superman's head where he was looking down or something, and I couldn't get the head right. I did it three or four times, but I had a mental block—I just couldn't get the head right. It was similar to a blind stare. And so, I turned it in and was off on another job, and the editor said, "Let's go have Murphy do this one." And [Anderson] put the head on Superman. It still wasn't the head *I* would've put in—it wasn't *my* head, you know. [*laughs*] That was the only time I can remember that anyone ever corrected my work. After 40 years, I guess I'm entitled to *one* mistake. [*laughs*] But when I did Superman, I did him as best I could, with my own anatomy.

There was a time when all of the top artists—Neal Adams, Gil Kane, Carmine Infantino, George Tuska—penciled some *Teen Titans* stories, and I inked them, in *my* style, you see? It's a lot different when you're inking somebody else's work.

EURY: Tell me how you composed a *Superman* cover.

CARDY: When I did the *Superman* covers—or *any* of the covers—the first thing I did was take the area where I was drawing and make these little impressionistic, little short-hand figures where the action would be. Say, a line going this way, where the figure would be. And then, say, if Superman was going from the lower left-hand corner to the upper right-hand corner, at that angle, I would build on that angle to make the composition.

I don't know if you're familiar with classical music, but you probably know Beethoven's *Fifth*.

EURY: Of course.

THE SUPERMAN MYTHOLOGY:
100-PAGE SUPER-SPECTACULARS

Cars may have gotten smaller during the gas rationing of the 1970s, but DC's reprints were super-sized! Squarebound treasure troves called *100-Page Super-Spectaculars* were readers' tickets to DC's rich past, priced at only 50 (later 60) cents. After a few experimental issues published in 1971 the 100-pagers returned, becoming so popular during the early to mid-1970s that several DC titles adopted the 100-page format each issue, with a mix of new and old stories.

Superman-related 100-Page Super-Spectaculars

DC-7 *Superman* #245 (Dec. 1971–Jan. 1972)

DC-10 *Adventure* #416 (Mar. 1972)

DC-12 *Superboy* #185 (May 1972)

DC-13 *Superman* #252 (June 1972)

DC-15 *Superboy* (Mar. 1973)

DC-18 *Superman* (July 1973)

DC-21 *Superboy* (Oct. 1973)

Superman #272 (Feb. 1974)

Superman Family #164 (Apr.–May 1974)

World's Finest #223 (May–June 1974)

Superboy #202 (May–June 1974)

Superman Family #165 (June–July 1974)

World's Finest #224 (July–Aug. 1974)

Action #437 (July 1974)

Superman #278 (Aug. 1974)

Superman Family #166 (Aug.–Sept. 1974)

World's Finest #225 (Sept.–Oct. 1974)

Superman Family #167 (Oct.–Nov. 1974)

World's Finest #226 (Nov.–Dec. 1974)

Superboy #205 (Nov.–Dec. 1974)

Superman Family #168 (Dec. 1974–Jan. 1975)

World's Finest #227 (Jan.–Feb. 1975)

Action #443 (Jan. 1975)

Superman Family #169 (Feb.–Mar. 1975)

Superman #284 (Feb. 1975)

World's Finest #228 (Mar.–Apr. 1975)

CARDY: He has the theme, [*singing opening notes from Beethoven's* Fifth Symphony] "buh-buh-buh-*baah*." Then he repeats it: "buh-buh-buh-*baah*." Then he has some other music, and then he'll have the "buh-buh-buh-*baah*" here and there—a lot of repetitions of that, so he never lets you forget the main theme.

So like that, if you have a figure going at one angle, it becomes the main line, the main "theme." Then you have a lot of other smaller figures, or other little compositions like clouds or scenery, going at the same angle at different places in the picture, like repetitions of the main them. And then you have these little angles that go against it, that move the picture around. It all adds up to a sound composition, you see.

With my covers, I wanted them to be simple and powerful. If you're at a newsstand, and you have rows and rows of comic books, you want your cover to have a two-second impact that catches the reader. And if you have a lot of confusing covers, the people are not looking at the drawings, they're just looking at the titles. But if you have a drawing that catches your eye—that's what *I* always wanted, for simplicity.

In other words, if you're looking at a display of a lot of colorful T-shirts, with all those colors and patterns, and you see a white T-shirt, it attracts your eye from all those colors. Or a *white* T-shirt with a bright red dot in the center—it's like a bull's-eye.

EURY: What are some of your favorite Superman covers?

CARDY: One of my favorites is where Superman's in the forest, and there's these two kids holding on to legs (*Superman* #257, Oct. 1972). A beam of sunlight is coming down from the sky, and his hands are resting on the shoulders of these kids—"There's nothing to worry about." But underground, there's this alien blasting his way up to the top. I liked that, because when you want something ethereal, anything straight upright—a cathedral-like effect, or a going-to-heaven effect, sitting on a throne—if you put something at an angle, you'll have action.

EURY: That's also an effective cover for reader participation. You let the readers in on a secret that the characters don't yet know.

CARDY: Oh, yes.

EURY: I'm amazed that you can remember these cover details so vividly over 30 years later.

CARDY: Well, you know, certain covers remain favorites. There's a *Teen Titans* one (issue #16, July–Aug. 1968) that's a big book, and Wonder Girl's being drawn into the book by these aliens. There's another one, an *Aquaman*, "When The Sea Dies!" (*Aquaman* #37, Jan.–Feb. 1968).

EURY: How did you go from drawing interiors to becoming a cover artist?

CARDY: After *Bat Lash* was cancelled, Carmine told me he didn't want my talents, didn't want *me*, to be wasted. So he said, "I've got to get you to do covers." [Editor's note: Cardy's critically acclaimed *Bat Lash* premiered in *Showcase* #76,

Original covers to *Action* #426 (Aug. 1973) and 435 (May 1974).
TM & © DC Comics.

Aug. 1968 and continued in *Bat Lash* #1–7, Oct.–Nov. 1968 through Oct.–Nov. 1969.]

EURY: Did you ever have any Superman covers that were rejected, that you had to redo?

CARDY: No, no, I never did. The closest I came was when I had that block with that Superman head and it had to be redrawn by Murphy Anderson.

Speaking of Murphy Anderson, you know, when I used to go up to DC, they'd have this radio on with this announcer. I'd always hear this deep voice on the radio. So one time when I went in and went to the room where the colorists and the artists were, I heard that voice and was looking around for the radio—but it was Murphy Anderson!

EURY: [*chuckles*] I *knew* where you were going with that story, because I've known Murphy for a long time—we're both from North Carolina—and he has the best voice, the deepest, most resonant voice, a voice that belongs on radio.

But it was a little strange for you, seeing a Murphy Anderson-drawn head on your Superman's body....

CARDY: Well, it wasn't disturbing, but I still can't get over what happened to me then, having a mental block and not being able to draw that head. I just couldn't get it to work. I like Murphy—as a man, and as an artist—but *his* Superman head didn't work on that cover, either. [*laughter*]

EURY: From your own critical perspective of your work, how did your art on your *Superman* covers differ from your earlier interior artwork?

CARDY: A cover is like doing a single painting, but a story is like directing a mini-movie. My work on *Superman* was a lot slicker than when I drew *Teen Titans*. My work was a lot tighter in the '50s, and it started loosening up when I did *Daniel Boone*. Then I tightened up on *Aquaman* [in the early '60s], but then I loosened up on that toward the end. With *Teen Titans*, I started a little tight and I loosened up, and the same with *Bat Lash*. I finally got what I felt comfortable with by the time I did the *Superman* covers.

With my covers, I wanted *impact*. There's a *Titans* cover where Aqualad is pissed off at Robin and is socking him (*Teen Titans* #28, July–Aug. 1970). Now, Aqualad is moving like an arrow towards Robin. Robin is bending back—he just got hit. The other figures are straight, in the background, like a wall, to support Robin. And then I left everything in the background *white*. Had I put any [background] color on that cover it would have slowed down the action. All the color was in Robin's costume and Aqualad's costume.

EURY: You weren't *coloring* your covers, were you?

CARDY: No. The covers would come to DC in lots, from different artists. Sol Harrison would hand them out to different colorists. If I was around the colorists, I'd tell them . . . say, I had a cover where there should be warm colors, I'd say, "Try to keep the colors in this range." And the next time I'd see it, I'd have a *purple* cover that's completely wrong. And I'd say, "How come you did a purple cover?" "Well, the color you wanted, he had it last month on the cover and we didn't want to use it." In a way, that made sense, but *purple*, for a warm cover? I don't think you have that kind of problem today.

EURY: Most covers today are pinups, and many are paintings, that are visually appealing but, unlike what you did on *Superman*, don't reveal anything about the story inside.

CARDY: Well, if you'd look at some of the covers that Carmine did, they didn't always show what the story was about. [*laughs*] I always felt the covers should be part of the story. It's got to be pertinent for you to be showing that.

EURY: You made another contribution to Superman's history: After you left DC in the mid-'70s, in 1977 you drew movie-poster roughs for *Superman: The Movie*. What can you tell me about that?

CARDY: When I was working with an agency, I was asked to do some pencil layouts for *Superman*. I did Trevor Howard and all the people on the council on Krypton, then I did Gene Hackman—I did loads of them, but there were only three or four that I could salvage … the studio kept the rest.

EURY: There's a great promo shot from *Superman* with Chris Reeve pointing skyward—wasn't that from one of your drawings?

CARDY: Yeah. I did hundreds of those sketches.

EURY: But none of those were used as the *Superman: The Movie* poster....

CARDY: For the first movie's poster they used the big shield [the "S" insignia] of Superman, and it was glowing, with flashes. I heard that Bob Peak, one of the best illustrators in the business, got $30,000 to do that Superman movie emblem. They never used the characters I did for the poster … but at least they paid me for them. [*laughs*]

Cardy's original "bullet" art for The Superman Family #164 (Apr.–May 1974), the first renumbered issue of the former Jimmy Olsen title, and the published version.

TM & © DC Comics. Art courtesy of Heritage Comics.

Cardy drew another Big Red "S" on the cover of Marvel's Crazy magazine #16 (Mar. 1976).

One of Nick Cardy's 1977 layouts for *Superman: The Movie*, and the Christopher Reeve promotional photo it inspired. Reprinted with the permission of the artist.

Cardy's sketch for "Licenseman," the Danish government's super-recruiter for its TV licensing campaign. Reprinted with the permission of the artist.

EURY: I'm sure the money paid by Hollywood dwarfed the rates you'd been used to in comics.

CARDY: At the time I was doing covers for DC, the rate was $45 a page or $60 for a cover. I think I got paid $2,000 for those Superman roughs—there were some 13" by 20" sketches, some of various sizes.

There was a lot of competition for the movie work. There were over 400 top illustrators—who did art for magazines, advertising, and movie posters—who were considered. To get a better chance of getting work, I thought that if I did humorous illustrations, that might help cut down the odds. There'd be maybe three artists in the humor field doing a finished version of a movie poster. We'd each get, say, $5,000 for these paintings. If the producers liked yours, you'd get an additional $5,000.

EURY: What's the strangest Superman drawing you ever did?

CARDY: Remember the Uncle Sam "I Want You" poster?

EURY: Sure. By James Montgomery Flagg.

CARDY: Yeah, Flagg. Well, there was this Danish outfit that paid me to draw a Superman-like figure pointing at the audience like Uncle Sam. In Denmark, they have to pay taxes to watch television each month. So this was a piece commissioned by the government to get people to pay those taxes. It had the character flying out of the television, but instead of it being Superman it was their leading singer, their Frank Sinatra. They sent me photographs of him, but said, "The hair's not right." So they flew me to Denmark to redo his head. [*laughs*]

EURY: I'll bet you're glad they didn't send Murphy Anderson to Denmark to do it! [*laughter*]

You didn't collaborate with any other artists on covers, did you?

CARDY: No. No one ever inked my covers. I inked all my covers.

EURY: Is there anything else you'd like to add about your Superman covers?

CARDY: Whenever you'd see a cover that Carmine had some influence with, the streets were always *slanted*. I did a cover where these soldiers are carrying Superman (*Superman* #265, July 1973).

EURY: That's a great cover. That was a downshot, wasn't it?

CARDY: Yeah, a downshot. I liked that, because it was very effective, especially with the rain. But that same pose was also used on an *Aquaman* cover (issue #30), carrying Aquaman the same way. I think Neal Adams did a similar cover. And they were all laid out by Carmine. Sometimes with Carmine, if he had a cover idea that was successful, he'd like to repeat the same pose. Maybe it was because he knew what would sell. Carmine was good on cover layouts. His layouts on *Flash* covers helped the sales on that book. Let's not forget that Carmine Infantino was a great comics *and* cover artist.

It's like what Julie Schwartz used to say, "You put a gorilla on a cover, and it sells well." Maybe that was true, because even *I* did some covers with gorillas, like the one in the courtroom, with a gorilla lawyer yelling at a gorilla jury.

EURY: Any closing words about your *Superman* covers?

CARDY: Carmine also knew that having a girl on a cover would sell. Me, I had the one where Batgirl is falling down from a building (*Superman* #279, Sept. 1974), and Superman flying up toward that.

I tried to go a little more forceful than Curt Swan. His figures were nice, but they were static.

On *Superman*, I tried to keep the faces open, not putting too many blacks in. Each comic book, and its various heroes, has its own mood and tempo. My *Teen Titans* covers were light, but my *Brave and Bold* covers were heavy, they were dark.

Each cover was a challenge. It was a challenge making each new cover forceful in design and layout. My Superman covers were a loving attempt to humbly add impact.

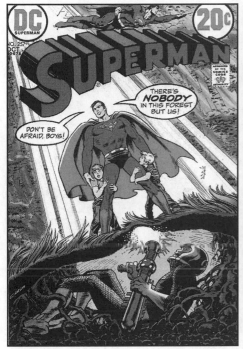

Superman #257 (Oct. 1972).

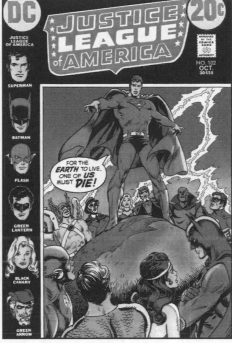

Justice League of America #102 (Oct. 1972).

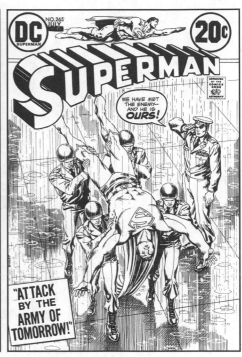

Superman #265 (July 1973).

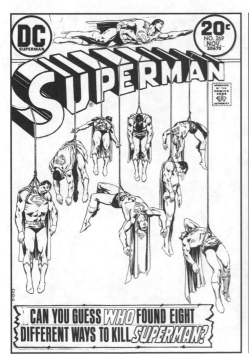

Superman #269 (Nov. 1973).

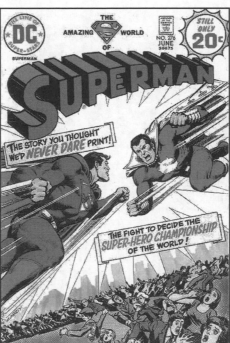

Superman #276 (June 1974).

Superman #279 (Sept. 1974).

THE SUPERMAN MYTHOLOGY:
THE GREAT PRETENDERS: WOULD-BE SUPERMEN

Were the Super-girls, -pets, and -Kandorians of Superman's Silver and Bronze Ages not enough, from 1958–1986 there were more Super-types buzzing the pop-culture skies than you could shake a Phantom Zone projector at! This collection celebrates many of these Mimickers of Steel, as well as a few characters that found the adjective "super" too enticing to ignore.

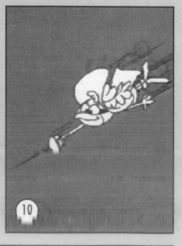

1. Mighty Mouse. © Viacom.

2. Super-Chief. TM & © DC Comics.

3. Underdog. © Total Television.

4. Super-Goof. © Disney.

5. Supercar. © ITC.

6. Herbie as the Fat Fury. © 1965 ACG.

7. Super Green Beret. © 1965 Lightning Comics.

8. Archie as Captain Pureheart (aka Pureheart the Powerful). © Archie.

9. Atom Ant. © Hanna-Barbera.

10. Super-Chicken, from TV's *George of the Jungle*. © Jay Ward.

11. Super President, star of his own short-lived TV cartoon. © DePatie-Freleng.

12. Paul Lynde as Super (Uncle) Arthur, *Bewitched*. © Sony.

13. Blaxploitation classic *Super Fly*. © Warner Bros.

14. Archie's adaptation of the movie *The Super Cops*. © MGM.

15. *Monty Python's Flying Circus'* "Bicycle Repairman" sketch. © BBC.

16. Former DC Comics office manager Dick Milgroom in George Reeves' Superman costume. Photo by Jack Adler. © 1975 DC Comics.

17. Dan Aykroyd as Nazi Superman; *Saturday Night Live*. © Broadway Video.

18. Action flick *Superchick*. © Marimark.

19. *Sesame Street*'s Super Grover. © CTW.

20. Bill Murray as Superman; *Saturday Night Live*. © Broadway Video.

21. Barbra Streisand's album *Superman*. © Sony.

22. Super Richie (Rich). © Harvey.

Len Wein Interview

Len Wein (b. 1948) is a one-man comic-book Who's Who. After breaking into the business as a writer in the late 1960s, he went on to write and/or edit virtually every major character for both DC and Marvel, also serving as Marvel's editor in chief in the mid-1970s. Known for his flair for dialogue, Wein co-created Swamp Thing, the Human Target, Wolverine, and the new X-Men, and has written *The Phantom Stranger*, *Batman*, *Superman*, *Justice League of America*, *The Amazing Spider-Man*, *The Incredible Hulk*, among many others. His most enduring contributions to the Superman mythos are S.T.A.R. Labs and Mongul.

Conducted by Michael Eury on February 7, 2006.

MICHAEL EURY: You first wrote *Superman* for Julie Schwartz after Denny O'Neil left the title; how did you land the assignment?

LEN WEIN: I guess I was next in line. I have a feeling that most of the assignments I received in my up-and-coming days happened because I seemed to be the next guy in line.

EURY: Had you voiced any particular interest in writing Superman?

WEIN: Nope. My preference was always Batman.

EURY: What was Julie's attitude about *Superman* at the time, since his "experiment" of revamping the character wasn't working?

WEIN: I can't speak for Julie, obviously, but with my decades-old memories, I think his problem was that Mort's stories had become very, very gimmicky. There was "Superman's an old man this time," or "Let's make him really fat," or Lois trying to figure out who he is for the ten millionth time. Julie was a *story* guy—more than anything, he was a story guy. I think this "experiment," as it's been called, of de-powering Superman a little bit was his way of doing the type of stories you couldn't do with a guy who could move the Earth.

EURY: Were you comfortable with other aspects of the revamp? For example, Clark Kent being a TV news broadcaster?

WEIN: It made some sense, but it was really never what Clark Kent was about. Trying to update the character—that happens with every character, even now. Everybody's constantly being revamped.

I'm a traditionalist. There were elements of the character that could have moved forward with the times, but there are certain aspects that make him who he is. I think Clark Kent ought to be a reporter. Newscasters aren't reporters—newscasters sit there and read off of a monitor. As a reporter, Clark could go anywhere, and do anything. As a newscaster, he had obligations—what if a volcano was about to erupt, just as he was about to deliver the six o'clock news?

EURY: Good point. Clark as a TV reporter inadvertently saddled the series with another gimmick—Clark having to sneak away from live broadcasts in order to become Superman.

WEIN: In *one* story, it's a fun bit—try to find a way to get off camera and save the world, then get back on camera ... but that would only work, in such a position.

Courtesy of Glen Cadigan.

Also, frankly, despite the fact that Christopher Reeve has arguably my all-time favorite super-hero moment on film, in the first *Superman* film, where he demonstrates that Clark Kent and Superman look *nothing* alike, if you're on TV every day, for *thirty minutes* a day, eventually people are going to go, "You know, that guy *does* kind of look like Superman!"

EURY: Denny O'Neil professed difficulty in writing Superman, while Elliot Maggin and Cary Bates found their voices through the character. What about you?

WEIN: He was always a secondary assignment for me. Despite the fact that I was writing Superman—there was an attitude of, "Oh, my God, this is the granddaddy of this whole megillah... We wouldn't be *in* this business if not for him!"—I liked writing *Superman*, but I *loved* writing *Batman*.

EURY: Was there pressure connected to writing the flagship character of the company?

WEIN: No, Julie was never that way. But I had the same reaction I had when Marvel assigned me *The Amazing Spider-Man*. At that point I was the third or fourth regular writer the book had in its run.

It was intimidating to man the flagship character of the line—*personally*, not professionally. Julie never made *Superman* difficult—he was always there to support me, to back me up, and help me get through it.

EURY: Describe for me a standard *Superman* plotting session with Julie Schwartz....

WEIN: It was give and take ... that was the best part. I often came in with a rough idea, or sometimes I'd hit him with a few ideas, and we'd give and take. "Here's what I want to do this month." "That sounds cool, *but...*" Julie would throw things out, and I'd throw things out—I don't mean "out," but that's the way a lot of them ended up. We'd go back and forth until we were both happy with where we were going. That was his favorite part of the process as an editor, the plotting.

EURY: Did he make many changes to your scripts?

WEIN: No ... I did. [*laughs*]

I think I our relationship changed when I did a story for him called "Whatever Happened to the Crimson Avenger?" They were doing this "Whatever Happened To?" series as a back-up [in *DC Comics Presents*], and he and I plotted this very detailed story about the death of the Crimson Avenger, about how he saved the Holland Tunnel. Except when I got home and started to write it, I realized that the plot we had worked out didn't work.

So I re-plotted the story entirely—now it had to do with explosives, and a tugboat—he died saving the city in a whole different way. So I turned in the script. Julie started reading it, and he got about halfway through it, then he stopped and went, "Wait a minute! This isn't the story we plotted. It's a whole different story!" I said, "Uh-huh." He said, "Why did you *change* it?" And I said, "Well, I started to write the script we'd worked out, and realized it didn't work, so I *fixed* it." And he looked at me with what has now come to be called the "*Springtime for Hitler*" look. You know, eyes wide, jaw slack, unable to believe what you've just seen or heard. [*laughs*]

Then he started to smile, and then he started to laugh. And I said, "What?" And he said, "You know, you're the *first* writer who's ever done that, and I couldn't be more pleased. I used to work with Gardner Fox, and every so often Gardner would turn

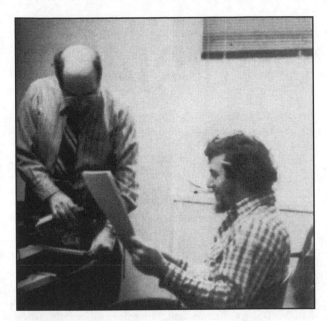

The writer (right) and his editor, mid-1970s.
Photo © 1975 DC Comics.

in a script that would not work at all, and I would ask, 'Why does this script not work?' And he'd say, 'Well, that's the way we plotted it.' *You're* the first guy who ever *fixed* something without me telling him to do so!"

EURY: [*laughs*] What a great story.

WEIN: Yeah. The relationship evolved from there.

EURY: At the time you did that Crimson Avenger story you had been writing for quite a while, and I suspect Julie trusted your instincts and talents more than he might have when you first did *Superman*.

WEIN: Julie would always edit one of my scripts that day, when I brought it in, so I could go over it with him. There are famous stories from some of his old '40s and '50s writers where, if you'd look at the script, you'd discover pencil lines through every line of dialogue, with new dialogue written above it … it was all Julie's dialogue. But on the very first script of mine where he changed something, he changed a word of dialogue, but then said, "I don't get it." And I said, "What?" And he said, "I changed this line, and now it doesn't work anymore. Why doesn't it work?" And I looked at it and said, "Oh, I know. You took out a three-syllable word and put in a two-syllable word." He said, "So?" I said, "I write for rhythm. There's a definite beat to how I write. If you take out a three-syllable word, you've got to put in a *new* three-syllable word." So I said, "Here, try *this* one." And he went, "Oh. Wow." [*laughter*]

So as we worked together longer, he'd changed less and less. Occasionally, he'd go, "Ha! I can put a *period* here instead of a *question mark*! I can put a double-dash here!" He would just love to do that, because it was fun. There was joy in that between us.

He turned to me one day and said, "You know, if I've got Curt Swan coming in to pick up a *Superman* script on a Friday at noon, I [usually] need to have the script on the previous Friday. But if Curt's coming in to pick up one of *your* scripts on Friday at noon, I need to have it in by *eleven* that same day." [*laughs*] That was the greatest compliment any editor ever gave me.

EURY: That's wonderful. Len, I'm curious about how you came up with S.T.A.R. Labs, which first appeared in *Superman* #246 (Dec. 1971). What's S.T.A.R.'s backstory?

WEIN: It was my own idea. No one suggested it. It was one of those fan moments. I mean, *every* month Luthor or Braniac or somebody else would attack some different scientific lab in Metropolis. Dear God—how many can there be?! [*laughs*] So I thought, "If they're going to attack a lab— it should be a *chain*! It should be a series of labs containing the stuff [*laughs*] that somebody intended to *steal*." So I came up with a chain of labs called Scientific and Technological Advanced Research and it spiraled from there.

EURY: Let's talk about Lex. Your second issue of *Superman*, #248 (Feb. 1972), featured "The Man Who Murdered the Earth!," one of my all-time favorite Lex Luthor stories. From your perspective, what made the Earth-One Luthor Superman's number-one enemy?

WEIN: Well, he was that before I got there. I don't believe for a moment it had to do with the hair. I always thought that was silly. I think it was best covered in what I believe was the first episode of *Lois & Clark*, the whole thing about Luthor being the "big guy in the highest tower in Metropolis who could look down on everyone." And Superman says to Luthor after their first confrontation, "If you want me, I'll be around. Just look up." And suddenly, Luthor isn't the tallest man in Metropolis.

EURY: So which Luthor do you prefer: The super-scientist or the white-collar criminal?

WEIN: The businessman. He makes much more sense. Marv [Wolfman] always used to say, "I loved the Earth-One Luthor. He would spend five million dollars to build a giant robot to steal $50,000 from a bank." [*laughter*] That never made any sense, none whatsoever.

EURY: You created one of the most powerful Superman villains of the 1970s, the Galactic Golem. What's the story behind this character?

WEIN: He came about because I needed somebody Superman could hit! [*laughs*] The problem with Superman's rogues' gallery was, they were all *thinkers* … they were scientists, or guys who built toys. With the Golem, he could hit Superman, and Superman could hit him back. Same thing with Mongul—he provided direct contact in a Superman villain. Most of the stories with Superman villains, Luthor especially, involved him making something to deal with Superman. Superman would stop it, swoop down and grab Luthor by the collar, and take him off to prison.

EURY: Do you think that during Superman's earliest days there might have been a reluctance to create an enemy that Superman could mix it up with?

WEIN: I just don't think that anybody ever *thought* of it. Remember my comment about Julie's reaction to my changing the script: "Nobody ever did that before!"

If you remember the old Superman stuff, especially Mort's, they always dealt with *puzzle* problems. *I* always wanted to see Superman duke it out with the aliens! But because Superman was so powerful, there was this approach, "I've become an old man. How do I deal with this?" Or, "I weigh a thousand pounds. How do I get around like this?" Here's a circumstance, a situation for Superman—how does he solve that problem? As opposed to, here's a threat that he can just hit with all his might, and have a great time doing it.

EURY: You're right. During the Weisinger years, there were very, very few menaces that actually posed a physical threat to Superman. One of my favorites is a rather goofy character, but one I love dearly, the Composite Superman. He made Superman and Batman duck for cover!

TM & © DC Comics.

WEIN: Yeah, he had the powers of the entire Legion of Super-Heroes. He was a threat.

EURY: What a great premise, but it lacked a satisfying resolution, because with the Composite Superman's two appearances, it took a gimmick to get Superman out of this dilemma.

WEIN: That's why I liked the Galactic Golem, because he gave Superman somebody he could deck, and vice versa. My thinking was, "Superman is powered by a yellow sun. Well, here's a character who's powered by every star in the sky."

EURY: Earlier you mentioned Mongul, the super-villain you introduced in *DC Comics Presents* #27 (Nov. 1980). Some people assume that Mongul was a Jim Starlin creation.

WEIN: Well, he had Starlin visuals, but he was my creation.

EURY: It's taken a couple of decades for that character to firmly take a toehold in the DC Universe. He was revamped early in his career....

WEIN: They got past his Warworld concept, as well.

EURY: But Warworld followed the character *outside* of comics, since it appeared in the *Superman* animated series.

I'VE SMASHED YOUR INVULNERABLE FORTRESS, SUPERMAN!

NOW I'LL SMASH YOU!

"FURY OF THE ENERGY-EATER!"

Nick Cardy's original cover art to *Superman* #258 (Nov. 1972), featuring Len Wein's hittable villain, the Galactic Golem

TM & © DC Comics. Art courtesy of Nick Cardy.

EURY: When he appeared a second time on TV, in *JLU* [Cartoon Network's *Justice League Unlimited*], they adapted Alan's story [Alan Moore and Dave Gibbons' *Superman Annual* #11, 1985], "For the Man Who Has Everything."

EURY: I'm a little puzzled over which Mongul is in comics now. The original one died, and his son took over—

WEIN: —his son who looks *exactly* like him, and is also named Mongul!

EURY: How about that? [*laughs*] Sort of like the George Foreman family....

WEIN: Whoever killed him, it was a terrible mistake. It was stupid. I don't remember what the story was, or who wrote it, but I remember I thought, "No, you've taken one of the few physical threats to Superman and gotten rid of him?" Now, I would've simply had him get better. I wouldn't have created a son. I would've had [Mongul's] neck broken, but have him come back as a tougher villain.

EURY: He would have been quite ticked off, too.

WEIN: But somebody else thought it'd be a good idea to bring in his kids—Mongul and Mon*girl*. But for all intents and purposes, the Mongul currently in the books is essentially the same character, but I like to think, not quite as potent.

EURY: Did you approach Superman differently when writing him in *Justice League of America* as opposed to writing his solo adventures?

WEIN: You have to think about *balance* in the JLA. One of the things that always drove me crazy in the old Gardner Fox [*JLA*] stories was that the Martian Manhunter was a regular. The Martian Manhunter essentially had *all* the powers of Superman, plus extra ones—the shapeshifting, the invisibility, and all that. And what was the super-power he used almost exclusively in *JLA*? His super-breath. [*laughs*] Gardner was afraid that if he used all his Superman-like powers, what's the point in the rest of the Justice League?

EURY: What would often happen in those early *Justice League*s is that Superman or Martian Manhunter would quickly encounter kryptonite or fire, to weaken them and give a more level playing field to the rest of the JLA.

WEIN: I could be remembering wrong, but I don't think I opted for kryptonite or fire too often.

EURY: After a handful of issues you disappeared from *Superman* for seven years. Why did you depart from the title in 1972?

WEIN: I think that's when I went to Marvel.

EURY: So there were no problems with working on *Superman*....

WEIN: There was never any frustration in working with Julie Schwartz. Julie Schwartz is beloved by me, and by most of the folks in the industry. Years before I met him, he affected my life. He literally changed my life. It wasn't just because I loved his stories. Because of his letters columns, I met Marv. Because of his letters columns, I discovered comics fandom, which he helped create, because he had been one of the guys who had created science-fiction fandom. He helped invent fanzines. He'd done these things *long* before I met him. And he became a dear friend, and taught me much about what I know as a writer. Here's a guy whose impact upon my life cannot be measured.

I would never have any problems working on *Superman*, or working with Julie. Every once and a while, we'd have a little fit, like anybody does. I remember one particular script, a plotting session, and it was a back and forth where he must have thrown out 25 ideas, and I nixed every one of them. I said, "No, this doesn't work, no, no, no." So finally, he looked up at me in sheer frustration and said, "What the *hell* am I bothering in coming up with all these ideas if all you do is throw them away?" And I said, "If we didn't figure out which ones to throw away, then we couldn't figure out which ones to keep." [*laughs*]

Page 2 of Wein and Neal Adams' unfinished Superman anti-pollution tale, from *The Amazing World of DC Comics Special Edition* #1 (Feb. 1976).
TM & © DC Comics.

Between his *Superman* stints Wein wrote these landmark Marvel issues.
© 2006 Marvel Characters, Inc.

EURY: Len, you came to Superman's rescue to help him overcome one of his greatest failures by enlarging the Bottle City of Kandor in *Superman* #338 (Aug. 1979). Do you consider this to be your most noteworthy addition to pre-Crisis Superman lore?

WEIN: This sounds weird, but I almost hope not. It seemed at the time that it was the time to do it. Although I like the ending of the story, I'm sorry I did the story.

EURY: Oh, really?

WEIN: Yeah. One of the things that has happened in comics over the last 20 or 30 years is, we're an industry, certainly editorially, of people who grew up on these books. And all of us, at some points of our careers as editors or writers, have said, "Oh, God, I am so tired of *that*," whatever "that" is, so we changed it or dropped it. But I don't think that any of us realized at the time that what was old to us was new to somebody just coming in. When I was doing Superman, in every issue that I could possibly manage it, I went out of my way to do a shot where Clark sees something about to happen, and pulls his shirt open and says, "This looks like a job … for Superman." Even now as I say it I get chills down my back. It's *the* seminal moment of what Superman is. Some people say, "But everyone's seen that." Well, everyone *hasn't* seen it.

So I came at Kandor thinking: "I'm so tired of this. It's been 20 years, 30 years, of that stupid city." So I came up with a story I thought might have some emotional impact. I pitched it to Julie and he said, "Sure," and we did it. And I regret that, because the idea of a bottle city of tiny people is a much cooler idea than what I left it as.

EURY: Often editors and writers, in efforts to reenergize a series, stray too far away from the original concept—and when they do, they always have to go back to the beginning.

WEIN: Also … how much was done with Kandor after I left it, and left the Kandorians, on a planet where I said they had to rebuild their civilization?

EURY: Some, but not much … that was in 1979, and just a few years later the whole thing was rebooted. And before long, they all hit the bottle again. [*laughter*]

So, what do you consider to be Julie Schwartz's most significant contribution to the Superman legend?

WEIN: His *run* on the book. I don't think there's any single moment. As with everyone, you go through and find what works and what doesn't work. He was adventurous to *try* some of these things: to try Clark Kent, TV reporter; to try the sand-monster and to do power him to some degree, to try and do things that *hadn't* been done before.

EURY: Julie's run is unmatchable—which I find curious from a newly discovered perspective. After speaking with so many people about Superman, it's become clear to me that Julie initially took the *Superman* assignment with some degree of trepidation. Did you ever get that impression?

WEIN: Julie never turned down a challenge. As intimidated as I was when I took over as writer—"Oh, my God, this is Superman!"—I think that even with Julie, there was that initial intimidation: "Can I make this work?" But with all things, you get past it.

EURY: You introduced the Earth-One version of Superman's Golden Age rogue J. Wilbur Wolfingham in *Superman* #341 (Nov. 1979). A W.C. Fields-like con man seemed an odd match for Superman in the late '70s—what appealed to you about this character?

WEIN: Two things: (A), I loved writing W.C. Fields, which, as you say, is who he really is, and (B), I love bringing back old characters to see how they play today. I did the same thing with … oh, how do I put this politely? Oh, yeah—*weird-ass* Batman villains. [*laughter*] Crazy-Quilt, the Kite-Man, characters like that, just to see if they could be made to work in today's world. Same with Wolfingham.

We had come up with an issue with two stories with similar titles—"The Man Who Could See Tomorrow," or something like that. So we did the lead story first, but not the Wolfingham one, although he wound up on the cover, as I recall. Then I had half a book to fill. This was the first time I had to write a two-story issue of *Superman*. So I remembered the character and thought, "Let's do a comedy story for a change." I thought, "If readers like him, I'll bring him back again."

You'll notice he never came back. [*laughter*]

EURY: You were the first writer to realize Chemo's value as a major villain, pitting him against the Man of Steel in *DC Comics Presents* #4 (Dec. 1978) and *Superman* #342 (Dec. 1979) and #370 (Apr. 1982). I take it you're a Metal Men fan.

WEIN: Oh, yeah, I love the Metal Men. The first time I used Chemo was in that Superman/Metal Men team-up I did for *DC Comics Presents*, like you said, where I also used an old Hawkman villain, I.Q. I realized after doing that first story that here was a villain that was a physical match against Superman, so I kept bringing him back. No one else was using him, and I was free and clear to use him. I didn't violate anything about what the character was—if there had ever been another *Metal Men* book, they could have taken him back easily, without any harm.

EURY: There are a few Ross Andru/Mike Esposito *Metal Men* covers with Chemo that are etched into my memory. Chemo's a visually dynamic villain.

WEIN: He's an unstoppable force.

EURY: Sort of the DC Universe's equivalent of Godzilla.

WEIN: Yeah, or the Hulk, without the rage. The big, unstoppable, essentially elemental character. There's not a whole lot of thought process going on, but enough to make him a danger.

EURY: Chemo was just dropped on a city as a bomb in *Infinite Crisis* #4 (2006). You showed others at DC that Chemo had value as a character outside of *Metal Men*.

WEIN: That's true of a lot of characters. I usurped Hawkman's Gentleman Ghost, as another example, and used him as a Batman villain.

EURY: If you had written the Earth-One Superman's last adventure instead of Alan Moore (the imaginary tale "Whatever Happened to the Man of Tomorrow?" in *Superman* #423 and *Action* #583, Sept. 1986), how would you have concluded Superman's story?

WEIN: I couldn't possibly have done a better job than "Whatever Happened to the Man of Tomorrow?"!

ELLIOT S! MAGGIN INTERVIEW

In 1971 a college treatise by Elliot S! Maggin opened the door for him at DC Comics. He quickly impressed editor Julius Schwartz and soon, *Superman*'s readers, with his insights into the Man of Steel's heroism, a philosophy he also exhibited with other characters, particularly Green Arrow.

One of the foremost Superman writers of the 1970s and 1980s, Maggin's contributions to the Superman mythos include his novels *Last Son of Krypton* and *Miracle Monday*.

Conducted by Michael Eury via e-mail on January 26, 2006.

MICHAEL EURY: Mr. Mxyztplk became Mr. Mxyzptlk because of a letterer's error, and your middle initial permanently earned an exclamation point after your own script typo. Are you, like Mxy, an imp from the Fifth Dimension?
ELLIOT S! MAGGIN: I'm not. I'm from the '60s.
EURY: I know you've told the tale many times, but the story of how you started writing for Julius Schwartz is fascinating. For the record, would you mind sharing it?
MAGGIN: I did a term paper at Brandeis for a history course on communications media. The point of the paper was to illustrate the premise

Photo © 1975 DC Comics.

that the comics medium was a viable political tool, as it was (maybe still is) being used extensively in South America. So I told the professor that the bulk of the paper would be an original script for a comic-book story. I wrote the script, wrote an explanation of what I meant for it to illustrate, and when I handed it in the professor was disappointed. He said he understood that I was going to draw it, too. He gave me a B-plus so I'd be disappointed, too. It was a Green Arrow story called "What Can One Man Do?," where Green Arrow decided to run for mayor of Star City, and I quoted Hemingway and everything. I thought I deserved better, so I sent the script to Carmine Infantino, who was the publisher at DC at the time. Carmine didn't read it, but gave it to Julie Schwartz. Julie didn't read it, but gave it to Neal Adams. Neal reads a lot. He told Julie that if he bought it, then he, Neal, would draw it. Julie read it, liked it and sent me a letter saying so. I shortened the script to his specifications, DC bought it and it turns out it's the only comic-book story I've written that Neal drew. [*Editor's note:* It was published in *Green Lantern/Green Arrow* #87 (Dec. 1971–Jan. 1972).]

So about five years later I got an invitation to come back to my old college to give a talk on making a living as a freelance writer. I went, and it turned out it was a terrible night. In New England you have these ferocious storms called nor'easters that can tear paint off your walls and enamel off your teeth with little knives of frozen rain. We had one of those that night. It turned out that fewer than a dozen people showed up for my little lecture, and one of them was my cousin Dave who lived nearby. Mostly the people who came wanted to know what Brandeis was like during the Vietnam War and did I know any of the famous people who'd gone to school there (Dave knew Louise Lasser and I kind of knew Abbie Hoffman, but only by phone). I talked about how I got into the comics business for awhile, but I spent most of the lecture gawking at this stunning young woman who sat near the front of the room. Finally she asked

me a question: who was the professor who gave you the B-plus, and I told her his name. "Oh, really" she said, "that's my husband."

I suspect there's a moral in there somewhere, although it eludes me.

EURY: Rumor has it that "Must There Be a Superman?," your first script for the character (*Superman* #247, Jan. 1972), was inspired by Jeph Loeb, then a young fan. What's the origin of this tale?
MAGGIN: The rumor seems to be true, but for the life of me I've been trying with no success to remember the incident for years. I've known Jeph since he was about 12, I think. His stepfather was a vice president of the university when I was in school and I was very fond of him and his family. When I sold my first story I went down to New York to see Julie, who asked me to think about an idea for a Superman story. This was right out of the box and people think that's odd these days, but Julie was new to Superman and almost no one was much excited about Superman in those days. Julie had no idea what he wanted to do with him—other than to put his best writer, Denny O'Neil, on the case.

But Denny didn't much like the character either. I did. So I went to dinner at Jeph's house and I mentioned that coming up with a few ideas for Superman stories was what I was working on just then. That's as much as I remember. Apparently Jeph wrote me a note a few days later with an idea for a story called "Why Must There Be a Superman?," which was precisely along the lines I thought I would have loved to take the character, but never thought they'd let me. I had often thought about the relationship—and I knew there needed to be one—between Superman and the Guardians, for example. But Jeph outlined this whole idea in this letter and a week or so later I went to see Julie with about eight or ten germs of ideas scratched on a legal pad and the story Jeph worked out was the one Julie pounced on. I remember I was thrilled that he liked the idea, it was the one I liked best and thought there was no chance he'd let me play around with the fundamental premises of the character like that. But I just didn't remember that Jeph had been involved with it. When he told me years later that he'd essentially been my collaborator I was horrified. I would at least have liked to give him some credit at the time, so now I do just that every chance I get, to the point where Jeph's embarrassed whenever it comes up. "Imagine how I feel," I keep telling him.

EURY: How did that question—"Must There Be a Superman?"— shape the many Superman stories you later wrote?
MAGGIN: It was the fountainhead, the pivot point on which I stood to determine what Superman's place in the Universe really was. The

BUT YOU MUST NOT COUNT ON A *SUPERMAN* TO PATCH UP YOUR LIVES EVERY TIME YOU HAVE A CRISIS-- OR DISASTER--

YOUNG MANUEL HERE-- HAS THE RIGHT IDEA! WHEN THE REST OF YOU BACKED DOWN TO HARLEY, MANUEL REFUSED TO KNUCKLE UNDER...

premises I set out in that one story pretty much defined the fundaments of everything I ever wrote about the character afterward.

Julie and Denny's approach to Superman at the time was to "de-power" him; to make him less powerful than he'd grown to be in order to bring him down to a more human scale. I disagreed with that approach. I disagreed with it, and still do, down to the ground. Every time since that anyone's gotten the chance to redefine Superman—and there've been more than just a few of these chances since 1970—the first thing they've thought to do was "de-power" him. Julie said, at the time, that he can't juggle planets any more, but he can juggle buildings. I didn't and don't see the point. It's been my point of view that Superman stories are not about power. They're about moral and ethical choices. Each one asks the question: *What does a good person do in a given situation if he's got all the power in the world?* Writers and artists and editors—and producers and directors and actors, for that matter—don't get to limit Superman's powers. Once you do that it's not the character you think you're dealing with any more. Every "superman" in every culture—Zeus and Odin; John Henry and Paul Bunyan; Beowulf and

Arthur—gets to decide the answer, in his own context, to that question. The success or failure of a storyteller's attempt to convey that is based on the degree to which the character gets to illustrate that for himself. If you start by "de-powering" such a character, then your mythology is flawed. You don't know which archetype it is you're really dealing with.

EURY: Describe a standard plotting session with Julie Schwartz.

MAGGIN: Predecessors of mine like John Broome and Gardner Fox, legend says, used to spend a day on a single story, going to lunch, working things out incident-by-incident, panel-by-panel, so that when they left the building Julie knew exactly what he would be getting on his desk a few days later. I never did that. In fact, I don't think I ever had lunch with Julie until I was in my thirties.

At the beginning I'd come in with half-a-dozen or more ideas and we'd vaguely work out the basics of the one that best struck his fancy. After awhile, I'd come to a plotting session almost cold. I'd say I ran into Kurt Vonnegut on the street and he told me it'd be all right if I put him in a Superman story. Or did you ever think that maybe some of the time travelers that went back in time to save Lincoln actually succeeded, and every time they do they push back the time and circumstances of Lincoln's death a little bit? Or what if Luthor's been breaking out of jail in mid-March because he's got this ritual he does every year that has nothing to do with Superman or anything we ever thought of, and what might that be? Or whatever.

So depending on his mood, Julie would yell at me for awhile and tell me I was a plot vampire, sucking all my ideas out his head, and we'd talk story for an hour or two and I'd go home and write. The trade-off for both of us for this relative freedom was that about a third of the time I'd come back with a story that wasn't quite the way Julie had envisioned it and—again depending on his mood and his deadline schedule—he might send me back to rewrite a little. After awhile I caught on that as often as not, asking me to do a rewrite was a way to keep me out of other editors' offices while Julie ate through his backlog a little. He always, always, always got his books in under deadline, which was a talent I envied when I became an editor sometime later.

EURY: Did Julie often edit your dialogue?

MAGGIN: He tried. We'd have yelling fights over that. I think I learned pretty much everything I know about story structure from Julie—although he claimed he didn't have any formal understanding of it. But as to dialogue, it seemed to me that the reason I was working for this guy was mostly that he felt out of touch with the quirks of the jargon of his young audience. I was there to provide that. When Julie wanted some quick repartee he'd get combative with me and jot down the best stuff I'd come up with. When he wanted to get some nerdy innocuous line for Clark he'd ask Cary Bates. Cary was from Ohio. Julie was from the Bronx, so he was good at inducing headaches.

EURY: In today's Superman continuity, and on TV's *Smallville*, Clark Kent is the "real" person and Superman is his manufactured identity—yet when you were writing the character, the opposite was true. Elaborate on this—why Superman needed the Kent guise, and the challenges, or perhaps limitations, his alter ego posed to you.

MAGGIN: I take issue with your premise. I like the *Smallville* show quite a lot and I don't think they subscribe to the notion that Clark is "real" and the super-powered guy is somehow an act. Clark Kent in *Smallville* is, just as we were at that age, wrestling with figuring out who he is. Eventually—as you did and I did—he'll catch on.

Superman is a mythological archetype. The hero is, by definition, the best self that the character is capable of being. Repeatedly in mythology we see stories of the hero presenting himself at first in a disguise—occasionally a disguise so vivid that it fools the hero himself. When he was the age of the Clark character in *Smallville*, King Arthur thought he was a lowly squire, the

---

METROPOLIS MAILBAG

S-784

Dear Editor:
I am very happy that new and interesting things are happening with *Superman*. He has passed a turning point in his life, and that is always intriguing.

Superman has always been the most interesting of all the DC characters—so interesting that he has forged a whole new American mythology around himself. I think it is time that National Periodicals be congratulated for making this very definite contribution to the American culture. One sees *Superman* and his efforts in every phase of American life. Professor Max Lerner, in *America as a Civilization*, cites *Superman* as a contemporary folk hero, even as were *King Arthur* and *Robin Hood* of another culture—even as *Paul Bunyan* and the heroes of the old West in our own culture. *Superman* is in the media—reruns of a television show rake in the residuals twenty years after they were made, and admen use the *Superman* theme all over newspapers and magazines.

The greatest compliment is imitation. *Superman* has been satirized and borrowed from for over thirty years. He is a legend, and one every bit as rich as the legends of the past. *Superman* is replete with the values of his contemporaries, and their weaknesses—humanity that will not be admitted to under an exterior of strength—a social conscience—reverence for human life—power and the daring to explore the unknown—the assertion of omnipotence. This is the legend of the *Superman*. This is the legend whose growth we of our generation are privileged to witness.

Now the legend grows again. The *Man of Steel* becomes a TV reporter. He loses an old weakness and finds a new one. He wrestles with the problems of law and justice. He struggles with the inner conflict of belonging—of wanting a place where he can live with people like himself. He could not cope with the simply human existence he would find in the city of *Kandor*. This is strength. He is dynamism. He is the man who has moved planets and draws his strength from the awesome powers of a bright young star. He has lived with strength and must live with his own kind—living forever—traversing dimensional barriers as barriers of air—learning—growing—always groping for what is right and of value for himself and those whom he is charged to protect.

This is *Superman*. This is the *Man of Steel* of our legend. In the '50's, when comics were being blamed for juvenile delinquency and street violence and all manner of social ills, I picked up a *Superman* comic at a candy store in Brooklyn's East New York. From that magazine—that brief encounter—came my imagination—my own social conscience and reverence for human life—my own daring to dream. It is time that I and a generation like me thanked National Periodicals for *Superman*. He has helped to make us *dream.*
Elliot S. Maggin, Brandeis University, Waltham, Mass.

(Well, King Arthur inspired Malory, Tennyson, Mark Twain and T.H. White. Robin Hood inspired Sir Walter Scott. And it seems Superman has inspired Elliot Maggin to write a moving essay. Super-Thanks, Elliot!—E.N.B.)

Dear Editor:
What I really love about Denny O'Neil's *Superman* is that O'Neil has not fallen prey to one of his greatest faults—one shared by many writers who are, like him, adept at *characterization*. When he took over *Green Arrow* and *The Atom*, his characterizations were excellent, but they were completely *different* from their previous ones! Happily, *Superman* is the same logical-minded intellectual he always was.

This is most notable where *Superman* is unable to legally save the islanders. Most heroes would either sit there helplessly or launch into a bitter tirade against "the Establishment." But not *Superman!* Like the reasonable man he is, he simply says, "There's a moral law that's above some man-made laws," and sets about saving the natives.

O'Neil can write really excellent plots, and this issue's was no exception. The new weakness, now fully defined, was used well. I certainly hope Murphy Anderson will continue to ink Curt Swan's pencils—as long as he does, I'll have no complaint with the art in this magazine.

It's really incredible how E. Nelson Bridwell can go through those hundreds of back issues and come up with a complete history of the final years of *Krypton*. "Prison-in-the-Sky" did a fine job in explaining the theory behind the criminals-into-space method of imprisonment. But is that a *black* man on page 5? It's not a bad idea—but since we've never seen any on *Krypton* before, it would mean that *Krypton* had a greater race problem than *Earth* ever did! I wouldn't want to think that of such an advanced civilization, so let's just call it a mistake, hmm?

Swan did well in inking his own pencils. All in all, the "new *Superman*" is the best revamping of a character I've ever seen.
Richard H. Morrissey, Framingham, Mass.

(That was *a black man—of a black civilization on Krypton. See the* Map of Krypton *in the current Giant Superman (#239) for another look at it. Remember—you see blacks in the U.S. because their ancestors were brought here as slaves. That never happened on Krypton.—E.N.B.)*

Dear Editor:
Isn't it true that the *dissolver-beam* that appeared in the *World of Krypton* story in issue #234 also appeared in Giant Superboy G-71 ("The Phantom Superboy")?
Jerry Cole, Grand Rapids, Mich.

(Correct! It was also mentioned in Giant Superman G-78 ("Father's Day on Planet Krypton"). Congratulations! You're the only reader who noted either of these recent reprints in connection with the dissolver.—E.N.B.)

Address all comments to METROPOLIS MAILBAG, National Periodical Publications, 909 Third Ave., New York, N.Y. 10022.

The original pasted-up lettercol of *Superman* #238 (June 1971), featuring an insightful letter from pro pro Maggin (as well as a missive from super fan rich morrissey)
TM & © DC Comics

adopted son of a great man and a servant to that man's goofy son. He learned better and so did the rest of us, in a very dramatic manner.

In our own tradition, stories of kings and heroes from the time of the invention of written English have a recurring theme of exalted beings dressing in sackcloth and going out among their subjects to see what life is really like. That's who Clark Kent is. He's the prince in *The Prince and the Pauper* who because of his experiences grows up to be a wise king. He's the rail-splitter who studied law by firelight who came to save the Union and free the slaves. Check out the new Lincoln biography by Doris Kearns Goodwin: the tall, plainspoken country bumpkin was the campaign narrative; the President was a certifiable genius.

Come to think of it, unless it gets banned where you live, check out Anne Rice's new book, *Christ the Lord*.

EURY: You co-wrote, with Cary Bates, a four-parter in *Superman* #296–299 (Feb.–May 1976) where the Man of Tomorrow evaluated the importance of both of his identities. He temporarily hung up his cape to be "Clark Kent *Forever*— Superman *Never!*" (issue #297), a story that hinted at Clark's intimacy with Lois Lane. In those days before *Superman II*'s Superman/Lois Fortress sleepover and the current comics' marriage of Clark and Lois, did they actually consummate their relationship?

MAGGIN: Of course they did.

EURY: Speaking of Cary Bates, when did you first meet him?

MAGGIN: I think it must have been 1971. I was down in New York every weekend I could spare and he'd just graduated from Ohio University.

EURY: You and Cary collaborated on quite a few Superman stories. What process did you use as co-writers?

The splash page to *Action* #455 (Jan. 1976), written by Elliot S! Maggin, with art by Curt Swan and Tex Blaisdell.

TM & © DC Comics. Wallace Harrington collection.

MAGGIN: In every case where we worked together, he wrote scene descriptions and I wrote dialogue to fit them. For a long time we lived less than a block away from each other. Eventually we got a couple of hand-held tape recorders, so he would pace his living room dictating page layouts and scene descriptions onto a cassette and I'd transcribe it filling in the text. We were each very facile in the portion of the work we chose. I think we broke a scriptwriting speed record one morning working that way.

EURY: On two occasions you guest-starred Batgirl in *Superman* (issues #268, Oct. 1973, and #279, Sept. 1974). Was this predicated upon your affinity for Batgirl or reader requests?

MAGGIN: I never really paid much attention to reader mail unless it was addressed to me. I'm sure I was just feeling in a Batgirl kind of mood at the time.

EURY: "Make Way for Captain Thunder!" (*Superman* #276, June 1974) was one of your most popular Superman tales of the 1970s (and a favorite of mine, too). But why the Captain Marvel proxy Captain Thunder, when DC was by that time publishing *Shazam!*?

MAGGIN: We were trying to do the traditional Fawcett-style Captain Marvel in the *Shazam!* book in those days. The style of artwork was different from Superman's. The degrees of suspension of disbelief in the two story threads—*Shazam!* as opposed to *Superman*—were different. I never really believed that Superman and Captain Marvel belonged in the same story and neither did Julie. The Captain Thunder story was a piece of speculation as to what Captain Marvel might be like if he lived in the "real world." I think Metropolis in the '70s was what we thought of as the real world at the time.

EURY: You liberated Krypto from the limbo kennel in *Superman* #287 (May 1975), and in 1999—when comics had become too "serious" for a flying canine—you featured Superdog in a novella titled *Starwinds Howl*. How would you define Krypto's importance to the Superman mythos?

MAGGIN: A man needs a dog. A superman needs a superdog. As far as I can tell, the two species are locked together by some kind of biological imperative we can maybe recognize but can't explain from inside the system.

EURY: You wrote some of the most significant Lex Luthor stories of the Bronze Age. What's your philosophy about this villain—why Luthor's continuing rivalry with Superman when he could have reaped great fortunes exploiting his intellect?

MAGGIN: In a world without a superman, Luthor is the most accomplished man on Earth. I think Luthor is aware of this supposed destiny from the moment he's conscious, and as soon as he is aware that there's a being in the world whose greatness he can't surpass, he has to be that being's enemy. Luthor's place in the world is displaced by Superman. I suppose I'd be driven by resentment, too.

EURY: There's a misconception that LexCorp (originally "Lexcorp") is a construct of the *Man of Steel* relaunch, but the little-known fact is, you coined the word in "The Ghost of Superman Future" in *Superman* #416 (Feb. 1986), just before the reboot….

MAGGIN: Yeah, Lexcorp is mine. I called Paul Levitz when they published *Who's Who in the DC Universe* and it said John Byrne had created Lexcorp and Paul acknowledged that I was right. It doesn't make that much difference, but I'm a big believer in justice. I've never been very good at pursuing justice on my own behalf. I'm kind of glad I pointed this out. Thanks for noticing.

EURY: With your interest in politics (Green Arrow's flirtation with elected office in your first published script, and your own congressional bid), what was your reaction to Luthor becoming the DC Universe's U.S. president in 2000?

MAGGIN: I think there's probably some unintentional resonance in portraying the President of the United States as a documented criminal, but I really don't think it's consistent with the literary value of the Luthor character. As I said, maybe Luthor would be president in a world without a Superman, but Superman's here to keep nonsense like that from going on.

EURY: Which of the other members of Superman's rogues' gallery did you find interesting to write, and why?

MAGGIN: I'm no big fan of the rogues' gallery. We exhumed about a dozen of them for *Superman* #299 at the climax of that series where Clark and Lois got it on. Frankly, I thought it fell flat. Characters need to be a function of story rather than the reverse, I think.

But my favorite characters to write were always Luthor and Perry White. Perry reminded me of Julie Schwartz, and I always liked him. Julie's is my personal rogues' gallery. I keep thinking he's going to make a surprise return appearance one of these days.

EURY: You penned one of the first super-hero novels, *Last Son of Krypton* (Warner Books, 1978). I understand that its genesis began with your treatment for a Superman film, predating 1978's *Superman: The Movie*....

MAGGIN: That's correct. I wrote a fat memo to Carmine Infantino sometime in 1974 explaining, with academic citations and everything, that now—the mid-'70s—the world was primed for a resurgence of the super-hero genre in film and literature. He seemed to be impressed with the memo. So I took the next step and went off and wrote a treatment for a Superman feature film.

Next thing I know one of my favorite writers in the world, Alfred Bester, is prowling around the office doing research for a Superman feature film. I was actually thrilled to meet Bester—although I'd hung out with him on the phone before and he advised me not to go to graduate school in journalism. It turned out that when I did go to journalism school my favorite professor there was a friend of Bester's. So it goes. Eventually Bester left the project and before I knew it Mario Puzo, of all people, is in the library with Nelson Bridwell looking through old Superman comics. Cary and I ended up spending two days in a conference room with Mario puffing on these enormous Cuban cigars and talking about Superman movies. Then sometime during the afternoon of the second day Mario furrowed his forehead and looked at the both of us and he said, as if it were a revelation, "Well, this thing is a Greek tragedy," and Cary and I looked at each other and then looked at Mario and one of us said, "That's what we've been trying to tell you." It was a scene out of a '50s sitcom.

At some point the three of us were talking about Hollywood. I remember asking Mario, "How do you get to be a hot-sh*t screenwriter?" and he snapped back, "Write a bestseller and wait for them to come to *you*." Then he thought about it a little and he said, "You know, if they didn't think they needed a big name on this project they'd have you guys write it," and Cary said, "For $5000 each we'd ghost-write it for you," and Mario laughed. It wasn't until later when I found out what he was getting paid for the screenplays that I realized he thought it was we who were joking. Who knows? If Cary had said $50,000 maybe he'd have taken the bait.

So a few days later I took my film treatment upstairs to the eighth floor where Warner Books was at the time and told them I wanted to write a Superman novel. It was not Mario's story, but through a series of accidents my book came to be released on the day the movie premiered.

EURY: Miracle Monday (1981), your second Superman novel (inspired by your "The

Miracle of Thirsty Thursday!" script in *Superman* #293, Nov. 1975), introduced Kristin Wells, a history professor from the future, who traveled to the 20th century and fought alongside the Man of Steel as Superwoman in two *DC Comics Presents Annual*s. Is there any chance this character will resurface?

MAGGIN: I don't see how it's likely. I actually have a contract giving DC Comics and me joint rights to the original characters in *Miracle Monday* including Kristin Wells. I'd have to come up with some boffo idea for her and convince them to let me run with it, or they'd have to ask me about some boffo idea for her that someone else had and I'd have to think it was boffo too. It's all about what you had for breakfast that day.

EURY: So, how is Miracle Monday celebrated in the Maggin household?

MAGGIN: Normally, people send me e-mail to remind me of the day. I don't usually need reminding. As it happens, I got to see the first published copy of my book on Miracle Monday the year it came out (1981, was it?) and invariably some of the more remarkable things that have happened in my life have happened on that day. I'd close on a house, or my wife and I would have a terrific dinner, or we'd find out she's pregnant, or I'd meet somebody who'd be president five or six years later. That sort of thing. This year my son is graduating from college around that time, but a week or so late. We'll see.

EURY: These novels were bestsellers but have been long out of print—weren't they supposed to be reprinted as part of your 1996 deal to write the *Kingdom Come* novel?

Page 1 of Maggin's Julie Schwartz tribute, from *Superman* #411 (Sept. 1985).
TM & © DC Comics. Art courtesy of Heritage Comics.

MAGGIN: They were. That was the understanding.

EURY: You wrote "The Last Earth-Prime Story" in _Superman_ #411 (Sept. 1985), the Julie Schwartz 70th birthday issue. Was this tribute your idea? And how on Earth did you and your co-conspirators pull this off without Julie catching wind of it?

MAGGIN: It was my idea. I was winding down my 15 years on Superman at the time, and so was Julie. I was living in New Hampshire and I called Paul Levitz and suggested the idea to him. He loved it. Paul loves a lot of ideas but he isn't always interested in publishing them. This one caught his fancy.

So I wrote the script and gave it to Bob Rozakis in the Production Department and Bob spirited the process along among the artists and the techies. And one day when the pencils came in I was sitting in Bob's office with the door closed, drooling over the art and giggling about whether we'd really be able to pull this off. Julie came barging in haranguing either Bob or me about somethingorother and I managed to change the subject rather gracefully in mid-sentence, and Bob gingerly slid a sheaf of papers over the pages on his desk and Julie's fit ran its course and he went away. That was the closest we came to being found out.

I didn't make it to New York the day they unveiled the book to its unsuspecting editor of record, but he called me up about an hour later, when he was first able to talk coherently. He just couldn't believe we'd managed to put that over on him. Neither could I, for that matter.

EURY: What would readers have seen if you had succeeded Julie Schwartz as the Superman editor?

MAGGIN: I don't know that I was ever in the running. Nobody in any position to make such a decision ever brought it up to me at the time. The folks making decisions about Superman actually seemed seriously desperate as to where to turn in those days and they were going out of their way not to listen to the likes of me.

A mid-1970s photo of (left to right) Bob Rozakis, Elliot Maggin, and Julie Schwartz.
Photo © 1975 DC Comics.

My suspicion is that if it had happened, though, fans would have seen more of Curt Swan and Ty Templeton and—get ready: Gray Morrow and Alex Toth drawing Superman. I'm almost certain Mark Waid and Jeph Loeb would both have been more involved in writing the book in those years. So would Cary Bates. And probably the events of the storylines would have taken on a more consciously classical nature. That is, there would have been more allusion to classic mythological themes and norms, but in the modern and the future world. More enchanted skyscrapers and haunted subway stops. You might have seen a President Luthor, but only in an alternate universe, and you would have seen more of alternate universes in general. I liked Earth-Prime, as it happens. You would also never have heard any hint of any silly "controversy" over whether Superman was disguised as Clark or Clark was disguised as Superman. But I doubt there is an alternate universe anywhere where any of that ever happened.

EURY: Who do you believe was the most underrated Superman artist of the 1970s/1980s?

MAGGIN: Ty Templeton. And, as it happens, I don't think I've ever met the man.

EURY: What do you consider to be Julie Schwartz's most significant contribution to the Superman legend?

MAGGIN: Saving the character from oblivion. I don't think anyone knew what to do with Superman when he got dropped on Julie's desk and there wasn't the wealth of licensing opportunities there is now to fall back on. Superman might have been canceled or—more likely—bought by another company. In fact, there's someone I was trying to convince to buy him around 1974 who could have done it if I'd been more convincing and he'd been more visionary. But the deal would have been to bring Julie with him. I never told Julie about that.

EURY: Same question, but in reference to _your_ work.

MAGGIN: In my darkest moments I get this idea kicking around my head that the most significant things I'll ever have done in my life might turn out to be what I did in my twenties. Then I remember my kids and it gets light out. I'm not sure what my biggest contribution to Superman was, but it may be an attitude that I wrote into the character in one of the books and several of the stories: the idea that there is a right and a wrong in the Universe and the difference is not very difficult to tell. Superman stories are about moral and ethical choices, not power. The trick is to figure out how to show a person of enormous power choosing between right and wrong. It's a Greek tragedy, see?

EURY: Is there a Superman story you never got a chance to tell?

MAGGIN: About a gazillion of them.

A manuscript page from Schwartz and Maggin's "Memoirs of a Time Traveller" series for _Amazing Stories_, 1990s.

© 2006 Elliot S! Maggin. Courtesy of Heritage Comics. J.S. Collection.

GERRY CONWAY INTERVIEW

Gerard F. "Gerry" Conway (b. 1952) co-created the Punisher, Firestorm, and Power Girl, and wrote the groundbreaking *Amazing Spider-Man* storyline featuring the deaths of Gwen Stacy and the Green Goblin. A former Marvel Comics editor in chief, Conway penned the *Superman vs. The Amazing Spider-Man* crossover in 1976. Outside of comics, he has authored science-fiction novels, the *Star Trek* newspaper strip, and movie screenplays, and has since become a successful TV writer/producer for such series as *Diagnosis Murder* and *Law & Order: Criminal Intent*.

Conducted by Michael Eury on February 13, 2006.

Courtesy of Glen Cadigan.

MICHAEL EURY: Like Jim Shooter and Cary Bates, you started writing comics while in your teens. How did you break in to the field, and how old were you at the time?

GERRY CONWAY: I was living in New York City, in Queens. During the time we're talking about, the late '60s, DC Comics had a tour every Thursday for fans, and usually five to ten people would show up. Once I found out about the tour, I went every week, and met people like Marv Wolfman and Len Wein, who also took the tour every week.

I discovered that if I went on the tour, I could sort of slip away and talk to the editors—which is what I did. I think I was about 15 years old. I found they were receptive to talking with me, but whether they thought I was somebody who would actually be able to write for them, I don't know. My primary motivation was my discovery that Jim Shooter was selling stories to Mort Weisinger at the age of 13, so I thought, "Well, *I* could do that!" My initial idea was to be an artist, but the editors suggested I try writing instead once they saw my art. I took that advice. [*laughter*]

Eventually, I connected with George Kashdan, who, at that point, was editing *Hawkman*. George was receptive to story ideas—he was actually very open to it. But I ended up

suggesting two or three Hawkman stories, I wrote a couple of paragraphs on each, sent them to him, and called up to see what he thought of them. He said he liked them, but he was not going to be editing the book anymore. In fact, he was not going to be editing at all. That's when Dick Giordano and Joe Orlando came in as editors. So I called Dick Giordano and sort of misrepresented myself, and said I was working with George Kashdan. [*laughs*] So he said, "Sure, come on in." And he had me submit some stories on spec. He told me later he thought I really didn't have what it took, but I was so enthusiastic, he felt sympathy toward me and kept letting me write—not buying anything.

At that point, the way DC's offices were set up, three editors shared an office: [in this case,] Joe Orlando, Dick Giordano, and Murray Boltinoff. Murray was an old pro, an old hack pro—and I say "hack" in a nice way. He did what needed doing and he ground it out. He'd been around for a while—before the comic-book business he'd been in pulps and in radio. Murray was one of these suit-and-tie-type guys, very professional, very dry. Not a warm and welcoming person, until you got to know him. But he saw me over there with Dick, and Murray, like the other editors, was under pressure to use new talent.

So one day, after Dick left to do something and I was still sitting at his desk, Murray asked me if I'd be interested in doing a story for him, apparently under the impression I was writing for Dick. And Murray's the kind of guy who would never, *ever* buy anybody's first project—you had to have been bedded by somebody else. So I ended up working on a three-page story for Murray for *Tales of the Unexpected* for the better part of an entire summer: I would write the story, bring it in, he'd give me extensive notes, detailed rewritings on the page … I'd go home, type that up, bring it in, he'd rewrite that … I'd go home, I'd retype that … [*laughs*] and that went on all summer. So finally, he either got tired of me or tired of it and accepted the story and asked me, "Okay, what's your rate?" I said, "I don't know. I don't have a rate." And the blood went right out of his face, as he realized he had taken my cherry. [*laughter*]

EURY: He really had no clue?

CONWAY: No idea it was the first story I ever sold. I didn't sell another story to him for ten years. [*laughter*] From that point on, after Dick found out I'd actually sold something, *he* bought some stories. Over the years I became one of Dick's top writers, and one of the top writers at DC, and went from there to Marvel, where I got some plum assignments.

EURY: You found your voice at Marvel in the early '70s....

CONWAY: At the time, my move from DC to Marvel was perceived as selling out.

EURY: Is that so?

CONWAY: Yeah. Don and Maggie Thompson, who used to do *The Comics Reader*, wrote an article or editorial in part where they criticized me for leaving DC, which in their view was obviously the more creative company, and said I'd sold out by going over to Marvel. Only, I thought, "But Marvel does the books I love. I was overjoyed. This is what I always wanted to do. It was a consolation prize." [*laughs*] I mean I'd was

Conway's Punisher drawn by John Byrne.
© 2006 Marvel Characters, Inc. Art courtesy of Heritage Comics.

doing great stuff. The stuff Denny O'Neil and Neal Adams were doing was phenomenal—

EURY: But that was the exception to the rule at the time.

CONWAY: Yeah. As a company, it was moribund. And Marvel was terrific. Well, that's a matter of personal opinion, but I really was attacked as a sellout.

EURY: What led you to jump from Marvel back to DC in the mid-'70s?

CONWAY: It came about from a series of unfortunate misunderstandings. I had been working at Marvel for five or six years as Roy's [Thomas] number-two guy. The understanding I had with Stan Lee, and the understanding Roy had with Stan, was that if Roy left as editor, I would be promoted to editor. I had even gone in at times when Roy was sick or was on vacation, and I would fill in for him. Well, Len Wein and Marv Wolfman were working at DC for most of this period—Len and I were good friends; he had been best man at my wedding, and we'd been roommates at one point—and I thought it'd be good for him to get over to Marvel. Marv had already made the move—Marv never ignited over at DC the way Len had, at that point, so he had less of an attachment to that company. Marv was hired as an editor to help Roy with the black-and-white books, because at that point Marvel was expanding phenomenally. Roy also needed an editorial assistant, someone with experience as a writer as well as an editor. So Marv and I suggested, "Let's bring Len in."

After this, Len and Marv were in the office every day. I was working at home. Roy and Stan had a falling out over a political issue. This happened while I was in California on vacation.

So Stan said to Roy, "Okay, you can stay, and write and edit your own books, but what do I do [about an editor in chief]?" Roy said, "Well, Gerry's next in line. You should make a deal with Gerry." When Marv and Len heard Roy had quit, they went in and insisted they be promoted, because they were the next in line officially. So Stan gave Len the job.

I came back from vacation and discovered I'd been passed over. In my view, I'd been stabbed in the back. I don't think Len did this out of any type of maliciousness—he probably thought it was the logical step. He hadn't been at the company that long—only three or four months—I guess he didn't know the history, that I was supposed to be the guy. So in a snit, I left. It came down to an issue over a contract, where I felt they reneged over some stuff, so I quit and went back to DC.

EURY: And you started at DC with a full plate: You were a writer/editor of a handful of titles—"Conway's Corner"— plus writing for other editors, including Julie Schwartz, on *Superman*.

CONWAY: That's right. I'd done some scripts for Julie earlier in my career—I'd done some *Superman*, some *Justice League*s. [In 1976,] DC's executives felt like they were losing all these people, and here I was, at the time Marvel's top writer after Roy, and I'd come over to DC. So it was like, "Boy, we made a coup. We got this guy." They threw everything at me, and I was happy to take it.

EURY: You weren't overwhelmed by the sheer volume of titles?

CONWAY: No. At that point, I was a fast writer. I think now, however, writing so much wasn't a good idea, because over time my ability to maintain the quality of my writing at that volume just wasn't there. It was not a good thing in the long run.

EURY: Did you ask to write Superman stories, or did Julie approach you? And how aware was Julie of what you'd done at Marvel?

CONWAY: Julie was sort of semi-aware. I don't think he looked too much outside of his own bailiwick, even at DC—I don't think he looked at what other editors were doing. But he knew me from before. I had actually known Julie since 1968. He knew I was a writer, that I was doing well. I think it was Carmine who

wanted to get me on their top books, and their top books were *Superman*, *Batman*, *Justice League*, and the like. I believe he urged Julie to give me a shot, and it worked out. I think it turned out fairly well.

EURY: I agree. When you first took over *Superman* with any regularity (issue #301, July 1976), you were paired with José Luis García-López as the *Superman* artist. His work was phenomenal.

CONWAY: Oh, of course. He's a terrific artist.

EURY: But strangely, he's often overlooked as a Superman artist. Do you have any opinions on why that might be the case?

CONWAY: I think it's because, while he's a terrific draftsman and did a fabulous job with the character, his Superman didn't look different. It looked like an extension of the DC house style. Because I worked with José very closely, I saw the depth he gave to the material, but if you only looked at his art cursorily, you could think this was somebody who was following in the path of Neal Adams and Dick Giordano, rather than finding the particular storytelling style García-López brought to it.

Page 8 of *Superman* #308 (Feb. 1977); Conway script, García-López pencils, and Frank Springer inks.
TM & © DC Comics. Bruce MacIntosh collection.

José was tremendously underrated. He did terrific work on that, terrific work on this miniseries we did together, *Cinder and Ashe*, and I don't think he ever really broke through. Part of the reason might be, he was a slow penciler, so he only did 18-page stories for *Superman*. He didn't become ubiquitous, and didn't get many covers, so he never became huge the way Neal Adams became huge, at least in part because Neal was drawing covers all over the place. It wasn't that Neal only did the occasional *Batman* story, he was doing, like, ten covers a month. García-López didn't do many covers outside of the books he worked on.

EURY: No, and like you're saying, many of the books he did work on had covers by other artists—including Neal Adams.

CONWAY: And that was a shame, because I really think José's Superman was among the best of that entire period. And because he was Hispanic, and English was his second language, he didn't go to conventions to meet people and develop a fan base. He wasn't interviewed as much, and it's just a shame. The work he did on *Superman*, the work he did on *Atari Force*, the work he did on *Cinder and Ashe*, was some of the best stuff DC did during the '70s and the '80s. But what are you gonna do? Ross Andru never got any respect, either, and he's one of the great artists.

EURY: Absolutely.

You introduced Dr. Jenet Klyburn as the head of S.T.A.R. Labs in *Superman* #304 (Oct. 1976). Was she based upon Jenette Kahn, who was coming in to DC as its president at that time?

CONWAY: Yep.

EURY: That seemed obvious, but I just wanted to hear it from you.

Let's talk about *Superman vs. The Amazing Spider-Man* (1976). Since you'd written both characters, you were the logical choice to script the story, but were there any other contenders?

CONWAY: Well, no. The way it broke down was, when they made the deal, DC agreed to provide the writers, and Marvel provided the artists. This happened almost immediately after I came back to DC. Carmine felt like Marvel was taking his best artists, so here I was, the writer they just hired away from Marvel, so I was the *only* choice in his eye. And I don't think, honestly, there was anybody else working at DC at the time who had written *Spider-Man*.

EURY: Was there anything you wanted to do in the crossover that was denied?

CONWAY: No, we pretty much had carte blanche. I've always had a sense of the absurdity of modern comics and super-heroes, as was apparent during my *Spider-Man* run in the '70s. So, for my money, there was no rational way we were going to justify this team-up. [*laughter*] I mean, in what Universe, on what world [did it take place]? We could've done Earth-12, but then Marvel and DC both would have said, "No, *we* want to be the original planet."

EURY: Some fans have said it took place on Earth-$.

CONWAY: Yeah. [*laughs*] I looked at it as a chance to do a story for the fans, a fun story. It was a chance to do the scenes I [as a fan] would like to see in this fantasy. It was an imaginary story that never happened. The goal was to have *fun* with it, to do the scene where Superman hits Spider-Man and Spider-Man flies through a building, of having Spider-Man do something Superman couldn't do—all those little "gift" moments you want to see.

EURY: You definitely delivered those. I admit, every few years, I reread that comic.

CONWAY: Really?

EURY: Yeah, because it rekindles that tingly little fan feeling I had all those years ago when I first read it. It still holds up, and it's exceptionally well drawn, which leads me to a question: In *BACK ISSUE* #11 (July 2005) it was revealed that Neal Adams secretly retouched some of Ross Andru's Superman figure pencils in the *Superman/Spider-Man* crossover. Were you aware of that at the time? Are you aware of it *now*?

CONWAY: I've never been officially informed. I knew that when Dick [Giordano] was inking it, he changed things, because you *had* to with Ross. The problem with Ross' pencils were … they were never remotely anatomically human. [*chuckles*] He was great at storytelling, he was really good at design, he drew great buildings—he was really good at all that technical stuff. But when it came to the human figure, that was not his forte. But he did it stylistically consistently, and dramatically. At Marvel, he would be redrawn by [John] Romita. Occasionally, when an issue passed over Romita's desk, he would see some face of Peter Parker, or some face of Spider-Man, that didn't look right to him, and would redo it. In some cases, John would redraw three or four panels.

And at DC, Dick was a fairly heavy inker—when he inked something, it looked like he had inked it, as opposed to some inkers who try to become invisible in the project. Dick at that time was very influenced by Neal Adams—even when Dick *penciled* something, you could see Neal's influence—so when I saw the finished work and it looked like Neal Adams' drawing, it didn't occur to me it might actually *be* Neal Adams' drawing.

Jenette Kahn, the inspiration for Conway's Jenet Klyburn, and Sol Harrison with a giant Superman birthday cake; Bob Rozakis looks on. From the 1976 Superman Super-Con at the Americana Hotel in NYC.

TM & © DC Comics.

EURY: That was my assumption as a reader. But thanks to Daniel Best's investigative journalism in *BACK ISSUE* #11, the story finally came out that Neal "inked with a pencil" some of the Superman figures on pages that Dick had left behind at Continuity Studios.

Dick mentioned to me after that article was published that he, not wanting to slight Andru's work, was sorry that this had come to light. In this very book, though, a number of people, yourself included, have praised Ross Andru's work, so I hope that makes amends for our revealing the "secret."

Next topic: You were involved with another big Superman event—the introduction of Power Girl in *All-Star Comics* #58 (Jan.–Feb. 1976). Let's talk about how she was created.…

CONWAY: The convoluted version of this is, when I went to DC, I had a conversation with Roy Thomas—we stayed friends through all of this—and he was a big DC fan in the early '60s … actually, since the '40s and '50s. He told me he'd really like it if I'd bring back the Justice Society. And I said, "But they're all a bunch of old guys." [*laughter*] Nobody thought about setting it back in the '40s, which is what Roy did later. So I came into this thinking, "How can I make this a young book?" I wanted to do something to feature these [classic] characters, which were cool characters, and I liked doing groups—this was before I did *Justice League*.

So I decided to come up with some young characters I could play around with on Earth-Two, and I realized Earth-Two didn't have a Supergirl. So I thought, "I'll do a Supergirl of Earth-Two, but I don't want her to be called 'Supergirl,' because then people would be wondering, 'Well, *which* Supergirl are we talking about?'" So I figured, "*Power Girl*—that would be cool." I actually designed her costume myself, even down to the circle on her chest.

EURY: Ah, the famous circle.…

CONWAY: Yeah. I did that for a variety of reasons. One, there was a theory at the time, and I sort of subscribed to it myself, that super-characters had to have symbols on their chests. I didn't want it to be a big "P" [*laughter*]. I kept looking at [the costume design], and looking at it, and finally thought, "You know, it would be kind of cool just to put a big circle on her chest." Then Wally Wood inked it, and Wally made it *really* look good! We all loved it, but Jenette Kahn didn't want Power Girl to look like that because she thought it was sexist, so we had to get rid of it … I think it was to the detriment of the character, because it became just a white shirt—she became "T-Shirt Girl." [*laughs*]

EURY: I was a teenager then, and I really *liked* that circle.

CONWAY: A lot of older guys did, too. [*laughter*]

EURY: Interestingly, during the '70s, Power Girl's popularity eclipsed Supergirl's. Even though she didn't have her own magazine, Power Girl had her *Showcase* run (issues #97–99, Feb.–Apr. 1978), and readers seemed more taken by this Earth-Two character.

CONWAY: Sure. You know, unlike Supergirl, Power Girl didn't have Superman's moderating influence growing up. She was a much more direct and contemporary character. That was fun.

EURY: Have you followed Power Girl's role in *Infinite Crisis* (#1–7, Dec. 2005–June 2006)? She's become a major player in the DC Universe again.

CONWAY: Good! Well, I'm not getting any money off of it. [*laughter*] If they put out a toy they'll probably send me something.…

EURY: Essentially, Power Girl was the entry point for DC bringing back Earth-Two.

CONWAY: Oh?

EURY: Yes. In the years after *Crisis* [*on Infinite Earths*, 1985–1986], DC had a hard time explaining where the character was from, but it's now being established that the stories you and Paul Levitz did were the gospel truth. The Golden Age Superman came back, too. Essentially the Crisis of 1985 was unraveled.

CONWAY: That makes sense. You have to do a major overhaul every 20 years or so to keep the characters fresh and contemporary. *Crisis* was 20 years after "The Flash of Two Worlds," which was 20 years after the end of the Justice Society—it's good they're doing that.

EURY: You wrote the *Superman vs. Wonder Woman* tabloid. Why was that set during World War II rather than the 1970s?

CONWAY: It was actually my interest in doing Wonder Woman as she had been done in the '40s. The Wonder Woman of 1960 on was pretty lame, in my view. But the Wonder Woman of the '40s had dynamism, and I was more interested in that version of the character. And the original *Wonder Woman* TV series certainly reminded us that [the '40s] was a good period for her, although the TV series took the '40s era and did the '60s character.

I like doing stories set in the past. I suspect I was influenced by Roy. Basically I was his surrogate at DC, doing the stories he would've wanted to do. I think he probably encouraged me to set it during World War II.

EURY: You worked with José again on that project, which is a beautiful, beautiful book. One thing that some fans have been distracted by, even to this day, is that he drew the Earth-*One* Superman in the book, but I'm guessing that was for character identification and no other reason.

CONWAY: Yeah.

EURY: You also wrote the first big Superman/Captain Marvel battle in the *Superman vs. Shazam!* Collectors' Edition (1978). That was the first actual crossover between these two characters, correct?

CONWAY: Yeah. It was another Roy Thomas-influenced story. Roy is a huge Captain Marvel fan.

EURY: I'm certainly aware of that, but am a little surprised that Roy didn't hold out this story for his own....

CONWAY: I don't think Roy ever thought he would go to DC. He came over after I left. But [at the time] he felt it was a universe he'd never touch. So seeing it in a vicarious way would've been fun [for him].

EURY: You had an on-again/off-again relationship with Superman in the '70s and '80s, writing *Superman* and *Action* for number of short stints. Why didn't you stay with the character longer?

CONWAY: Uh … I honestly don't know. I think at least part of it was the way Julie was working. With the exception of *Justice League*, which he may have felt was too complicated for more than one writer to be working on, Julie liked to have several writers on his books—which, of course, was diametrically opposed to the way I like to work, with continuity from one issue to the next. So over time, he wanted to do it one way and I wanted to do it a different way, and it just didn't work out. But I enjoyed writing it at the time—I had a lot of fun with *Superman*.

And another thing: José was slow … [*chuckles*] he's always been very slow. It got to the point where if I wanted to continue working on the book, I might've had to work with someone else, and that didn't feel right.

EURY: Although on some of your *Superman* and *Action* stories, Gerry, you were paired with Curt Swan.

CONWAY: Yes.

EURY: How did you approach Superman differently when writing him in *Justice League* as opposed to writing his solo adventures?

CONWAY: I don't think I tried to write the character differently—I tried to keep him consistent. But Superman is so powerful, and so overwhelming, and such a personality. Let's face it: If you were in a room with all these characters in real life, the one you'd be looking at—the *only* one you'd be looking at—is Superman.

Okay, maybe Wonder Woman. [*laughs*]

But Superman's the most charismatic and dynamic. That's not to say his *character* is that interesting, but he's just so overpowering. So portraying him in *Justice League* was always difficult, because I'd have to find a way to sort of neutralize him, or find a way to use him that didn't overpower the other characters.

EURY: What would you consider your most significant contribution to the Superman Legend?

CONWAY: None that I remember. [*laughs*] My problem is, I don't remember the *stories* that well—I remember the experience of working on them, but I don't remember the specific stories. I think what I *did* like the most, now that I think of it, was creating a sense of continuity for the character. I did try to do storylines that would extend from issue to issue to issue. In that sense, *that* was something I contributed.

EURY: Which must've been frustrating, since that was contrary to Julie's style.

CONWAY: Yeah, he didn't quite get it. He'd work with me a little bit, because I was the new guy, but that was my primary motivation.

One of the things that anybody who looks at my stuff over a period of time will probably pick up on, is that I'm really not that compelled by the super-heroics, or the super-powers. Somebody like John Byrne can sit down and figure out how all this stuff works and make it consistent and interesting, but I don't really care. My favorite character is Green Lantern, because all he has to do is wish for something and it happens.

So I don't care about that part of it. The part I care about is the characters themselves—Clark Kent, Lois Lane, you know, people behind the scenes—so the *real* story in any comic I've written is the *subplot*. In some cases, like my second run on *Spider-Man*, it became all about the subplot, to the point where there was practically no story. [*laughter*] It became, "Okay, this issue we're going to do 12 pages of Robbie Robertson." [*laughter*] For me, that was a dream situation, when I was allowed to do that.

So to the extent I added some emphasis to the secondary characters, that was my contribution.

EURY: What about Lana Lang? She worked fine when she was the belle of the ball in *Superboy*, but always seemed a bit out of place in *Superman*.

CONWAY: Well, I've got a thing for redheads in comics.

EURY: Like Mary Jane Watson…?

CONWAY: Yeah. People are always asking me, "Why'd you kill Gwen Stacy?" Well, I wanted to keep the *redhead*! [*laughs*]

EURY: Anything closing comments about Superman?

CONWAY: I enjoyed writing the character, I enjoyed working with José, and I have fond memories of it. The truth is, writing *Action* wasn't my primary drive while I was at DC, but it was fun to do.

Gerry Conway's super-heroine the Vixen was intended to star in her own title in the late 1970s. The "DC Implosion" shelved her series, but Gerry finally introduced her in *Action* #521 [July 1981]. Art by Swan and Chiaramonte.

TM & © DC Comics. W. Wm. Huntington Hall

THE SUPERMAN MYTHOLOGY:
SUPERMAN TEAM-UPS

For years, *World's Finest Comics* co-starred Superman and Batman, "your two favorite heroes in one adventure *together*." Once Julius Schwartz inherited *World's Finest* from Mort Weisinger, the series' format changed, with Batman stepping aside for other Superman teammates. Batman returned after two years, but Superman continued to meet—and sometimes fight—other super-heroes in a number of tabloid-sized specials and, beginning in 1978, his own team-up series, *DC Comics Presents*.

Superman vs. Green Lantern in a commissioned illustration by Paul Smith.

World's Finest Comics (1970–1972)
Starring Superman and:
#198: the Flash
#199: the Flash
#200: Robin
#201: Green Lantern
#202: Batman
#203: Aquaman
#204: Wonder Woman
#205: the Teen Titans
#206: Batman (reprint Giant)
#207: Batman
#208: Dr. Fate
#209: Hawkman
#210: Green Arrow
#211: Batman
#212: the Martian Manhunter
#213: the Atom
#214: the Vigilante

DC/Marvel Crossovers
Superman vs. the Amazing Spider Man (1976)
Marvel Treasury Edition #28 (1981): Superman and Spider-Man

All-New Collectors Edition (1978)
#C-54: Superman vs. Wonder Woman
#C-56: Superman vs. Muhammad Ali
#C-58: Superman vs. Shazam!

DC Comics Presents (1978–1986)
Starring Superman and:
#1: the Flash
#2: the Flash
#3: Adam Strange
#4: the Metal Men
#5: Aquaman
#6: Green Lantern
#7: the Red Tornado
#8: Swamp Thing
#9: Wonder Woman
#10: Sgt. Rock
#11: Hawkman
#12: Mister Miracle
#13: the Legion of Super-Heroes
#14: Superboy
#15: the Atom
#16: Black Lightning
#17: Firestorm
#18: Zatanna
#19: Batgirl
#20: Green Arrow
#21: the Elongated Man
#22: Captain Comet
#23: Doctor Fate
#24: Deadman
#25: the Phantom Stranger
#26: Green Lantern
#27: Manhunter from Mars
#28: Supergirl
#29: the Spectre
#30: Black Canary
#31: Robin the Teen Wonder
#32: Wonder Woman
#33: Shazam!
#34: the Shazam! Family
#35: Man-Bat
#36: Starman
#37: Hawkgirl
#38: the Flash
#39: Plastic Man
#40: Metamorpho the Element Man
#41: the Joker
#42: the Unknown Soldier
#43: the Legion of Super-Heroes
#44: Dial "H" for Hero
#45: Firestorm
#46: the Global Guardians
#47: the Masters of the Universe
#48: Aquaman
#49: Shazam!
#50: Clark Kent
#51: the Atom
#52: the Doom Patrol
#53: the House of Mystery
#54: Green Arrow
#55: Air Wave
#56: Power Girl
#57: the Atomic Knights
#58: Robin the Teen Wonder and the Elongated Man
#59: the Legion of Substitute Heroes
#60: the Guardians of the Universe
#61: OMAC, One Man Army Corps
#62: the Freedom Fighters
#63: Amethyst, Princess of Gemworld
#64: Kamandi, the Last Boy on Earth
#65: Madame Xanadu
#66: the Demon
#67: Santa Claus
#68: Vixen
#69: Blackhawk
#70: the Metal Men
#71: Bizarro
#72: the Phantom Stranger and the Joker
#73: the Flash
#74: Hawkman
#75: Arion, Lord of Atlantis
#76: Wonder Woman
#77: the Forgotten Heroes (Animal-Man, Dolphin, and Congorilla)
#78: the Forgotten Villains
#79: Clark Kent
#80: the Legion of Super-Heroes
#81: Ambush Bug
#82: Adam Strange
#83: Batman and the Outsiders
#84: the Challengers of the Unknown
#85: Swamp Thing
#86: Supergirl
#87: Superboy
#88: the Creeper
#89: the Omega Men
#90: Firestorm and Captain Atom
#91: Captain Comet
#92: the Vigilante
#93: the Elastic Four (Jimmy Olsen as Elastic Lad, Plastic Man, the Elongated Man, and a stretchable menace)
#94: Harbinger, Lady Quark, and Pariah
#95: Hawkman
#96: Blue Devil
#97: the Phantom Zone Criminals

DC Comics Presents Annual
#1 (1982): Superman and the Golden Age Superman
#2 (1983): Superman introduces Superwoman
#3 (1984): Superman and Shazam!
#4 (1985): Superman and Superwoman

JOSE LUIS GARCIA-LOPEZ INTERVIEW

José Luis García-López's (b. 1948) lithe, realistic rendition of Superman enviorated the Man of Steel's covers and interior pages during the mid- to late 1970s. Born in Spain but reared in Argentina, García-López relocated to the United States in 1975 to work in the American comics business, and has been in demand as an artist ever since. Joining his landmark work on *Superman vs. Wonder Woman* and *DC Comics Presents* are his memorable series *Cinder and Ashe*, *Deadman*, *Atari Force*, various *Batman* tales, and, as of the mid-2000s, *JLA Classified*.

Recommended reading: *Modern Masters vol. 5: José Luis García-López*, edited by Eric Nolen-Weathington (TwoMorrows, 2005).

Conducted by Michael Eury via e-mail on February 20, 2006.

MICHAEL EURY: When were you first exposed to Superman?
JOSÉ LUIS GARCÍA-LÓPEZ: It was in Argentina and I was very young, about seven. I have this uncle who brought me Superman and Batman magazines in black-and-white. These were translated and published in Argentina. We also had Mexican editions in full color, but I don't remember seeing Superman in those.

Courtesy of Glen Cadigan.

EURY: Your first work for DC Comics was as an inker, on a Dick Dillin Atom story in *Action Comics* #448 (June 1975) and a Curt Swan "Private Life of Clark Kent" story in *Superman* #289 (July 1975), published three weeks apart. Which of these jobs did you produce first?
GARCÍA-LÓPEZ: The Clark Kent story was the very first. I got that assignment from Julie Schwartz during my first visit to DC's offices.

EURY: How long had you been living in New York when you got that Clark Kent story?
GARCÍA-LÓPEZ: About five days. I was very methodic, and my first task was to get a place to live, where I could work. When I was done with that, I just went out to look for work.

EURY: How was your English when you moved to the U.S.?
GARCÍA-LÓPEZ: Very bad, and today it's not much better (you have proof of that in front of you). [*laughs*] However, I had no major problems. Most of the people I met were very kind and did not make me feel bad because of my broken English.

I remember doing a lot of work for Joe Orlando in those first months, and I had problems understanding him. Curiously, I had nothing like that with Paul Levitz. Paul was "translating" Joe for me, in a way.

EURY: Did your limited English at the time affect your ability to interpret script directions?
GARCÍA-LÓPEZ: I don't think so. I was working with a dictionary at my side and a little book with American modernisms. If I did find problems with the occasional slang, I never hesitated to ask the editor.

EURY: Were you a fan of Curt Swan's art prior to inking him?
GARCÍA-LÓPEZ: Not really. You have to remember that my contact with Superman was in my early childhood, and I don't think the character was published any more in Argentina when I was in my teens, and besides, I wasn't into super-hero stuff. I got familiar with Mr. Swan here, and grew fond and appreciative of his style.

EURY: Who do you think was Swan's best inker?
GARCÍA-LÓPEZ: I have to say Bob Oksner. He was a great inker and a wonderful artist himself.

EURY: By mid-1976 Julie Schwartz was assigning you *Action* and *Superman* covers and interiors. Did you perceive Superman as a prestigious assignment?
GARCÍA-LÓPEZ: At that time I was not aware if there was prestige involved with certain characters. For me it was mainly a challenge—super-heroes were something new for me. I had to learn it as a new language. I was lucky my comic-book art improved faster than my English. [*laughs*]

EURY: Do you have any anecdotes about working with Julie Schwartz?
GARCÍA-LÓPEZ: Having a relationship with him was an anecdote in itself. He was very funny and 100% professional, the best editor you could have. Besides, as a bonus, through him you had the chance to be introduced to people like Isaac Asimov, among others. Julie was great.

Mid-1970s sample *Big Ben Bolt* newspaper strips by García-López; these *Bolt* samples helped the artist get hired at DC.

TM & © King Features Syndicate. Art courtesy of Modern Masters.

EURY: Your Superman was nimble and athletic, not the Herculean muscleman that most artists drew (and still draw today) ... very Christopher Reeve-like, even before Reeve played Superman in the movies. What was your motivation for drawing Superman this way?

GARCÍA-LÓPEZ: No motivation at all. There was not any plan, mine or from the editor, to push me in a certain direction.

I came from the Alex Raymond "school," and that may explain the way I draw and move the figure. Raymond was a master of "elegance." You have to take a look to his *Flash Gordon* to see how graceful his figures were. However, I was not the first, of course—remember that Superman, in the beginning, was modeled after Flash Gordon and Tarzan.

EURY: Which of Superman's classic artists most influenced your work?

GARCÍA-LÓPEZ: Curt Swan and Neal Adams. Perhaps Adams was not a "classic" at that time, but he came also from Raymond through Stan Drake. So for me they were the people to have in mind when drawing the "big guy."

Superman TM & © DC Comics. Corgi ® is a registered trademark of Corgi Toys.

EURY: You illustrated the famous—or perhaps infamous—cover to *Action #481* (Mar. 1978), featuring Superman "driving" his Supermobile (based upon a Corgi toy vehicle). Were you involved with designing the Supermobile, or did you work from Corgi's designs?

GARCÍA-LÓPEZ: I wasn't aware that it was a "famous" cover. [*laughs*] I'm happy to say that I had *nothing* to do with the Supermobile ... and you're right, it was horrible. I can bet that the design came from the toy's maker, and that no comic-strip artist was ever involved in the "crime"!

EURY: Super-villains Amazo, Solomon Grundy, Lex Luthor, Brainiac, Metallo, and Mr. Mxyzptlk were among the bad guys you drew in stories and on covers. Which was your favorite villain to draw?

GARCÍA-LÓPEZ: I don't remember having a favorite villain. If you ask me now, I'd say Luthor and Mr. Mxyzptlk. You can have fun and play with those two.

EURY: Even though you weren't the first artist to draw S.T.A.R. Labs' Dr. Jenet Klyburn (Curt Swan was, in *Superman #304*, Oct. 1976), your rendition of the character was beloved by fans....

GARCÍA-LÓPEZ: Again, you surprise me with this news. I just did the best I could.

Smart and sexy Dr. Jenet Klyburn, from 1988's *Who's Who Update #1*.
TM & © DC Comics.

Superman vs. Wonder Woman cover line art. García-López pencils/Dan Adkins inks.
TM & © DC Comics. Art courtesy of *Modern Masters*.

EURY: I assumed you were aware that fans liked the way you drew her. Gerry Conway had Jenette Kahn in mind when he created Dr. Klyburn—did you base her appearance upon Jenette?

GARCÍA-LÓPEZ: No, she wasn't [visually] inspired by Jenette Kahn.

EURY: Let's talk about the *Superman vs. Wonder Woman* tabloid (*All-New Collectors' Edition* #C-54, 1978) you drew, which was one of DC's big events of the late '70s. Was this drawn at standard comic-art size or larger?

GARCÍA-LÓPEZ: It was slightly larger than the regular comic-book page.

EURY: *Superman vs. Wonder Woman* was set during World War II. Were you knowledgeable of war history before this assignment?

GARCÍA-LÓPEZ: I was more interested in the politics of

war than in the war itself, and besides, it's a genre I don't feel comfortable doing. But I did the required homework to get it right, even if it was a "super-hero war style."

EURY: Being a 1940s period piece, *Superman vs. Wonder Woman* presumably took place on Earth-Two, yet you drew the more recognizable Earth-One version of Superman. Were you aware of DC's multiple Earths at the time?

GARCÍA-LÓPEZ: Anything you want to know about multiple Earths, *I'm* the guy to ask. [*laughs*] No, I wasn't, not then and not even now. It has to do with quantum physics, right? [*laughs*]

EURY: So, around the same time he fought Wonder Woman, Superman also duked it out with Spider-Man, Muhammad Ali, and Captain Marvel. Why couldn't Superman get along with anyone back then? [*laughs*]

GARCÍA-LÓPEZ: [*laughs*] Seriously, what happens is that without conflict you have no story. Anyway, I liked the one with Muhammad Ali, and its idea that all of us are "Earth beings"—no whites, blacks, Catholics, Muslims, French, or Germans, etc., you get the idea. We only realized that when confronting something not from our common Mother Earth, and Supes and Ali were pushed to fight by those outside powers.

EURY: Since you weren't fond of drawing super-heroes, was it difficult being the artist of the Superman team-up book *DC Comics Presents* (*DCCP*)?

GARCÍA-LÓPEZ: I took everything DC gave me. It was all new for me, and I was not aware it was a team-up book, or whatever you call it. I just did a few [*DCCP*s] for the simple reason I've couldn't keep up with deadlines. The same happened with other projects they gave me.

EURY: Of your various inkers on Superman titles, who best matched your style, and why?

GARCÍA-LÓPEZ: The best inker I ever had in super-hero comics was Dick Giordano. Now, I don't remember if I had him on the Superman titles, but if I didn't, then I'd choose Dan Adkins—he really did a great job in those first *DC Comics Presents* issues.

EURY: Many fans expected you to be the heir apparent to Curt Swan and become *the* Superman artist. Why didn't that happen?

GARCÍA-LÓPEZ: I've never expected that honor, and if some editor had that idea they soon realized that I was not able to do a regular monthly book.

EURY: Instead of becoming *the* Superman artist you became *the* DC licensing artist, your style epitomizing the company's look in merchandising and style guides. How did you get involved with licensing?

GARCÍA-LÓPEZ: DC chose my pencils and Giordano's inks for the first guide. I guess that between the two of us we have a kind of "generic" style appropriate for the project. Now, this wasn't the first licensing work we did together—around 1978 we did several illustrations to promote the use of the chief DC characters to sell merchandise.

EURY: You recently drew Superman and his fellow Justice Leaguers in a *JLA Classified* story arc (issues #16–21, 2005–2006). Any chance we'll see you drawing a *solo* Superman story again?

GARCÍA-LÓPEZ: Maybe… Let me tell you, *I* don't choose to draw Superman, *he* is the one who insists in choosing *me*.

García-López layouts for a *Heroes Against Hunger* (1986) page, from which Jerry Ordway provided finished art.
TM & © DC Comics. Art courtesy of Jerry Ordway.

A powerhouse page from *Superman #301* (July 1976), penciled by García-López; figure inks by Bob Oksner, background inks by Terry Austin.
TM & © DC Comics. Jeff Amason collection.

MARTIN PASKO INTERVIEW

Readers who criticized the Man of Tomorrow's rogues' gallery for being unworthy of the hero were forced to eat their words when Martin Pasko became the *Superman* scribe in the mid- to late 1970s. Under Pasko's guidance, formerly laughable villains such as Bizarro and Titano were retooled as credible threats, and new menaces including the Atomic Skull were introduced. Pasko has written scripts for such versatile TV series as *The Twilight Zone* (mid-'80s version), *Roseanne*, *Batman: The Animated Series*, and *The Tick*, and returned to the Man of Steel in 2006 to pen the comic-book adaptation of the movie *Superman Returns*.

Conducted by Michael Eury via e-mail on March 21, 2006.

MICHAEL EURY: You wrote several back-up stories (for "The Private Life of Clark Kent," "The Sporting Life of Steve Lombard," etc.) while you were cutting your scripting teeth before graduating to full-length Superman stories. Was Julie Schwartz tough on you?
MARTIN PASKO: I'm not sure what you mean by "tough," but Julie did have a tendency to rewrite heavily anyone he considered a beginner—something most editors of his generation did. So there was quite a lot of clunky, unnecessary, and clichéd dialogue that the credited writer had nothing to do with—text

Photo courtesy of Martin Pasko.

that the writers were often frankly embarrassed and annoyed to see in print under their byline. In my case, it was about three years before I'd gained enough of Julie's confidence—and he had heard enough compliments from other editors on my ear for dialogue—that he was willing to trust my draft. By the end of my working relationship with him, the stuff was seeing print almost entirely as I wrote it.

He could be difficult to plot for, too, since he insisted on taking a very active role in breaking the story. And everything was plot, plot, plot, gimmick, gimmick, gimmick to him—not that I fault him for that; he was a product of his time. But that kind of superficiality is what makes the overwhelming majority of mainstream comics published in the 20th century dramatically unsatisfying to all but the least-demanding readers, those whose taste runs exclusively to mindless escapism. Most super-hero "characterization"—with the possible exception of Batman, whose motives and personality are plausibly rooted in psychopathology—is non-existent. Or so preposterous that a truly sophisticated, naturalistic, character-driven story is virtually impos-

sible to achieve unless you ignore most of the ill-conceived back-story and reimagine it, or discard it altogether and start over from scratch. (Which is not often possible in a market that sees a hidebound fidelity to continuity as a selling point. Sadly, that situation has gotten so ridiculously out-of-hand that it's no longer possible to revise your predecessors' unsuccessful ideas without turning the changes into an over-publicized pseudo-event.)

But Julie would never have bought into the idea of trying to create something "sophisticated" in the first place. His generation held that comics were strictly for pre-teens. So the only tool kit a writer was left with in that environment was a grab bag of gimmicks, *shtiklach*, misdirections, and twists, and the writer's job was to figure out how to appeal to an outmoded editorial sensibility without descending into the realm of the Weisingeresque.

All this was further complicated by the fact that after over 30 years of editing comics, Julie was pretty jaded. Consequently, his efforts to be original (although what he described as originality often struck me as needless convolution) sometimes led him to embrace ideas that were over the top. He was so seduced by the perceived freshness of some of his own premises or plot moves that he couldn't see that the reason no one had tried them before was that they were, frankly, silly. Occasionally he needed someone to remind him that the shortest, and best, distance between two story points is a straight throughline. Denny O'Neil could sell him on ways to avoid kitchen-sinking, but not me. For all the plum assignments Julie threw my way, I never did achieve with him the credibility necessary to persuade him that in plotting, at least, less can be more.

EURY: Which of Superman's classic writers and artists most influenced your Superman work?
PASKO: I don't really know how a writer of comics is influenced by artists as opposed to other writers, and while I can vividly remember my favorite Superman stories from childhood, I was never terribly interested in looking up who wrote what (all but the last two years of the Weisinger stuff is uncredited). Why? Because I would learn nothing: stylistically, the writing all read pretty much the same. I got to know many people who worked for Weisinger, and they had an interesting explanation for why all the stories had such a recognizably consistent tone and style.

It was due, not merely to Weisinger's aggressive rewriting, but to a common practice in the 1950s which, by all reports, was ethically challenged even by the standards of that less talent-friendly era. Allegedly, Weisinger would take pitches from one writer, reject all the premises the writer would pitch, then hand the guy one of his "own" ideas to develop. The writer never complained or questioned because he left with a guaranteed assignment. Then another writer would come in and the process would be repeated, with the second writer never knowing that "Weisinger's" concept was actually one of the "rejected" premises pitched by the writer who preceded him. The writers were slow to catch on because everything had been given "the Weisinger touch," which usually involved building in logical flaws, absurd twists, or unlikely cross-promotions.

JULIUS SCHWARTZ
Editor

An autographed Julius Schwartz trading card, from a 1990s comic promo trading set. Courtesy of Heritage Comics, J.S. Collection.

EURY: In your first full-length Superman story (*Superman* #305, Nov. 1976) you started off with a bang, having the original Toyman murder the jester-clad Toyman II by blowing him up with a booby-trapped cuckoo clock! That was an audacious move for comics of the day. Did your story spark any controversy?

PASKO: None that ever came to my attention. Julie wasn't married to Cary Bates' revamp of the character, and all I wanted to do was clear the way for contemporizing the original; I'd always been fascinated by the creepy incongruity of a criminal mind lurking behind that avuncular, Ed Wynn exterior. And even then, the way to contemporize a villain was to "darken" him from a con man to a killer. But the notion that we were being "audacious" never entered our minds. You have to remember that when I started with Julie, all comics were returnable and the direct market was in its infancy: the earliest comics shops had barely opened for business and DC was only just experimenting with direct sales via a van that toured parking lots like a library bus. The only real criterion for success was percentage of print run that sold through at newsstand, and the industry's profile of the average reader dictated that appealing to a fan sensibility was not only a non-starter, but anathema. Fans, it was said, were older than the "real" readers, read every issue, and knew everything there was to know about the characters and continuity. As opposed to the vast majority of the audience, who were supposedly only casual readers: small children, servicemen, functionary illiterates, and non-English speakers who picked up maybe three or four issues a year at most. Veteran editors like Schwartz actually counseled *against* writing for fans. Julie gave all his writers lectures about how stories had to be crafted to be accessible to people who'd never seen a comic book before. It was a mindset so far removed from how the business operates today that it can scarcely be imagined by those who've come up in the slavishly fan-centric, non-returnable environment.

EURY: You're aware that your killing Toyman II didn't stop him from appearing on *Challenge of the Super Friends* in 1978.

PASKO: No, but I'm not surprised. Then, as now, only hardcore comic-book fans value that degree of fidelity to the source material in mass-media adaptations.

EURY: Bizarro was transformed from comic relief to a major menace in your next issue, #306 (Dec. 1976), and you revitalized the former one-hit wonder Metallo in *Superman* #310 (Apr. 1977). Were these more threatening takes on classic Super-foes your idea, or were you encouraged by Julie to make them more dangerous?

PASKO: Those were my takes. From the beginning of Julie's editorial tenure on *Superman* to my arrival, a rogues' gallery was, with a few exceptions, conspicuously absent. Luthor appeared a handful of times, Cary "retconned" the Toyman and created Terra-Man, and Superman would get a worthy opponent whenever Len Wein did a fill-in. But there was little beyond that. Somehow Julie had become convinced that there weren't any viable villains, and so Cary and Elliot Maggin did story after story pitting Supes against balding guys in jackets and ties. Gerry Conway and I came to *Superman* determined to change all that. But, unlike Gerry, I believed

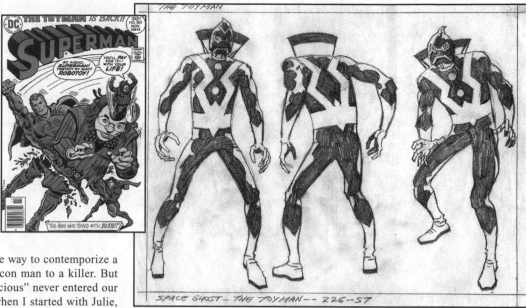

Pasko's first full-length story, in *Superman* #305 (Nov. 1976). Unconnected to either of DC's Toymen is this Jack Kirby-designed Toyman from the Space Ghost revival, part of Hanna-Barbera's *Space-Stars* TV series (1981–1982).

TM & © DC Comics. © 2006 Hanna-Barbera. Art courtesy of Heritage Comics.

that the only problem with most of the existing villains was that they needed to be made "bigger"—more powerful, more grandiose, more desperate—to give Supes a real challenge. The only exception to that was the Prankster, who could only be played for comedy in my judgment, so I relegated him to 8-pagers and one sequence in the *World's Greatest Super-Heroes* syndicated strip, where I gave him a civilian name, Oswald Loomis. In any event, my goal was to take the old villains that Julie disdained and give them an edge, in hopes of attracting new, older readers. I seem to have succeeded in doing that, since the numbers on *Superman* went up while *Action*'s sales plateaued, and the only difference in the creative teams on the two books was the writer.

I also continually pressured Julie to let me make *Superman* as different from *Action* as humanly possible, and do it by giving the book more of a serial structure, with multi-issue story arcs, "B"-stories, and runners that would continue for half a year or more—in short, a structure more familiar to readers of Marvel, who at that time had finally eclipsed DC in sales after a decade of nipping at its heels. This was necessary to give us enough space to cut loose with the action.

Another thing I did was simply take advantage of the fact that Julie's innovations —eliminating kryptonite and making Superman less powerful—had been largely ignored by the other editors who inherited Weisinger titles. Julie was starting to back off from his changes because they were confusing people who were reading the entire Superman line. All I did was push the already-opened door a bit further open, using kryptonite liberally and building a rogues' gallery that better matched the newly "re-powered" Man of Steel. Both Gerry and I were into going for more extreme action—Superman and the villain knocking each other through buildings and planets, that sort of thing. Gerry's results were generally more effective because most of his scripts were assigned to guys like J.L. García-López and Ross Andru, who had a much better sense than Curt Swan of how to use extreme angles, detailed backgrounds, forced perspective, and movement into and away from camera to make the action look as dynamic as possible.

EURY: You created the Atomic Skull in *Superman* #323 (May 1978), turning S.T.A.R. Labs' Dr. Albert Michaels into "the Man with the Self-Destruct Mind." Was Dr. Michaels' transformation planned from his first appearance (in the Gerry Conway-scripted *Superman* #303, Sept. 1976), or was this your embellishment (and if so, how did Gerry react to his supporting-cast member being turned bad)?

PASKO: There were no long-term plans for the character, as I recall; we already had the recurring S.T.A.R. contact in Dr. Klyburn. "Flipping" Michaels was my idea, to get a potentially recurring costumed villain out of the Skull Gang, which were more or less conceived as one-shots. I don't think Gerry even noticed; we were hanging out together a lot during that time, and I think I'd remember if he'd ever commented.

EURY: What can you share with me about your creation of the Atomic Skull?

PASKO: Not much. I remember feeling, after I reread the first story, that the character was nothing special. Even then, the term "atomic" was starting to sound too retro.

EURY: Speaking of character creation, is it true that you coined the name "Ookla" for the sidekick of TV's Thundarr the Barbarian?

PASKO: Yup. Steve Gerber was the co-creator and developer of that show, and an old friend and collaborator from New York (I'd written for *Crazy* magazine when he edited it and had helped him plot a *Howard the Duck*). Steve had developed an urge to share a transplanted New Yorker's take on the insanity of LA with a like-minded dinner companion. So we would meet almost once a week, sometimes in West LA where I was living. On one of those occasions, before I'd begun to write for *Thundaar*, we were wandering around Westwood as Steve was telling me about how the network was frustrating him with its insistence on a Wookiee-like character. He had worked out how the creature could be made to seem somewhat less derivative, but was stuck for a name for it. Just then, we passed one of the entrances to the UCLA campus and when I saw the acronym on signage, the phonetic pronunciation leapt to mind. Entirely facetiously, I said, "Why not call him Oo-clah?" Steve did the unexpected and bit. And this, God help me, I will have on my tombstone.

That was the first of two times that I did that in connection with a Ruby-Spears show. The second was a few years later, when Gerber and I were developing the animated *Mr. T*. The creative exec producer, Joe Ruby, was a freak for dogs and, having created *Scooby-Doo* for Hanna-Barbera with his partner, Ken Spears, Joe usually wanted to put a dog in everything, almost as some kind of good-luck charm. He would also wax rhapsodic whenever he saw what he thought was a clever use of dogs in other people's shows; when Hanna-Barbera did an animated version of *Happy Days*, Joe thought they'd achieved some kind of cartoon brilliance by giving Fonzie a pit bull with a leather jacket. So when, in a conference, Joe started wondering what kind of dog Mr. T would have, I said—again, entirely as a joke—"a dog with a gold chain collar and a Mohawk." Steve started sliding off his seat with laughter, but Ruby was already calling Jack Kirby at his studio and asking him to do preliminary sketches. As it turned out, the dog, a rottweiler or some such named 'Dozer (as in "bulldozer"), became the second biggest seller in the toy line after Mr. T himself. As the one piece of merchandise whose revenue stream the studio didn't have to split with NBC, Universal TV, and the creator of *The A Team*, it made a boatload of money for Ruby-Spears that I never saw a dime of. I've since adopted a motto paraphrasing an old saying: "Be careful what you pitch for; you might get it."

EURY: I've got to thank you for bringing back Titano the Super-Ape in *Superman* #324 (June 1978). You were the only Superman writer during Julie's tenure to touch Titano.

PASKO: Which act—your delight notwithstanding—was eclipsed in sheer madness only by the creation of 'Dozer. As I said earlier, there was a need for antagonists who could keep Superman jumping, and I thought—foolishly, in retrospect—that I might be able to treat a giant ape that shot kryptonite energy from its eyes with the same straight face I brought to Bizarro. I couldn't, and matters were not helped by the art. We kept forgetting that what you got when you called upon the hyper-realistic and earthbound Curt Swan to draw menacing giant monsters invariably looked cute and cuddly at best, and at worst, like something that reminded you of an old Toho movie and made you look for the zipper. I seem to recall that the mall suggested that Titano was one Weisingerism that was best relegated to obscurity.

EURY: What inspired you to pit Superman against a lady pirate, Peg-Leg Portia, who appeared in *Superman* #318 (Jan. 1978)?

PASKO: That was a case of needing to find a character and situation to externalize a theme. One of the things I tried to do wherever possible was find fresh story areas by taking the previously unchallenged conventions of the feature and standing them on their heads. In this case, the convention being questioned was Superman's pledge never to kill, which over the years had been expanded to include always doing whatever it took to save any life in jeopardy. The pitch I hooked Julie with was, *What would happen if Superman were confronted with a situation in which saving a life is not the morally defensible thing to do?* In essence, it was a euthanasia story. This meant Superman needed to confront a throwaway character who could die with Superman's permission—a character whose existence was so wretched that he or she begged for the release of death. I wanted something bizarre and full of weird incongruities, to help give the other-worldly setting the same familiar-but-strange quality of certain planets in the original *Star Trek* series—you know, civilizations modeled on remnants of Earth cultures. I was brainstorming while listening to a Harry Chapin song called "Dogtown"—about the despair of Gloucester fishermen's wives who are left alone for months on end while their husbands are at sea, with no other companionship than the man's dog. The nautical imagery and the song's creepy description of the silently staring dogs intrigued me, and in a

TM & © DC Comics.

few minutes I had the pirate character and the odd juxtaposition of the telekinetic mastiffs.

EURY: What's your assessment of Curt Swan?

PASKO: Curt struck me as a very sweet-natured and astonishingly professional guy whose interior life was at odds with his work. He was more of a draftsman than a cartoonist. Like many comics artists of his generation, he got trapped in what started out as just a temporary gig. What he *really* aspired to be was a realistic magazine illustrator, working in line-art the way Norman Rockwell or Kelly Freas did in oils. He was literal-minded in that same way, too, and flights of fancy that required him to cheat perspective or imagine structures that didn't exist in real life never came easily to him. So being known for over three decades as the unlikely candidate for visualizing an invulnerable man flying through space had to have been difficult for him. But when you needed reality and clear storytelling, Curt was The Man. I was always proud and deeply appreciative of the way he handled the emotional dramatic scenes I wrote for him, or even the comic-relief scenes that were carried mostly in dialogue; his "acting" was impeccable—meaning no one could capture as broad a range of subtle, even mixed, emotions as he could. He could even "play an opposite": you could write a character lying, or saying things that conflicted with his real mood, and Curt could "sell" it. He always knew exactly where to "place his camera," too, and when to move it, but, more importantly, when *not* to. But, even though he was genuinely gratified by how much his work had meant to so many people, his personal taste seemed not to run toward the fantastic. I always sensed a tension when he was called upon to draw truly imaginary stuff. Odd, because the ideas Julie was throwing at him were way more believable than all those Porcupine Jimmy Olsens and Big-Head Lois Lanes he was forced to draw in the '60s.

Anyway, I learned that my instincts about Curt were right one day when I noticed a pencil page that had what looked like color notes in the margin that had been written in pencil and erased. They were scribbled next to a gimmick-driven sequence I wrote that required Superman to take off his boots while in the middle of falling out of the sky (don't ask). I asked Julie what it was, and he uncomfortably explained that sometimes, when Curt would get frustrated, he would vent in marginal comments that he would erase before turning in the pages. Over Julie's objections, I got a magnifying glass to read the impression. It said something like, "This is the most ridiculous thing I've been asked to draw in a long time." I just laughed and told Julie that Curt was absolutely right.

EURY: You also worked with José Luis García-López, who drew some of your *Superman* covers and team-ups in *DC Comics Presents*. Were there any language barriers that affected his translation of your scripts?

PASKO: None. At that time, we believed José to be fluent in written English; he just didn't speak it much. But, despite a charismatic presence that made him look like he'd just stepped out of a Sergio Leone movie, he had a reputation for being one of the calmest, most easy-going people in the business. He patiently suffered many indignities from well-meaning but awkward colleagues trying to overcome the language barrier. Without realizing it, Julie had taken to speaking to him very loudly, as people sometimes do when insecure about whether they'll be understood. It was the only time I heard José speak a sentence in perfect English. He took the cheroot from his mouth and quietly said, "Julie, I am Argentinean, not deaf."

The Pasko-scripted splash to *Superman* #316 (Oct. 1977), drawn by Swan and Adkins.

TM & © DC Comics. Art courtesy of Heritage Comics.

Page 15 of Pasko's Superman/Joker team-up from *DC Comics Presents* #41 (Jan. 1982). Art by José Luis García-López and Frank McLaughlin.

EURY: You were writing *Superman* when *Superman: The Movie* was released in December 1978. As a result, did your work fall under the scrutiny of protective higher-ups at DC and the suits at Warner Bros.?

PASKO: Not that I was ever told about. But the culture of DC's corporate parent was much different then; today's conventional wisdom about how to manage branded entertainment properties wasn't a factor. All the previous media incarnations of Superman (except the Kirk Alyn serials which, in the late '70s, were tied up in a legal dispute) were available to the public at the same time. The idea of "branding," and the corollary that there should be only one conception of a property in the public's mind at any one time, hadn't yet taken hold, so DC was left pretty much to do as it wished. After all, it had been in the Superman business for 40 years by then, so it wasn't like there was any fear that they'd screw it up.

EURY: How did Christopher Reeve's performance imprint DC's vision of Superman?

PASKO: Not much. We ignored the new super-powers or *shtik* the movies introduced, like using the "S" shield as a detachable weapon, and couldn't even figure out some of what Supes was supposed to be doing in the strange climax of the second feature, set in the Fortress. And the comics didn't pick up on the "standing in mid-air" thing till Byrne borrowed it. García-López and Dick Giordano, who was heavily influenced by inking José, were already modeling the face on someone who had features similar to Reeve's. Curt's version—his model sheets were the swipe for just about everybody who wasn't looking at Schaffenberger (or for Nick Cardy, who was always on his own planet)—was a combination of George Reeves and the approach of Win Mortimer, who'd preceded Curt as the primary Superman cover artist. I personally was disinclined to be influenced by the first two films because I didn't like them at all—not for any reasons having to do with the treatment of the character, but just because I found them bad as movies: the wild tone shifts, the erratic pacing, each performer acting in a different style, and cheesy production values because Marlon (I'll Read My Dialogue Off Strips Of Paper Glued to the Props) Brando was eating up the budget—literally, to judge by the look of him. I liked the third one even less, and didn't even bother seeing the fourth one, but by then, I was in Hollywood doing television and very little comics work.

EURY: Did you meet Chris Reeve during his preparation for the role?

PASKO: Yes, Cary and I met with him and DC's president at the time, Sol Harrison, right after Reeve signed for the part. He was skinny and had sandy-blond hair, and didn't look like anybody's idea of Superman, but they swore they had a plan to fix that. I remember that Reeve's questions indicated he was going to try to approach the role internally (the poor guy hadn't yet seen the script, which seemed to be the product of writers unfamiliar with the concept of subtext). Having an acting background, I kind of sensed what sort of hooks Reeve was looking for, and I told him about the idea Nelson Bridwell had had that, as Clark, Kal-El compressed his spine a bit in an attempt to seem shorter than Superman. Reeve, who was well over 6 feet, seemed to spark to that. I remember wondering at a screening whether that meeting was responsible for the now famous angle on Clark's back when Lois demands he come clean on whether he's Superman, and Clark's posture straightens to his full height before he turns around to face her.

EURY: I've been told that DC was hopeful that *Superman: The Movie* would help "save" the comics industry, whose sales figures had been shrinking for some time. Is this your recollection?

PASKO: That may have been the case—the whole industry had the same hope for *Batman* ten years later—but no company officer ever said such a thing in my presence.

EURY: Most of your *Action Comics* stories were back-ups, but Julie assigned you to pen "The Life Story of Superman" in the landmark issue #500 (Oct. 1979). What challenges did that 64-page story present? Do you consider "Life Story" to be your most significant contribution to the Superman Legend? And if not, what would you say is?

PASKO: The only minor challenge was crafting a framing story that would allow the exposition to come up naturally. Once Julie bought my pitch for a subplot that played during a tour through the Superman Museum, it wasn't much of a challenge.

As for significant contribution, I guess that from a fan's perspective, the "Life Story" probably is it; the Tor Books black-and-white reprint is still widely available and enthusiastically recommended as a comprehensive overview of the "pre-Byrne" continuity.

The World's Greatest Super-Heroes daily from Feb. 8, 1979, written by Martin Pasko and drawn by George Tuska and Vince Colletta.

What *I'm* proudest of, however, is that I feel I succeeded in thinking about and writing the characters in a dramatically different way from my predecessors, and perhaps even many of my contemporaries. I can't speak to whether I influenced anyone else; I haven't seen much evidence of that. I'm just gratified that I got away with it at all. The fantasy elements and derring-do were never my primary interest; indeed, if Curt were drawing the job, the more spectacular you made the stunts, the sillier they'd look in that near-photorealistic style. I was more interested in trying to get at how these characters would logically behave if they were real people, to the extent possible within the limitations imposed by the editorial biases. So I'm proudest of little things, like the way Superman disabused Lana Lang of her hope that they could ever have a serious relationship; the dilemmas I put Superman in that forced him to re-examine his own overly simplistic, morally unambiguous world view; and the back-up stories that took up themes like ageism and anti-Semitism in a low-key and indirect way, rejecting the on-the-nose approach that characterized the "relevant" comics of the early '70s.

I think the real challenge in doing Superman even somewhat naturalistically is to get at the inner conflicts beneath the do-gooder exterior. It seems to me that the only way you can take the "Boy Scout" curse off Superman, or transcend the sophomoric and dishonest nature of heroic fiction tropes, is to explore the character's tragic dimensions—the isolation and loneliness, and the terrible burden of the responsibility thrust on him by an accident of birth. I wasn't as successful at taking the material in that direction as I would have liked because, at the time I was writing the book, I didn't have the emotional maturity, nor the kind of craft that comes with experience, that it takes to construct a believable interior life for a fantasy figure. Today I think I could bring a depth to the character that might impress some readers, but I'm not sure that it would be commercial; today the average fan seems to want "fun" comics, and is slow to embrace anything that at least *tries* to be serious-minded or thought-provoking. But back when I did my two-year run on *Superman*, the closest I could get to humanizing the strange visitor was in what I could extrapolate from my personal experience—having been adopted by people who were much older than my contemporaries' parents; having been brought from my birthplace to another country; being singled out as "gifted."

But there's still the possibility that someone, someday, will come to the character with enough objectivity and detachment, as well as maturity and wisdom, to make it understandable and believable in human terms, if readers even want that. The popularity of such alienating and anti-cathartic conceits as "meta-humans"—a concept that militates against making the characters relatable in normal human terms—suggests that today's readership doesn't. So perhaps it doesn't matter whether anyone has yet been able to get Superman to make sense as a real person.

And I'm not sure that anyone has, though a few of the better writers who've tackled the character, like Alan Moore or Mark Waid, have come close. In mass media, the various screenwriters have lacked the ability or inclination to dig deeper than the "iconic" image, so their idea of being true to the character reduces him to a boring if not downright corny Goody Two-Shoes. And, sadly, most comics writers, even the highly regarded ones, are comics fans first and writers second. That strikes me as a handicap: I believe that the only way you can get into new, deeper character-territory is to *challenge* genre conventions rather than celebrate or serve them. But to be a comics fan is to be addicted to those clichés; what seduces people into becoming fans in the first place is the "givens" of the genre—such as the belief that volition can continually trump hard wiring; that instincts from the cerebral cortex, like self-preservation, can ever be overridden except in fleeting moments of great urgency, at least in an individual whose thinking is not already disordered; or the notion that sane people run around calling themselves "heroes" or "adventurers" as if those were job titles. I don't believe anything truly meaningful or worthwhile can be written by the types who indulge in that endless and excruciatingly tedious debate about what does or doesn't constitute "heroic" behavior.

EURY: Same question, but in reference to Julie Schwartz's editorial tenure....

PASKO: Perhaps against his better judgment, Julie allowed Superman to be done by writers and artists who didn't think of super-hero comics as the exclusive province of small children. By doing so, he provided the bridge between the high-concept silliness (or "campiness," if you will) of the Weisinger years and what would be produced in the '90s and later. Without Julie paving the way, subsequent developments like John Byrne's relaunch, and the burst of creativity that followed it under Mike Carlin's guidance, would not have been possible. So Julie is probably just as responsible as anyone for the fact that the character is still viable today.

RICH BUCKLER INTERVIEW

Detroit native Richard Buckler (b. 1949) began penciling mystery and back-up stories in the early 1970s. Throughout the 1970s and 1980s Buckler was a virtual comics whirlwind, illustrating a host of Marvel and DC titles, including *Fantastic Four*, *Astonishing Tales* (featuring his creation Deathlok the Demolisher), *World's Finest*, and *All-Star Squadron*. He has drawn Superman covers and stories on several occasions, chief among them the 1978 *Superman vs. Shazam!* tabloid.

Conducted by Michael Eury via e-mail on February 28, 2006.

MICHAEL EURY: Were you a Superman fan before you broke into comics?
RICH BUCKLER: Of course I was! *Superman* was the first comic book I read, and for years he was my favorite character. I loved the Curt Swan version of Superman and used to practice my drawing by tracing and copying all the Superman poses from the comics (I was around ten years old when I first started drawing). As I expanded my reading and collecting to include just about all of the DC and Marvel characters, Superman remained one of my absolute favorites.

EURY: Other than Curt Swan, which of Superman's classic artists most inspired your interpretation of the character?
BUCKLER: Neal Adams' version knocked me out! But I loved Jack Kirby's treatment of Superman, too! The one that was definitive for me, though, was Curt Swan's Superman.

EURY: I first remember your art in Superman family titles on "Rose and the Thorn" in *Lois Lane* #117 (Dec. 1971). Was this your earliest Superman-related work?
BUCKLER: Yes, this was my first "super-hero" work for DC. It just happened to be something that appeared in a Superman-related title. I was lucky, too. It was a sort of feminist character, and [later] Jenette Kahn was really into this Robert Kanigher creation—plus, it seems, I was one of Jenette's favorites for awhile, and she really loved my treatment of the character. I was quickly promoted to other assignments featuring Superman.

EURY: Did you ever work with Mort Weisinger?
BUCKLER: No, that was before my time.

EURY: When did you meet Julie Schwartz?
BUCKLER: Around 1968–69. This was before I got work at DC Comics. I was turned down at least a half-dozen times before I finally got my first break. I met him during one of my annual treks from Detroit to New York, showing samples of my art, hoping to get hired eventually.

EURY: You went back and forth between Marvel and DC during the 1970s, sometimes working for both simultaneously. What were the pros and cons of the companies during that time?
BUCKLER: I think I've already gone on record with this, but I'll repeat it here. My ambition was to be like Jack Kirby (my all-time favorite comic-book artist/creator) and to somehow eventually draw every character at every company, in every genre. While I could never hope to achieve the speed and versatility of my idol, it was a fun trip that lasted for years—and I think that during my career (of 30-plus years) I nearly accomplished that goal!

EURY: Beginning in the late 1970s and continuing through the early 1980s, you penciled many *Superman* and *Action* (and other Superman family titles) covers. In the early to mid-'80s, Ed Hannigan designed many of DC's covers. Did Ed, or someone else, lay out your Superman covers, or were you designing them yourself?
BUCKLER: It was actually the other way around, in that I used to lay out many of Ed Hannigan's covers (at Marvel, anyway—by the time he moved to DC he knew his way around fairly well). I don't think I was working at DC at the time he was [designing covers]. All of my assignments came to me by way of Vince Colletta or Julie Schwartz. I always worked up my own ideas, with the exception of one or two that were laid out by Ross Andru.

EURY: What challenges did Superman covers present to you, as opposed to covers you drew for other characters and series?

A Rich Buckler/Grey Adams illo of Buckler's creation Deathlok. Deathlok © 2006 Marvel Characters, Inc. Art courtesy of Heritage Comics.

BUCKLER: Well, the challenge was to draw Superman "right." That is, suitably heroic and dynamic, but always with the same "character." What I went for was a sort of Curt Swan/Neal Adams look (I know, always the fan, but that was/is *my* character—the super-fanboy).

The biggest challenge, always, was getting that big "S" right. Julie Schwartz was always busting my chops to get it right. I remember that, one time, he even went to the trouble of sketching out for me the "S" in a carefully constructed diagram, so that I could use it as a template.

The other challenge was trying to "find" a good cover scene in the photocopies of the story that I was given to work up my idea for. Sometimes it was only a few pages. Frequently, the idea (or story situation) would be suggested by Julie (who usually knew what he wanted). He would tell me something like, "Here is what I want. All right, maybe it could be more visual, but you get the idea!" Julie always left it up to me to come up with a way to get his idea across dynamically.

EURY: What are some of your favorite Superman covers you drew, and why?

BUCKLER: Probably my favorites were the covers (and stories) for *DC Comics Presents* featuring Superman and the Shazam Family (issues #33 and 34, May and June 1981)—also the giant tabloid comic featuring *Superman/Shazam* (*All-New Collectors' Edition* #C-58, 1978). I thought at the time that some of the covers I did for Julie Schwartz were kind of nutty or bland … but now I look back on that work and it was pretty cool.

I was very comfortable with the Superman material. More importantly, Julie never had to hand anything back to me and say, "Would Superman do something like that?" or "It doesn't fit for the character." He trusted that I knew and loved the characters.

EURY: One of *my* favorites was *World's Finest* #283 (Sept. 1982) … you managed to make the Composite Superman look utterly menacing—no easy task, as this villain often came off as goofy.

BUCKLER: I'm not sure how to reply to that. I never thought *any* of the characters were "goofy" (well, sometimes the story situations were a little goofy—but that was part of the fun!). I always took my work very seriously regarding the craft of it. Hey, these were characters that appeared in stories for DC's flagship character! I absolutely loved every minute of working on any and all of the Superman books!

EURY: Dick Giordano, Bob Oksner, and Frank Giacoia were among your Superman inkers—who do you think was your best inker?

BUCKLER: That's a tough choice. You just named three of the finest talents in the comics!

EURY: Let's discuss that *Superman vs. Shazam!* tabloid you penciled. This was the first-ever meeting between Superman and Captain Marvel. Did you know much about Captain Marvel before DC's *Shazam!* revival?

BUCKLER: I was thoroughly familiar with Captain Marvel, even though the character flourished at least a generation before mine. Thanks to Roy Thomas and his magazine *Alter-Ego* I was introduced to the character during my early collector/fan days (this was in the '60s). I was exposed to tons of the material via microfilm versions produced by Jerry Bails.

EURY: Was *Superman vs. Shazam!* drawn at regular comic-art dimensions or at a larger size?

BUCKLER: It was drawn on oversized paper, as I recall. I don't remember the exact size and dimensions, but it was bigger than an original page for the regular comic books, so as to allow some photographic reduction to sharpen up detail.

EURY: *Superman vs. Shazam!* was an impressive 72 pages. How long did it take you to pencil it?

BUCKLER: Approximately the time it took me to draw three regular-sized comics. Maybe a little longer, since I was working with the larger page size.

EURY: You brought up your Superman/Marvel Family team-up … it included Hoppy the Marvel Bunny. Was it difficult portraying Hoppy in a realistic manner?

BUCKLER: Funny you should mention that. I'm not a "big foot" type of cartoonist. Throw a funny animal character into a story—Bugs Bunny, or Mickey Mouse—and a "little foot" cartoonist like me is usually thrown for a loop.

Yeah, that was a bit challenging. But after about a quarter of a million figures under my belt, I had developed the ability to sort of "think in 3-D" and visualize just about anything. It was a slow start at first, but I managed to figure out as I went along how to make it work. It turned out to be the most fun part of drawing the story!

EURY: Another major Superman story you drew was "Crisis on Three Earths!" in *DC Comics Presents Annual* #1 (1982), the team-up between Superman and the Golden Age Superman. Cosmetic differences (mainly graying

Original cover art to *Action* #478 (Dec. 1977), by Buckler and Bob Oksner.
TM & © DC Comics. Art courtesy of Heritage Comics.

temples and an altered "S" insignia) aside, how did you approach each Superman to keep them unique?

BUCKLER: That's a hard one to explain. What I do (and I am sure other comics artists use a similar technique) is internalize a lot—that is, in my imagination I will let a scene play as if the people in the story were real. What I ended up portraying was a "youthful" Superman and a more "mature" Superman. Both had the same personality—just different stages of personality development.

EURY: Of the various Superman writers you worked with, whose take on the character did you most appreciate?

BUCKLER: Well, Roy Thomas is my all-time favorite writer. Then again, Gerry Conway was always on and never, *ever* slacked off!

EURY: It seems like everyone who worked for him has a good Julie Schwartz story. How about you?

BUCKLER: I remember sitting in Julie's office and getting my first assignment from him. He was always known to "bust chops," so you really had to be up to it for a one-on-one with him. Anyway, he asked me, point blank, "Rich, what makes you think you're good enough to work for me? Do you really think you can compete with comics artists here that have been drawing for 30–40 years?"

To this day, I remember my answer, word for word, which was, "Do I think I'm good enough to compete with these guys? Yes! Absolutely! And if, somehow, I'm not *yet*—I *will* be, next week, or next month!" Quite a bold statement for a 20-year-old upstart. But I meant every word of it. I think he saw how hard-working and determined I was, and it seemed to me that I had earned a small amount of admiration and respect from him at that moment. Maybe, just for a moment, I had reminded him of his youthful years when he first started. I don't know.

But I remember another time, a year or so later, when I was working at a desk space in the DC Comics offices—right across the hall from Julie, as a matter of fact—he handed me a couple of cover assignments and said something like, "We need these by three o'clock! Think you can do it?" "Of course I can. No problem," I answered (in fact, that was *always* my answer!).

When I worked up two cover sketches, which I insisted that I get paid for separately—prior to that time, the sketch or "cover rough" was considered part of the work of penciling the actual cover—I raced into his office and handed them to him. He quipped, "That was about 20 minutes. What took you so long?" I answered that I had to sharpen a few pencils.

Anyway, he did some quick mental math and said something like, "You just earned about three dollars a minute. You think that's fair?" And I answered, "Sure. I thought up the [cover] idea. If you like it, then I'll draw it!" He thought that over, and I threw in, "Besides, I don't get paid for the quality of my line. I get paid for the quality of my *thought*." I think he liked that idea. And I always appreciated the quality of *his* thought.

He was an amazing man—and one of the best editors I ever worked for.

BOOK: SUPERMAN VS. SHAZAM   C-58   ISSUE & DATE: 3-2800   PAGE: 64

A 2000s Superman illustration by Rich Buckler.

BOB ROZAKIS INTERVIEW

Bob Rozakis, for years known as DC Comics' "Answer Man," began writing puzzles and activity pages for the company in the 1970s before taking a staff position there. During his quarter-century DC tenure, Rozakis spent 17 years heading its Production Department, where he was influential in steering the publisher toward the use of computers for color separations and other phases of comic-book composition.

The co-creator of the fondly remembered series *'Mazing Man*, Rozakis wrote many full-length and back-up Superman stories during the late 1970s and early to mid-1980s, including the chronicles of the hero's college days, the miniseries *Superman: The Secret Years*.

Conducted by Michael Eury via e-mail on February 7, 2006.

MICHAEL EURY: You were a letterhack before becoming a comics pro. Where was your first letter published?

BOB ROZAKIS: My first letter was published in *Adventure Comics* #321, the June 1964 issue. It was about Monel metal, which had characteristics similar to the hero of the same name.

EURY: Through your correspondence with Julie Schwartz you arranged a 1973 tour of the DC offices, a fan's dream come true. Walk me through that day....

ROZAKIS: I had been writing letters to Julie's books for quite awhile, so he knew my name when I called and asked if I could come and visit. He said yes and so I went up to the offices on a Friday afternoon in either March or April of 1973. He showed me

Photo courtesy of Bob Rozakis.

around and I remember meeting Murphy Anderson. Murphy was sitting at a desk in the production bullpen, working on a "John Carter" story for Joe Kubert at the time; I remember him saying that Kubert preferred artists doing pencils and inks.

The key event of the afternoon, however, was that I had brought along some crossword and word-find puzzles I was doing for a fanzine. I thought that E. Nelson Bridwell would enjoy them. When Julie saw them, he grabbed them and went to find Sol Harrison. Next thing I knew, Sol was there, saying, "If you can make up ones just about Superman and Batman, we'll buy them!"

We talked a bit more and agreed I would produce three each for Superman, Batman, and the Justice League. I was back the following Monday with nine puzzles! I wanted to get them done and turned in before somebody changed their mind!

A couple of weeks later, I got a call from Sol asking for Tarzan puzzles, again needing them over a weekend. Those puzzles saw print, in the first *Tarzan Limited Collector's Edition*, before the other puzzles I'd created.

EURY: When did you pick up the hobby of puzzle-making?

ROZAKIS: I had done a couple for a former girlfriend who needed something different to entertain the class during her student-teaching. From there, I decided to do some that were comics-related and submitted them to a couple of fanzines. One, *The New York Review of Comics*, used a few until it disappeared from the scene.

EURY: Is Will Shortz your idol?

ROZAKIS: Will Weng and Eugene Maleska, who preceded Shortz as the *New York Times* puzzle editors, actually.

EURY: Comics readers of the 1970s were familiar with the Batmobile, the Supermobile, and the Spider-Mobile, but you drove the comics-shop-on-wheels, the Comicmobile. What's the story behind that Super-van, and how long was it on the road? And what role did it play in your getting a job at DC?

ROZAKIS: The Comicmobile was "Solly's Folly." The premise was the same as an ice-cream truck—drive up and down the streets selling comic books. I was graduating from Hofstra University (with a BBA in Accounting) and asked Sol Harrison about a job. At the time, Michael Uslan was driving the Comicmobile, but Sol decided I could take that over.

Mike did much better than I did; he was able to get permits to park at local beaches and parks in New Jersey. On Long Island, I was prohibited from going near any of them, along with schools and any other place you might expect kids to gather.

Initially, though, I was hired as a production assistant and helped move the company from 909 Third Avenue to 75 Rockefeller Plaza. Then I drove the Comicmobile for about six weeks. When it was shipped off to Bruce Hamilton in Arizona, I returned to working in the office, this time as an assistant editor to Julie.

EURY: Was *Superman Family* really the result of lack of Comicmobile fan recognition of *Jimmy Olsen* and other Super-titles?

ROZAKIS: Mike and I had lots of research from what we sold and didn't sell. *Plop!* was far and away our bestselling title. *The Brave and the Bold*, with Batman teaming up with another

Bob "Superman" Rozakis and wife Laurie "Wonder Woman" Rozakis, and the Comicmobile; 1974
Photo © 1974 DC Comics

character, sold much better than *Batman* or *Detective Comics*. The Superman titles sold if there was something interesting involving Supes on the cover. The kids certainly didn't know the difference between *Jimmy Olsen* or *Action* or *Superman*. If it had the Man of Steel on the cover, it was a Superman comic.

EURY: What kind of reaction did you get from gas-station attendants when you drove in for a fill-up?

ROZAKIS: Some of them would ask for free comics. I said if I could have free gas, they could have free comics. They never saw the connection.

EURY: What eventually happened to the Comicmobile?

ROZAKIS: Bruce Hamilton had an up-close-and-personal encounter with a semi. And that was the end of the Comicmobile.

EURY: What was Julie like as a boss?

ROZAKIS: Julie liked people to think he was a lot gruffer than he actually was. I learned a lot about plotting a story from him. One of his standards: When you have a mystery in a story, throw out the first five answers you come up with because those are the ones the readers will think of. The one you come up with after that will surprise everybody.

EURY: At first, as Superman editor, Julie Schwartz wasn't intimate with the Man of Steel's history—but his associate editor E. Nelson Bridwell knew Superman (and comics) lore better than possibly anyone. Did Julie and Nelson often butt heads over continuity?

ROZAKIS: Nelson was great for digging up an old issue to prove or disprove a point. He had an encyclopedic memory when it came to comic-book trivia and he knew exactly which issue to pull out. The only times he and Julie would butt heads would be if there was something in a script that contradicted an old story and Julie would decide it didn't matter.

I used to use this type of example: Cary Bates submits a script in which Superman is turned into limburger cheese by red kryptonite. Nelson insists it can't happen because in the June 1957 issue he was turned into cheddar cheese. Julie says it doesn't matter. Nelson argues that it does, citing six other instances, pulling out all the old issues to prove his point. Ultimately, Julie does what he wants.

EURY: Got any good E.N.B. stories to share?

ROZAKIS: Nelson used to fall asleep in the office sometimes. One day, I was walking down the hall and saw him in his office, sprawled across the desk, like a dead man. As I was staring, wondering if I should call the police, Paul Levitz came by. Paul couldn't see Nelson at first, just the look on my face.

I think he nudged Nelson to see if he was still alive and that was enough to wake him up. Somewhat embarrassed, Nelson could only say, "I dropped my pencil."

EURY: You moved from DC's Editorial to Production Departments in 1976. How'd that happen?

ROZAKIS: There were some people who wanted me out of the Editorial Department. Rather than go freelance, I moved into the slot of proofreader and assistant production manager under Jack Adler. When Jack retired in 1981, I took over Production for the next 17 years.

Given the major role I played in developing the formats for the offset books as well as championing the computerized coloring and separations, I think it worked out much better for DC than if I'd stayed in Editorial.

EURY: Long-time readers fondly remember the *Daily Planet* house-ad pages you wrote, where your alter ego of the Answer Man was born. *The Daily Planet* was your idea, wasn't it?

ROZAKIS: Yes, it was. I suggested it to Sol Harrison as a way to hype more of the books. Since I was the proofreader, I knew what was going on in all of them. Sol particularly liked the idea because I would do it on staff and it would not cost anything. I

added the Answer Man column as an extra feature and then got the company to spring for paying Fred Hembeck for his comic strip. (I think he got $15 apiece.)

EURY: Were you involved with another of DC's promo tools, the Hot-Line?

ROZAKIS: I voiced some of the weekly Hot-Line ads. I remember how we would practice them a few times, trying to get as much info into 60 seconds as we could. I wish there was an outtakes reel because sometimes we really messed up.

EURY: How about "The Great Superman Movie Contest"?

ROZAKIS: Yes, I had a hand in that as well. I was the one who "graded" all the postcard entries and got to meet Christopher Reeve when he came to visit the office and pick the winner. (There were only a couple of dozen people who got all the answers correct, by the way.)

A 1977 house ad for DC's Hot-Line (phone number no longer valid), with art by Kurt Schaffenberger.
TM & © DC Comics.

Christopher Reeve pulls the winning postcard for the 1978 "Great Superman Movie Contest," observed by Bob Rozakis (left) and Sol Harrison.
Photo courtesy of Bob Rozakis.

THE SUPERMAN MYTHOLOGY: BEWARE OF PURPLE KRYPTONITE

Run an Internet search for "kryptonite" and you'll discover data about *purple kryptonite*, the variation which, according to Web posts, either imbues non-super Kryptonians with super-powers or gives them short-term mind-over-matter control.

Having a hard time recalling purple K? There's a reason: there's no such animal.

Well-intentioned but mistaken fans have posted erroneous information about purple K, connected to two vintage Superman tales:

The first was an Imaginary Story by Edmond Hamilton in *Superman* #159 (Feb. 1963), where Earthwoman Lois Lane became the heroine Supermaid of Krypton; her exposure to purple "earthite" permanently transferred her super-abilities to the powerless Kryptonian Kal-El.

The second was a "Private Life of Clark Kent" back-up titled "Mind Over Money," written by Bob Rozakis and published in *Superman* #371 (May 1982), where the Metropolis Marvel temporarily gained enhanced mental faculties after encountering a purple *sun*.

Special thanks to Mark Waid and John Wells.

Another thing I did with the contests was come up with the "DC grab-bag" as an alternative prize to the free one-year subscription that had been promised. I put together bundles of 20 books—all leftovers from the DC library—would flag down any freelancers I could to autograph some whenever they came in, and even included foreign editions.

Sol loved it because it cost the company less than all those subs would have … and it cleaned out the library!

EURY: After penning scripts for *Detective Comics* and *Freedom Fighters*, among other titles, you got your first shot at the Superman family by writing a Perry White tale for *Action* #461 (July 1976), "The Toughest Newsboy in Town." Perry's not exactly the most dynamic character to star in "amazing exploits." Why was he chosen for a back-up?

ROZAKIS: Despite what it says in the recent [*Daily Planet*] TPB that includes the story, I did not write it. I got a credit as "Cub Editor" because I did a substantial rewrite (with Julie's approval) on the script. The person who wrote the story opted to not have his name on it … hence the confusion.

So, I guess my first Superman family story is actually the Krypto tale (pardon the pun) in *Action* #467, "A Superman's Best Friend is His Superdog."

EURY: For a couple of years you wrote *Action* back-ups, including Air Wave, where you were often paired with Alex Saviuk. I always felt Alex was underrated as an artist. What can you tell me about Alex?

ROZAKIS: Alex is a great guy and a fine artist. I thought he was overlooked at DC because his work wasn't flashy. If he'd been born 20 years earlier, I think he would have been one of the mainstays of the industry.

I guess if you tallied up who drew the most of my stories, it would be neck-and-neck between Alex and Stephen DeStefano.

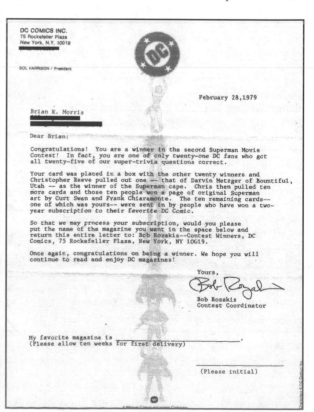

Rozakis' letter to *Krypton Companion* contributor and Superman contest winner Brian K. Morris. (Naturally, Brian chose *Superman* as his subscription!)

Courtesy of Brian K. Morris

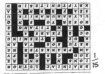

The *Superman* Sunday strip from Jan. 15, 1984. Written by Rozakis, penciled by Jose Delbo, inked by Sal Trapani.

EURY: In the early 1980s you wrote many of the rotating back-up series in *Superman*, among them "Superman: The In-Between Years," "Superman 2020," and my personal favorite, the imaginary series "Bruce (Superman) Wayne." By this point of his career, was Julie still deeply involved with story plotting, or did you have more leeway with your scripting?

ROZAKIS: Julie was always heavily involved in the plotting. You didn't get a go-ahead to write a script unless he approved the plot first. But I had a lot of fun with those back-up series, because they were a way to expand the Superman universe to places no one else was working.

Julie did give me a little more leeway when I wrote the *Superman: The Secret Years* miniseries, but I'd worked out the whole four issues in order to get it put on the schedule.

EURY: Many of your back-ups were drawn by Curt Swan. Did you know Curt well?

ROZAKIS: I knew Curt the way I knew most of the guys from the previous generation, which is to say, as a friendly professional. I enjoyed his work long before I ever had the honor of having him draw one of my scripts.

EURY: During your days as a Superman

contributor, Julie assigned a lot of different inkers to Curt: Tex Blaisdell, Bob Oksner, and Frank Chiaramonte, to name a few. Which of Curt's late-1970s/early 1980s inkers do you think best meshed with his style? And which didn't?

ROZAKIS: Of the three, I'd probably say Bob Oksner. I felt Chiaramonte's inks overpowered Curt's pencils and Tex's weren't strong enough. Of course, they were all trying to replace Murphy Anderson, who would easily be my choice if you'd included him on the list.

But the one I liked was Kurt Schaffenberger, who I got to ink Curt's pencils on *The Secret Years*.

EURY: Your first full-length Superman issues were co-written with Paul Kupperberg and featured the villain the Planeteer in *Superman* #387 and *Action* #547 (Sept. 1983). Creating a villain worthy of Superman is no easy matter, but the Planeteer was a heavy-hitting, Galactus-level menace. What was the genesis of the Planeteer?

ROZAKIS: The story was actually done for a German publisher named Ehapa. DC had a deal to produce a number of extra-length

(left) Note the logo changes between *Superman* issues #385 and 386.
TM & © DC Comics.

stories specifically for them. Julie decided to team up Kupps and me to do that story—spread the wealth a bit.

To be honest, I don't remember how we came up with him, but it was undoubtedly in a plotting session with Julie. And I'll bet it was Julie who came up with the name.

Over the next few years, I worked on a few more of the stories for Ehapa, most of which never saw print in the U.S.

EURY: You created another Super-foe, the genie-like Yellow Peri, in *New Adventures of Superboy* #34 (Oct. 1982), then brought her into Superman's life beginning with *Action* #559 (Sept. 1984). She even made it onto TV, in the second season of *Superboy*. Were you consulted for this episode?

ROZAKIS: The Yellow Peri was another character that started with a name. Julie and I were walking to a luncheon one day and he suddenly said to me, "The Yellow Peri! I want you to use that as the name of a character." So I used her in *Superboy* and then had her grow up to return in the Superman stories.

And no, I was not consulted about her use in the TV series.

EURY: You also wrote the *Superman* newspaper strip for a while. When, and who was the artist?

ROZAKIS: Well, I didn't write the strip; I wrote *The Superman Sunday Special*, which was a potpourri of puzzles, trivia and (of course) Answer Man answers. It ran every Sunday for two years, but never made it into a New York paper, so I never saw it in print until my aunt in Cleveland sent me a couple of comics sections for the *Plain Dealer*. Jose Delbo was the penciler and Sal Trapani did the inks.

EURY: Superman's logo was slightly modified in 1983, between *Superman* #385 and 386, with some of the characters— particularly the "U"—being rounded out. It was a change that I suspect most folks didn't pick up on, but eagle-eyed geeks like me noticed. You were heading up Production at that time—what was the reason for the logo change?

ROZAKIS: I don't remember. A desire to streamline it just a little?

EURY: In *Superman* #411 (Sept. 1985), the Julie Schwartz 70th birthday issue, you wrote that "Julie turns up in the most inopportune places at times" in regard to your colluding with Dick Giordano and others to orchestrate this "top secret" tribute issue. You *must* have some juicy stories about Julie near-misses or other bumps in the road in the production of this issue behind the editor's back....

ROZAKIS: The one I particularly remember: Elliot Maggin was sitting at my desk in the Production Department and we were talking through the plot. (Who better to plot a Julie story than someone who had worked as Julie's assistant editor?) All of a sudden, Julie barges into the department and is startled to see Elliot in there. Elliot did a "hummina hummina" and walked out.

Julie asked me later what Elliot and I were talking about and I said he'd had an income-tax question, a logical thing to be asking someone with an accounting degree. Julie bought that and it wasn't until we surprised him with the book that he said, "Aha! I *knew* it wasn't a tax question!"

EURY: Last question: After the Crisis, did 'Mazing Man inherit Jimmy Olsen's Superman signal watch?

ROZAKIS: Yes, and both the watch and 'Mazing Man are off in some parallel dimension—along with all my other contributions to the legend of the Man of Steel.

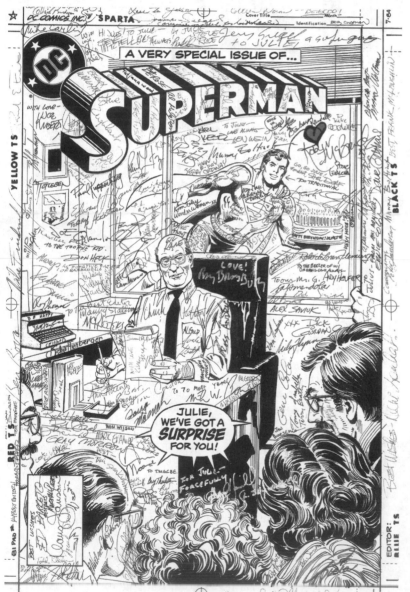

"DobRo" was one of the masterminds behind the Julie Schwartz birthday issue, *Superman* #411. Schwartz was presented with the original cover art to the issue, signed by DC staff and creative personnel.
TM & © DC Comics. Art courtesy of Heritage Comics.

Story pages 1, 4, and 17 of "Partners in Peril," scripted by Rozakis (over a Bridwell plot) and drawn by Alex Saviuk and Frank Chiaramonte, for an Ehapa publication.

CURT SWAN INKERS ROUNDTABLE

Interviews conducted by Brian K. Morris in March 2006.

During Curt Swan's decades-long association with the Man of Tomorrow, a variety of great artists embellished his pencils, all excellent illustrators in their own rights. And when fans of *the* Superman artist want to learn more about the pencils that brought the world's greatest hero to life, who better to ask than the men who inked them?

"Gathered" together via individually conducted telephone and/or e-mail interviews, the participants in this roundtable are, in alphabetical order:

Joe Giella

Joe Giella (b. 1928) has inked not just Superman, but almost every Silver Age DC hero from his collaboration with penciler Dick Dillin on *Justice League of America* and *World's Finest Comics*. A mainstay of Julius Schwartz's inking stable, Giella has also worked in many fields of art, including syndicated newspaper strips like *Batman* in the 1960s and *Mary Worth* in the 1990s and 2000s. In addition to inking Swan in *Superman* #219 (Aug. 1969), Giella inked Curt in *Action Comics* #484 (June 1978), featuring the wedding of the Earth-Two Clark Kent and Lois Lane.

Dick Giordano

Aside from being one of the most innovative editors at Charlton and DC Comics, as well as one of comics' finest illustrators, Dick Giordano (b. 1932) has embellished more pencilers than this finite space allows to mention, trained some of the best inkers around, won awards from fandom and his fellow professionals, and demonstrated his talents in not only comics, but also in advertising and commercial art. He inked Curt Swan in *Superman* #240 (July 1971) and #275 (May 1975), and several on covers.
Recommended reading: *Dick Giordano: Changing Comics, One Day At a Time* by Michael Eury (TwoMorrows, 2003).

Dave Hunt

After laying himself off as a Senior Designer at Crowell-Collier-MacMillan, Dave Hunt's (b. 1947) samples earned him a staff job at Marvel Comics, doing corrections as well as backgrounds for Frank Giacoia, Joe Sinnott, Mike Esposito, and others before moving on to ink numerous Marvel titles. When DC made him an offer he couldn't refuse in 1978, Hunt wound up inking a variety of great pencilers such as Swan, Irv Novick, Don Newton, Bob Oksner, Alex Saviuk, Gene Colan, and his friend Kurt Schaffenberger, among others. He also has the distinction of inking Wayne Boring's last Superman stories in *Action Comics* #561 (Nov. 1984) and 572 (Oct. 1985).

Bob Oksner

From his early days at Timely (Marvel) Comics, Bob Oksner (b. 1916) made his way to DC Comics, showing his penchant for strong storytelling and drawing pretty women. Oksner's art graced DC's humor titles for many years before he became a DC mainstay in the 1970s on "Supergirl" and as a cover artist. During his illustrious career, Oksner also wrote and/or drew syndicated newspaper strips such as *Miss Cairo Jones*, *I Love Lucy*, and *Dondi*; worked in advertising; and won awards from the Academy of Comic Book Artists and the National Cartoonists Society. Bob succeeded Murphy Anderson as Curt Swan's chief inker in the pages of *Superman* and *Action Comics* in 1973 and stayed at the post until 1976.
Recommended reading: Supergirl history in *BACK ISSUE* #17 (TwoMorrows, Aug. 2006).

Dick Giordano inks, Swan pencils, from *Superman* #240 (July 1971).

Ty Templeton

Two of the funniest comic books to come out during the 1980s were the cult classics *Stig's Inferno* and *Kelvin Mace* ("A Man Who Has No Business Being Anyone's Role Model"), both by Ty Templeton (b. 1963). Once he came to DC, he also showed a talent for dramatic storytelling. The long-time writer and artist of DC's "animated" *Batman* stories, as well as projects from Marvel Comics, Fantagraphics, and the mid-2000s *HeroScape* inserts, Templeton's impressive résumé includes inking Curt Swan in comics such as *Who's Who in the Legion of Super-Heroes* and in *Superboy*, based on the syndicated television series.

BRIAN K. MORRIS: How did you get the job of inking Curt Swan?
JOE GIELLA: Mort Weisinger would borrow me from Julius Schwartz to work with him on certain projects. It wasn't so temporary when he asked me to pencil and ink the *Batman* syndicated strip. That assignment lasted four years. This played havoc with Julie's schedule. Anything that altered his schedule made him very angry. Mort would say to me, "Joe, I have a very important job for you." I was not in the habit of turning editors down. I probably would say, "Okay, no problem." You don't dictate to the editors, they tell *you* what to do. [*laughs*] That's what happened.
DICK GIORDANO: It's not a job, per se; it's an assignment that an editor makes for a particular story. It normally is made on a case-by-case basis and doesn't necessarily extend beyond the assignment at hand. I don't recall why I was given these assignments... too many years ago and I rarely asked "Why me?" anyway.

DAVE HUNT: My regular book started out as *Legion of Super-Heroes*. I had no idea how hot that was at the time. I hadn't read comics in a long time. In fact, I'll tell you, I didn't know anything about many of the Marvel characters when I started [at Marvel]. I kind of grew up with the DC characters. I knew Batman and Superman real well, but I had never read a *Legion of Super-Heroes*. And also, I did "Green Arrow" with [Alex] Saviuk and I didn't know they were the A-line books that they were. But I think maybe a year or two, I don't recall, they set me down in the waiting room and Paul Levitz was running around. I was waiting and waiting, waiting, waiting; and I heard a lot of talk outside. And Paul came in with a Curt Swan story and he said, "You want to do this?" And I said, "Uh, okay." [*laughs*] So he introduced me to Julie Schwartz and the rest is history. [*laughs*]

I didn't know anything about [Schwartz], I didn't know who he was, I didn't know that I had loved his work as a kid, growing up. [*laughs*] All I knew is he was sort of a grouchy guy, or he *seemed* to be, and he was very businesslike. He sat me down and said, "Well, do your best. Make it as photographic as possible," because Julie, his mind was all in the writing. He knew good art in a way, but it wasn't his strong suit.

Yeah, he handed me a 22-page Superman story by Curt Swan. And that's why I said, "Okay. Oh, sure." [*laughs*] Because of my history, I knew Curt's work very well and in fact, when I was a kid, I had no intention of being a comic artist. But I did copy one or two people. One was Wally Wood and the other was Curt Swan. So you could imagine… [*laughs*]

BOB OKSNER: I was doing humor magazines like *Jerry Lewis* and I think I had some of the longest runs of any humor magazines there. However, in about 1970 or 1971, they took [*Jerry Lewis*] off [the schedule]. I guess there was no call, no market. And Carmine Infantino and Joe Orlando were editors at DC; they put me on Curt Swan's work almost right away and that's how I started on Curt Swan. I appreciated his art; he was great.

TY TEMPLETON: No story here, I'm afraid. I was inking stuff for Mike Carlin out of the Superman office at the time—over Byrne on *Action*, over [Jim] Mooney on *Superboy*, and over [Dan] Jurgens on *Adventures of Superman*—when I got the assignment to ink Swan. No fanfare, just another day on the job, more or less. Of course, it was a personal thrill for me, but there wasn't any sort of lobbying on my part.

MORRIS: How did you approach the job of inking Curt? Trepidation? Eagerness? Just another job?

GIORDANO: A little of each, really. To look at Curt's pencils was to want to ink them. Trepidation because it was a challenge that I wasn't sure I could meet—I didn't!—as I'd always thought that Curt hadn't often been inked well, and that maybe I was the guy? And, yes, another job. I was working exclusively for DC at this period and one job followed the other. I never turned down an assignment unless the deadline was impossible to meet. My workload came from four or five different editors.

OKSNER: I'd rather, of course, have been doing humor, but I had to eat, I had to earn money. But DC had been very, very helpful to me, and good, because I left them several times, and came back, and they put me right straight to work. I never had any problems at DC.

GIELLA: A little of each. Every job is different. I psyche myself up prior to starting. It is very similar to painting and carpentry, which I love to do. A lot of the work is in the planning. Whether it's carpentry, painting, or comics, the joy in seeing a project materialize from its infancy stage to completion has kept me going all these years. I never get bored.

HUNT: Yeah, I guess I'd say so. I remember being a little scared, sort of like, "I've got to do this. Don't screw it up, Dave." I knew it was really important. I went home and I started work on it, and I settled into it really fast. I was surprised. I remember feeling

like, "Hey, wait a minute! I know Curt Swan's work so well. I've been looking at this for 30 years." [*laughs*] And so it became very natural for me to ink Swan.

TEMPLETON: I approached it with tremendous eagerness *and* fear. Swan was one of the five or six seminal artists of my childhood. Before I knew the names of different artists, I had long known Swan was the "good" Superman artist. At this point in my career, I had inked over John Byrne and Dan Jurgens for a while and I felt like a solid professional … but inking over Swan was playing in the big leagues in a way that working with my very talented contemporaries was not.

I had a similar reaction the first time I inked Jim Mooney and Irv Novick. The folks that came before us in the biz will always remain legends to me because of

Bob Oksner in the 1970s.
Photo courtesy of Bob Oksner.

Bob Oksner inks, Swan pencils, from *Action* #438 (Aug. 1974).
TM & © DC Comics. Art courtesy of Heritage Comics.

their power to inspire. As much as I *love* the work of say, Jerry Ordway—whom I inked once or twice—there's something magical about working with a childhood hero.

Kirby, Wood, Kurtzman, Swan, Gil Kane, and Will Eisner were the six artists who used to blow my mind when I was a kid. Later I discovered Moebius, Toth, Kubert, etc. Although I've met most of them once or twice over the years, I only ever got a chance to work with Swan professionally, and for that I always thank my lucky stars.

MORRIS: Curt's pencils are known to be clean and richly detailed. Did this make them easier or more difficult to ink?
TEMPLETON: Curt's pencils are richly detailed, but I'm not sure I would describe them as "clean." Curt had a strange habit of not erasing lines he wasn't happy with. You'd often come across a figure with an extra hand—seriously—because Curt had thought better of the gesture and redrawn the arm … but the silly man didn't erase the original gesture. He did that a lot with more subtle lines as well, perhaps drawing three different jawline contours in a closeup. Of course, it wasn't hard to figure out which was the "right" line, since it was clearly much darker than the other lines. Sometimes the inker had to choose which line Curt meant. I found it a very pleasant way to work, since I wasn't just tracing lines, but making decisions.

Also, Curt had the other strange habit of roughing in the word balloons in the pencil stage, and not penciling anything in that space. From time to time, the letterer would put the balloon in a different spot in the panel, and the inker had to finish the blank spot. I remember one panel had a character with no foot since Curt assumed the word balloon was going there. He had a leg … but no foot. As inker, I had to draw that foot in there, and I used to dutifully find similar Swan panels, and do my best to "swipe" a Swan shot so the missing parts of the art would stay consistent.

But the basic drawing, the anatomy, the light and shadow, the backgrounds, and especially those living, expressive faces, was *all* there. There was never a moment, as the inker, where you felt you could improve the drawing, just live up to its potential.
GIELLA: Curt knew what he was doing. He was more of an illustrator. I didn't have to correct anything. For me, his pencils were difficult to ink. In order to do a decent job on Curt's work, you really should know how to draw. I don't think any of us originally started out as inkers. For monetary reasons, many of the artists decided to ink. As far as I am concerned, I can ink much faster than I can pencil. For the last 15 years, I have been doing the *Mary Worth* strip. Penciling the strip is a lot slower, but I make time on the inks. I'm sure the opposite is true with many of the artists.
GIORDANO: They were clean and detailed but also quite "soft." Nothing had a hard edge to it. More realistic than is always appropriate for fantasy work. I found them difficult to ink.
HUNT: You know, Joe [Giella] and I have talked about that very thing. We have talked about inking Curt and the funny thing is I will describe his penciling as much rougher than you might expect. Because his inkers make him look pretty similar, you might think his pencils are very tight, but they weren't. The key to Curt Swan was that there may be several lines in there, but the

Kurt Schaffenberger, Curt Swan, and Murphy Anderson, circa 1994–1995. Autographed to their friend and collaborator Dave Hunt.
Photo courtesy of Dave Hunt.

right one was in there. Gil Kane, he might have had ten lines in there and you never were quite sure which was the right line.

Actually, it made it easier for someone like me. Inkers who can draw like the wiggle room. One of the hardest things to do is ink a penciler who digs in the paper and you have to ink in the grooves. That's a Frank Giacoia ism, "ink in the grooves." That's hard.

Well, okay, I won't mention any names, but there are some pencilers who dig it in. They think they're inking with their pencil and then it's very hard for an inker. I mean, aesthetically, it's hard because very often, the line isn't in the right place and we are obligated. What are you going to do? Are you going to white it out?

MORRIS: How much extra work do you want to put in on this, right?

HUNT: Exactly. And of course, we don't make big bucks in comics, so…

We did a couple of stories with Terra Man and one of the stories started out as a full-page splash of a shoot-out in a barroom with like a million characters. And Curt penciled in the margins, "Sorry, Dave." It took forever to ink that, it must have taken forever to draw it. But I wish I had not erased that. [*laughs*]

OKSNER: [The detail] made them enjoyable to ink. Easier and everything was there; and enjoyable, working on a good artist's pencils. You didn't have to create anything where things were lacking. They were not lacking in his pencils, nothing. I believe it's because the pencils were so good, that they were so wonderful to work on.

MORRIS: Since Curt's pencils were so complete, what did you try to bring of your own style to the jobs?

GIORDANO: Curt's anatomy, perspective, and compositions were impeccable but that didn't make them complete. He did not pencil for black-and-white line inking but instead drew like an illustrator drawing gray areas mixed with some indicated black-and-white. Since we weren't using washes, the gray areas had to be converted to either black or white or using black line work to suggest gray.

I used my ink style on every job I inked. Curt's were no exception. The weighted lines to suggest mass, clothing folds, and hair rendering among other of my techniques went into every job of Curt's. Alas, to no avail. I joined the legion of inkers who couldn't ink Curt well!

GIELLA: Well, I wanted to do a good solid job and still try to maintain Curt Swan's style. That was not an easy task. I remember our production manager Sol Harrison telling us because the reproduction left a lot to be desired, we should thicken our lines and add more blacks. I learned this working with Dan Barry on *Flash Gordon*. He was a great designer and he really knew his reproduction. Dan's influence really helped me in this field, especially on Curt Swan jobs.

TEMPLETON: I wouldn't have wanted the slightest hint of my own style to the job. I was working with a legend, why should I want to impose upon it? No, I tried as hard as I could to reproduce the styles of George Klein and Murphy Anderson, who were my favorite inkers on Swan … and I probably added touches of Joe Sinnott and Wally Wood, my two favorite inkers of all time.

Of course, all of that failed, and I ended up doing it in my style, whatever that is. Wally Wood once said that an artist's style is the accident that happens when he unsuccessfully attempts someone else's style and fails.

OKSNER: Well, I was just beginning to do Superman stories, Superman art. There was nothing I felt I could bring to it. If he had to draw a girl or something like that, I could try to make her prettier, although they were already gorgeous.

I'd just begun. When you're beginning with a top-flight penciler, you don't think of adding anything in the beginning. Later on, I may have, but it happened so long ago that I can't recall anything that I added to Curt's.

HUNT: I never saw him do a breakdown. He always did a full job. I would add blacks, I would spot blacks, that used to be kind of taken for granted that's what an inker did. It was rare way, way, way back that a penciler would really spot blacks to any extent and it was up to the inker. Well, you know, I'm talking about a way of thinking that's years and years old. This is not the modern-type comic art. You know because you're sort of my

Dick Giordano pencils *and* inks for a mid-1970s Superman puzzle.
TM & © DC Comics. Art courtesy of Heritage Comics.

Bob Oksner pencils *and* inks: cover art to (left to right) *Supergirl* #9 (Dec. 1973–Jan. 1974), *Action* #453 (Nov. 1975), and *Action* #455 (Jan. 1976).
TM & © DC Comics. Art courtesy of Heritage Comics.

generation, in a way, and it was called "the black-and-white style," and it came out of [Milton] Caniff and on and on.

MORRIS: How did Curt's pencils, or his approach to story-telling, compare to other pencilers you've inked?

OKSNER: First of all, he didn't originate muscles, or create muscles where no muscles were, and cartoonists did. And his pencils had a feeling of weight. They were solid and he was wonderful to ink.

TEMPLETON: As a storyteller, he was amongst the best. At the time I was inking him, the dominant style had moved to very dynamic panel layouts, which Curt wasn't big on. He was a meat-and-potatoes storyteller, and by that, I mean he got the job done without excessive flash, which is often distracting. I'd say that *no one* was as good at meat-and-potatoes storytelling as Curt was.

I look at it this way—Curt was *so* good at creating realistic scenes, human faces and expressive and engaging body language, that he didn't *need* the flash that lesser pencilers rely on. Take Todd McFarlane, for example, or even Jim Lee. I'm fond of their work, but it's nothing *but* flash, with fairly weak storytelling for the most part. There's something very attractive about those dynamic pages we see nowadays, but if you asked a modern artist to tell a story in square panels, six to a page, like Curt preferred, you'd see their shortcomings in a right hurry.

Curt's basic drawing *had* no shortcomings, so he felt he didn't need to distract you with flash.

HUNT: Well, that's a complicated question. A lot of it really had to do with the writing of Superman. There's a lot of people standing around at *The Daily Planet*, talking in rooms, head shots. But Curt's pictures of Superman flying through the air are as dynamic as anybody's, today or yesterday. That was incredible.

The storytelling was visual. That's the trick. I used to think of the inker as being like the art director in a movie. You know, I light scenes, I set the mood. The writer and the penciler put the characters in a room, but the rest of it is up to me.

GIELLA: In comparing Curt Swan to *Justice League of America* artist Dick Dillin, I know they were both great artists

but I felt more comfortable and relaxed working on Dick Dillin's pencils. His style was closer to mine.

Curt may have been a better artist, and I remember joking with Frank Giacoia, "I need a few drinks before I start working on Curt's job." He really put a lot of detail in the scenes. No faking.

GIORDANO: Curt's approach to storytelling was clear and straightforward, but not as dynamic as Irv Novick, Mike Sekowsky, or, of course, Neal Adams. But you know what? It didn't matter. Curt's work had a unique charm of its own!

MORRIS: For those who inked Curt Swan on a regular basis, why did you eventually move on?

OKSNER: I guess I got other assignments. I was doing covers, *Superman* covers, *Action* covers. And I started to do Captain Marvel [in *Shazam!*]; I enjoyed drawing Mary Marvel. I enjoyed drawing anything that had either a girl in it or some humor. And of course, during those years, I did many covers and *Welcome Back, Kotter*.

HUNT: Remember when John Byrne took over Superman? That's why *I* left the series. I was doing Superman and I got this memo. Everybody associated with Superman came in on a certain day and time, so we did. Now picture this; this is the Valhalla or the pantheon [*laughs*] … this is all tongue-in-cheek, by the way. There's me, there's Curt Swan, there's Kurt Schaffenberger; right there, you've got a hundred years' worth of skill and experience. There's Julie Schwartz—okay, there's *200* years. [*laughs*] There's Alex Saviuk and others. So Dick [Giordano] said—pretty much, this is a quote—"None of you are ever going to work with Superman again." You can imagine what a chill went through that room. He said, "John Byrne is coming in and we're revamping the whole thing."

It was a really short meeting, not a lot of discussion and explanation. He said, "We have to change direction with *Superman*. It's not selling that well."

MORRIS: Did you have a page/panel/story that stands out in your mind as a particular favorite? Any that you wish you could get another chance at?

Ty Templeton inks, Swan pencils, from *Action Comics Weekly* #642 (Mar. 14, 1989).
TM & © DC Comics.

TEMPLETON: Favorite panel, hands down was the last panel in *Action Comics Weekly* #642 (Mar. 14, 1989). It was a drawing of Clark looking at the reader and winking. Such an iconic panel, and I got to work on it … *ahhh*.

The last panel of the Legion of Super-Heroes Clubhouse story was another good one, because it featured all 25 members of Curt's Legion, waving at the reader. It was Curt's last full Legion story. I gave the page to Mark Waid when Curt passed away. It's one of the *Secret Origins* issues (#46, Dec. 1989).

My favorite story was a two-parter with Luthor and Superboy in another dimension, where Supes had lost his powers (*Superboy* #9 and 10, Oct. and Nov. 1990). It was the fifth or sixth story I had done with Curt, and I was finally feeling confident, rather than nervous. Those two issues turned out very well, though they printed a little blotchy. Curt told me once that he really appreciated the work I'd done on that two-parter. He actually requested me on a specific story after that job.

GIORDANO: No favorites that I can remember … we're talking 25–30 years ago on some of these jobs. I can't think of a job, Curt Swan's or any one else's, that I wouldn't wish to have another shot at. Curt's more than any one else, though, because I felt that I didn't do him justice.

GIELLA: Almost every comic job that I have ever done, I wish I could do over. I feel this is especially true at comic conventions, signing books for the fans. It sure brings back a lot of memories for me, over 50 years in the business.

OKSNER: Not really, no. They were all so good. [*chuckles*] If I could, I would recall the name of it. In those days, as I said, I never had a day when I didn't work, or seldom a day [*chuckles*] and that was of my own volition, not from lack of work. So with all the stuff I did then, I have no memories of the particular stories that I inked.

MORRIS: Did you ever get to meet Curt? What were your impressions of him as a person?

GIORDANO: This was the era of all the work being used by DC was done by people living in the Tri-state area and artists and writers delivered their work to the DC offices often in those pre-FedEx Days. Curt also lived in Connecticut as I did, and we attended the same social functions.

THE TARANTULA'S BACK IN TOWN— AND SPIDER-MAN HAS HIM!

30

Dave Hunt and Mike Esposito inking Ross Andru on a Gerry Conway story (a gathering of Supermen!), from *Amazing Spider-Man* #147 (Aug. 1975).
© 2006 Marvel Characters, Inc. Art courtesy of Heritage Comics.

Curt was mild-mannered, soft-spoken, and very easy to get along with. He laughed easily and enjoyed life in his quiet way. And like many of the Westport artists, loved to play golf.

TEMPLETON: I spoke to him on the phone a couple of times, but got to meet him only once. It was at the DC offices, years ago when [Mark] Waid was an editor there. I was hanging around Waid's office and Curt came in to deliver a job and Mark introduced us. He looked like a living Curt Swan drawing.

In my life, I've only ever asked three comic pros for their autographs: Neal Adams, Murphy Anderson, and Curt Swan; and Curt was the only artist I've ever asked for an autograph since I became a pro. Neal and Murphy were at conventions when I was a teenager. I've met Stan Lee, Jack Kirby, Steranko, Eisner, Jim Lee, Mike Mignola, etc. etc. etc. … but I've never felt the need to ask for a signature, except with Swan. I don't know why, but meeting him unexpectedly, like that, I was flustered and thrown and I hunted down a copy of a *Superman* comic in the office and had him sign it. It was like meeting the Pope, or a movie star or something.

Joe Giella, Dave Hunt, and Joe Kubert, plus Julie Schwartz (seated). Date unknown.

Photo courtesy of Dave Hunt.

OKSNER: I never got to meet him. He lived in Connecticut and I lived in New Jersey. And we brought the work into the office and [left the building] at different times. So I never really saw him.

HUNT: No, not very often at all.

I felt about him kind of like an uncle, in a way. My Uncle Bill had been in the Army and Curt had been in the Army and that's where he started drawing for *Stars and Stripes*, I believe. However, he wasn't that much older than I was and yet I had grown up loving his work. I was reading *Superboy* around, say, 1950 to '52. There would occasionally be a Curt Swan story in *Superboy* and I just loved those. That's where I pretty much first saw his work. Most of the *Superboy* [art] was George Papp or others in a much more cartoony style. But when Curt would draw a story—"*Wow*, look at that! Wow!"

GIELLA: I did go to a few Christmas parties with Curt. He loved to dance and he always had a smile on his face. We got along very well.

When my dad passed away, I couldn't get anyone to help me on the *Batman* strip. Curt came to my rescue. I drove to his home in Connecticut. He seemed a little nervous. Maybe he thought he had to duplicate my style. I told Curt the wake and funeral was going to take about four days. "Here is the script and reference, have fun!" I was not going to dictate to Curt Swan.

I was lucky to have him do a complete *Batman* week for me. He did a beautiful job. What a talented man.

MORRIS: I guess he was a Superman in real life. too.

GIELLA: With *me*, he *was* Superman. [*laughs*]

MORRIS: What does Curt Swan or his art have to teach other artists?

GIELLA: That's a good question. Occasionally, art students ask me to look at their work, I try to allocate a little time for them. Don't tell this to King Features, but I have never been able to get ahead on my *Mary Worth* schedule.

I always bring up the comic greats. Curt is definitely among them. My comments to the students are, "Don't imitate the hot artist of the month. Study their work and see what each artist is contributing to the field. Eventually, you will develop your own style."

Some will listen, some won't. *I* should talk. I went through the same stage.

OKSNER: Well, if they would look at Curt's work, I guess the reality and the solidity of the draftsmanship that he had, that would help them. But I think the market [today] is different, totally different. It's probably much more exciting, but artistically, not great. I mean, there are some of them [who are great], I should think.

HUNT: Oooh! [*thinks*] Okay, learn to draw, period!

I learned a lot from inking Curt, about how to draw people, let's put it that way. It sounds like a cheap book—*How to Draw Realistic People, How to Draw Children So They Don't Look Like Little Adults*—Curt could do that; how to draw clothes on figures as they don't look like they're made out of sheet iron. Look at a lot of comics today. You'll see a lot of sheet iron going on there.

A page from Templeton's *Stig's Inferno* #6 (1984).
© 1984 Ty Templeton.

They're not paying much, they're all fanboys, they're all brought in by their buddy-boys who happen to be editors.

GIORDANO: I think I'll pass on this one except to say *all* artists learn from those who went before … but not *all* that went before.

TEMPLETON: Skill is the best solution to any problem. If you know what you're doing, you'll last forever, and people will always respond to you. Curt was all about the skill and the mastery.

MORRIS: What did I forget to ask you?

HUNT: What about Kurt Schaffenberger? We would always trade Christmas cards and he would always drew his Christmas cards and you can see [Kurt's wife] Dorothy in those drawings. Kurt drew himself all the time. Incredible!

Kurt was always a gentleman. He really was what we would call a gentleman, always courteous and not terribly formal, but always very cordial, a very nice guy. [*chuckles*]

OKSNER: Nothing I can think of.

GIORDANO: How much I'm going to bill you for this! Hee hee hee.

GIELLA: You keep coming up with these good questions. [*laughs*] God, I don't know. I think you got it all. [*laughs*]

TEMPLETON: How's my driving?

Many thanks to our participants for their time and fact-checking, as well as good buddies Michael Eury, Jim Amash, and R. C. Harvey for assistance and advice above and beyond the call.

BRIAN K. MORRIS, *fastest ear in the Midwest, transcribes interviews for Alter Ego magazine and turns a hist job for all things Kryptonian into articles for* **BACK ISSUE,** *including "The Makeover of Steel" (BACK ISSUE #12, October 2005), exploring Superman's 1991 revamp.*

Mike Esposito inks, Swan pencils, from *Lois Lane* #103 (Aug. 1970).

Frank Giacoia inks, Swan pencils, from the 1974 Aurora *Comic Scenes* insert comic.

Tex Blaisdell inks, Swan pencils, from *Action* #471 (May 1977).

Frank Chiaramonte inks, Swan pencils, from *Superman* #328 (Oct. 1978).

Tony DeZuniga inks, Swan pencils, from *DC Comics Presents* #53 (Jan, 1983).

Al Williamson inks, Swan pencils, from *Superman* #413 (Nov. 1985).

CHAPTER 4

WHATEVER HAPPENED TO THE MAN OF TOMORROW?

SUPERMAN COMICS OF 1980-1986

Comic books were changing in the 1980s—new talent, new directions, new formats, new venues … but the same old Superman. The Man of Steel's DC franchise reliably marched along, month after month, with rarely more than increasing issue numbers distinguishing the editions from the ones that preceded them. Despite the hero's omnipresence as a pop-culture institution, with his big red "S" plastered on everything from movie billboards to peanut-butter jars, Superman's comics now lacked the punch to enthrall readers as they did in earlier decades.

Not that some creators didn't remind fans that Superman's fatigue could be cured with a heaping dose of imagination; four of them are interviewed in the pages following. Also winging to the hero's rescue was writer Alan Moore, whose all-too-few Superman stories left readers breathless and gasping for more. Yet the Man of Tomorrow was suffering from tired blood, his knees buckling under the burden of his own history.

After a decade of being number-two-with-a-bullet behind industry leader Marvel Comics, DC Comics dedicated itself to resuscitating its icons starting with its 50th anniversary event, 1985's *Crisis on Infinite Earths*, followed by a Superman reboot that began with the 1986 *Man of Steel* miniseries.

This chapter analyzes the final years of Julius Schwartz's editorial tenure, and includes a roundtable discussion where 16 writers, artists, and editors—most of whom guided Superman's adventures during or after the hero's 1986 revamp—discuss the influences of their forerunners upon their own work.

A 50th anniversary Superman illustration produced by Curt Swan in June 1988.

Superman TM & © DC Comics.

1980

Action Comics #503–514
(#507: "The Miraculous Return
of Jonathan Kent")
Superman #343–354

DC Comics Presents #17–28
(#27: first Mongul)
Justice League of America #174–185
Legion of Super-Heroes #259
(Superboy leaves the Legion)
The New Adventures of Superboy
#1–12 (new solo series)
Superboy Spectacular #1
Super Friends #28–39
The Superman Family #199–204
World's Finest Comics #260–265

Best of DC Blue Ribbon Digest #3
(Super Friends), 5 (Year's Best Comics
Stories), 6 (Superman/Daily Planet),
7 (Superboy), 8 (Superman)
The Brave and the Bold #160
(Batman and Supergirl team-up)
DC Special Blue Ribbon Digest #1
(LSH), 3 (Justice Society, with
Superman), 5 (Secret Origins of
Super-Heroes)
DC Special Series #21 (Super-Star
Holiday Special, with Superboy &
LSH story)
Superman Radio Shack giveaway
The Super Friends Hour (ABC-TV
cartoon revamp)

1981

Action Comics #515–526
(#521: first Vixen)
(#525: first Neutron)
Superman #355–366

DC Comics Presents #29–40
The Krypton Chronicles #1–3 (miniseries)
Justice League of America #186–197
Legion of Super-Heroes #277–279
(Superboy as Reflecto)
The New Adventures of Superboy #13–24
Secrets of the Legion of Super-Heroes
#1–3 (miniseries)
Super Friends #40–47 (#47: last issue)
Super Friends Special #1
The Superman Family #205–213
World's Finest Comics #266–274

Best of DC Blue Ribbon Digest #10
(Secret Origins of Super-Villains),
11 (Year's Best Comics Stories),
12 (Superman), 13 (DC Comics
Presents), 15 (Superboy), 16 (Superman),
17 (Supergirl), 19 (Superman)
The Brave and the Bold #175
(Batman and Lois Lane team-up)
DC Special Blue Ribbon Digest #8
(LSH featuring Superboy), 9 (Secret
Origins of Super-Heroes), 11 (JLA),
13 (Strange Sports Stories), 15 (Secret
Origins of Super-Villains)
DC Special Series #23 (World's Finest
digest), 25 (*Superman II* tabloid),
26 (Superman and His Incredible
Fortress of Solitude tabloid)
*The Great Superman Comic Book
Collection* hardcover reprint edition
Superman and Supergirl Radio
Shack giveaway
Superman II U.S. theatrical release
Superman: Miracle Monday novel

1982

Action Comics #527–538
(#527: first Lord Satanis and Syrene)
(#535: first Omega Men)
Superman #367–378
(#371: first Kandor II)
(#376: *Daring New Adventures of
Supergirl* preview)

DC Comics Presents #41–52, Annual #1
(#52: first Ambush Bug)
*The Daring New Adventures of
Supergirl* #1–2 (new solo series)
Justice League of America #198–209
The New Adventures of Superboy
#25–36
The Phantom Zone #1–4 (miniseries)
The Superman Family #214–222
(#222: last issue)
World's Finest Comics #275–286

Adventure Comics (digest,
LSH reprints) #491–495
Best of DC Blue Ribbon Digest #20
(World's Finest Comics), 21 (JSA, with
Earth-Two Superman),
22 (Christmas with the Super-Heroes),
23 (Year's Best Comics Stories), 24
(LSH), 25 (Superman), 27 (Superman
vs. Luthor), 31 (JLA)
The Brave and the Bold #192
(Batman and Superboy team-up)
*Captain Carrot and His Amazing Zoo
Crew* #1 (Superman appearance)
DC Special Blue Ribbon Digest #22
(Secret Origins of Super-Heroes)
Superman and Wonder Woman Radio
Shack giveaway

1983

Action Comics #539–550
  (#544: 45th anniversary issue; first
  new Luthor and Brainiac)
Superman #379–390, Annual #9
Superman Special #1

DC Comics Presents #53–64, Annual #2
(first Superwoman)
*The Daring New Adventures of
Supergirl* #3–13 (retitled *Supergirl*
with #14)
Justice League of America #210–221,
Annual #1
Legion of Super-Heroes #300,
Annual #2 (Superboy and
Supergirl appearances)
The New Adventures of Superboy #37–48
Supergirl #14
World's Finest Comics #287–298

Adventure Comics (digest, LSH
reprints) #496–503 (#503: last issue)
All-Star Squadron #21 (Earth-Two
Superman appearance)
Batman and the Outsiders #1
(Superman appearance)
Best of DC Blue Ribbon Digest #32
(Superman), 33 (Secret Origins of LSH),
35 (Year's Best Comics Stories),
36 (Superman vs. Kryptonite),
38 (Superman), 40 (Superman/World of
Krypton), 42 (Superman vs. Aliens)
DC Sampler #1 (Superman and Supergirl)
Infinity, Inc. #9 (Earth-Two
Superman appearance)
Superman III U.S. theatrical release
Superman III DC Comics adaptation
Superman Sunday Special newspaper
Sunday strip becomes puzzle page
*Superman From the Thirties to
the Eighties* updated version of
hardcover reprint

1984

Action Comics #551–562
  (#554: Siegel and Shuster tribute)
  (#555: Supergirl's 25th anniversary)
Superman #391–402, Annual #10
  (#400: double-sized anniversary issue
  with guest contributors)
Superman Special #2

DC Comics Presents #65–76, Annual #3
Justice League of America #222–224
The New Adventures of Superboy #49–54
  (#54: last issue)
Supergirl #15–23 (#23: last issue)
World's Finest Comics #299–310

Batman and the Outsiders #19
(Superman appearance)
Best of DC Blue Ribbon Digest
#44 (Secret Origins of LSH),
46 (Jimmy Olsen), 48 (Superman
Team-Up Action), 50 (Year's Best
Superman Stories), 54 (Superman
Battles Weird Villains)
Blue Devil #3 (Superman appearance)
DC Sampler #2–3 (Superman
appearances)
Jemm, Son of Saturn #4 (Superman
appearance)
Supergirl American Honda comics special
Super Powers #1–5 (miniseries)
*Super Friends: The Legendary Super
Powers Show* (ABC-TV
cartoon revamp)

1985

Action Comics #563–574
Superman #403–414, Annual #11
  (#411: Julie Schwartz birthday tribute)
Superman Special #3

DC Comics Presents #77–88, Annual #4
  (#87: first Superboy of Earth-Prime)
Legion of Super-Heroes #6, 11–16
(Superboy and Supergirl cameos or
appearances)
Supergirl Movie Special
Superman: The Secret Years #1–4
(miniseries)
World's Finest Comics #311–322

All-Star Squadron #53 (Earth-Two
Superman appearance)
America vs. the Justice Society #1–4
(miniseries, Earth-Two
Superman appearances)
Best of DC Blue Ribbon Digest #56
(Superman vs. More Aliens),
57 (LSH), 58 (Super Juniors),
59 (Superman Sagas), 61 (Year's Best
Comics Stories), 64 (LSH),
66 (Superman Team-Up Action),
67 (LSH)

Crisis on Infinite Earths #1–9
  (#7: death of Supergirl)
DC Challenge #1–2 (maxiseries,
Superman appearances)
New Teen Titans Annual #1
(Superman appearance)
Red Tornado #1–2 (miniseries,
Superman appearances)
Super Powers vol. 2 #1–4 (miniseries)
*The Super Powers Team: Galactic
Guardians* (ABC-TV cartoon revamp)

1986

Action Comics #575–583
  (#583: last Earth-One Superman issue)
Superman #415–423, Annual #12
  (#423: last Earth-One Superman issue)

DC Comics Presents #89–97
  (#97: last issue)
Legion of Super-Heroes #23 (Superboy)
Lois Lane #1–2 (miniseries)
World's Finest Comics #323 (last issue)

Best of DC Blue Ribbon Digest #69
(Year's Best Team Stories),
71 (Year's Best Comics Stories)
Booster Gold #7 (Superman appearance)
Crisis on Infinite Earths #10–12
DC Challenge #3–12 (maxiseries,
Superman appearances)
Heroes Against Hunger Special
*The Last Days of the Justice Society
Special* #1 (Earth-Two Superman
appearance)
Secret Origins #1 (Earth-Two Superman)
Super Powers vol. 2 #5–6
(miniseries, cont'd.)

MARV WOLFMAN INTERVIEW

Brooklyn native Marvin Wolfman (b. 1946), the creator or co-creator of numerous comics characters including Blade the Vampire Slayer, Daredevil's nemesis Bullseye, and the New Teen Titans' Cyborg, Raven, and Starfire, emerged from comics fandom in the late 1960s to ultimately become one of the medium's top writers. A one-time Marvel Comics editor in chief, Wolfman's credits also include the celebrated horror series *Tomb of Dracula* and DC's 50th-anniversary crossover *Crisis on Infinite Earths*. He has written Superman before and after the *Crisis,* including the 2006 novelization of the film *Superman Returns.*

Conducted by Michael Eury via e-mail on February 8, 2006.

MICHAEL EURY: You've previously stated that Superman is your favorite super-hero of all time. Why?
MARV WOLFMAN: Possibly because he was the first super-hero I saw. I was a kid watching the *Superman* TV show. In the closing credits it said something like, "Superman is based on the copyrighted character appearing in *Superman* and *Action Comics* magazines." Right after the show was over, my friend and I immediately went to the corner store and bought our first Superman comics.

But I think the real reason is he's the most pure, the perfect wish-fulfillment concept. He represents the basics, truth and justice, like no other hero.

Photo courtesy of Glen Cadigan.

EURY: Which of Superman's classic writers and artists most influenced your Superman work?
WOLFMAN: Jerry Siegel. It's probably the PC thing to say since he created it, but in reality he wrote my favorite issues, which I only discovered much, much later. He also had a solid, rough-and-ready approach to the original Superman (1938–1940), which I really love. That Superman is my all-time favorite. But then he also wrote the original "Death of Superman" story, which may be the best super-hero comic written in the '50s–'60s.
EURY: Mort Weisinger was headed toward retirement when you were breaking into comics. Did you have any encounters with him?
WOLFMAN: I met Mort a few times and I know I pitched him several early stories. I don't remember if he bought any, so I don't think we worked together. But I'd met him when taking the DC tour and I met him while interning up at DC.
EURY: You started writing Superman stories for Julius Schwartz in 1980, at approximately the same time as the launch of *The New Teen Titans*. Did Julie seek you out, or did you voice interest in writing the character?

(right) Marv Wolfman's "Fabulous World of Krypton" story was indeed drawn by Dave Cockrum, and was the *Superboy and the Legion* and *X-Men* artist's first solo pro art job, in *Superman* #248 (Feb. 1972). This is an alternate version of the story's first page, which Cockrum redrew for publication.
TM & © DC Comics. All Rights Reserved.

WOLFMAN: I actually wrote some Superman material for Julie early on in the early '70s, including a "Fabulous World of Krypton" story which I think may have been drawn by Dave Cockrum. When I came back to DC in 1980 I sought out Julie because I really wanted to work on Superman.
EURY: I understand that Vandal Savage, the villain in your stories in *Action* #515 and 516 (Jan. and Feb. 1981), wasn't your original choice as the adversary in that two-parter....
WOLFMAN: Actually, the story goes back further than those two issues. Julie wanted a refiguring of both Luthor and Brainiac. I came in with ideas for both, including the corporate Luthor take. Julie felt at the time that I should do only one and Cary Bates, who'd been writing Superman for nearly two decades, should do the other. That seemed fair to me as well. My Brainiac revamp was taken and Cary's super-suited Luthor concept was used.

I think for the time period the businessman Luthor was a bit too cerebral for the comic, and certainly much harder to explain, whereas Cary's idea of the super-suited Luthor was direct. When my Luthor idea was rejected, I just turned the concept over to Vandal Savage, who I had head up a corporation called Abraxas. It didn't work as well with Savage as it would have with Luthor because so few people actually knew who Savage was. It didn't have the same impact.

Interestingly, I told DC at the time that if the new concept for Luthor was used, he would take over the series. And he did [beginning with the 1986 *Man of Steel* revamp]. I'm extremely pleased, because it gave him more depth and let him become a real villain as opposed to the mad scientist he'd been for a decade or two.

EURY: Had this new take on Luthor been accepted when you first pitched it, do you think it might have paved a path of change for Superman which would have allowed him to bypass the 1986 reboot?

WOLFMAN: No, I don't. I think in fact it may have gotten lost in the changes. By doing everyone over at once it made for a bigger story.

One note on my Luthor concept that I don't think I've mentioned before aside from convention appearances: as I've always stated I hated the idea of the '50s/'60s Luthor who would be in prison at the beginning of every story, break out somehow, always in his prison grays, wear those grays throughout the story (did he know Superman was going to toss him behind bars, so he didn't bother to change?), go to his hideout which was hidden somewhere in Metropolis (how many secret hideouts did he have?), activate a giant robot, and rob a bank or something. I kept thinking: (A) "If I had giant robots, I could sell them for more than I could steal," and (B) "How many millions did I have in order to have all those secret hideouts and labs?"

So I thought my revamp—remember we were starting Supes over [in 1986]—could explain where Luthor got that money. In other words, he was a businessman at the beginning of his career (illegal, of course) and he made zillions. Later, after he was arrested, he'd have had all those millions to have his secret hideouts.

EURY: Tell me the stories behind the creation of two of your additions to Superman's rogues' gallery, Neutron (first seen in *Action* #525, Nov. 1981) and Lord Satanis (*Action* #527, Jan. 1982).

WOLFMAN: I've always created villains and supporting characters in every series I've ever done. I find it hard to believe there are writers who only want to regurgitate old characters when you can create new ideas. With Neutron it was a matter of coming up with someone potentially more powerful and deadly than Superman had ever faced, and with Satanis it was using Supes' weakness to magic/sorcery as the basis for the villain.

Both were designed to be able to go one on one against Superman and survive. I thought for the most part Superman's enemies were pretty lame. I'm not sure but I think I may have used Neutron once before, in the Aurora comics story I wrote for the Superman model kit, but my memory on that is very shaky and I don't have easy access to my Aurora comics to find out if that was indeed Neutron. [*Editor's note:* It was.]

EURY: You wrote several Brainiac stories prior to over-hauling the character in *Action* #544 (June 1983). What about the original Brainiac appealed to you?

Wolfman's eventual *Action* partner Gil Kane penciled the cover to *Jimmy Olsen* #152 (Sept. 1972), which was inked by Bob Oksner.
TM & © DC Comics. Art courtesy of Heritage Comics.

Kane's cover pencils to *Superman Special* #1 (1983); Gil also wrote the issue.
TM & © DC Comics. Courtesy of David Hamilton.

Preliminary *Captain Marvel* art by Wayne Boring. Marv Wolfman wrote the second (#23, Nov. 1972) of three *Captain Marvel* issues penciled by the former Superman artist.

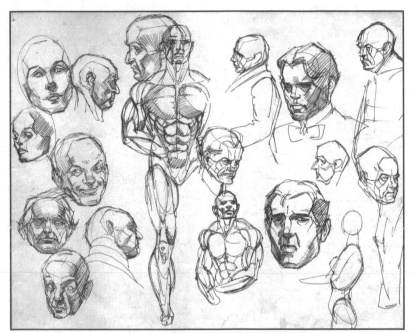

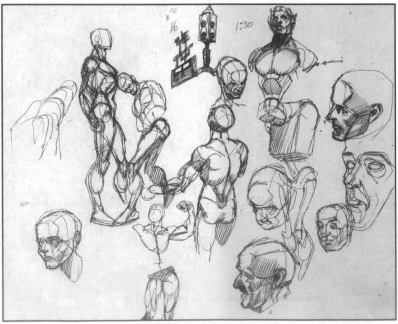

(above) Anatomy sketches by Gil Kane. Don Juleman(?)

WOLFMAN: There was something about the concept of the computer villain that interested me from the moment it was revealed that Brainiac—who, if I recall, had been around for awhile—was a computer. I can't explain why but I really liked him. When I had to come up with a revamp, I wanted to make him cold and deadly and to use computers—the systematic and emotionless—as his basis because I thought that singular approach would make him completely different from every other villain at the time in any book. I also thought of Brainiac not only as the body we saw, but the entire ship—which is why he was plugged in. It was *all* Brainiac.

EURY: Ed Hannigan designed Brainiac's new appearance, correct?

WOLFMAN: Yes. Ed and I worked together. I wanted a H.R. Giger approach and Ed developed that look, which is brilliant.

EURY: At a time when many readers regarded Superman as boring, you, with Gil Kane, revitalized his adventures beginning with *Action* #539 (Jan. 1983). How did this creative pairing occur?

WOLFMAN: Julie put us together. Simple as that. I had been a huge fan of Gil's when I was growing up. In one of my early fanzines I said I thought he was the best super-hero artist at DC. I also absolutely loved his work on *Green Lantern*. When I knew I was going to work with him, I realized I could do stories I could never do with anyone else. We could do an action/character-based Superman instead of a talky plot-driven story.

Because I could put Marvel-like action in the story, and I had a firm idea what Superman can and cannot do, I think we were able to make him "cool." It's not hard. I just think a lot of writers are intimidated by the character. I love the character, but I'm not at all intimidated by him. He has all these powers, but you need to play him as a person having to deal with the problems he faces.

EURY: What strengths did Gil bring to Superman?

WOLFMAN: Gil brought a dynamic that hadn't been seen in *Superman* since the very early issues. You looked at his Superman and it was exciting.

EURY: Despite Kane's energetic interpretation of the Man of Steel, oddly, he's not regarded by many as "a Superman artist." Any theories on why his Superman work is sometimes overlooked? (Incidentally, it's not overlooked by me—his *Action* art was nothing short of brilliant!)

WOLFMAN: I think if Gil and I had stayed on the book together another year or so he might have been "discovered" by the fans. But I do have to say when we did *Action Comics* together it was the first time in years that *Action* outsold *Superman*. People were discovering us and enjoying the harder-edged material we were doing. Had we stayed on longer I think we could have made more of an impact.

EURY: Lana Lang was a semi-regular Superman supporting-cast member during the 1980s, although some readers contend that she best belonged in Superboy's stories. What did Lana contribute to Super*man*?

WOLFMAN: Not much. She was just another character. I think we could have done more with her, playing her more as a confidant to Clark since he'd known her for so long.

EURY: Your salute to Jerry Siegel and Joe Shuster, "If Superman Didn't Exist…" in *Action* #554 (Apr. 1984), is fondly remembered by many. Did you hear from Siegel and Shuster in response to your tribute?

WOLFMAN: Yes, I received a very nice letter from Jerry and Joe thanking me. I still have it. Let's face it, they not only created the best super-hero ever done, but the first. Everything that has come came from what they did. Also, I think Joe's Superman art was vital and powerful, and still the best interpretation of the character ever done, and Jerry used to write some incredibly powerful and emotional stories.

For instance, as a kid I loved a comic called *Mr. Muscles*. I think it ran two or three issues and came out from Charlton, I believe. It was about someone who had polio (in the news at the time) who refused to let the polio cripple him. Years later I discovered Jerry wrote it. I also used to get this comic from England called *The Spider*—it appeared in trade-paperback size. Every so often there was a story that blew me away. There were no credits. A year or so later the editor mentioned that Jerry had written those issues.

So I think we should all be honoring Jerry and Joe even more than we have. I loved that story.

EURY: After writing perhaps the most poignant and powerful Supergirl story *ever* in *Crisis on Infinite Earths* #7 (Oct. 1985, below), how do you feel about Kara's return in current DC continuity?

WOLFMAN: Thanks. I worked hard on that one and having George [Pérez]'s art accompanying the words wasn't too shabby either. As for her return, I always assumed she would come back. The idea was to start the universe over. If Supergirl never existed then a new one could be recreated. I'm surprised it took this long.

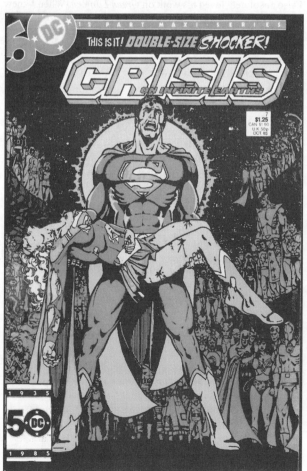

EURY: Are there any plans to bring your 1988 *Superman* animated series to DVD?

WOLFMAN: God, I'd love to see that as a DVD. I could easily do commentary on it. I have all the episodes on tape—from the studio—and occasionally look at them. We had lots of difficulties with that series, including a network head who hated super-heroes and wanted some of the dumbest ideas I've ever seen, and Standards and Practices that was still mired in the old ways so we could not actually have Superman punch anything, including robots. Real action was verboten so there were severe limitations on what we could and could not do. But I think we still got some good stories, though. It's a shame the series as a whole was forgotten.

EURY: You co-plotted a story with TV's first Jimmy Olsen, actor Jack Larson, for the unpublished *Neverending Battle* Superman Museum benefit comic. What was its plot?

WOLFMAN: You know, I don't remember the details, but Jack had come up with the idea of Jimmy going back in time to discover who William Shakespeare was talking about when he dedicated his sonnets to someone with the initials WH (my memory is bad so I may be misremembering the initials).

Numerous animation cels from decades of Superman cartoons are on display in the Superman Museum in Metropolis, Illinois.
Photo © 2004 Cookie Morris.

A guest-star-packed Wolfman/Kane page from *Action* #546 (Aug. 1983).
TM & © DC Comics. Art courtesy of Heritage Comics.

IT WAS A HELLUVA RIDE, JULIE— IF WE DO IT AGAIN— I RIDE ON TOP! HAPPY BIRTHDAY— LOVE— GIL KANE

A birthday card to Julie Schwartz, drawn by Gil Kane. Date unknown.
© 2006 Gil Kane estate. Art courtesy of Heritage Comics. J.S. collection.

Nobody has ever figured out who the dedication is to. Jack is not only an actor but a writer, poet, etc., and he thought it would be a good story for Superman and Jimmy to go back in time to unravel the mystery.

I was thrilled to work with him—he came to my house. Later on we drove in his MG to dinner. For someone who got involved with comics solely because of the *Superman* TV show to spend time with "Jimmy" was a complete thrill.

Interestingly, according to the IMDB, Jack is playing Bibbo, the bartender of Ace O' Clubs bar [in *Superman Returns*]. Well, Bibbo and the Ace O' Clubs were introduced in one of my (and Jerry Ordway's) *Adventures of Superman* stories, so Jack is playing one of my characters.

EURY: What was Julie Schwartz's most significant contribution to the Superman mythos?

WOLFMAN: Julie got rid of a lot of the sillier stuff that Mort had done in the '50s and '60s that no longer worked in the '70s and '80s. Julie was great to work for. My respect for him as an editor and a person is enormous, but I often think *Superman* was not necessarily the right book for him. I think he worked best on comics more grounded in reality and in SF than Superman.

But Julie opened up the series and allowed us to do a lot of different kinds of stories. He also sensed how much I loved Superman and he let me do things that I think he might not have let others try. I wish we could have worked together on other series, too, but by the time I got to DC all he was doing was Superman.

EURY: Same question, in regard to your work.

WOLFMAN: I know I'll be known as the writer who redesigned Luthor and Brainiac, but I'd also like to be thought of for trying to infuse life into Superman with a sense of action of character, of making him more of a person with worries and concerns that have nothing to do with his powers. I would like to think that the stories I did with Gil, Curt, and later Jerry showed that the character could still be modern and fun and the stories could be based on something more than Superman fighting giant robots. That there was something about the character himself who was much more than the bland Boy Scout most people wrote him as.

I'd also like it to be remembered that I created Cat Grant, who was the first regular female to find Clark attractive. Her interest in Clark made him more realistic and cool. In fact, we actually got Clark out of his blue suit and into cooler clothing. Cat quickly became infused with the Superman mythos and wound up on *Lois & Clark* for a season, and I thought she was a great character.

The one character I'm always surprised that continued is Professor Hamilton, who went on to *Lois & Clark* as well as *Smallville* and is still in the comic, 25 years after I created him.

But mainly, I think my main contribution was in showing that Superman did not have to be the stodgy old character he was long portrayed as. He could be as vital and interesting to read as any other more modern character. You just have to think of him as a hero second and as a man first.

KEITH GIFFEN INTERVIEW

One would be hard-pressed to find a comics character that hasn't been plotted, written, or illustrated by Keith Giffen (b. 1952). Known for his unbridled imagination and acerbic sense of humor, Giffen began drawing comics in the mid-1970s, doing pencils or layouts on series such as *All-Star Comics*, *Kobra*, and *The Defenders* before making his mark in the early 1980s as the penciler of *Legion of Super-Heroes* and later, as the plotter of *Justice League* and as the creator of Lobo. During Julie Schwartz's waning years as Superman editor, Giffen created one of comics' most irreverent characters, Ambush Bug.

Conducted by Michael Eury on February 21, 2006.

MICHAEL EURY: When and how did you start working with Julie Schwartz?
KEITH GIFFEN: I don't recall when and how, but I do recall *what* happened. I was on *Legion of Super-Heroes*, I was the hot shot at DC. And I was doing a story for either *Action Comics* or *DC* [*Comics*] *Presents*, I don't recall which, and I'd just handed in my last batch of pages to Julie—and he was *killing* me! Every page he looked at, he just *sneered*! It was *horrifying*! It was this *nightmare*! He completely rattled my confidence. Every horrifying thing you'd ever thought about an editor was *right there*! He had this look on his face like I'd just crapped on the paper and rubbed it around. He threw them in the corner of the room on the floor! I thought, "Holy sh*t, my career is *over*!"

And he reaches into his drawer, and I figured, "He's going for a gun, he's gonna execute me on the spot." And he pulls out that stupid jar he had of those pink mints, and he says, "Want a mint?" [*laughter*] And I go, "*Excuse me*?!" And he goes, "What're we doing *next*?" And I go, "Are you kidding me? After all that?" And he goes, "Hey, hey, hey—*first* you see the *bear*. I don't need to work with guys who fall apart with a little bit of criticism." And from then on, he was a mentor and a friend. [*laughs*]

He did that to Bob Fleming, too. He didn't want guys whose egos couldn't stand up to criticism. He didn't want gossamer talents. He wanted people who could withstand the criticism, because it's part of being a professional. But … oh, Lord! That stands as one of the most unnerving experiences in my entire comic-book career!

EURY: Wow! Through the wringer!
GIFFEN: You have no idea. I would go home and look at my wife, and go, [*mock stammering*] "I-I-I don't know what to do to please him."
EURY: So, did you have to run home and take a shower after that?
GIFFEN: Of course. They had to clean up the *slop* I left behind.
EURY: [*laughs*] Maintenance! Mop-up in Schwartz's office!

GIFFEN: Yeah. [*laughs*] But after that, the change was remarkable! He turned into the Julie who, when you walked into his office, he made sure your check was waiting for you, right there in his drawer. The Julie who could look at a page and go, "That doesn't work," and you'd go, "Yes, it does—wow, it *doesn't*, does it?"

I do stand proud of one moment: Through Julie Schwartz, I was responsible for what Andy Helfer calls "the single most humiliating moment of [Helfer's] entire career."
EURY: And what would that be?
GIFFEN: Well, Julie was in his late 60s, early 70s then, and as Andy puts it, "I had to go into his office and explain in detail to a 70-year-old man why he couldn't use the Vietnamese province of 'Poon Tang' in a story [by Giffen]." [*laughter*] But when [Andy] told me, he just had this look on his face, like, "I'm gonna *get*cha!" [*laughter*] That's one of things I can point to with pride and go, "Got 'im!"

But after the first time I worked with Julie, I honestly believed that I was never going to work with him again. I really thought, "This man hates my guts."

EURY: So, Keith, you ignored Jim Croce's warning "You don't tug on Superman's cape" and lampooned the Man of Steel. What made the Superman of the early '80s the perfect target for satire?
GIFFEN: Superman was the perfect straight man. As super-heroes go, he was the straightest "line drawn down the middle" guy. He was the perfect straight man to play against Ambush Bug. You knew that there was really nothing anybody could do to hurt Superman—unless you're hiding that big chunk of green rock—and it was fun to see someone that supremely confident get a little flustered.

We never did anything to actually mock Superman or hold him up to ridicule. We had so much affection for

Courtesy of Glen Cadigan.

HEY, CHECK IT *OUT!* I'M LEAPING TALL BUILDINGS WITH A SINGLE *BOUND!*

STAY RIGHT WHERE YOU *ARE!* I'VE GOTTA LOCATE A *SPEEDING BULLET!*

TM & © DC Comics.

all of the characters in the Ambush Bug stories that we tried to never cross that line and go, "This guy's stupid." But Superman in the '80s, he very much epitomized that idea, "Superman's a Boy Scout." I guess Ambush Bug was the lunatic kid on the campout. It was fun to do. Ultimately, if I remember correctly, Superman usually wound up with the last laugh.

EURY: Yeah, true.

GIFFEN: The only time I think we stepped over the line is one of the few things I regret having done during my career. It was the *DC* [*Comics*] *Presents* where we had Superman and Ambush Bug switch bodies. The problem was not because of Superman but because of Kobra. Mike Barr had discovered we were going to use Kobra, and he was about to use Kobra in *The Outsiders*. He stopped me in the corridor and said, "Please don't demolish the character too badly, because I'm trying to revive the character, and want a dignified starting point." And I said, "Don't worry! Don't worry! We'll treat 'im good!" And we *demolished* that character. Mike Barr was pissed off at me good, probably to this day, and you know what? He's right. I did him bad.

But that said, I think that was one of the funniest Superman/Ambush Bug stories we ever did, with the switching of the bodies. My favorite scene was when Ambush Bug discovers Superman's heat vision. And when it goes on, the sound effect is "click." [*laughter*]

Come o-o-on … we were having *fun* with the characters. I really think it was a breath of fresh air seeing Superman get a little crazy,

Joe Shuster's "scrappy" original version of Superman, seen here in a sketch done by the artist in the 1940s, is framed by Keith Giffen, who drew the final cover.

get a little flustered, and be the Bud Abbott to Ambush Bug's Lou Costello.

EURY: I found those stories funny, too, but they stood in stark contrast with how other writers handled the DC characters. Other than the Kobra situation you mentioned, how was your take on Superman received by the other writers and artists who were treating him seriously? Did they understand what you were doing?

GIFFEN: With Ambush Bug, there were a lot of people who took what we did too seriously and didn't understand what we were doing, and I disagree with them wholeheartedly. I can't mention their names, because it would sound like I'm dumping on them, and I would be. For every shot we'd take at … say, Gerry Conway—I mention Gerry [as an example] because I know we *didn't* take any shots at him—we would take three or four at ourselves. If we were merciless to anyone, it would be to each other. With some people, I think the gags cut a bit too close to what they thought was the truth, but we never did anything with any deliberate malice.

EURY: I agree with all that, too, and as you know, at the very end of Ambush Bug, I was part of the process [as editor], and I, like the rest of the team, took some shots in *Ambush Bug Nothing Special* (1992).

GIFFEN: Hats off to Al Gordon for letting us do that "a call from Al" running gag in *Nothing Special*. [*laughter*] But it was a more open time back then, before everyone became rock stars and before egos became so delicate. You know, Julie Schwartz could find joy in becoming the free-rolling Julie head that's become Eclipsoed. A lot of people went, "In *Ambush Bug Nothing Special* you tore apart a major crossover event from DC [1992's *Eclipso: The Darkness Within*]." Yeah—but *I* was doing it! I was doing the *Eclipso* series, with you and with Bob!

EURY: I guess this was an instance of some people just not getting the joke.

GIFFEN: There's always that. But even in our *Justice League* stuff, whenever we dealt with somebody else's characters, it was never, *ever* done with malice. It still is not, like with *Defenders*. I couldn't do that kind of humor with characters I genuinely disliked. I mean, characters I genuinely dislike, like … oh, Karate Kid … I tend to kill! [*laughter*] How does this apply to Superman?

EURY: I … don't … know. [*laughter*]

GIFFEN: Well, Superman—Superman was basically Ambush Bug's godfather. We could've never gotten that character off the ground without Superman being there as the straight guy. And of course, that translates over to Julie Schwartz being willing to let us take these chances, to Paul Levitz for legitimizing the character by letting him be part of the story with the Legion of Substitute Heroes [*DC Comics Presents* #59, July 1983], and so on and so forth. It was a time when we all had a sense of humor. It was more innocent then. That's a reason why Ambush Bug and Superman worked so well together—they were both genuinely innocent characters.

EURY: I never thought of it that way, but you're right.

GIFFEN: Ambush Bug was innocent in that *Candide*, trail-of-destruction kind of way, and Superman was innocent in that firm belief in life, liberty, and the pursuit of happiness, and truth, justice, and the American way. So I guess they *were* on a collision course.

EURY: You drew Superman in the style of Joe Shuster.

GIFFEN: Absolutely!

EURY: So from where you stand, nobody did him better?

GIFFEN: Nobody did him better, and nobody's done him better since … or *will* do him better. I was also [inspired by] the Max Fleischer cartoons. That's exactly where I stop with Superman. If I were to do a Superman story today, I'd *still* draw it in that style. To me, *that's* Superman: he squints, he's got that big jaw with the bull neck, you know, and he's a *squat* little guy.

EURY: How tall is he?

GIFFEN: I'll give him maybe 6 feet if he's standing up straight. But 5 feet, 11 inches, maybe 5-foot-10. He's like the Thing. Everybody thinks of the Thing as this huge, hulking guy, but if you look at the early *FF*s, he's shorter than Reed Richards. So Superman to me has always been that skyscraper-leaping, scrappy guy.

EURY: Most people would think of Superman as a towering figure.

GIFFEN: To me, Superman's always leaping around, not standing still. If he slowed down, you'd see that he's actually like one of us. We're always looking up to Superman like he's an icon, a god, a being that inspires awe or fear. But with *my* Superman, you'd say to him, "Hey, Superman, you just defeated that group of saboteurs trying to undermine the American war effort. What's next?" "I'm going to Disney World!" [*laughter*] *My* Superman could say that. A more innocent Superman. That's gone now. But life goes on. That probably explains why I'm not doing Superman today. [*laughs*]

EURY: Yeah, but there are some people who like revisiting those earlier days—that's why I'm interviewing you today.

Julie even bossed around the Man of Steel! Actor Christopher Reeve consults with Super-editor Schwartz prior to the filming of 1978's *Superman: The Movie*.
Photo courtesy of Heritage Comics. J.S. collection.

GIFFEN: Possibly … the possibility's there. You see, I don't believe you can approach the future by marching lockstep into the past. Revisiting ideas: wonderful, absolutely wonderful. But bring in something *new*.

As an example, look at Marvel's *Ultimate* books—and DC's counterparts, the *All Star* books. I'm not gonna criticize anything that anybody's doing on them, because criticism usually means, "That's not the way *I* would've done it," and that's not fair.

But look at *Blue Beetle*. [DC executive editor Dan] DiDio said to me, "You can have the name and the scarab. You want it?" "Hell, yeah!" I'd like to think that if somebody had given me an *All Star* book [*under breath*] (fat chance) like *Green Lantern*, I'd say, "Just give me the *ring*."

EURY: Just the name and the ring.

GIFFEN: Well, for marketing concerns, they might say it'd have to keep the costume and be Hal Jordan, but I'd still start over. I can guarantee you, it'd have nothing to do with Oa, and introducing Sinestro would be an *event*. How cool would it be to do anything you want with the name and the character?

EURY: Let's say you'd been given *All Star Superman* from issue #1. What would you have done?

GIFFEN: I'd have no idea. Develop paralysis, I'd be so shocked.

EURY: [*laughs*] So the paralysis wears off. *Then* what would you have done with the character?

GIFFEN: I can tell you what I *wouldn't* have done. I would keep the iconic stuff that makes him Superman, because he is a junk-culture icon—Lois, Perry, that kind of stuff—but I would not feel the same obligation toward the *Daily Planet*. I might feel the same obligation to the triangle of Clark, Lois, and Superman, but with the rest of it, it'd probably bear as much similarity to Superman as *New Gods* did to *Thor*—same basic tenor, same basic feel, but this ain't Asgard!

EURY: And Superman would be 5-foot-10.

GIFFEN: Yeah, if I drew it. [*laughs*] I might do the *Kingdom Come* "S," with the black under the red, and do "nothing short of a shell can burst his skin," that sort of thing. But writing *Superman* month after month has got to be like writing "*The Adventures of God*," because there's no way to stop him—except magic … purple things … and, oh yeah, cat dander! [*laughs*]

EURY: I had a similar conversation with Denny O'Neil, who had this very problem. And the fans at that time, 35 years ago, rejected his and Julie's premise of weakening Superman.

GIFFEN: Denny didn't get a chance to take it far enough. Fans are really willing to accept the reality with which you present them, so long as you don't violate your own laws of physics.

EURY: Denny said the same thing. At the time, Julie Schwartz wasn't editing the other Superman titles. It seemed like DC didn't mean business since the changes were not reflected outside of *Superman*.

GIFFEN: At DC *now*, when a character goes through a major change and the character is a multiple-book character or you're dealing with a major change in the entire DC Universe, [it's

Shuster's influence upon Giffen is evident in this page from *DC Comics Presents* #52 (Dec. 1982), inked by Sal Trapani.
TM & © DC Comics. Art courtesy of Heritage Comics.

THE SUPERMAN MYTHOLOGY: SUPER-TURTLE

"Super-Turtle," a 2/3-page sequential cartoon strip randomly packaged throughout various DC Comics Silver Age titles, was the creation of Henry Boltinoff (1914–2001), the cartoonist responsible for other DC fillers such as "Cap's Hobby Hints" and "Casey the Cop," as well as *Hocus Pocus*, the long-running newspaper cartoon which challenged readers to find differences between two similar panels. Bearing no relation to the Man of Steel (or the Legion of Super-Pets) other than his red cape (adorned with a yellow "T" insignia), Super-Turtle's frolicsome adventures provided a quick diversion between stories or story chapters. The character's powers were essentially the same as Superman's, and he concealed his identity behind a pair of eyeglasses.

Super-Turtle Appearances

Action Comics #299, 301, 305, 309, 318, 321, 336, 374, 381

Adventure Comics #304, 312, 316–317, 326, 329, 341–342, 363, 377, 379

Ambush Bug #1, 3

The Brave and the Bold #70

Silver Age 80-Page Giant #1

Silver Age Secret Files #1

Superboy #103, 105, 107–108, 110, 113–114, 127, 130, 156

Superman #159, 162, 170, 175, 181, 188, 190

Superman and Batman: World's Funnest

Superman's Pal Jimmy Olsen #90–91, 115

World's Finest Comics #149, 151–152, 154, 156, 158, 166, 181

Special thanks to John Wells for the Super-Turtle checklist.

A 1992 Wonder-Con panel, featuring (left to right) *Legion* penciler Jason Pearson, editor Michael Eury, writers Mary and Tom Bierbaum, plotter Giffen, *Timber Wolf* penciler Joe Phillips, and *Legionnaires* penciler Chris Sprouse.

Photo courtesy of Rose Rummel-Eury.

everywhere]. DiDio, when he walked in, he grabbed [editors] by the neck and said, "You're gonna walk in step, and I'm gonna beat out the keys." He'd say, "You can't have Batman with a girl Robin in one book and Dick Grayson as Robin or Tim Drake as Robin in another." Now, I'm not coming down on [the side of] continuity, because I think that continuity is a stranglehold, but *consistency* would be nice. Consistency of character. Consistency of tone. If I'd come on to *Spider-Man* and all of a sudden said, "Now he shoots webs out of his butt," fans wouldn't accept that. But if I started an all-new *Ultimate Spider-Man* book where Spider-Man shot webs out of his butt, then fans would be more willing to accept that particular version of Spider-Man.

EURY: I'm betting that there are a lot of grade-school boys who would think that Spider-Man shooting webs out of his butt is a cool idea. [*laughs*]

So, Keith, when you were lampooning Superman through *Ambush Bug*, did Julie take any flak?

GIFFEN: I can't think of *anybody* who could've walked in and given Julie any flak. But Julie used to put on this innocent face when it came to Ambush Bug: "I didn't know what they were doing! They sit over there and laugh at their own stuff! They're crazy!" But I think he knew what we were doing.

EURY: He was sort of a covert co-conspirator…?

GIFFEN: I think so. He'd go, "I don't know what they're doing! They're insane! It's all that hippie sh*t!" [*laughter*] But I think deep down he was going, "You're taking me off the Superman books? *I'll* show you taking me off the Superman books."

Sometimes he'd look at a page, and look up over the top of the page, and he'd give me this look, "How *dare* you do this?" Then he'd say to me, "I don't get it." And I'm thinking, "*Yeah*, you did."

EURY: Let's go back to your comment about Julie being taken off the Superman books. Privately, did he disclose any problems with adjusting to the editorial changeover?

GIFFEN: Nothing I know of, nothing I can point to that showed that Julie was feeling disgruntled. *But*—put yourself in that place. There's no way on Earth you could possibly be AOK with it.

There's nothing I can point to that said he was angry, but I think he might've thought, "You're making all of these changes. *I* could've made those changes, too." That's a gut feeling.

EURY: Interestingly, the legend is, at first Julie reluctantly accepted the *Superman* assignment.

GIFFEN: *Very* reluctantly, yeah. He was someone whose books were based upon science, and Superman's world had a certain amount of fantasy, and Julie didn't like going there. As he moved on, he would mold himself to the requirements of the job at hand. When I was doing Superman stories for him, he was always asking questions. There was always that little bit of digging to see if the story could satisfy him—"Okay, there's this vampire … but where did it *come* from?"

But at the end, he was like the king who was being asked to step down from the throne. And nobody does that entirely willingly.

EURY: But he did it with grace.

GIFFEN: Of course, but what choice did he have? And it wasn't like he was being shown the door. [*Editor's note: Schwartz remained a consultant for DC and became the company's unofficial "goodwill ambassador."*]

You know, I always thought that when the king was being asked to vacate the throne, when he stood up there was this "SHWUCK!" Velcro sound. [*laughter*]

EURY: How did he react when you first pitched Ambush Bug?

GIFFEN: He accepted it on the spot. But keep in mind that the first time Ambush Bug appeared was in a *DC* [*Comics*] *Presents*, with the Doom Patrol. We pitched him as "Bugs Bunny as a super-villain." And he *was* a villain back then, no doubt about it. You remember, he used to keep these itty, bitty bugs in his antenna pods? That was because Julie needed that [visual] shot: "If he's gonna teleport, how does he do it?" So we put that terminal there. As he went on, it became more, he could pop in, he could pop out. But at first, with Julie, it had to make some kind of sense to him.

The second time, I wanted to bring him back with the Substitute Heroes, and Julie was okay with that. And then the mail started to come in, and all the talk was about Ambush Bug. So I said to Julie, "You know, you're doing these Air Wave things in the back of *Action*." And he said, "Well, they're not doing very good." And I said, "So why not do Ambush Bug occasionally?" And that's what started it—we were doing back-ups, then suddenly he's on the cover, and the response to the character was staggering.

EURY: And then his own miniseries.

GIFFEN: Now *there's* a weird story. When I was doing *Legion of Super-Heroes*, [then-editorial director] Dick Giordano called me into his office and said, "So, what do you want to do next?" And I always believe that I should ask for something I don't stand a chance in hell getting, because then I can bargain down to what I really want. I wanted *Thriller*. But I asked for *Ambush Bug*. And Dick went, "Okay," and I said, [*incredulous tone*] "*Excuse me?!*" [*laughter*] I outsmarted myself. I never got *Thriller*, but I got *Ambush Bug*.

Julie was never anything other than supportive of *Ambush Bug*. He never made me go back and change a single page. Even when we were bringing back all those characters they were trying to get rid of in *Crisis*.

EURY: And even odder ones, like Egg Fu.

GIFFEN: Oh, yeah, Egg Fu was there, too.

You know that Julie loved to talk through his plots with his writers. When it was time to do the fourth issue of *Ambush Bug*, I said, "Hey, Julie, are you ready to plot the fourth issue of *Ambush Bug*?" Julie put down his papers, he looked me right in the eye and went … "Why? You haven't done a single thing we've ever talked about, except draw Ambush Bug in the issue. *Why?!* Get out of here!" [*laughter*]

When Bob Fleming would come into the office to get pages [to dialogue], he and I would sit over in the corner and laugh and laugh at the pages. At one point Kurt Schaffenberger was in the office with Julie, and Bob and I were over in the corner laughing at *Ambush Bug*. And Julie slams his hand down on his desk and says, "See? *See* what I have to put up with? They laugh at their own work! They just sit over their and laugh at their own pages! They'd laugh at *anything*! They'd laugh at the nose on my face…"

EURY: [*laughs*] He set himself up for that one, didn't he?

GIFFEN: Exactly. Bob and I just looked at one another, and brayed laughter like donkeys. Yeah, Julie was good for those moments.

It's interesting that so much of my take on Superman is connected to Julie, because my preferred take on Superman is

Writer J. M. Lofficier and penciler Giffen lampooned the French comic *Asterix* in *Action* #579 (May 1986).
Asterix © Hemmets Journal AB.

the Siegel and Shuster Superman. Go figure that one out—contradictions abound!

EURY: How did Robert Loren Fleming come on board as the Ambush Bug dialoguer?

GIFFEN: Paul Kupperberg dialogued the first Ambush Bug story in the Superman/Doom Patrol team-up, then Paul Levitz dialogued the Superman/Substitute Heroes *DC [Comics] Presents*. I was the only consistent one there. When we were planning the next *Ambush Bug* and I was wanting to take him into the goofy hero bit, I'd been reading Bob Fleming's *Thriller*. I thought he was a real good writer, and plus, he had the only office at DC [as proofreader] with an ashtray, and I smoked then, and I'd go in and goof around with him. I realized he had my kind of sense of humor. We just understood where each other was coming from.

With Bob, I was not helping him [dialogue *Ambush Bug* pages], I was not giving him *anything*. He'd call me and say, "Why's he eating sushi on this page?" and I'd just hang up on him. [*chuckles*] I wasn't helping him … if anything, I was a saboteur. He'd ask, "What about these guys in the warehouse? Who are they?" "How the hell should I know?! Figure it out!" I'd draw Ambush Bug holding a baseball bat all of a sudden, and Bob would say, "Where'd he get the baseball bat?" "I don't know!"

EURY: You both *did* have this uncanny knack for being on the same page.…

GIFFEN: I think he and I did a damn good Superman! For what we needed Superman to do, he worked. [*under breath*] But I'm sure most of fandom is not gonna agree with that.

EURY: Tell me about working with Bob Oksner, your *Ambush Bug* inker.…

GIFFEN: Bob was *such* a part of the process, and you sometimes don't think of inkers as being part of the process. You know, here's a guy who'd been involved with the business for ages, and he was being handed these *lunatic* pages, and *man*, did he get it right. I'm astonished by some of his inking on *Ambush Bug*. Then he retired. And I kind of knew deep down that when Bob Oksner retired, so did Irwin Schwab [Ambush Bug's alter ego]. As good as a job as Al Gordon did on the *Nothing Special*, it just wasn't the same.

EURY: It was sort of the series finale, after a couple of the cast members had already retired.

GIFFEN: It was like a TV series that went one season too long. We didn't quite jump the shark, but man, did we come close. I mean, sometimes, teams work, and when all the components aren't there—walk away. My *Lobo Unbound* with Alan Grant was like Lobo White. When it works, it works.

EURY: That's a good closing remark, unless you've got something else to add about Superman.

GIFFEN: I do have one more point to make about Superman: Lighten up, folks. There's nothing wrong with being a Boy Scout.

THE SUPERMAN MYTHOLOGY:
CLARK KENT: MARVEL MOONLIGHTER

If zipping about the galaxy as Superman and around the globe as WGBS-TV's star reporter weren't enough to muss a hero's spitcurl, Clark Kent occasionally managed to find time to drop in on the pages of Marvel Comics.

A famous mild-mannered reporter pays a visit to *The Daily Bugle* in *Marvel Team-Up #79* (Mar. 1979).
© 2006 Marvel Characters, Inc.

The Thunder God, trying out a new alter ego, bumps into Clark in *Thor #341* (Mar. 1984).
© 2006 Marvel Characters, Inc.

Clark Kent, Lois Lane, and Julius Schwartz (lower left of panel) sneak into *X-Men #98* (Apr. 1976).
© 2006 Marvel Characters, Inc.

(top right) Recognize the TV broadcaster in *Secret Wars II #7* (Jan. 1986)? (bottom right) This panel from *X-Men Annual #10* (1986) features cameos by Clark, Lois, and the Joker.
© 2006 Marvel Characters, Inc.

Look closely and you'll spot also Clark Kent and/or Superman cameos in these non-crossover Marvel titles:
Amazing Spider-Man Annual #23
Avengers #228, 296, 327
Captain America #260
Daredevil vol. 2 #8

Excalibur vol. 1 #8
Marvels #4
Ultimates #3
Uncanny X-Men #245
Web of Spider-Man #75

Special thanks to John Wells for list.

194

STEVE GERBER INTERVIEW

Writer Steve Gerber (b. 1947) captivated Marvel Comics readers in the mid-1970s with offbeat, satirically laced series such as *Man-Thing*, *Omega the Unknown*, *The Defenders*, and his most famous creation, *Howard the Duck*. Since then, his has been one of comics' freshest, most unpredictable voices, on titles as diverse as *Metal Men*, *KISS*, *Destroyer Duck*, *Void Indigo*, and *Hard Time*. Gerber's contribution to the Superman mythos during the Julius Schwartz era occurred through his *Phantom Zone* miniseries and its follow-up in *DC Comics Presents* #97.

Conducted by Michael Eury via e-mail on March 19, 2006.

MICHAEL EURY: Most readers assumed that the *Phantom Zone* miniseries (#1–4, Jan.–Apr. 1982) was DC's response to the Phantom Zone villains appearing in the movie *Superman II*, but given the peculiarities of scheduling, that might not be the case. Was the *Phantom Zone* comic indeed inspired by the movie's success?
STEVE GERBER: The short answer is "yes." I'm glad we stuck

Photo courtesy of stevegerber.com.

with the comics version of the villains, though, even if Zod's Italian fascist-inspired uniform looked a little goofy.
EURY: You'd done very little work for DC prior to this, most notably *Metal Men* #45 in 1976 and a three-issue run of *Mister Miracle* in 1978. How were you chosen to write *Phantom Zone*?
GERBER: As best I recall, Dick Giordano approached me about it. It's not something I would've come up with myself, because I was never a big fan of the PZ villains.
EURY: *Phantom Zone* was edited by Dick Giordano. Why didn't Superman line editor Julie Schwartz oversee it?
GERBER: Again, this is a guess: Dick may have thought I would have had difficulty working with Julie, whose approach to story and character was very different from my own. I would probably have agreed with that judgment, and so, probably, would Julie. Much as I liked and admired Julie, I don't think we would have been a good fit as editor and writer over the long term.
EURY: Did you bring your former *Howard the Duck* collaborator Gene Colan on board, or was he Dick's pick?
GERBER: As I recall, I asked for Gene, and Dick immediately agreed. I knew exactly what Gene's Superman would look like before he even set pencil to paper, and he didn't disappoint me. What really blew me away was Gene's Clark Kent! He looked real and human, maybe for the first time in the character's history. Gene was suffering a

Adventure into Fear #17 (Oct. 1973), introducing Steve Gerber's Superman homage, Wundarr.
© 2006 Marvel Characters, Inc.

little from typecasting at both Marvel and DC. At Marvel, he'd become the *Dracula* guy; as a result, at DC, he became the *Batman* guy for a while. They thought of him as an artist who could create a certain kind of eeriness and mood. Which was true, of course, but it hardly defined Gene's limits. He was capable of doing really wonderful sci-fi-flavored action stuff, too.

EURY: You had written a Superman pastiche almost ten years earlier when you introduced Wundarr into the Man-Thing series in *Adventure into Fear* #17 (Oct. 1973). What's the story behind Wundarr's creation?
GERBER: Nothing except my love of the Superman character and my desire to do a little parody/homage.
EURY: According to Roy Thomas, Stan Lee was miffed over Wundarr. Did you catch any heat from Stan or Roy?
GERBER: Actually, it was DC who was miffed. Marvel was the miffee. What I had intended as parody, DC saw as plagiarism. From what I was told, there were angry words exchanged, but it never got anywhere near a courtroom. Marvel agreed to do another Wundarr story that would set him drastically apart from Superman—which is what I had always intended—and that was that. (Wundarr's home planet never exploded. His father *was* the alarmist the Krypton elders supposed Jor-El to be.) I'm sure Roy must have conveyed to me Stan's displeasure with the incident. Under the circumstances, of course, Stan had every right to be displeased. I'm still amazed, though, that DC took it so seriously.
EURY: *The Phantom Zone* reintroduced *Daily Planet* employee Charlie Kweskill, formerly the Zone villain Quex-Ul, whose powers and memories were erased by gold kryptonite in his sole prior appearance in *Superman* #157 (Nov. 1962). Were you aware of this character prior to your developing *Phantom Zone*, or was Kweskill a discovery during your research?
GERBER: I'd read the story when it was originally published, but the strangeness of it really popped out in the research stage. Here was this Kryptonian, living and working among humans, even believing himself to be human, but carrying deeply repressed memories of a prior—and villainous—existence on another world. These huge concepts were tossed around very casually during the Weisinger years. Quex-Ul never appeared again, nor was his presence at the *Daily Planet* ever mentioned. For me he became the "hook" that made the PZ villains understandable on a human level, the character who could lead the others out of the realm of caricature.
EURY: While on that topic, how well versed were you in Superman's Kryptonian history before *Phantom Zone*?

(left) *Omega the Unknown*, co-created in 1975 by Gerber and Mary Skrenes, also bore subtle similarities to Superman, including interior artwork by one-time Supergirl and Superman artist Jim Mooney.
© 2006 Marvel Characters, Inc.

GERBER: As well-versed as anyone who grew up reading and loving the Superman books of the late '50s and early '60s. I vividly remember reading the first Phantom Zone story—which actually appeared in *Superboy* or *Adventure Comics*, if I recall—when it was originally published. Well-versed enough to remember that the "Map of Krypton" printed in the first *Superman Annual*, a comic book I hadn't looked at for almost two decades, made reference to a place described as the oldest city on Krypton. I can't recall the name of that city at the moment, but the very notion that it existed seemed to open up huge new possibilities. It suggested that different locales on Krypton might have different cultures, different architectures, different economic and sociological realities. I've always been skeptical of the one planet/one culture concept.

EURY: *Phantom Zone* #1's cover copy asked, "A Humane Method of Criminal Confinement … or a *Dimension without Hope*?" How did *Phantom Zone* reflect your personal views of the real world's penal system?

GERBER: I didn't write the cover copy for that issue and didn't see it before it reached the stands. To be honest, I wasn't thinking much about earthly penal systems at that time. I *was* trying to decide whether Jor-El had created a humane system or a really easy way to warehouse criminals out of sight and mind.

EURY: The often-violent *Phantom Zone* pushed the envelope for DC super-hero fare of the day, examples being Colan's depiction of man-hater Faora Hu-Ul's victims in issue #1 and pyrotic Az-Rel setting Nam-Ek on fire in #2. Any problems with the Comics Code during the miniseries?

GERBER: None that I know of.

EURY: In issue #2, members of the Metropolis S.W.A.T. team are wounded by their own bullets, ricocheting off of Kryptonian villains they were firing upon. This type of realism had long been absent from Superman stories. What was Julie Schwartz's reaction to your darker handling of Superman's world?

GERBER: I can only speculate. There must have been *something* about it that he liked, or he wouldn't have invited me to write the last issue of *DC Comics Presents* a few years later.

EURY: The Kryptonian escapees come close to igniting World War III, their actions triggering a nuclear exchange between the U.S. and what was then the U.S.S.R. Did this spark any controversy during this pre-*Watchmen* DC era?

GERBER: Again, not that I recall.

EURY: How do you respond to readers who argue that the Phantom Zone villains and other Kryptonian survivors—Krypto, Supergirl, the Kandorians, etc.—weakened Superman's appeal as the "Last Son of Krypton"?

GERBER: I think they were right, to some extent. At age 13 or so, I could get past Krypto, Supergirl, the PZers, and even the entire city of Kandor. They were interesting concepts. They generated interesting stories. For me, the line was crossed when Supergirl's parents turned up alive. When that happened, I pretty much gave up on the Superman books. I didn't want to stick around long enough to find out Jor-El and Lara had survived, too.

EURY: You penned a sequel to your miniseries, *DC Comics Presents* #97's (Sept. 1986) "Phantom Zone: The Final Chapter," penciled by Rick Veitch and inked by Bob Smith. This time you worked with editor Schwartz, on

(left) Supergirl takes to the skies on page 10 of *Phantom Zone #2* (Feb. 1982), scanned from a photocopy of Gene Colan's pencils.
TM & ® DC Comics.

one of his last Superman stories. What was Julie's attitude about the impending changes with the character he had edited for 16 years?

GERBER: Just a guess, but from talking to him at the time, I think he felt a kind of relief, as if a burden had been lifted. He never asked for the Superman books. I think he would've been very content to edit his revival characters, *JLA*, and *Strange Adventures* for his entire career.

EURY: In "Final Chapter" you revealed the Zone's *sentience*, a fascinating concept. For the benefit of those who didn't read this tale, would you offer a recap?

GERBER: As best I remember: The Phantom Zone, it turned out, was not a separate dimension, but a field of consciousness surrounding a being called Aethyr. That field had physical limits, so it was actually possible to cross the landscape of Aethyr's consciousness and come out on the "other side" of the Phantom Zone. That was the basic idea. The ramifications of it were much more complex.

EURY: While *DCCP* #97 was published concurrently with Alan Moore's imaginary tale "Whatever Happened to the Man of Tomorrow?," your "Final Chapter" was the *in-continuity* send-off to Superman's pre-Crisis adventures, with the Bizarro World, Mr. Mxyzptlk's fifth dimension, and Argo City being destroyed. Looking back on "Final Chapter" 20 years later, I realize that your story would have provided

a fresh starting point for Superman, *without* the necessity of the *Man of Steel* reboot. Do you agree?

GERBER: Not *that* story, exactly, but something like it, told in an extended format and greater depth, might have worked. The series was suffocating under decades' worth of accumulated clutter and needed a thorough housecleaning, but I felt the reboot threw away a lot of good stuff along with the junk.

EURY: I'm curious about the proposed revamping of Superman you pitched to DC in 1985 with Frank Miller. What were your plans?

GERBER: That would take hours. Conceptually, what we wanted to do was recreate the character with a contemporary sensibility, while adhering as closely as possible to the *spirit* of the Siegel and Shuster original. That's vague, I know, but it had to do with Superman's place among humanity and his role as a force for social justice, a theme that, judging from the character's first year, was very important to Jerry Siegel.

More Colan pencils from *Phantom Zone* #2, with Green Lantern in pursuit of escaping Zoners.
TM & © DC Comics.

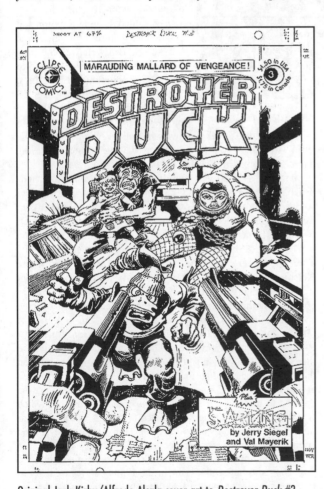

Original Jack Kirby/Alfredo Alcala cover art to *Destroyer Duck* #3 (June 1983). Note the back-up series written by Jerry Siegel. *Destroyer Duck* was produced as a fundraiser to assist Gerber in his legal battles with Marvel over ownership of Howard the Duck and to increase awareness for creators' rights.
TM & © 2006 Steve Gerber.

PAUL KUPPERBERG INTERVIEW

The writer of over 700 comic-book stories, Paul Kupperberg co-created DC Comics' *Arion, Lord of Atlantis* and *Checkmate* and wrote *Doom Patrol*, *The Vigilante*, and *Masters of the Universe*, among other series. Counting media tie-ins from *Star Trek* to *Powerpuff Girls* among his credits, Kupperberg is also no stranger to Superman, having scripted the *World of Krypton* miniseries, *Supergirl* and *Superboy* stories, and the hero's syndicated newspaper strip.

Conducted by Michael Eury via e-mail on March 10, 2006.

MICHAEL EURY: You started writing Super-stories in *Superman Family* #182 (Mar.–Apr. 1977). How did you land in Julie Schwartz's stable?

PAUL KUPPERBERG: That was my first story for DC Comics, a "Fabulous World of Krypton" ten-pager called "The Stranger," a kind of Christmas-on-Krypton story. Before that I'd sold a half-dozen horror stories to Charlton Comics and had been trying to break in at DC, where, fortunately, I knew people from my fanzine connections, including Paul Levitz, an old friend with whom I'd published fanzines (*The Comic Reader*,

Photo courtesy of Paul Kupperberg.

Etcetera) over the years who was now on staff as an assistant editor. He called me and said Denny O'Neil, who he was assisting, as I recall, and who edited *Superman Family* at the time, was looking for World of Krypton stories, so I went up, pitched some ideas, and Denny bought "The Stranger."

God bless the DC Dollar Comics of the mid-'70s. Along with all the anthology titles DC published in those days, like *House of Mystery*, *Weird War Tales*, and *Ghosts*, there was plenty of room for the new writers of the time like myself to cut our teeth and learn our trade on short stories. Six-page mystery and romance stories, ten-page super-hero back-ups, whatever. There were seven or eight stories in that issue of *Superman Family*, so as bad as "The Stranger" was, it was just one of many and could kind of get lost in the crowd. The art, on the other hand, by another newcomer, Marshall Rogers, and inker Frank Springer, was very nice.

Anyway, as I say, Denny O'Neil was the *Superman Family* editor at the time. Then I believe I wrote the Nightwing and Flamebird feature, beginning in #183 (May–June 1977), for Nelson Bridwell. That ran for about a dozen installments. I came back to *Superman Family* with #215 (Feb. 1982), taking over the Jimmy Olsen feature from Martin Pasko, also for Nelson, who was also Julie's assistant. So *Superman Family* got me on Julie's radar.

I couldn't tell you why Julie finally tapped ᵐᵉ ᵗᵒ ʷʳⁱᵗᵉ ᴬⁿ ʰᵉ ᵉᵈⁱᵗᵉᵈ ᴴᵉ ᶜᵒᵘᵈ ʰᵃᵛᵉ ᵏⁿᵒʷⁿ ᵐᵉ

my work or maybe he'd just seen me and heard me around the offices—I wasn't exactly a quiet, shrinking violet, especially in those days—and thought there was something to my attitude that would translate to the writing.

EURY: You scripted the first comic-book miniseries, *The World of Krypton* (#1–3, July–Sept. 1979), for editor E. Nelson Bridwell. What's the story behind this series? And was the term "miniseries" coined at that time?

KUPPERBERG: The *World of Krypton* miniseries was originally scheduled to be an arc in the then-recently revived *Showcase* title. I'd written the first three issues of the new *Showcase* (the New Doom Patrol, #94–96), followed by Paul Levitz's Power Girl arc (#97–99), our collaborative *Showcase* #100 (featuring practically everyone who had ever appeared in the title in a very *Crisis on Infinite Earths*-type story, only done in 38 pages instead of 12 issues), followed by three issues of Hawkman, and a one-shot "Tales of the O.S.S." *World of Krypton* was supposed to be *Showcase* #105–107, but the book was cancelled, leaving Krypton and some other features up in the air.

Nelson Bridwell was the *only* person who would have wanted to edit a book like that in those days. It was all about tying together all the bits and pieces of Jor-El's life on Krypton that had appeared in dozens of stories over the years. It was *everything*, from the major stuff like how he met Lara to some nitpicks like the name of his cousin, Cru-El, the nasty kid. No. *Really*.

Anyway, Nelson was one of the original fanboys-turned-pro, having been a diehard fan from the '40s and '50s who had sold some stories to *MAD* Magazine and been hired as an assistant to the Superman editor of the time, Mort Weisinger. Nelson had an encyclopedic memory for everything comics (and the Bible and Shakespeare, too) and he just loved continuity. There were many instances in stories I wrote for him where Nelson would edit some bit of continuity trivia into the script that would then require footnotes to explain. He just had to connect all the dots, so he was the perfect guy to oversee something like *World of Krypton* (and, later on, a *Secrets of the Legion of Super-Heroes* miniseries that I wrote for him).

1979 was the aftermath of 1978's *Superman: The Movie*, so there was still interest in getting more Superman-related titles on the stands. I imagine that since DC had this book mostly finished at the time of the *Showcase* cancellation, the powers-that-be decided to throw it out there on its own as a miniseries, which was what we were calling it even back then. This was a couple or three years after *Roots* and *Rich Man, Poor Man* on TV [added "miniseries" to the American vernacular].

EURY: While most long-time readers will remember you as a Superboy and Supergirl scribe in the 1980s—series we'll get to in a moment—you wrote a handful of Superman stories for Julie Schwartz. Wasn't your first actual Superman script a team-up with *Masters of the Universe*'s He-Man (*DC Comics Presents* #47, July 1982)?

KUPPERBERG: Yep, although, technically, Julie was only "consulting" editor on the *Masters of the Universe* job. Dave Manak was editing the MOTU project.

TM & © DC Comics.

A sketch of *Masters of the Universe's* He-Man by George Tuska.
He-Man TM & © Mattel. Dewey Cassell collection.

A page from Paul Kupperberg's *World of Krypton* #1 (July 1979). Art by Howard Chaykin and Murphy Anderson.
TM & © DC Comics.

Just like writing for DC Comics was what every newbie writer aimed for, writing Superman for the legendary Julie Schwartz was what you aspired to once you did break into DC. When I finally asked Julie about it years later, he couldn't remember, but something tells me that since my first Superman writing for him was as part of the *Masters of the Universe* licensed tie-in deal, he must have figured it wasn't like a "real" Superman story. Seeing that I didn't screw up too badly on that, I suppose he must have figured I was competent enough that he didn't have to worry about me doing too much damage to the character. I think my next story for him was another issue of *DC Comics Presents* (#52, Dec. 1982), a Doom Patrol team-up.

EURY: You also wrote Radio Shack's *Superman and Wonder Woman: The Computer Masters of Metropolis* (1982), one of several "custom comics" DC produced for advertisers in the early 1980s. How did writing a custom comic vary from writing a traditional comics script?

KUPPERBERG: There's not really that much of a difference, certainly not in the "old days" of single-issue stories, other than having to shoehorn the information that the clients are paying to get across into the story without turning it into a technical manual or a catalogue. Then, as now, DC was fairly protective of their characters, especially the big guns like Superman and Wonder Woman, so they were played straight even if the corporate-sponsored story might have been sort of goofy. I believe Joe Orlando, who was in charge of Special Projects, edited that particular story. I also wound up writing at least one more Radio Shack comic as a result of that one, for Archie Comics, which Radio Shack contracted with after their deal with DC was done.

EURY: You wrote two stories featuring Terra-Man (in *Superman* #377, Nov. 1982 and *Action* #557, July 1984), making you the one of the few writers outside of the villain's creator, Cary Bates, to handle the character. Terra-Man is either loved or hated by readers—what appealed to you about this cosmic cowboy?

KUPPERBERG: I like cowboys … what can I tell you? Terra-Man was just a wacky, fun character. And he was different from the rest of Superman's rogues' gallery. Besides, where else could I have someone call people "bushwackers" or "snakes in the grass"?

EURY: The tribute to Edmond Hamilton, the super-villain Colonel Future (*Superman* #378, Dec. 1982), was your creation. Remind readers of who that villain was, and tell us how he was created.

KUPPERBERG: Allow me to correct you, as Julie liked to say. Colonel Future was *co*-created by me with considerable kibitzing by Mr. Schwartz. As I recall, he wasn't exactly a villain, more of a good guy who had to do villainous things to make his powers work. I came in with a vague idea for a bad guy who possessed a psychic power to "see" futuristic technology but only when his life was in imminent danger. Julie liked the basic idea but, as always, had a way to make it better.

Way back in the *real* olden days of the 1930s, Julie had been, as everyone should know, a literary agent in the science-fiction field. One of the writers he handled was the author Edmond Hamilton, who also wrote, throughout the '40s, '50s, and into the '60s, comics. One of Hamilton's pulp characters was Captain Future, who, as I recall, was the inspiration for Captain Comet, which Julie introduced in *Strange Adventures* #9 (June 1951).

Anyway, as an homage to his old friend, Julie thought we should (A) give Hamilton's Captain Future a promotion to Colonel, and (B) use Hamilton's name as the secret identity of Colonel Future. Once we had those pieces in place, filling in the rest of Colonel Future story was pretty simple.

EURY: You and collaborating writer Bob Rozakis introduced another addition to Superman's rogues' gallery, the Planeteer, in *Superman* #387 and *Action* #547 (Sept. 1983). What's the backstory behind the Planeteer and his conception?

KUPPERBERG: …I don't remember … at least not any specifics, although, now that I think about the circumstances of that story, BobRo may be the better man to tell this story.

See, in the early '80s, despite the fact that DC was producing three monthly Superman titles, some of the overseas licensors wanted even more material than we were producing, particularly a German publisher called Ehapa, which is now a part of the Danish publishing giant, Egmont, I

believe. So DC started producing these 40-plus-page graphic novels, what they called albums, for that market. I think there were about a dozen done altogether, four of 'em by Bob and myself, and at least one by me solo. The idea was, we'd provide Ehapa with their albums, then reprint the stories as two-parters in the regular monthlies. The Planeteer was one of those jobs. As I recall, on the jobs we did together, Bob plotted out the stories and I scripted them.

DC did publish one of those stories as a stand alone one-shot album, 8.5" x 11" format with a cardboard covers, *Superman Spectacular* (1982 Series), which reprinted one of those German stories, called something like "The Startling Saga of Superman-Red and Superman-Blue" (next to bridge, pea soup, and puns, Julie loved alliteration best), which somehow involved Luthor splitting Superman into two individuals, riffing on the classic (and one of my all-time favorite Superman stories) "The Amazing Story of Superman-Red and Superman-Blue" from *Superman* #162 (July 1963).

Anyway, long-winded digression aside, since Bob plotted the story, the Planeteer was most likely his baby. I just put words in his mouth.

EURY: In the mid-1980s, the biggest surprise in each issue of *Action* and *Superman* was not the identity of the villain of the month, but just who would write the issue, with you, Bates, Rozakis, Elliot Maggin, Mike W. Barr, Joey Cavalieri, and Robert Loren Fleming among the writers rotating in and out. Was this "revolving door" Julie's policy during the day, or was he searching for a new scribe among you?

KUPPERBERG: ["Revolving door"] seemed to be the policy. I think Julie liked the variety of writers and what they could bring to Superman. He'd been working on the character for 15 years by then—and it wasn't just one monthly title, but a whole slate of books, *Superman*, *Action*, *DC Comics Presents*, *Superboy*, *Supergirl*, and the odd other project, like the Ehapa stories, Annuals, and the syndicated strip. Julie loved the process of dragging a story out of the mess of ideas that would fly around whenever we plotted.

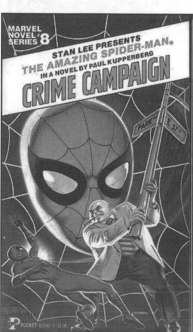

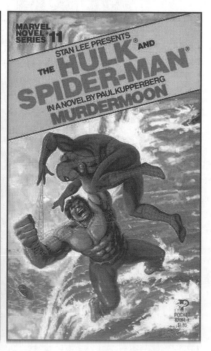

Two 1979 Marvel super-hero novels written by Kupperberg, for editors (and fellow Superman titles) Len Wein and Marv Wolfman

A collection of Julie Schwartz's badges from 1990s convention appearances

Courtesy of Heritage Comics

EURY: Describe your working relationship with Julie Schwartz....

KUPPERBERG: Well, I kind of went through an evolutionary series of stages in my working relationships with Julie, beginning with Terror, then Awe, then Submission, followed by Rebellion, and ending in, I hope, Mutual Respect. And Friendship. Julie was a special person in my life, especially in his later years when we got to know each other better. Julie would come in to DC once a week, he was editor emeritus and had an office to come to, and I made sure to visit with him on most weeks and call if I hadn't seen him in a while. I even got to be his traveling companion once, out to a convention in Kansas City when the person he usually traveled with, Brian Thomsen, who co-wrote Julie's memoirs, couldn't make it.

Anyway, not to get sloppy or weird, but Julie was a presence in my life growing up through the comics he edited. I loved everything he did, and I'm talking about the very early 1960s, at the height of his powers as an editor. *Justice League of America*, *The Flash*, *Green Lantern*, *The Atom*, *Mystery in Space*, *Strange Adventures*, *Batman* … Holy Moley, could there be a better time for a fan? He was High King Lord Editor, he was doing what everyone else was copying if they even bothered trying. So when I started writing for him, I was intimidated as all hell. I actually never used his name at first because I thought I'd sound like an idiot calling him Mr. Schwartz and couldn't bring myself to call him Julie.

At first, I would come in with story idea pitches and he would twist them 180 degrees away from what I had in mind, but I went wherever he sent it because this was *Julius Schwartz*! After a while, once I got comfortable and learned that for all his tough, gruff, Perry White shtick, the man was a sweetheart. I started arguing for my ideas, some of which he'd go with, some not, but he always gave me a fair hearing. Finally, we reached the Mutual Respect where I'd come in and pitch something, like the Madame Xanadu crossover in *DC Comics Presents* (#65, Jan. 1984), which wasn't really his cup of tea, but he trusted me enough to let me go ahead with it anyway and, when it was finished, left it pretty much alone except for some line editing.

I once said to him, "Julie, every month I bring in my scripts, you take them, you edit them, they get printed, and you never tell me if you liked it or not." And he just gave me a don't-be-an-idiot look and said, "If I *didn't* like it, you'd know it!" He wasn't effusive with his praise, but he'd compliment you by not totally rewriting you and by handing you your check.

EURY: Do you have any stories to share about working on *DC Comics Presents* with artists like Gray Morrow and Don Newton, illustrators not normally associated with the Man of Steel?

KUPPERBERG: I've been real lucky. At the time I got into comics, most of the artists I grew up reading were still working, so I've had stories drawn by guys like Carmine Infantino, Gil Kane, Steve Ditko, Jack Kirby, Ross Andru, Don Heck, Irv Novick, Curt Swan, Jerry Grandenetti, Kurt Schaffenberger, George Tuska, George Evans … a slew of great artists.

But if I had to pick favorite story based solely on the way the art worked so perfectly with the story, it would have to be the Gray Morrow issue of *DCCP* (the Superman/Madame Xanadu team-up). I'm very proud of that script, but Gray's art just made the story. It was a very human story and he made Clark look so *real life* and drew such great facial expressions. It's an amazing piece of art especially considering, as you say, Superman wasn't Gray's usual territory. I didn't have any contact with Gray over the story … I didn't know he was drawing it until the day I walked into his office and Julie showed me the art. I nearly plotzed.

Don Newton was another great, great artist. I'm very lucky to have had him draw several of my stories, several "Green Lantern Corps" back-ups including the story that introduced Ch'p, a short run on *Aquaman,* and several gorgeous issues of *DCCP*. Most of which I wished the scripts had been up to. Don was a very talented man who I met only a few times at comic-book conventions, but we did get to spend some time together during the shows and he was a good guy. It was a shock and shame, his dying so young. I used to love his *Phantom* at Charlton, not to mention his fanzine work, long before I ever got to meet him.

EURY: Speaking of illustrators not normally associated with Superman, Carmine Infantino penciled your "Born to Be Superman" script for *Superman* #404 (Feb. 1985), one of his few Superman tales. Regarding that story's "13

In addition to Kupperberg's *Superman* #404, Carmine Infantino—inked by Murphy Anderson—also drew the Man of Steel in a story sequence in *Heroes Against Hunger* (1986).

Panel 1: WHERE ARE YOU GOING, MR. KENT--?! / HAVE TO, er... GET PEOPLE **ON** THIS STORY--FAST!

Panel 2: ...BECAUSE THIS REPORT SAYS *SUPERMAN'S* GONE ON A RAMPAGE UPSTATE--

Panel 3: --BUT THAT CAN'T BE RIGHT-- / --AND *I* OUGHT TO KNOW!

© DC COMICS INC., 1983
Dist. by Tribune Company Syndicate, Inc.

P. KUPPERBERG
DELBO/TRAPANI

A *World's Greatest Super-Heroes* Superman daily written by Kupperberg and drawn by Jose Delbo and Sal Trapani, from July 28, 1983.
TM & © DC Comics. Art courtesy of Heritage Comics.

years after Superman disappeared" premise, how did you feel when a similar idea became the basic concept behind the movie *Superman Returns*?

KUPPERBERG: As far as I'm concerned, Carmine could draw anything I wrote any day of the week. I think he's one of the best designers and storytellers in the business with a unique, quirky style. I've always loved his stuff, right from when I started reading him on *The Flash* and "Adam Strange" in the early '60s. In fact, Carmine was the very first artist whose style I learned to identify at sight. Just a wonderful artist and, while I know there were those who didn't like him inking himself, he penciled and inked a few "Tales of the Green Lantern Corps" stories I wrote in the '80s that are just beautiful.

I don't know why Julie gave him the "Born to Be Superman" script … it was probably something as simple as Carmine happened to need work and that was the script sitting on Julie's desk at the moment, but I'm so happy he did. It's one of my favorite of my Superman stories and Carmine did a beautiful job on it. As always.

As far as any similarity with *Superman Returns*, it's a big world and there really are only seven plots in it. I can't tell you how many movies and TV shows I've seen where I could make a case that the idea came from a story I wrote. And I've seen just as many where the writers of the movie or TV could make the case I ripped them off. I mean, you want to get technical, look at a movie like *The Return of Martin Guerre* (1982) … a French peasant goes off to war and when he returns, years later after being presumed dead, nobody's quite sure he is who he claims to be. I didn't see the movie until years later, but there's that similarity in stories.

EURY: Tell me about writing the *Superman* syndicated newspaper strip….

KUPPERBERG: That was your basic dream come true. You go way back, to the very beginning of comic books, and every writer and artist in the field was only working in comics until they could sell a newspaper strip. Well, in that grand tradition…!

Martin Pasko was the initial writer of the strip, which

Tom & Jerry TM & © 2006 Turner Entertainment.

Superman and came out around the time of the first Superman movie. Paul Levitz then took it over and I ghosted a two- or three-month sequence during his run, which led to my being offered the gig when Paul gave it up. I wrote it for, boy, three or four years, I think, and I loved it. Once I found the rhythm of writing a daily and Sunday continuity (although near the end of the run I lost the Sunday page from the continuity, which was converted to a fun and activity page written by Bob Rozakis), it was a blast to do. The adventure strip was a dying breed even then so it was nice to get my licks in before it went away altogether. Several years later I wrote a humor strip for a while, the *Tom & Jerry* syndicated strip for Editor's Syndicate, and while that was fun to do, it didn't have the same thrill as the Superman strip. And, man, I don't know how guys like Charles Schulz and the rest can do a humor strip for decades … writing six funny three-panel gags a day is a killer!

By the time I took it over, the strip had gone from being, essentially, a JLA strip to starring Superman with the occasional guest-star … I remember one continuity guest-starred Wonder Woman, for instance. Julie Schwartz, for whom I was already writing *Superman*, *DC Comics Presents*, *Superboy*, and *Supergirl*, was the editor, so our working relationship was an established and well-oiled machine. I'd come in, pitch an idea, run it around the block a few times with Julie throwing in his ideas and suggestions, and then go home and write. And, like any series, some storylines worked better than others.

EURY: When you took over *The New Adventures of Superboy* in 1982, you introduced teenage Clark Kent's girlfriend, Lisa Davis. Like your "Born to Be Superman" was prescient of *Superman Returns*, your character of Lisa added a *Smallville*-like romantic dynamic to Superboy's stories. Tell me about Lisa.

KUPPERBERG: I grew up reading the Mort Weisinger Superman, the guy who acted like a complete wuss and pretended to be afraid to cross the street without holding someone's hand "Hmm, if I don't hold Perry's hand while crossing this street, someone might suspect that Clark Kent and Superman are one and the same!"

Basically, I was sick to death of the whole bit. I mean, it worked early on for the character and it was cute even through the Weisinger years, but this was the 1980s, for crying out loud. It was clichéd by then and I wanted to stop it, at least in *Superboy*, where I was the sole writer and could keep things consistent. So I had Clark try acting like, y'know … a normal teenager—play some touch football, not be a dweeb—and no one batted an eye.

And it was so time for a girlfriend who wasn't Lana. The Clark-Lana dynamic was such that their dating kind of didn't really work, at least not for me, so I came up with Lisa. Besides, adding a new regular cast member helped to stir things up all around and gave us someone new to mess with, plus made Lana jealous, which was fun.

As I recall, Lisa's dad was a politician, a city councilman who, it would have turned out, was in on some shady dealings that Pa Kent ran for office to try and fight, leading to attempts on his life, etc. Finally, when the whole scheme unraveled—without any interference from Superboy; this was a Jonathan Kent subplot all the way—her dad was to either get killed or go to prison, I forget, and the family would leave town.

EURY: Didn't you plan to do a Superman story where the adult Lisa returned to Clark's life?

KUPPERBERG: Yep. The idea was that Lisa would show up at the *Daily Planet* and tell Clark she needed Superman's help and when he says he'll try to contact him for her she tells him she's known since they were dating that he was Superboy. She never told anyone. We were going to tease a renewal of the relationship, even get them back together, then something horrible was supposed to happen to her. I don't know if we planned exactly what that far ahead. But … *Crisis*. Ah, well.

EURY: It's my understanding that you found Clark more fun to write than Superboy. Why?

KUPPERBERG: Superman's an archetype, an icon. You see the costume and that "S"-shield and there's a certain expectation of how the character will act and react. He's Superman, the world's biggest Boy Scout. Clark, on the other hand, is a regular guy, or at least could he handled as a regular guy. For instance, I once wrote a line of dialogue for Superman that began, "I'm afraid I don't know the answer to that," or somesuch, and Julie edited it because "Superman is never afraid!" Well, I'm afraid of everything, so I'm going to relate to meek, mild-mannered Clark Kent way better than to Superman.

EURY: While we mentioned that Carmine Infantino isn't known as a Superman artist, he drew many of your *Supergirl* stories. What unique qualities did he bring to the character?

KUPPERBERG: Sheer storytelling ability and a mastery of draftsmanship. In a lot of ways, I felt the same about Carmine as I did about Julie, at least on a professional level. Carmine is just one of the best ever, just a comic-book god to me. I saw him a couple of weeks ago at a convention and took my nine-year-old son over to say hello. I introduced Carmine to Max by telling him that this was one of the best artists ever in comics.

EURY: Eduardo Barreto, who illustrated some of your stories, was an up-and-coming artist at the time you were writing for Julie. Where was he from? Do you recall how he was recruited to DC?

KUPPERBERG: Uruguay. I have no idea how he connected with DC but he was talented enough that even if he had sent in

Carmine Infantino's lettered pencils for page 2 of Paul Kupperberg's Superboy story from the unpublished *Double Comics #1*.

TM & © DC Comics. All *Double Comics* art courtesy of Paul Kupperberg.

Page 14 of the Supergirl tale from the unpublished *Double Comics* #1 returns Kara to New Krypton, home to the liberated Kandorians. Script by Kupperberg, pencils by Eduardo Barreto.

samples, he would have been snapped up. Eduardo's a wickedly good artist. He just got the knack of telling the story and he always gave me exactly what I asked for, only about 17 times better.

In a lot of ways, he was like Curt Swan that way, another of those guys who I was lucky enough to work with and who you didn't ask me about, shame on you.

EURY: *Okay, okay—tell me about working with Curt Swan…*

KUPPERBERG: Curt was a quieter, more restrained artist, but he put everything you needed and wanted in a panel in each and every panel.

EURY: Your *Supergirl* supporting cast included a character named John Ostrander. This *has* to be more than a coincidence—presumably you were friends with John before he became a comics pro.

KUPPERBERG: Not a coincidence at all. I moved to Chicago from my native New York in 1979 and, purely by chance, found an apartment in a building across the street from John, who I knew through mutual friends. John was, at the time, a playwright and actor in the very active Chicago theater scene and a huge comic-book fan. This was several years before he got into comics at First Comics. Anyway, when I took over the Supergirl feature, I moved her to Chicago and, just for grins, gave her my old address—although her apartment was way nicer than mine!—so I thought it'd be fun to make Johnny-O Linda's neighbor. It's the kind of thing we do all the time, putting our friends in stories. In John's case, he happened to make the move into comics himself.

EURY: Did the Earth-One John Ostrander survive the *Crisis*?

KUPPERBERG: Yes, he did. I believe he went on to running a pet-grooming saloon, but we lost touch shortly after.

EURY: You were also attached to the *Double Comics* (aka *Double Action*) title, a proposed merger of the *Superboy* and *Supergirl* series. What are some of the storylines you'd planned for the Boy and Girl of Steel in this title?

KUPPERBERG: Superboy was going to become a team book with a group called the Galaxians or something like that. The first half-dozen issues of *Double Comics* was supposed to introduce the new heroes for the group while warding off a futuristic menace. We'd also follow the Jonathan Kent subplot, along with the Clark/Lisa romance.

Supergirl was going to spend a while out in space, first on New Krypton, where the people of Kandor, including her parents, had gone to live once Superman finally enlarged the bottled city.

EURY: How did you react when you were informed of Supergirl's addition to *Crisis*' "death list"?

KUPPERBERG: Not in happiness. As I said, we had some fun plans in store for her with in *Double Comics* that I would have liked to see come to fruition, but, hey, I was a hired gun working on someone else's property, so I rolled with the punches and moved on to writing other things.

EURY: Which of your contributions to the Superman mythos are you most proud of?

KUPPERBERG: I don't know how much I contributed to the mythos. Unfortunately, I felt like my best stuff was yet to come, especially on *Superboy*. We had a direction to go in with the book and the character, but, overall, I did a handful of stories I'm very proud of, including "Born to be Superman," the Madame Xanadu issue of *DC Comics Presents*, a few others. And, hey, I got to be one of the principal writers on *Superman* there for a few years there, I wrote the *Superman* syndicated strip as well as *Superboy* and *Supergirl*, had Swan, Infantino, Schaffenberger, and Oksner routinely draw my stories, worked with Julie Schwartz … all in all, I can't complain.

(right) Supergirl receives a lesson in Klurkor … and in humility.
TM & © DC Comics.

Superboy and Krypto tangle with Temporal Rangers on page 10 of this unpublished Kupperberg/Infantino tale.
TM & © DC Comics.

(right) Dick Dillin (1929–1980) drew Superman in *Justice League of America* from 1968 until his death in 1980; he also penciled numerous issues of *World's Finest*. Dillin and inker Joe Giella's *JLA* #66 cover, seen here, was rejected by DC but eventually published in 1977 as the back cover to *The Amazing World of DC Comics* #14. (far right) A commission by Ramona Fradon, who drew Superman and other DC super-heroes from 1977–1980 in *Super Friends*.

TM & © DC Comics. Art courtesy of Heritage Comics.

TM & © DC Comics. Wallace Harrington collection.

(right) From the late 1970s through the mid-1980s, Joe Staton penciled a variety of Superman, Superboy, and Legion adventures. This Staton-drawn page, inked by Frank Chiaramonte, is from *Superman Family* #196 (July–Aug. 1979). (far right) Before his heart-stopping Batman vs. Superman slugfest in the climax of 1986's *The Dark Knight Returns*, Frank Miller illustrated this cover for *New Adventures of Superboy* #51 (Mar. 1984).

TM & © DC Comics. Art courtesy of Heritage Comics.

TM & © DC Comics. Art courtesy of Heritage Comics.

TM & © DC Comics. David Hamilton collection.

TM & © DC Comics. Art courtesy of Heritage Comics.

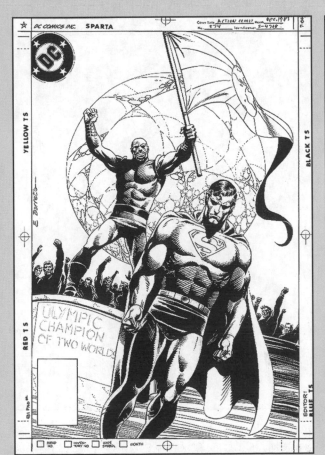

TM & © DC Comics. Art courtesy of Heritage Comics.

TM & © DC Comics. Art courtesy of Jerry Ordway.

(top left) Howard Bender, a Superman fan-turned-pro, drew a handful of Super-stories and covers in the mid-1980s. Pictured here are his cover pencils (later inked by Jerry Ordway) to *Action* #568 (June 1985). (top right) Rick Veitch penciled some of the Man of Steel's most unique tales, such as this Superman/Swamp Thing team-up, written by Alan Moore and inked by Al Williamson, from *DC Comics Presents* #85 (Sept. 1985). (left) Fans took notice of Eduardo Barreto's art on a variety of Superman covers and stories in the mid-1980s. Presented here is Barreto's original cover art to *Action* #574 (Dec. 1985). (above) Bernie Wrightson's model sheet for the Master, the menace in 1986's *Heroes Against Hunger* one-shot.

SUPERMAN ROUNDTABLE DISCUSSION
Moderated by Myk-El of the Kryptonian History Council, Kandor

Via the miracle of Kandorian technology, 16 Superman writers, artists, and editors have gathered to discuss Superman comic books from the Mort Weisinger and Julius Schwartz dynasties. The distinguished participants:

Jon Bogdanove (1990s *Superman: The Man of Steel* penciler)

Kurt Busiek (writer of *Superman: Secret Identity*; 2000s *Superman* writer)

John Byrne (writer/artist of 1986 *Man of Steel* revamp and late 1980s *Superman* and *Action*; 2000s *Action* artist)

Mike Carlin (1980s/1990s Superman group editor)

Jackson Guice (1990s *Action Comics* penciler)

Dan Jurgens (1980s/1990s *Superman* writer/artist; *Superman/Doomsday* writer/artist)

Karl Kesel (1980s *Superman* inker; 1990s *Adventures of Superman* and *Superboy* writer)

Jeph Loeb (2000s *Superman* and *Superman/Batman* writer; *Smallville* writer/supervising producer)

David Mandel (writer of "The Bizarro Jerry" episode of *Seinfeld*)

Jerry Ordway (1980s/1990s *Adventures of Superman* and *Superman* writer/artist)

Alex Ross (artist of *Kingdom Come*, *Superman: Peace on Earth*, and *Justice*)

Gail Simone (2000s *Action* and *Villains United* writer)

Walter Simonson (1990s writer/artist of *Superman Special #1*; writer of *Superman: The Last God of Krypton*)

Roger Stern (1980s/1990s *Action* and *Superman* writer)

Roy Thomas (1980s *All-Star Squadron* and *DC Comics Presents* writer)

Mark Waid (writer of *Kingdom Come*, *Superman: Birthright*, and *Legion of Super-Heroes*)

MYK-EL: What's your earliest Superman memory?

JOHN BYRNE: George Reeves on *The Adventures of Superman* television series, which I first saw in England as a child, aged about six.

JERRY ORDWAY: My earliest memories are of seeing *coverless* Superman comics from the early '60s, like the Giant reprints. We didn't have a comic source in our neighborhood, but a friend of the family dumped a grocery sack of coverless *Superman* and *Action Comics* on my brothers and me. I was maybe five years old at the time.

DAN JURGENS: The first comic I ever bought was *Superman #189*, way back in (Aug.) 1966, for a whopping 12 cents. For a mere dime and two pennies, I unlocked the door to an entire universe and future. Not a bad investment.

ROGER STERN: Oh, that's an easy one. My earliest memory of Superman goes back to the *Adventures of Superman* television show. Long before I could read, I was watching as George Reeves loosened his tie and ducked into a storeroom to change to Superman. I still hear a distant echo of his voice whenever I write dialogue for Clark Kent.

As far as comics go … hmm … that's a lot harder to pin down. I know that I saw a number of Superman comics, and probably thumbed through several before I ever found one

I know that I forked over my dime for the first Brainiac story—*Action Comics #242* (July 1958)—because I remember being puzzled that the green guy had a snazzier wardrobe on the cover (by the great Curt Swan, of course) than he did in the story inside (drawn by Al Plastino).

I recall reading earlier stories, but I might be remembering them from later reprintings in Annuals and Specials.

ROY THOMAS: Only that he and Batman were some of the earliest comics my mother bought me (at my begging) at age 4, probably in early 1945. I thought his name was Soup-erman and that he got his powers from eating soup.

GAIL SIMONE: It's a little odd, but I grew up on a small farm, and we didn't get much television reception, but the channel we did get carried the *I Love Lucy* show, and I adored the episode where Superman guest-starred. Enough so that I really wanted to put a crazy redhead and her Latin hubby in my *Action* run.

From "Lucy Meets Superman," *I Love Lucy* episode #166, original airdate Jan. 14, 1957.
I Love Lucy TM & © Desilu Productions

DAVID MANDEL: Yeah, my earliest memory of Superman is when George Reeves appeared on *I Love Lucy* at Little Ricky's birthday. That's the first time I ever saw Superman. Then I used to watch the old reruns of the *Superman* show, and eventually found comic books, thank God.

MARK WAID: Watching him fight an evil twin—*World's Finest Comics* #159 (Aug. 1966), which was my first exposure to the Man of Steel. I was drawn into comics by the *Batman* TV show, but it didn't take long for me to start picking up Superman's books, as well.

ALEX ROSS: That's a hard one. All I know is I have the evidence of some of the earliest comics I drew when I was about four or five, on folded-over 8" x 10" sheets of paper, with a full cover drawn on them. Clearly I knew who Superman was. That may have been because I had one of the Curt Swan-drawn comics, or I saw him on *Super Friends*. Or even still, there's a good chance I saw him on *Sesame Street*, where there was a kind of interstitial cartoon piece with him, where I believe he was carrying a giant ocean liner. It's a memory I have not confirmed since, but from memory I know this is something they would rerun for years and years on *Sesame Street*, and that might have been my first introduction.

I know that in the early '70s I'd also see reruns of the *Batman* TV show, and I know the George Reeves *Superman* show was right in there as well. By the time Superman was crossing over with Spider-Man in 1976, he was one of the primary characters I knew the most about, hand-in-hand with Spider-Man and Batman—I knew everything one needed to know at a very young age about a character like that.

MIKE CARLIN: Woke up on a hospital gurney—having just had my tonsils removed, at 2 years old—to a copy of *Superman Annual* #1 (1960) on my lap. My mom (*the* biggest Superman and Wonder Woman fan of *her* generation) had had her tonsils out the same day—and made sure I had the comic to keep me company. I haven't been far from the Man of Steel since!

JEPH LOEB: Watching the George Reeves show in glorious black-and-white after school. We lived outside of New York City and there was a host for the show named Officer Joe Bolten—a cop who claimed he knew the Three Stooges. Somehow, *The Adventures of Superman* was part of his afternoon lineup. I only really remember him in "cop" uniform, night stick, hat, telling us that we should never try the stunts that Superman did on the show. Since I already had X-ray vision, I didn't know what he was talking about.

KARL KESEL: I may have seen Superman on TV first, but my strongest, early memories of him are from the comics. Two in particular: an issue of *World's Finest* where Superman and Batman are on the cover changing the Batmobile's tire, with Supergirl and Batgirl snickering at them from behind a fence. I have no idea what the story was, but I still remember that cover. [*Editor's note:* "The Supergirl-Batgirl Plot!" in *World's Finest Comics* #169 (Sept. 1967).]

Making an even stronger impression on my young mind was an issue of *Action* where Superman came down with kryptonite leprosy! That story scared the crap out of me as a kid! And I only read the first part—I didn't get the next issue until years later—so for the longest time the image that lingered in my mind was a disease-ravaged Superman being blasted into the sun to be *burned alive* as far as I was concerned! [*Editor's note:* See the "Virus X" serial in *Action Comics* #363 (May 1968) through 366 (Aug. 1968).]

WALTER SIMONSON: I'm not sure, but I remember buying the Superman story that introduced Supergirl into the mythos (*Action Comics* #252, Apr. 1959). I'm sure I was reading Superman's adventures before that, but that's the first story I remember. That and the introduction of Metallo.

JACKSON GUICE: It was probably an issue of *World's Finest*—somewhere around issue #150 or #160. It certainly was published in the late '60s, as I was just beginning to get into comics then.

KURT BUSIEK: I honestly don't remember. My parents didn't allow us to read super-hero comics when I was a kid, but I can't remember a time I didn't know who Superman was. I do remember reading old coverless *Jimmy Olsen* comics at the barber shop, but even then, I already knew who Superman was.

But I guess that's going to have to be it—I can't think of anything older than that.

JON BOGDANOVE: Age 5, watching *Superman and the Mole Men* while "flying" on the oak table top, on my stomach, arms and legs outstretched, towel tied around my neck. Our TV was black-and-white, as was the man in tights.

Thereafter, I went to kindergarten every day wearing my own, self-made Superman costume under my regular clothes. (I was very warm in school.) The costume consisted of my long-sleeve, cowboy-print winter pajamas with red briefs worn outside, sock feet, towel, and big, gold belt swiped from my mom's old "fancy" dress. I made the "S" with crayons and scissors and pinned it to my shirt.

As soon as the bell rang after school, while all the other kids were putting on their coats and hats, I would move surreptitiously to the closet door. Glancing over my shoulder, I'd touch the rim of my perpetually tape-and-string-mended spectacles and duck into the closet! There, thrashing about for ten minutes in the dark, cramped space, I'd heroically struggle out of my mortal clothes finally to burst forth into the now-empty classroom, ready to save the little girl with the brown pigtails on whom I had a terrific crush.

I flew a couple of laps around the playground, where big kids were having recess, but my "Lois" was long gone. If I was wounded by the jeers my appearance evoked, I gave no outward sign. I knew the meaning of the word "invulnerable."

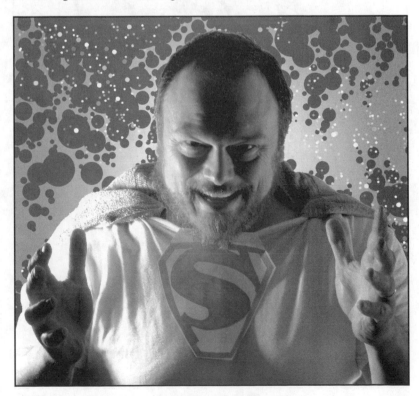

Jon Bogdanove: Still dressing up as Superman, after all these years.
Photo courtesy of Judy Bogdanove.

I never saved the little girl with the brown pigtails, but it was on one of these days that my eyes were opened to the power of color-vision. Arms outstretched, my face set in George Reeves' expression of kind vigilance, I was patrolling the six blocks or so homeward from school.

About a block from Ballantine Road, I passed a rich kid playing Superman in his yard. I assumed he was a rich kid because he was wearing a store-bought Superman costume! It was the first one I'd ever seen, and I was astounded to discover that it was so brightly colored. I was amazed by the blue! From my television, I had surmised that Superman's cape, boots, and briefs were red. I had guessed that the yellow parts were white, and that the tights themselves were beige.

Raising one eyebrow quizzically, I banked toward this kid's yard and swooped in for a dramatic landing. Crashing mightily through a low hedge of boxwood, I assumed "the Stance" and hailed my fellow super-being. The startled kid was nonplussed by my appearance, and proceeded to point out that my "tights" were pale yellow, with a goofy cowboy print all over them.

Jon Bogdanove's Man of Steel, from the 2006 Superman Style Guide.

Exhibiting the same gentle tolerance and benign fatherliness that George always displayed to the likes of Jimmy Olsen, I proceeded to correct the lad as to the color scheme of his outfit, pointing out that Superman's suit was tan, not blue. Taking issue with my assertion, he offered to prove me wrong.

Together, we flew into his basement, where he produced his stash of *Superman* comics. I had never seen a comic book before, but I understood from TV that these "magazines" were Superman's medium of origin. Because of this, I had to acknowledge, manfully, that I was indeed wrong. He acknowledged that my gold lamé belt was cool.

We spent the afternoon together, fighting crime in his backyard and reading his stack of comics in his treehouse. His mom made us peanut butter and butter sandwiches (gross!) and Hi C juice (red!). She may have also called my mom; I don't know.

Some months later—perhaps a year—I was given a comic of my very own by my babysitter, Peggy Flayton. It was a profoundly meaningful gift, and I'll never forget her for it. The comic was an "Imaginary Story" in which Superman and Batman had a fight.

From my perspective then, it was a terrible story, because I did not want to see two heroes fight when they should overcome their differences and be friends ... just like the kid with the store-bought Superman suit and I had done on the afternoon I learned that Superman wore blue.

MYK-EL: Tell me why *you're* a bigger Superman fan than the other members of this roundtable...
BYRNE: I would not be so presumptuous as to think I was.
LOEB: I can't. Waid is sitting at the table. I concede.
THOMAS: I'm not ... though I consider him far and away the most important super-hero ever. Batman isn't even in the running.
BUSIEK: Now, now. Would Superman say it's about being bigger than the other guy? Or simply doing your best, regardless of the circumstances?
GUICE: Because, following Superman's fine example, I have my own Lois Lane room, as well.
ORDWAY: I can't play that game at all. The first *Superman* movie is the most influential part of my love for the character, as I was an avowed Marvelmaniac as a teen.
STERN: With this group, I don't know that I am. Especially not with Waid and Bogdanove around. Doesn't Mark know Clark Kent's Social Security number? And Jon named his son Kal-El, for cryin' out loud! Long before Nicolas Cage did the same, it should be noted. And I don't believe I ever tied a bath towel around my neck and pretended to be Superman.

But, hey, when I was a lad, I used to go to Hayden's Drugstore just about every Friday evening. And if there was a new issue of *Superman*, *Action*, or *World's Finest* to be found there, I bought it. Sometimes, I'd even settle for an issue of *Lois Lane* or *Jimmy Olsen*.
SIMONSON: I'm not. I bow to Jon Bogdanove. Anybody who names his son Kal-El takes the prize in my book.
BOGDANOVE: "Bigger fan"? I probably *weigh* more than any of these other guys.
CARLIN: Have you seen the size of *me*? C'mon...!
SIMONE: Because I fell in love with the comics version very late in life, while they're all trying to recapture their childhoods, the poor bastards. I'm kidding, but it's true that I wasn't the biggest Superman fan until I got a chance to write him, as pathetic as that sounds. It's not at all that I thought my take was so original ... it's that when I started writing the book, I was simply amazed at how incredible the cast was, and how powerful a character Superman was. It was somewhat revelatory.
WAID: I have my own Superman costume and I wear it all the time. Oh, wait, that's Alex Ross' answer

Alex Ross' Earth-2 Superman card from the 2006 *Infinite Crisis Vs* set.
TM & © DC Comics. Courtesy of Ilke Hincer.

ROSS: I probably have bigger Superman toys [*laughs*]. Who here amongst us has a life-sized, wax-works statue of Superman in their home? Have any of the rest of you [*laughs*]?

I have a little painting I did of Superman hanging above my fireplace in my living room. And as I married a similarly Superman-driven fan, my wife is also an enabler of Superman. In fact, a good portion of gifts I get her are related to Superman iconography. We are an equal opportunity Superman-loving household [*laughs*].

JURGENS: I can't. Sadly, I probably have to defer to Waid on that. We may all have to do so.

WAID: I know you're expecting some answer from me involving the words "twelve kinds of kryptonite" or "Social Security number," but I'm perfectly willing to share the title of "biggest Superman fan" with my peers here. On the other hand, anyone who says they're a BIGGER fan than I—them's fighting words.

I always liked Superman, but my lifelong attachment to him began January 26, 1979—at about three o'clock in the afternoon, if you want to be that specific. That was the afternoon I saw *Superman: The Movie*, and it literally transformed my life. Walking into that theater, I was a directionless, unhappy, borderline-suicidal kid with no one to look up to and with a real dearth of inspirational figures in his life. Walking out—after two consecutive showings—I was transformed. Christopher Reeve—like Curt Swan, Superman's defining artist during my youth—found a way to take this alien being from a far-off galaxy and make him utterly human.

KESEL: *I'm not!* I know for a fact that Mark Waid, John Byrne, Dan Jurgens, and Jon Bogdanove are *much* bigger Super-fans than I am! Probably everyone else here is, too.

The truth is, Superman was never my favorite character (let's face it—he's no Challengers of the Unknown!), and when I

Roy Thomas and Marie Severin poke fun at the "Stupor"-family in *Not Brand Echh #7* (Apr. 1968).
© 2006 Marvel Characters, Inc.

wrote him I really did try to write "Superman stories for people who don't like Superman." Over the years, I've come to appreciate him much more than I used to. I was phenomenally lucky to have worked on him—both as an inker during John Byrne's run, and as a writer later on—and have come to realize that his powers really are the least interesting thing about him. Much more interesting is his human side. Superman has the best supporting cast in comics (and the worst rogues' gallery; we'll get to that later), but more importantly: Superman is the Ultimate Immigrant to America. He's lost more, come farther, and rose to greater heights than anyone else. He really is the promise of America writ large. And that's pretty powerful stuff for a writer to work with.

MYK-EL: Some believe that Weisinger's expansion of Superman's super-powered family weakened Superman's uniqueness. Agree or disagree?

STERN: Oh, it definitely did. By the time Mort retired, it almost seemed as though more Kryptonians had survived the destruction of their planet than had died there.

Now, having said that, I can guess why Mort did it. It added characters—and potential titles—to his growing editorial fiefdom. A lot of those stories still have a charm to them. And, boy, they sure sold a lot of comics.

Still, in the long run, I think that all of those super-dogs, cats, monkeys, horses, rats, bats, aardvarks, and gorillas just watered things down. I know that, even as a young pre-teen reader, I was already getting sick of them.

GUICE: I would be inclined to disagree. While it can certainly be argued the expansion weakened Superman's status as the "...sole survivor of a doomed planet," the Super-family were my favorite elements of the comic when I first discovered the character.

It's easy to look back on those stories now and mock them for the general silliness and naïve 1950s wholesomeness they contain, but as a kid of that era, I ate it all up.

CARLIN: I'm one of the folks who agrees with that statement. There was a point where there was a Supergirl, a Super-Monkey, a Super-Intendant ... a Super-Everything ... but you all know that! This was a period where every Tom, Dick, and Mon-El had the exact same powers as Superman. (But, to be fair, this wasn't *just* the case with Superman—this was a DC Disease back then. There wasn't *one* Green Lantern—there was a whole Corps! There wasn't *one* Hawkman—there was a planet full! Even Flash couldn't escape all the speedsters in that particular marathon.)

SIMONE: Completely disagree. While cutting away the allegedly "silly" aspects of Superman's mythology, we quite forgot that there's likely a large potential readership that might really enjoy a story about a superbaby or a flying horse.

We all thought that stuff was cornball junk that needed to go, but I'll tell you right now, a lot of young girls would like Supergirl more if she had a flying horse.

BOGDANOVE: Of course it did! But that does not mean it was inappropriate for its time. Some good stories came out of it, plus some charming kitsch, and plenty of high-Freudian weirdness.

JURGENS: Rather than look at it from the perspective of today, or even an adult perspective, I prefer to gauge it by my reaction as a reader at the time. For the most part, I thought it was great, but I do remember thinking that Streaky the Super-Cat pushed things a bit too far.

ROSS: It certainly did not weaken his appeal in reality. It only weakens it when you're trying to take it way too seriously, like most of us on this roundtable probably have over the course of our careers.

The last 20 years of storytelling have only been a replay of the original history of Superman, starting from the simplicity of just having the one man coming from Krypton, and then by slowly bringing in those elements of his mythology, expanded to every conceivable concept, whether it be sister, brother, cousin, dog, horse, cat—all of these applied with the *fun* that radiates from the concept of Superman.

All Weisinger did—other than trying to figure out ways to sell comics—is he expanded the joy that surrounded the Superman mythos to not be trapped into the storytelling of just the one man. You could even argue by the time that he was doing this, Superman had been creatively tapped of what could be told of the one man from Krypton living in the world by himself.

BUSIEK: Both. There's a power to Superman being the last survivor of Krypton, to being the "Last Son" in the sense that there are no other survivors. That sense of isolation, of loneliness, of being the only being like himself in the entire universe, has a grand and operatic power that works really well.

At the same time, though, there's a different kind of power, of emotional zing, to Superman as the center of an extended web, with Supergirl, the Phantom Zone criminals, the Bottle City, and yes, even the dog and the monkey. That Superman is the "Last Son" in the sense that he was born of Krypton's destruction, that he was the last child born on Krypton. Zod was born earlier, Supergirl somewhere else, and so on. But there's a richness, a feeling of Superman as the center of a pantheon, that we get out of the Weisinger Super-family approach, and that's made for a lot of great stories, too.

So both ideas have their strengths, and the character can stand out either way. We got Superman as a solo act for 20 years, and then Superman as a pantheon for over 30, and then went back to Superman as a solo for 20 years. The pendulum seems to be swinging the other way now, and that's fine with me— I think there's a lot to be had in both, and if one's been explored long enough, maybe it's time to try the other for a while.

ORDWAY: I think it clearly was a gimmick, but, like Ace the Bat-Hound, I don't think Krypto weakened the concept. So many of the offshoot characters are endearing, but Superman is still the main focus. Is he the "Last Son of Krypton" anymore with them? Probably not. But as a little kid looking at the coverless 80-Page Giants, I thought it was all cool.

SIMONSON: I don't know the answer viewed as history. But as a kid, I bought (and have since lost—relax, everybody) the Supes issue in which Supergirl first appeared. I can still remember thinking it was going to be some sort of fake/imaginary/not-real story. And was amazed (and rather delighted) that it wasn't. So as far as I was concerned, as a young reader, the expansion was fine by me.

THOMAS: Yes, it weakened his uniqueness ... but it made the comics more interesting, and probably preserved the character's popularity during the post-TV years. It's just that it was wearing thin by the '60s.

MANDEL: Did it make Superman less unique? Technically, yes, but they told so many great stories using all those Super-characters plus the Bottle City of Kandor and even Krypto. It's all about the stories. Whether he was unique or not didn't matter.

KESEL: I'm sure many here will disagree with me, but Superman being the Last Son of Krypton is *not* what makes him unique. There are a ton of characters that are alone and cut off in one way or another. Isolation and alienation are strong themes in a lot of super-hero comics. But when you add in Supergirl and Krypto and Kandor and the Phantom Zone—you have a family, and even more: a displaced community of refugees (touching on that immigrant theme again), and *that's* unique in comics. Weisinger went too far (Beppo, anyone?) and in some very wrong directions (although there is an undeniable charm to even the wackiest stories ... *especially* the wackiest stories), but— whether done on purpose or not—the underlying idea of Superman as the Moses-like de facto leader of a lost people was brilliant. If you ask me.

WAID: Agree—but who cares? [*Dodges things thrown by others at the table.*] Is there anyone out there who can really, truly say that they were less interested in reading a Superman story because he wasn't the only comics character who had heat vision or could fly?

Look, it's all in how you frame the word "unique." The trade-off—which, I'll argue with my dying breath was, based on sales figures, obviously the right one to make—was this: Kal-El was no longer "uniquely" the last survivor of Krypton (though he hadn't been since about 1950). Instead, he was surrounded by a replacement "family" that was unique in its charm. There was something subconsciously very poignant about watching

Superman, the loneliest man in the universe, be rewarded in his virtue with a cousin and a dog. If you want to rag on the monkey and the cat, be my guest, but bear in mind that as much keening and wailing is done over them by more "sophisticated" readers, the monkey appeared a grand total of about eight times in 15 years and the cat not much more often. Hardly a crime against culture and literacy.

LOEB: You're talking about the guy who brought Supergirl, Bizarro #1, and Krypto back into the mythos after Mr. Byrne wiped them from memory. Cool is cool. Those ideas were cool and still are. Look at the success those characters have found.

BYRNE: If we agree that the word "unique" means "the only one of its kind," the answer to this question is self-evident, isn't it?

MYK-EL: What's your favorite Imaginary Story, and why?

JURGENS: There are many, but I've always been fond of "The Death of Lois Lane" from *Superman* #194 (Feb. 1967). I enjoyed anything where we saw Superman married, with family, down the road, and this one had a very effective, bittersweet feel to it.

A very, very close second would be *World's Finest* #172 (Dec. 1967), in which Jonathan and Martha Kent adopt the orphaned Bruce Wayne and raise him and Clark as brothers. Really a wonderful story, with Curt Swan at his finest.

GUICE: Pretty much all of them. I love those cheese-ball stories, particularly when they involve "future" tales of Lois and Superman married—like *Superman* #131 (Aug. 1959), "Superman's Future Wife"—or giant bald heads.

STERN: Definitely "The Death of Superman" from *Superman* #149 (Nov. 1961) ... a powerful, powerful Jerry Siegel story complemented perfectly by the Curt Swan/Shelly Moldoff art. Nothing even comes close.

But I would give an honorable mention to "Superman's Other Life," the first "Imaginary Story" from *Superman* #132 (Oct.1959). Great art by Wayne Boring and Stan Kaye, and a solid story by Otto Binder. And it even set up a framework for why we were seeing this alternate version of our hero's life on a Krypton that didn't explode—it was all a computer simulation!

Hey, remember when only Superman and Batman had their own personal computers? Computers the size of Mack trucks!

ORDWAY: I like the old "Death of Superman" storyline, mainly because it was mostly a Lex Luthor "what if." I just think it was a well-plotted story with clever twists, like Lex being a hero.

BUSIEK: I gotta go with "The Death of Superman," just for that great parade of mourners, as we see Superman's friends, family, colleagues, and even ambassadors from other planets pay their respects to the departed hero.

There was something so perfectly elegiac about it, that when you cut to those cheerful, happy criminals celebrating the death, it seems like an utter insult. It's a very mannered story, as so many of them were, but it's one where the very formality of it is a strength—it's full of ritual and a kind of stately inevitability that really serves the story well. Plus, that panel with Krypto just chokes me up every time.

SIMONSON: The story I remember is the one in which a dying Superman, poisoned by kryptonite, was being blasted off the Earth in a rocket ship as he was turning green. (Or at least, that's how I remember it.)

WAID: Is Walt remembering the Virus X story as an imaginary tale? Because if he's not, figuring out what story he *is* referring to is gonna eat up pretty much the rest of my afternoon. Thanks, Walt!

TM & © DC Comics.

Writer/artists Dan Jurgens and Walter Simonson.
Photo courtesy of Dan Jurgens.
Photo courtesy of Glen Cadigan.

KESEL: I can't say I remember many Imaginary Stories in detail, but I do remember a lot of concepts that I thought were cool. Bruce Wayne and Clark Kent being raised by the Kents as brothers comes to mind—I always thought that was a great idea. (No idea if it was a good story, however.) And, of course, who *doesn't* love the Super-Sons?!

LOEB: I loved the Super-Sons stuff! And for a kid who didn't know he had father issues, I guess *I* had father issues!

WAID: So many to choose from, but avoiding the obvious, my dead-heat tie is between "The New Superman-Batman Team" (*World's Finest* #167, June 1967) and "Superman and Batman—Brothers!" (*World's Finest* #172, Dec. 1967). The first was delightful because it crammed just everyone and everything from the Superman mythos into it, from Braniac to Supergirl to gold kryptonite; the second was a genuinely good story because it was full of emotion. It *was* a good story, Karl!

CARLIN: "Superman 2965," the Superman of the Future (*Superman* #181, Nov. 1965) ... but mostly 'cause I thought that Superman's hair was hipper!

BYRNE: "The Death of Superman." Incredibly powerful when I was a kid. The ending still makes me cry.

In the colorful tradition of Superman-Red/-Blue were Jeph Loeb and Tim Sale's Marvel miniseries *Daredevil: Yellow* (2001–2002), *Spider-Man: Blue* (2002), and *Hulk: Gray* (2003–2004).
© 2006 Marvel Characters, Inc.

Walt Simonson pencil art from *Superman Special* #1 (1992).
TM & © DC Comics. Courtesy of David Hamilton.

ROSS: The big one, "The Amazing Story of Superman-Red and Superman-Blue" (*Superman* #162, July 1963). But if I thought of this as looking at an entertaining piece of drama, then it'd probably be the *Superman Annual* (#11, 1985) written by Alan Moore that wasn't exactly a fantasy, but was a fantasy inside of Superman's head, where he was given that vision of what if he had never left Krypton. But for nostalgia's sake, from what I read as a young boy, the digest comics reprint of "Superman-Red and Superman-Blue," together figuring out how to fix the entire world, is no end of fun.

MANDEL: "Superman-Red and Superman-Blue." It had everything. Can't choose between Lois and Lana? Choose them both.

SIMONE: I'm a poor Superman scholar in most ways, so I'll have to go with an obvious choice, "Superman-Red/Superman-Blue." Still a fun story all these years later.

BOGDANOVE: I don't have a favorite, simply because when I was a kid I was alienated by the idea of "imaginary" stories. I found them disturbing. Now, of course, I understand the attraction for writers and artists to play outside of continuity. But I still prefer an "other dimensional" explanation, like Mike Carlin's *Elseworlds* concept.

CARLIN: Actually, Jon, I'd credit Mark Waid (editor) and Brian Augustyn (writer) with

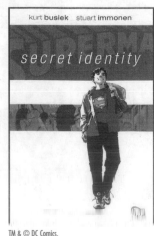

kurt **busiek** stuart **immonen**

secret identity

TM & © DC Comics.

doing the first (unlabelled) Elseworlds ... and Denny O'Neil with coining the phrase (AND writing the blurb of explanation we use to this day)!

THOMAS: I don't really remember any of them that well, or with any special fondness. Too old, I guess.

MYK-EL: Do you have a "lost" Imaginary Story, the tale Mort or Julie *didn't* tell?

SIMONE: Several, but they're all about sexual dysfunction.

STERN: Nah, I always preferred the real ones.

CARLIN: I do ... but ... this *is* embarrassing ... I lost it.

BYRNE: I'd still like to do a *Superman/Captain America* as a companion piece to the *Batman & Captain America* one-shot I did a few years back.

BUSIEK: Does *Superman: Secret Identity* count? No?

I did have an idea awhile back that felt to me like a big, complete-in-one-three-part-novel Weisinger story, but it's not an Imaginary Tale, and with luck, I'll actually get to tell it in *Superman*. So I'll keep it to myself.

JURGENS: Hmm ... I would have played around with Kandor a lot more. I always thought that was underutilized for both "real" and "imaginary" stories.

BOGDANOVE: Sort of—see my answer to your penultimate question.

ORDWAY: No, but I bet Alan Moore still has. I think it would be really hard to do something like that, at least for me. I'd like to read

214

someone else's attempt, though.

MANDEL: Baby Kal-El never landed on a truly alien crazy planet as far as I remember. I would have liked to have seen a Tarzan-like story where the baby is raised by the squid aliens. Then later on, he helps invade Earth. Or something like that.

WAID: Actually, next to the Alan Moore finale, that *was* the last Imaginary Story that Julie ran: *Superman* #417 (Mar. 1986), by Elliot Maggin and Curt Swan, where baby Kal-El landed on Mars instead of Earth. John Carter, not Tarzan, Dave, but very close.

GUICE: Sammy the Super-Ferret? I mean—is there really an Imaginary Tale still left that Mort and Julie didn't mine at some point?

KESEL: Like I've read all of them that they *did* tell? This looks like a job for Mark Waid...

WAID: I think by the time we got to "What if the Waynes had adopted Kal-El?" late in Julie's run, the well was pretty much tapped. Also see, "Baby Kal-El lands on Mars instead of Earth."

THOMAS: Sorry, no. I guess I'm not much use in this roundtable.

MYK-EL: Now, now, Roy, we'll have none of *that* kind of talk—we're one big, happy Super-family here.

Next question: **Which of Superman's classic writers and artists most influenced your work, on Superman and on other series?**

THOMAS: None, really, since I wrote relatively little Superman. But I did love Jerry Siegel's early '40s stories when I discovered them as "old comics" in the late 1940s.

BUSIEK: I'm a huge Cary Bates fan, and my sample scripts that got me my first work in the industry were mostly Bates pastiches, but over the years, I think I've been more influenced by Jim Shooter and Len Wein, when it comes to Superman writers. Not by their Superman work, largely, but by stuff they did elsewhere.

STERN: First and foremost, Jerry Siegel. He not only co-created Superman, he wrote some of the best Superman stories of my youth. I've already mentioned "The Death of Superman," but he also wrote "Superman's Return to Krypton" from *Superman* #141 (Nov. 1960). And then there's Bill Finger, who—in addition to co-creating the Batman—wrote the first, and still the best, Lori Lemaris story. Also Otto Binder and Ed Hamilton. Oh, and Jim Shooter, even though he was a year younger than me, the bum!

SIMONSON: I don't know that I took any direct influence from the writers and artists who worked on Superman over the years, but I am a huge admirer of Curt Swan! And as a kid, I always liked Wayne Boring's work. There was a hint of ritual about the way he always drew Superman landing with one foot drawn up, and ritual is important to children.

John Byrne and Curt Swan, 1986. Byrne remarks: "That was 'The Great Handoff,' Julie Schwartz's idea. You can't really see it, but Curt is handing me his pencil—passing the baton, as it were."
Photo courtesy of John Byrne.

BYRNE: I certainly felt Curt Swan looking over my shoulder as I drew Superman. Curt made the character so real it was as if I was trying to capture the likeness of an actual human. Something at which I basically suck, so in the end I had to find "my" Superman face. Since there were no credits in the days when Superman was having the greatest impact on me, it's hard to say which writers most informed my take on the character.

ROSS: I would say, just in the immediacy of what you see me do, it would be the combination of Joe Shuster and Max Fleischer. Of course, Max Fleischer is more for the [1940s animation] company name than an individual's name, because I don't think that Max was the illustrator on any of that stuff. Basically it was like seeing Joe Shuster twice—all Fleischer did was translate what Shuster did in comics form into animation. It was a direct translation, with a minor augmentation of the chest symbol—but really, that was what Joe was drawing.

It's sort of like my backlash to the many years of the style given to the character after Wayne Boring, going through Curt Swan, and even Chris Reeve, through any of the art styles that were seen in print, up until I got my chance with it, that I wanted to remind people more of the visual roots it had come from. You know, the certain shape of head and body that Superman had, the

An unnamed Lucy Lane makes a rare non-comic-book appearance in this Nov. 12, 1965 *Superman* daily drawn by Wayne Boring.
TM & © DC Comics.

The variant cover to *Superman* vol. 2 #150 (Nov. 1999), a personal favorite of its penciler, Dan Jurgens; inks by Kevin Nowlan.

TM & © DC Comics. Art courtesy of Dan Jurgens.

working with Jerry and Joe in 1939! [*laughs*] He got me into the business, showed me the ropes, and encouraged me in ways that we can blame him for me being here.

KESEL: Denny O'Neil and Jack Kirby. The "Kryptonite Nevermore" storyline and Kirby's *Jimmy Olsen* comics were the first time I really couldn't wait to get the next issue of a comic with Superman in it. There was a real air of excitement and anything-might-happen to both of them. Neither run lasted long enough—but then, the good stuff never does.

WAID: Elliot Maggin, as I've made no secret, is my primary guiding light, and his two Superman novels (*Last Son of Krypton* and *Miracle Monday*) are textbooks for me. That said, Marty Pasko wrote the best Superman "moments" and was a gargantuan influence on all my future work with this one line from *Action Comics* #500 (Oct. 1979), referring to Superboy's joy at finding Krypto and finally having someone with which to share the things in his world: "They were little things—they may not seem so important to you ... things like the feeling of the wind in your face—in a way no one else in the world can feel it ... or the sound bullets make when they bounce off living flesh." That's page 32—I know this because the original art is framed above my desk—and that one line is inarguably the single greatest influence on the way I write today, by starting inside the characters.

BOGDANOVE: Nowadays, I try to consciously incorporate as many influences from the Golden Age and Silver Age as possible, without copying any individual artist (unless I'm hired to do so).

My goal is to distill a quintessential contemporary Superman reflecting the taste of the times, but informed by the best of DC's past. The work I've been doing lately for Matt Denk and Janice Walker in DC's Licensing Department has a lot to do with that.

ORDWAY: For me, the strongest influence is the very first Superman story by Siegel and Shuster. I love the look of the Joe Shuster Superman, which was refined by the great Jack Burnley. And all the classic elements are in Jerry Siegel's early stories.

CARLIN: Curt Swan for sure ... and obviously Jerry Siegel.

MANDEL: I have to say Curt Swan. I'm not in the comics biz, but he so defined how Superman, how everyone in Superman's world, looked, that everything I think about Superman comes from that.

SIMONE: John Byrne and Dan Jurgens were big influences. It's irritating when great artists can also write so well.

JURGENS: I think all of the writers. It's really so hard to isolate them as they all contributed to the Superman mythos. As for artists, Curt Swan is the one who made Superman live and breathe for me.

When I first started working for DC, current Vertigo editor Karen Berger was editorial coordinator. She called me up one day and asked me if I could draw Superman. I said, "No. Only Curt Swan can draw Superman."

I still feel that way to this day.

MYK-EL: Curt Swan's best inker: George Klein or Murphy Anderson?

KESEL: Well, um ... *I* inked Curt Swan a few times and didn't do too bad a job. But seriously—and without being too namby-pamby—it's impossible for me to say. Murphy's is the look that comes to my mind as the classic Swan-Superman. I love Klein's work—in fact, I prefer it to Murphy's, stylistically, 'cause I love a good, fluid brush line—but Murphy's is the look from my childhood. This is like asking who's stronger: Hulk or Thor? Different answers at different times.

LOEB: Swanderson. C'mon, is this a question?

certain expression he'd bring with him—those things to me really infect the character with a completely different kind of mood than we think of him having, because we've gotten used to, as you point out in your later question, the Superman who's a friend, the sort of kind, blue-eyed, benevolent face, which many people sadly dismiss as being a naïve face. When you look back at the old Superman that they created, there's nothing naïve about this guy. He's very sure of himself—he's a man with powers and a purpose, and momentum, and that's something I wanted to show that he's got within himself.

GUICE: Wayne Boring and Stan Kaye—easily. I have a great fondness for that tree-trunk waist they drew on Superman. No other super-hero before or since has had that physique.

LOEB: I'm not sure if I'd call him "classic," but Elliot or Maggin did it for me. Classic makes him sound like he was

MANDEL: I have to go a little bit for me, no more Swan Swan

CARLIN: I'm a Swanderson man ... but I do like Klein, too!

BUSIEK: On a Superman solo story, Anderson. On the Legion, Klein!

GUICE: I always enjoyed the Swan/Klein art combination more, personally, but I think the Swan/Anderson team is truly the definitive look for the character during that period.

BOGDANOVE: Can't decide. Both were wonderful.

WAID: With all due respect to Murphy, one of the finest gentlemen I've ever met, there's a crispness to Klein's line that, to my eye, complimented Swan's softness—but I freely admit that I'm making that judgment through the eyes of nostalgia and that this is a Sunday. If you asked me on a Saturday or a Monday, I might have said Anderson; it's that close a call. Most underrated Swan inker: Dan Adkins.

JURGENS: That is *so* hard. But I'd probably have to say George Klein, no disrespect at all to Murphy who was every bit as good and effective. But I think Klein was probably more true to the pencils.

SIMONSON: I don't know George's work well enough to have an opinion here, but I always enjoyed Murphy on Curt.

ROSS: Yikes! I guess I'd have to say George Klein, as he's credited with the art style of "Superman-Red, Superman-Blue." That simplistic style is the most charming era of Curt Swan.

BYRNE: Curt Swan. If those *Jimmy Olsen* stories I've been told he inked himself were, indeed, Curt, I would chose him as his own best inker.

THOMAS: Both were great ... Anderson more decorative ... but though I admired Curt Swan's talent, I always felt his work was too static, and there were too many lines in Superman's face, especially in the Swanderson version, making him look too old.

ORDWAY: My personal preference is with Murphy Anderson, but in the '80s it was the handful of terrific jobs by Al Williamson that showed a whole new dynamic to Curt Swan's pencils.

STERN: "Or"? I'm not going to make a choice between those two. Klein was Curt's best inker in the '60s, and Murph was his best inker in the '70s.

And in addition to those talented gentlemen, I would add Al Williamson ... and brother Ordway sitting over there, who also inked Curt's pencils a time or two.

In fact, allow me to embarrass Jerry just a little more. In the late 1980s, the Smithsonian put together a Superman exhibit that eventually went on the road and appeared at several museums around the country. When the exhibit came to the Strong Museum in Rochester, New York, the curator there had the inspired idea to ask Curt Swan to speak at the opening. Rochester is just a short drive from where I live, so my wife and I and a friend of ours drove up to see Curt and take in the exhibit. Curt was absolutely wonderful, of course, but he wasn't used to speaking before a crowd on his own, so—long story short— he asked me to join him up on stage to talk about any newer Superman projects that he might not be up on. Yeah, like *I'm* a great public speaker. But I was flattered and everyone seemed to have a good time. Well, at one point during the discussion, someone asked about younger artists, and Curt was extremely complimentary to all of the then-current Superman artists. He felt they all did fine work, but his personal favorite was Jerry. And then he vented a little frustration about our Mr. Ordway: "As talented as he is, he's even more modest. You can*not* give that man a compliment."

And I just grinned because Curt was exactly the same way. He was such a good artist, and a great, great man. One of the biggest thrills of my career was when he called to tell me that he enjoyed the stories I was writing for him (for the "Superman" strip in *Action Comics Weekly*).

MYK-EL: Who's the most underrated of Superman's Silver and Bronze Age artists, and why?

An iconic rendering of Marvel's Thunder God from Jurgens' *Thor* (Annual) *1999*; inks by Klaus Janson.
© 2006 Marvel Characters, Inc. Art courtesy of Heritage Comics.

SIMONSON: Kurt Schaffenberger, maybe, although I'm not sure what "underrated" means here. Everybody I know loves his stuff! [*laughs*] There was a real beauty to it.

BYRNE: Superman in the Silver Age is, to me, Curt Swan and Wayne Boring. Everyone else is in their shadows and so, I suppose by definition, "underrated."

CARLIN: Think most of the good guys are rated just fine ... Jack Burnley, Al Plastino, Kurt Schaffenberger, and Jim Mooney ... but they live under the Super-shadows of Wayne Boring and Curt Swan, I guess!

ROSS: I don't hear enough people speaking of José Luis García-López's work, although I know everybody respects him. The *Superman* issues he did in the '70s are, for me, the most infinitely desirable and collectible. They have a wonderful figure-drawing quality. It was sort of like, "Yeah, we didn't get Neal Adams on that monthly book, but here's a guy who has all the depth and talent that Neal has." And a few talents that Neal *didn't* have. When you see the *Superman vs. Wonder Woman* book that García-López did, you realize that a very important artist who we don't often consciously think about had something to do with Superman in the '70s.

WAID: Not many people recall that José Luis García-López was being groomed by Julie to backstop Curt Swan, and even as JLG was just breaking in, his work was stellar. It's a shame he

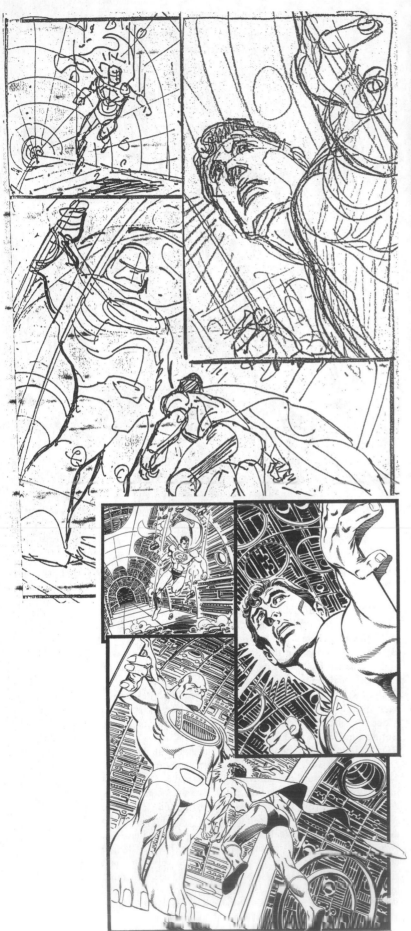

Art Saaf's 1979 cover painting for Gold Key's *UFO and Outer Space* #23. Saaf started drawing comics in the Golden Age and continued in the business for decades, taking on *Lois Lane* and *Supergirl* in the early 1970s.

did only a handful of Superman stories. Also, Ross Andru doesn't get his props despite his (and inker Mike Esposito's) solid run on *World's Finest Comics*.

BUSIEK: Are any of them really underrated? We're talking Swan, Schaffenberger, Boring, Plastino—there doesn't seem to be anyone on the list who's unfairly dismissed. Guys like John Forte and George Papp don't get the props the others do, but I don't think that's unfair. Jim Mooney, Bob Brown ... Ross Andru's not well-known for the Super-stories he did, but he's well-loved for other work.

In the end, I guess I'd pick Mike Sekowsky or Art Saaf, who were far more attached to Supergirl than Superman. But Sekowsky had a wonky, energetic charm that I don't think is as widely appreciated as it should be, and Saaf may have been quiet, but handled emotional scenes more subtly and well than I think most people notice. But for the most part, I think the Super-artists of the Silver and Bronze Age got rated pretty fairly.

STERN: I would probably give that nod to Kurt Schaffenberger. Kurt was usually thought of as being "*the* Lois Lane artist," but Superman was as much a part of those stories as Lois. And Kurt's Superman looked every bit as heroic as his Captain Marvel.

Bronze Age, huh? I've never been certain just what years that covered ... after Mort's retirement and before Julie stepped down as Super-editor? If that's the case, then I'd probably go with José Luis García-López. He didn't draw all that many Superman stories, but those that he did were choice.

José Luis García-López layouts (top left) with Jerry Ordway finishes (bottom left), from *Heroes Against Hunger* (1986).

A 1993 Curt Swan/Sheldon Moldoff recreation of their cover art to *Action* #283 (Mar. 1962).

Jerry Ordway's 2006 reimagining of the Swan/Klein cover to *Superman* #164 (Oct. 1963)

KESEL: Bob Oksner. While he was ideally suited for "Supergirl," I enjoyed his work on the other Super-books, too. Lively, engaging, always enjoyable to look at—*especially* his perky gals! He really brought a fun, innocent, Gil Elvgren-eque sexiness to the women he drew.

MANDEL: I have a soft spot for Al Plastino. There was a cool goofiness to his art.

BOGDANOVE: Al Plastino. His faces had great character.

ORDWAY: Wow, I think it's easy to forget the great work of Kurt Schaffenberger on titles like *Lois Lane*. Also, I always loved the way Ross Andru drew Superman.

JURGENS: For me, the answer would be Ross Andru. He opened things up a bit more than Swan did in terms of action, foreshortening, and layout technique, slightly "Marvelizing" Superman a bit. People don't associate Ross with Superman too much, but he had a nice little run.

GUICE: Ross Andru. Ross was magic. He could sell any story action no matter how complicated and make it look embarrassingly easy. He should be cited by many instead of mentioned by few, because he drew an enormous volume of high-quality work over the years.

THOMAS: Gil Kane. The stories he did in the '80s, mostly with Marv Wolfman, were great.

LOEB: Swanderson. Honestly. Ask someone under the age of 40 who Curt Swan was. That's why we named the character that Chris Reeve played on *Smallville* Dr. Swann. Sometimes these things need to be put into the memory banks in different ways.

MYK-EL: Other than Lex Luthor, who is the Earth-One Superman's best villain?

WAID: Steve Lombard. Okay, also, Brainiac.

CARLIN: Brainiac.

JURGENS: Brainiac. I love the idea of shrinking cities!

STERN: Brainiac, no question. Superman could thwart his plans, but he could never stop him for long.

BYRNE: I always liked Brainiac as a kid—although I must confess the character lost some of his mystique for me when I one day realized his name was "Brainiac" and not, as I had been pronouncing it, "Branek." He became a wee bit goofy at that point.

SIMONSON: As a kid, I was liked Brainiac. I'd also have to put Bizarro—who wasn't exactly a villain, really—in the "memorable" category. But there was something about Braniac's little hairnet of electrodes I just thought was great!

ROSS: It's not much of a debate: It's Brainiac.

There's an aggravation about Brainiac not getting his turn in cinema—this is just dragging on too long. They missed the boat in the movies when Brainiac didn't appear in the third film, because we'd already been through the whole Lex Luthor thing, and the Kryptonian villains all made sense, but it was *time*. In a way they forsook Brainiac's character introduction for not wanting to steal screen time away from Richard Pryor, because they paid a lot of money to get Richard Pryor, but to what effect? It was one of the first great compromises of what these movies could do.

BUSIEK: Brainiac! Aside from being a distinctive and memorable foe, his connection to the Super-mythos both through Kandor and the Legion gave him an effect felt beyond his presence on-stage, and cemented his role as one of Superman's Top Two Bad Guys.

THOMAS: No favorites, though Brainiac was a great name and concept. And I liked Mr. Mxyzptlk, even if I can't spell it.

LOEB: While I favor Brainiac, my heart belongs to Mxy, too. Better stories in the end. But nobody touches Lex.

MANDEL: I am contractually obligated to say Bizarro Superman. But, deep down, Brainiac was really great.

ORDWAY: I always enjoyed Bizarro stories, so that would be my vote.

GUICE: He's not really a villain, but I always loved Titano the Super-Ape whenever he made an appearance.

SIMONE: I actually have a soft spot for Terra-Man. I desperately wanted to bring him back, but didn't have the space.

BOGDANOVE: Parasite. Jim Shooter's original story was kick-ass.

KESEL: I've said it before and I'll say it again: Superman has the best supporting cast, and the worst rogues' gallery—probably because so many of the Silver Age stories had him playing tricks on his friends instead of fighting crime! I don't think he really had a "best" villain—they were all pretty lame. Toyman? Prankster? The Invisible Destroyer (or whatever he was called)? Please. Even Lex in the battlesuit—just thinking about it makes me yawn.

Many of this roundtable's participants have worked on *Fantastic Four*. Seen here: *FF #277* (Apr. 1985), written and pencilled by Byrne, inked by Ordway, and edited by Carlin.
© 2006 Marvel Characters, Inc. Art courtesy of Heritage Comics.

The roundtable's top pick for a 1960s TV Superman: Clint Walker.

Back in the day, I liked the *idea* of Terra-Man—a sci-fi cowboy—but even as I read the stories I winced at the silly ways that concept played out. Of course, there's Metallo—clunky design, but brilliant idea. Gotta love a guy with a kryptonite heart! Byrne's revamp of him was spot-on. (Makes you wonder what would have happened if Kirby had somehow ended up working on the Super-books under Weisinger instead of going to Marvel; can you imagine a Kirby-designed Metallo?)

WAID: Actually, the rumor for a long time has been that Metallo was Jack's one contribution to the Silver Age Superman, purportedly a suggestion he gave to his neighbor Robert Bernstein, who's credited with the first Metallo script.

KESEL: Probably the best match for the Silver Age Superman was Mr. Mxyzptlk—great visuals, anything goes, Superman wins by outwitting, not out-hitting. Plus, it showed on a grand scale that no one's a better straight man than Superman!

MYK-EL: Let's pretend that the success of the Adam West *Batman* TV show had inspired a new live-action *Superman* series. Which 1960s actor would have been best suited to wear the big red "S"?

JURGENS: Ron Ely. Forget Tarzan and put him in the cape!

SIMONE: Bill Bixby.

KESEL: I've often wondered how different comics and TV—even the entire world as we know it—would be if William Shatner had been Clark Kent instead of Captain Kirk! I can see it so clearly—as if it really happened. Shatner's unique vocal stylings over the opening credits: "Look! Up in the ... sky!" Leonard Nimoy as the drolly unflappable Inspector Henderson ... a young Christopher Reeve as Jimmy Olsen ... and who could forget DeForest Kelley as Perry White with his often said and now-famous line: "He's dead, Jimmy!"

Jerry Ordway reveals why he draws Superman with a big jaw.

ORDWAY: I'm going to go out on a limb here and say Clint Walker, of the TV show *Cheyenne* fame. He had a tall, muscular frame, and would've looked like a George Tuska-drawn Superman. But given that a campy tone would have been more likely then, I'm afraid my head might explode if I ponder it anymore.

ROSS: Clint Walker. He's the one guy I've seen from that era who had the looks and the build to match Superman.

You know, they never quite get a guy who's actually *built* like Superman to play him—George Reeves didn't really look like the comic-book Superman, Chris Reeve was the skinny guy you never would've thought of as Superman, and the same with the new guy [Brandon Routh].

GUICE: No question in my mind ... it would be Clint Walker.

SIMONSON: I would *love* to have seen Clint Walker as Superman. Don't quite know how he would have disguised himself as Clark Kent since he seems to have been a big man, but I still love the idea. He would have kicked ass as Superman!

BOGDANOVE: George Reeves' impact was so strong, I don't think anyone could have pulled it off successfully. It took most of two decades and Christopher Reeve to come close. However, theoretically, if they did a camp *Superman* on 1966 television, I might have expected to see Clint Walker or Mike Henry play the Man of Steel. There are probably some others, but I'm dubious of anyone's ability to do as immortal a spoof as Adam West and Burt Ward did with *Batman*.

MANDEL: Rock Hudson. Pre-*McMillan and Wife*.

CARLIN: Dick Gautier (Hymie the Robot from *Get Smart*) ... as long as this *is* a campy show!

BYRNE: Peter Lupus. I used to watch *Mission: Impossible* thinking he was a perfect Wayne Boring Superman.

STERN: Oh, now you're asking me to recall likely available actors from 40 years ago? That's rough, because you'd really be looking for a good journeyman actor who was ready to make the leap from playing supporting roles to leading man. Like Adam West did when he was signed to play Batman, or like James Arness did when he landed *Gunsmoke*. Before he got the part of Matt Dillon, Arness was known mainly for playing heavies and henchmen and the alien creature in *The Thing*.

Who played Superman on Broadway back then? Bob Holiday? [*Shakes head.*] No, we wouldn't be doing *Superman* as a musical, and I'd hope that we'd be playing this hypothetical show more seriously than *Batman*.

Better to look for some big strapping guy like Victor Lundin. He played Klingons on the original *Star Trek*, and even had some bit parts on *Batman*, usually playing henchmen to guest villains. (And just to add another Adam West connection, they both had

Roger Stern and Jackson Oulo.

supporting roles in *Robinson Crusoe on Mars*.) I'm not sure Lundin had the chops to pull off playing Superman/Clark Kent around 1967, but he had the height, the jaw, and a lot more hair back then. He'd have been worth a screen test.

Or ... hey, here's an idea! How about Lyle Waggoner? He was up for the part of Batman, but lost out to West. Of course, he later wound up playing Steve Trevor to Lynda Carter's Wonder Woman ... and I thought he would have made a great Blackhawk. Yeah ... Waggoner as Superman ... that would have worked.

WAID: Lyle Waggoner; he was available.

BUSIEK: Uh ... uh ... Lyle Waggoner. He'll do.

MYK-EL: Superman trivia pop quiz: What's a "drang"?

ROSS: God only knows.

MANDEL: No idea.

JURGENS: The answer I give to a question I can't answer!

ORDWAY: Um, is it a coffeemaker on Krypton?

BYRNE: Past tense of a "dring"?

KESEL: Karl am so excellent at pop quizzes, he am having no idea of answer!

SIMONSON: Not a clue. However, it's not always so much what you know as who you know. And with a quick call to either Kurt Busiek or Mark Waid, I could solve this one in a heartbeat.

BUSIEK: I'm guessing some sort of powerful Kryptonian beast.

GUICE: Best I can recall, it was a Kryptonian monster.

SIMONE: I don't know, but I *did* put a snagriff in *Action* #835 (Jan. 2006)!

BOGDANOVE: I think it's some kind of monster that Superman got turned into ... a red kryptonite thing, wasn't it—like a Chinese dragon?

TM & © DC Comics.

CARLIN: Sturm's sidekick?

STERN: That's Sturm's *partner*. "Sturm and Drang ... she's a philosophy professor ... he's a plumber ... they're detectives! Sturm and Drang ... this fall on NBC."

Sorry. Isn't a drang some sort of Kryptonian horned serpent? If it's the creature I'm thinking of, a chunk of red kryptonite once turned Superman into one ... in some old issue of *Action*, I think. I'm not sure, though. I probably read that story as a reprint. I do recall that Supergirl was in the story. Waid can probably tell us what issue it was.

WAID: A big, flying snake with a white horn, of course, not to be confused with a snagriff or a rondor. My God, what are they teaching you kids in school today?

STERN: There, *see*? I *told* you he'd know! Hey, Mark, what's Superman's blood type?

WAID: If I knew, I'd be synthesizing it in my lab, 'cause transfusions of the stuff give temporary super-powers, remember?

MYK-EL: This one's for Jeph Loeb: Tell me about your connection to Elliot S! Maggin's famous *Superman* tale, "Must There Be a Superman?"

LOEB: This is a story that I would rather *not* be repeating since it's now become "legend" largely because Elliot feels some compulsion to keep telling it. Give it up, Maggin! I love you! I really, really love you! I should point out that even though Elliot has all this guilt about it—I was and still am *thrilled* to have been a small part of a great story. I was something like 12. I had met Elliot through my stepfather since Elliot went to Brandeis University where my step-dad worked. Elliot came to dinner, I fawned, he was amused, and he offered to read something I had written should I ever want to.

Cut to: I sent him a script for story called "Why Must There Be A Superman?", where Superman goes to see the Guardians (why them? They were like the Watcher and I knew Marvel better at this point) because they think his presence on Earth is stunting man's evolutionary growth. I'm sure it was more like "You bad Superman." Superman then doubted what he was doing and then the entire thing devolved into a story that I ripped right out of *Spider-Man* #100 and Elliot called me on it. He wrote me this great note that you could steal from plays, movies, TV, but not from other comics. I learned a great lesson.

Some time after that, I read "Must There Be A Superman" and BOOM—there's the idea for the story. I'm incredibly flattered—

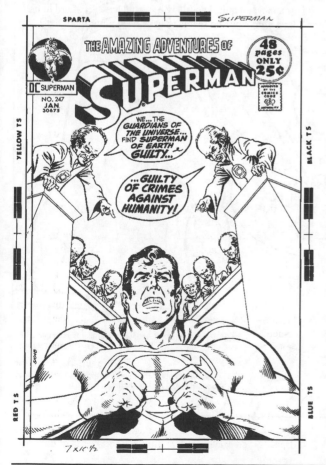

(left) The original Swanderson cover art to *Superman* #247 (Jan. 1972), and (above) two Jack Kirby/Steve Ditko panels from page 13 of *Fantastic Four* #13 (Apr. 1963), introducing the Watcher.

TM & © DC Comics. Art courtesy of Albert Moy.

© 2006 Marvel Characters, Inc.

Brainiac was featured in this late-1970s Whitman coloring book. Artist unknown.

thrilled—that Elliot saw something in my writing to use. I knew nothing of how he pitched it, forgot my story, and essentially all that stuff that's in the forward of the *Kingdom Come* novel.

I have, however, been told that "Must There Be a Superman" influenced Mark Waid into becoming a comic-book writer, so I'll gladly take credit for inventing Waid. [*laughs*]

MYK-EL: I have a question for David Mandel: Why the Bizarro fixation?

MANDEL: It was just one of those things that always stuck with me—especially those early stories of Bizarro having a baby and the baby is human-looking. I never forgot those. Plus the backwards-ness was so arbitrary it really made me laugh. The Bizarro planet may have been a square, but it still had gravity. Why? Things weren't upside-down. They had "cold dogs" instead of "hot dogs." Why not "cold cats"? I used to think about this a lot and when I became a comedy writer, I kept trying to put it in shows. I felt like since *I* think it's funny, I will force the world to learn about Bizarro.

At *Saturday Night Live* we used to joke about a Sunday-morning talk show that would discuss and debate the Bizarro World. I wrote a Superman funeral sketch when Sinbad hosted and tried to have Bizarro in there laughing—but we couldn't get the make-up right. When I got to *Seinfeld*, with Jerry always talking about Superman, it was too perfect a place. And once Jerry heard the idea he pushed me to run with it and put it hardcore Bizarro jokes—like "Me so happy me want to cry" at the end of the episode. But for me, the real victory was hearing people start talking about Bizarro more, using the word "Bizarro," and eventually, having him return to the comics.

MYK-EL: Discounting Darkseid, which of Kirby's Fourth World creations best benefited Superman lore?

BYRNE: All of them.

CARLIN: Goody Rickels.

GUICE: I vote Goody Rickels, too. Only in a Kirby comic would you run across that concept.

SIMONE: I enjoyed having Glorious Godfrey speak with Superman. His gift of gab is very good contrasting stuff for Superman's taciturn nature.

BUSIEK: Morgan Edge. He didn't work out the way Kirby had intended, but as a tough boss for Clark Kent who wasn't as idealistic as the rest of the gang, who wanted ratings and profits and didn't have much truck with reporters who tended to vanish at dramatic moments, he energized things in a way that worked well, and lasted a good long time.

JURGENS: Morgan Edge, hands down.

ORDWAY: Without a doubt, I think it was Morgan Edge. I really wish Kirby had done a final Morgan Edge/Darkseid story, though.

THOMAS: I liked the updating of the Newsboy Legion in *Jimmy Olsen*, mostly because it brought in the Guardian.

WAID: Tough one. I was never a huge fan of that stuff—my failing, not Kirby's—and am tempted to say "Flippa Dippa" just to get those words into this book somewhere.

KESEL: Clearly, the DNA Project has become an important part of Superman lore by this point. Hey—there wouldn't be the new Superboy without it! Thanks, Jack!

MANDEL: I'm not a big Fourth World guy, sorry.

SIMONSON: Project Cadmus and all the stuff that went with it.

ROSS: In a weird way, the cop character he created that would ultimately face off against Kalibak—"Terrible" Turpin—that in itself was an important contribution, mainly because he would eventually be worked into the *Superman* animated series as a parallel for Kirby himself. He was very close to Kirby as a man when Kirby did it, then when he was animated, they treated him as ... Kirby! When he faced off against Darkseid, not Kalibak, in the cartoon and was ultimately taken down, his death became one of the major moments in cartoon history, where he was treated with a glorious funeral—and I don't believe funerals commonly happen on *any* cartoon show.

A two-day Bizarro sequence from *The World's Greatest Super-Heroes* strip, from Mar. 28 and 29, 1984. Written by Paul Kupperberg and drawn by Jose Delbo and Sal Trapani.
TM & © DC Comics. Art courtesy of Heritage Comics.

It was a great moment, because it was an homage to Kirby and his Fourth World mythology. Because Jack Kirby made such a fan of Bruce Timm as a young boy, Bruce took every part of the Fourth World and made it intrinsically important to the Superman mythos, in a way deepening the Superman mythos by connecting it to a very palpable *Star Wars*-like war that would come across the galaxy to his world and his life. And I'm happy to say that my father and I got animated into the funeral sequence of that episode! They also had characters like the out-of-costume Fantastic Four, Orion, Big Barda, and Mr. Miracle—countless characters and professionals.

Kirby had something to contribute to Superman that really isn't appreciated, because nobody got to see it as it really was. His way of drawing Superman was great—there was no reason to fix it! But back then DC was stuck in "There's only one way of drawing something—it's got to be on model."

STERN: I have to go with Inspector Turpin. You can never have too many tough, crusty cops in Metropolis. That's why "Terrible" Turpin became a recurring supporting character in the Superman books over the past 20 years.

BOGDANOVE: The Weisinger era, pre-Kirby *Jimmy Olsen*s are arguably the weirdest comics of the Silver Age. At the time, I found them nearly unreadable. It was years before I developed an adult sensitivity toward their thematic subtexts of gender dysphoria and psycho-sexual fetishism. Although I can appreciate the subversiveness of those comics now—in their cultural context of repression, censorship, and denial in that era of post-Wertham Comics Code-approved sterility—I was not a fan of *Jimmy Olsen* comics at the time.

Kirby changed all that. He instantly restored Superman to the grandeur I sensed in the character when I was five years old and flying around the neighborhood with a towel around my neck.

Goody Rickels meets Don Rickles, by Jack Kirby and Vince Colletta, from *Jimmy Olsen* #141 (Sept. 1971).
TM & © DC Comics.

Bruce

cap.

mark Evanier

Tony Starts

It was not simply that Jack's Superman (even with those pasted-on faces that Carmine insisted on) was the most dynamic and heroic super-hero to cross a page of DC art since the 1940s—or that his stories were so fast-paced, majestic, more mythic in scale than anything DC had ever done—it was simply that his imagination was so incredibly wild and deep and rich.

In Kirby's hands, Metropolis stopped being this safe little cardboard-and-spackle town where nothing really serious or dangerous ever happened. Suddenly it was a real city, a vast stage for super-hero drama. Kirby's depiction had texture and flavor informed by his Lower East Side childhood. Kirby's Metropolis was a broad-shouldered Sandburgian collection of neighborhoods with elevated trains of iron and rivets and underground worlds of conduits and steam. Thanks to Jack, we discovered that Metropolis had slums, and dangerous dark corners—a global corporation with links to organized crime, and Apokolips bought out the *Daily Planet*, ending its age of purity and unchallenged innocence. The greater Metropolitan area had mysterious Wildlands, populated by Hairies, and a Zoomway roamed by the mysterious Mountain of Judgment.

Jack made Metropolis an epic place of biblical scale, a place with endless story potential. He literally opened up Superman's world and made it feel real. By doing so, he raised the stakes for the character, renewing his potential for drama and adventure. It took a while for other writers and artists to catch on, but it could be argued that the end of the Silver Age for Superman happened not with *Superman* #233, but when Kirby took on the Man of Steel in *Jimmy Olsen* comics.

Certainly the exciting, dangerous, high-stakes world that Superman thrives in now has its roots in Jack's revamp of Metropolis.

LOEB: Yep, it all did. Jack did what Jack does. He took the Superman mythos and ran it through his brain and created the Fourth World. I can't explain it, but you can't have any of that without Superman.

MYK-EL: Got a good Julie Schwartz story to share?
BOGDANOVE: Not really, I came aboard a little late for that.
LOEB: Only that I'm tired of people telling me I look like him—and this was when he was very *old* and I was *not*.
GUICE: All the stories I know were shared before, I'm afraid.
STERN: Oh, yeah?

Julie, as you may know, carried a supply of Superman S-emblem pins with him at all times. He always wore one on the lapel of his jacket, and if another gent admired his pin, he would reach into his pocket and present the fellow with an S-pin. But if an attractive young lady admired his pin, Julie would make a big show of removing his own personal pin and insisting that she take it. "Here, let me give you my personal Superman pin." This would invariably charm the young lady, and often win Julie an affectionate kiss on the cheek. Or, if he was seated, atop his bald pate. Of course, once the sweet young thing had departed, Julie would pull another pin out of his pocket and attach it to his lapel. (Lather. Rinse. Repeat.)

Okay, knowing that, we pulled a fast one on Julie at the 1988 Superman Expo in Cleveland, Ohio. Jerry and Mike will remember this. In fact, I think Mike was the one who set it up.

(left and opposite page) Bruce Timm's cameo-packed drawings from the animated Superman's Terrible Turpin funeral. Alex Ross is the bearded, long-haired figure in the top left image, with his father behind him, over his right shoulder.

Julie's birthday coincided with the Expo, and all of the DC folk in attendance got together for a group photo with him. And as the shutters began to click, we all pulled S-pins out of our pockets and started pinning them to his shirt. "Here, let me give you my personal Superman pin!" [*laughs*] Julie didn't know what was going on at first, but he took the gag in good stride. Plus he wound up with an extra dozen or so pins to offer young ladies.

That was also the day my wife Carmela and I discovered that Julie's birthday was the same day as our anniversary. When Julie found out, he was so happy, you'd have thought that he'd introduced us. (By the way, Julie's birthday is also Moe Howard's and Lou Gehrig's birthdays. And they say there's nothing to astrology!)

I miss Julie. He was a true original. You know how you'll hear people say, "If not for him, I wouldn't be here"? Well, if not for people like Julie, "here" wouldn't be here.

ROSS: I had dinner with him once, and he knew who I was and was familiar with my work. Given the fact that my career is relatively recent when compared to most, and how it seems unlikely that I would have crossed paths with some of the greats who formed this medium, that's enough of a Julie Schwartz story for me!

JURGENS: Somewhere during the mid-'80s, Julie asked me to draw a *Justice League* story. Now you must understand that even then, working for Julie was sort of like working for a legend. You didn't want to let him down.

I put so much pressure on myself that even today, I'm not happy with the results, though Julie said he was very happy with it. It was a flashback story to the original seven JLA members that has yet to see print. Probably just as well, too.

But to this day I believe that if I had drawn that same story for any other editor but Julie, I would have done a better job.

THOMAS: My first story for DC that I plotted was the second part of the Superman/Capt. Marvel crossover in *DC [Comics] Presents* ... Gerry Conway had, for legal reasons, plotted the first part from my concept. The second part is the story that, among other things, brought in Hoppy the Marvel Bunny. I did a set-up with the same line being repeated three times by a character ... and the last time, another character says, "You keep saying that." But Julie's assistant Nelson Bridwell took out the second of the two setups, which made it less effective ... so one of the first "discussions" I had with Julie about working for DC was a complaint about bad editing. But I did like both Julie and Nelson.

SIMONSON: My Julie story is not about Superman. During my early years in comics, I drew one Batman story for Julie, a tale by Elliot S! Maggin called "The Cape and Cowl Deathtrap" (*Detective Comics* #450, Aug. 1975). The splash page showed Batman menacing a fat guy in a cave. I drew the Batman with a smile because I thought that was much creepier than a standard frown, the way clowns, in another context, seem really scary. Julie had me change it to a frown. Years later when the story was reprinted by DC in a book of my work, I changed it back to a smile.

I'm still not sure which of us was right. But I liked my way better. Sorry, Julie. ;-)

ORDWAY: Well, at any comics convention where I signed books alongside Julie, he always edited or commented on the covers of my *Superman* comics while I signed them. Comments like "I would have flopped this image" to "We could never get away with this in Weisinger's day" cracked me up. He just never stopped. It was never mean-spirited, and always endearing. I only worked for him on a handful of covers and a *DC [Comics] Presents Annual*, but he seemed like a real taskmaster.

Curt Swan used to marvel at the fact that artists would be treated to lunch by an editor like Mike Carlin, as it never happened in his day. *He* bought the lunch to insure Julie or some other editor would keep him busy.

Legendary editors Julius Schwartz and Archie Goodwin, 1994.

Photo courtesy of Heritage Comics. J.S. collection.

KESEL: I wish I did. Having the opportunity to actually work with Julie was one of the true high points of my entire career, but right now no memorable anecdotes come to mind.

WAID: Without Julie's mentoring and encouragement, I'd probably be working in a loan office somewhere today, or running a super-hero-porn website or something. Julie never, ever lost sight of the fact that he got his start through fandom and was always a fan at heart, so among the DC editors of the '80s, he was often the most willing to give "new kids" like me a break. I'd been interviewing him for the fan press, so he knew who I was—kinda—but I was still a total tyro when I walked sheepishly into his office in October of 1984 and pitched my best idea for a Superman story. I was ready for him to shoot it down, but instead, he ran with it, we knocked ideas back and forth—this, by the way, was like boxing with Hemingway—and I left with the assignment and an immeasurable lift in confidence. Julie gave me what was and always will be the greatest day of my professional life.

Years later, long after he retired as an active editor, we forged another unique bond. Knowing how studious I am about DC's history—not only regarding the characters but the company and its staff and its workings—he'd seek me out whenever he recalled some long-forgotten piece of history or some fresh anecdote about, say, John Broome or Eddie Herron, and the delight of my expression as I listened to him tell it was always reflected in Julie's grin as he did the telling. Like a magician showing off some new trick in front of other magicians, Julie delighted in telling "the kid who knows everything about DC" something he didn't know.

"Jump the shark" is a moment when a character strays from his roots and his series begins to go downhill. The term comes from the *Happy Days* episode where Fonzie, on water skis, jumps over a shark. ("A shark in a *lake*, no less," adds Kurt Busiek.)

Happy Days TM & © Paramount Television. Fonzie figure © 2004 Classic TV Toys.

MANDEL: I tried to introduce myself to Julie and talk about Bizarro Superman. He didn't really listen to a word I said, but he gave me a Julie Schwartz trading card that he signed to me. So that was nice.

CARLIN: I do ... but it just might *be* my "lost" Imaginary Tale! Imagine me having to tie Julie Schwartz's tuxedo tie at the premiere in Cleveland of *Superman IV*! Not a hoax! Not a dream!

BUSIEK: I never did any work for Julie—the closest I came was that two of my sample scripts were given to him, and E. Nelson Bridwell pronounced them both perfectly usable, except for the unfortunate circumstances that one of them was for a Supergirl series they were revamping completely and the other was for a back-up series that had just been canceled. So I wound up pitching Julie a bunch of ideas he didn't like, and then working up another sample script from a plot of his that he handed me, and not impressing him there, either. And it was always good to talk to him at cons, but I was too intimidated ever to pitch him another story.

So I guess the answer is, no, sadly, I don't.

MYK-EL: When did the Earth-One Superman jump the shark and become the character that needed the 1986 reboot?

BYRNE: The day he ceased to be the "*sole* survivor of the doomed planet Krypton."

JURGENS: I don't think he ever did. The reboot wasn't needed, in my opinion. They could have brought John Byrne in to simply energize the books, without the reboot, and been just as effective.

THOMAS: I also don't think he ever needed the 1986 reboot, and while I liked the art on the latter, I hated most of the new concepts: the Kents being alive, Superman's costume being relatively vulnerable, etc.

BUSIEK: I don't think he ever did, either, not in the sense of there being a "jump the shark" moment. I think the series ran out of steam in its last few years, after nice runs on both *Superman* and *Action* by Cary Bates and Marv Wolfman, but I don't know whether it was fading because there was nothing that could be done but reboot it, or whether Julie knew a reboot was coming and was marking time rather than trying to rejuvenate something that was already facing an end.

But I think that in the right creative hands, the Earth-One Superman could have continued just fine. Which isn't to say the reboot wasn't a good plan, just that it wasn't the only one that would have worked.

LOEB: With all due respect to the fine fellows who did the reboot, I do not think it was needed. I thought Walt Simonson's "fix" that the reboot turns out to be all false memories that Jor-El placed in Superman's head from a crystal in the rocket so he would never yearn for his home planet was brilliant. With Walt's permission, that's how we did the Superman "Return to Krypton" storyline. Most successful Superman story I've written (in the monthly).

BOGDANOVE: Superman has jumped *lots* of sharks over the years. The first time was when DC made a conscious effort to redesign him during their legal fight against Siegel and Shuster. They made a deliberate attempt to relaunch the character by commissioning Wayne Boring's thick-waisted reinterpretation of Shuster's original model. It was the beginning of a DC tradition

Superman editors of two worlds, Mike Carlin and Julie Schwartz, 1994.

Photo courtesy of Heritage Comics. J.S. collection.

the periodic "Do-Over," which allows every generation to have its own version of these classic characters, through events like *Infinite Crisis*.

Although many Golden Age fans may feel this domesticated and denatured the character, it also ushered in the first wave of the Silver Age (marked by the first time DC rebooted its characters) and all the charming zaniness that entailed. It could be argued that the entire Silver Age, where Superman is concerned, was one big, fun shark-jump-fest, but by the mid-'80s that kind of thing had long been played out. I'm very fond of the Curt Swan/Julius Schwartz era, but in my opinion, John Byrne and Mike Carlin saved Superman.

GUICE: The early '80s were it for me. The character was crumbling under the massive weight of his own history by that point.

WAID: The series needed some sort of shot in the arm after about 1982 because, according to Julie, that's when the edict came down from his bosses to keep the stories simple and "kid-friendly" and to stop worrying about capturing older readers. But the character? C'mon, you know the answer to that as well as I do—there's nothing wrong with any character that the right writer can't fix. Ask Alan Moore if Superman ever "jumped the shark."

STERN: I don't know if he did. Of course, between 1980 and 1986, I'd mostly lost track of what was happening with Superman ... except maybe for an occasional issue of *DC Comics Presents*.

Besides, it was the Crisis on Infinite Earths event that led to all the myriad reboots. I wasn't there at the time, but from what I've read or been told, the original plan was for all of the books to start over at the end of *Crisis*. And when that didn't happen, the characters were rebooted in sort of a piecemeal fashion, starting with Superman.

CARLIN: My vote would be for just *after* Denny O'Neil's run for Julie.

ORDWAY: If you look at the covers on *Superman* through the '60s, they might as well be from the 1950s to me. Compared to Marvel, they look pretty dated. When Kirby hit DC in 1970, Superman got a boost, and there were some decent stories there. In the late '70s, I think they could have capitalized on José Luis García-López more, and moved Curt to another title to energize him as well. García-López was the great hope, to me as a fan of the right age then, looking for something like what I saw in the *Superman* film. I love Curt's work, but he was so identified as *the* Superman artist of the '50s and '60s, it's hard not to take him for granted.

Probably the great strength was Julie Schwartz, but he was also the problem as well, because he was loyal to his guys. But really, if things hadn't gone along that way, there would not have been the drastic, yet good, changes Byrne's *Man of Steel* brought to Superman.

ROSS: Without picking too much on the newscaster phase from the 1970s, they probably should have done a more dramatic reworking at least by 1980. The fact that they were still just running forward with the same teams showed a homogeny that just wasn't fitting with the times. This is why Marv Wolfman and George Pérez's work on *The New Teen Titans* was so dramatic— it was a bold step forward for a company that often did play it too safe. There were also some bold things happening at Marvel. Boundaries were being pushed elsewhere, but with Superman, such a high-profile vehicle, they waited until pretty much the rest of comicdom shamed them into change. [*Man of Steel*] followed *Crisis*, which was a very strong plan for the company, but that type of creative direction could have been given far earlier.

I think that when Neal Adams did his magnificent *Superman vs. Muhammad Ali* book, *that* was the time to change everything. They should have thrown a lot of money at

Neal at the time, when the *Superman* movie was coming out, and said, "Neal, you're the guy. Give us one year on *Superman*. Quadruple our sales."

SIMONSON: When fans became obsessed enough with "continuity" that it was no longer possible to tell a good story in comics that didn't acknowledge a character's entire history, instead of just ignoring the bad parts and moving on. That would have been about the early/mid-'80s.

KESEL: No idea when the Super-books really took a wrong turn, but they were clearly, completely lost by the issue of *Action* (issue #454, Dec. 1975) where, on the cover, Superman is shoveling a huge platter of fast-food burgers into his mouth at super-speed. What were they thinking?!? That was public-access-TV bad. No—it was worse.

MANDEL: Personally, I hated, hated, *hated* when Clark went to work for a TV news station. That was the beginning of the end of for me. Also in the late '70s, early '80s, there was another super-guy [Vartox] hanging with Superman. He had a secret identity, too, but a weird porn mustache and chest hair. That needed rebooting, too.

MYK-EL: Question for John Byrne (you've been asked this before, but it's a topic worth revisiting): Using the "super-power" of hindsight, 20 years after *Man of Steel*, what, if anything, should you have done differently?

STERN: Besides getting more promises in writing! [*grins*]

BYRNE: I would have kept Superboy as part of the mythos. When I first came aboard, my understanding was that I would be allowed to work with a Superman who was "new at the job" and still learning his way. Then, when the contracts were signed, DC basically pulled the rug out from under me and said "No, that can only be in *Man of Steel*. By the first issue of *Superman* he has to be totally up to speed." So, if my time machine was working, I would go back and insist that the third title be *Superboy*, so I could have that still-learning-the-ropes version to play with.

MYK-EL: And one for Mike Carlin: Did the semi-retired "goodwill ambassador" Julie Schwartz ever offer his editorial input to you after you took over the Superman titles?

TM & © DC Comics.

Karl Kesel (modeling his Super-jacket) wrote and drew "The Secrets of the Cadmus DNA Project" for *Secret Origins* #49 (June 1990), edited by Mark Waid.

Photo courtesy of Karl Kesel.　　TM & © DC Comics.

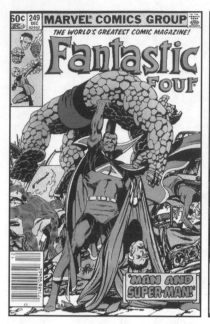

John Byrne cover déjà vu: Gladiator, Marvel's super-strong member of the Imperial Guard, from *Fantastic Four #249* (Dec. 1982), and the Man of Steel aping his cover pose, with Legionnaire FF surrogates, from *Superman* vol. 2 #8 (Aug. 1987).

CARLIN: Only to suggest that every single cover I'd commission would look better flopped (reversed)!

No. I'd *ask* Julie to read our work and comment ... but, to his credit, he wouldn't do it. One of the best things I learned from him, I think: For your own sake as well as the folks who take over after you ... let your "children" go!

MYK-EL: Superman went from Boy Scout to father figure in the Silver Age, then became a "friend" thanks to Christopher Reeve. How would you describe Superman today?

LOEB: The same. It's just how you play him. I wish he wasn't married. It's enormously restricting since the best comic-book stories are the melodrama of the human experience, and when love is limited to one person (in fiction) there's only so many corners you can paint the character into.

CARLIN: A cool guy to have on yer team.

BYRNE: Conflicted whiner. Basically a caricature of the way he was portrayed in the second Christopher Reeve movie.

SIMONSON: How about as "an old married guy"? ;-)

WAID: Way too blessed.

THOMAS: Haven't read a Superman story in years ... and I'll certainly never accept Luthor as anything but an evil scientist.

ROSS: That one stumps me. I recently ran into a young girl fan from whom I was buying some Superman merchandise for my wife, and she said, "You know, I really find that Superman is kinda arrogant these days!" And that struck me as being a real opinion from someone who had no idea who I was, and wasn't filtering anything for my benefit, and that right now there's something to be regained by Superman. The way that Superman is today is still yet to be defined.

The Superman that has most been seen during the past five years is the one from the romantic TV show, the entertaining *Smallville* drama. So beyond that, what the [*Superman Returns*] film may bring to us, and what the comics may do, is still yet to be seen. But Superman often falls back into the mold of being not so much the father figure, but instead your father's Oldsmobile, a character that a lot of old-fart collectors like. But for the brash young folks I think it all comes down to the delivery: the writing, the art, the message of those

who create it, and often, there's not much liberty given to those who work on the book.

GUICE: Pre-"One Year Later" relaunch ... as the guy dating your sister. He's around your house all the time pretending he's really cool, but in reality he needs a bath and a job.

After the latest relaunch ... well, I've got my fingers crossed on that one.

BUSIEK: A fighter. It's a rougher, more troubled world in a lot of ways, and that sense of security, that all Superman needed to do was maintain the status quo against outside threats, just doesn't seem like enough anymore. Superman needs some of that original, scrappy, Siegel-and-Shuster spirit, as the guy who'll take on entrenched power in the name of the little guy, and win through.

He's still a friend, but in a shakier world, you need a friend who'll dig in a little more, who'll help fix what needs fixing. That's Superman—and that's Clark, too, with the *Daily Planet* behind him. Clark reminds us that the world is what we make of it, and Superman helps make sure we have the chance to try.

KESEL: My current take on Superman—and, admittedly, it's just mine—goes back to Siegel and Shuster's original intent, in some ways, of Superman as a wish-fulfillment character. It's just that my wish is for Superman to lead by example, to think before he acts, to fix his mistakes, and to take full responsibility for his actions. I think that's what anyone who's the world's greatest super-power should do. But of course, that's just a fantasy.

JURGENS: I think Superman is still something of a father figure and always will be because of his stature within the industry. You can't escape it.

ORDWAY: I almost hate to say this, but he seems like too much of a "victim" these days. I am not sure any one creator has left a strong mark on the character in a long time. When the Byrne revamp happened, it also offered a great opportunity for the relaunched books to scream out to the fans, "Look at me, look at me!" In this day of every storyline having to be "important" it's hard to get noticed, I suppose, even if you are doing good work, what with all the other titles getting more attention.

STERN: Let's back up there a minute. Feel free to correct me on this, but I don't ever recall Superman being depicted in the comics as a "Boy Scout." That is one of those "truthiness" descriptions ... like writers talking about Spider-Man suffering from acne—which he never did. Or people remembering "when comics cost only a nickel"—which, aside from *Nickel Comics*, they never did. "Father figure," I might grant you. But I always saw Superman as more of a cool uncle or big brother figure ... a big brother in a good way, not in a "Big Brother is watching you" way.

I'm not sure how I'd describe the Superman of the current comics, since he and his entire universe again seem to be in a state of flux. But I can tell you how *I* see him...

Superman is the hero that we wish we could be, especially when the going gets rough. You know, like when a space shuttle has a hole in its wing, we wish that we could just take a deep breath and fly up to the rescue. Or when sailors are trapped in a submarine on the ocean floor, we wish that we could dive down there and bring them safely to the surface. And since we're not Superman—since we're not faster than a speeding bullet and more powerful than a locomotive—we wish that there was a hero like him to be there by our side.

Because, just like Boston Blackie, Superman is a "friend to those who have no friends, and an enemy only to those who would make him an enemy." And he doesn't spend half his life wondering if he's doing the right thing; he's too busy, *doing* the right thing.

BOGDANOVE: Certainly Superman has become a national icon. All you need to do is visit the Midwest, especially Metropolis, Illinois, to experience the nearly religious nature of people's love for him. I perceive that the vast numbers of

DOUBLE PAGE SPREAD: CUT AS SHOWN, ABUT PAGE EDGES, TAPE ON BACK, DO NOT OVERLAP   CUT LEFT HAND PAGE AT THIS LINE →

John Byrne pencils, from *Action* #828 (Aug. 2005), written by Gail Simone.

Americans he ranks somewhere between Elvis and Jesus. Many people overlay biblical parallels on Superman, drawing out the similarities in his story with the stories of Moses and Jesus. Much has also been written about Superman as an expression of our idealized national character.

Clearly Superman resonates deeply through our culture—at least the idea of him does. Yet, only a fraction of Americans read his comics. Why?

It may be that the weight of being an American icon is too big a burden for the character. For most writers or artists, it may be too difficult to write or draw stories, or versions of the character, that consistently fulfill everyone's heartfelt vision.

Superman means so much to so many people that it is a rare comic that can satisfy them all. There are so many expectations and so much baggage, the status quo of the classic myth is too sacred to challenge.

But drama requires challenging the status quo, even if it is ultimately restored. It's hard to make an interesting story that won't violate someone's idea of what Superman should be. Similarly, it's difficult and challenging, if not impossible, to draw a personal interpretation of Superman that won't completely miss the mark for some fans.

For me, as an artist, this challenge is part of the fun. On *Man of Steel* I struggled for years to find an interpretation of Superman that fulfilled my own heartfelt vision. I was never terribly satisfied with it, and neither were many fans. My struggling seems obvious to me when I look back at much of my work—but I also came pretty close sometimes, and I always drew authentically, from the heart, with passion, love, and respect. I think the fans who liked my work, liked it because of that. Clearly they were highly perceptive people.

My quest continues long after I left the book. For several years now, the folks in DC's Licensing Department have turned to me for vintage style guide art. I have developed a high degree of skill at imitating old guys—artists from DC's Golden, Silver, and Bronze Ages. I've learned well how to distinguish and identify the characteristic style elements of numerous uncredited artists of the past (thanks, in Superman's case, to the education and erudition of Rich Morrissey, who was an extraordinary fan and scholar), and I have developed the ability to create original work that amalgamates any combination of artists and styles from any period of DC history. It's been fun, challenging, and enormously educational work.

It has also guided me toward a better contemporary interpretation of the character. This year, I've graduated into doing more contemporary work, drawing 2006 style guide art for Superman and JLA characters. Each project requires a different modern style and approach to fill the needs of various clients and licensees—but all this work has one thing in common: It must represent DC's characters, including Superman, to the general, non-comics-reading populace—that larger audience of people for whom Superman is a national icon.

I've come to learn that DC Licensing carries the burden of Superman's iconic nature even more than Editorial does. They have no story to carry them, only individual, all-inclusive illustrations. Their character art must be able to stand alone and stand out in any theme park or on any lunch box. Every picture of Superman I draw for them must not only be instantly identifiable, but universally identified with. Regardless of style, I must draw a quintessential Superman—one that satisfies the maximum number of personal heartfelt versions out there. That means incorporating and amalgamating trace elements from the Golden and Silver Ages, with bits from current Superman artists, plus the influences of George Reeves, Chris Reeve—Tom Welling and even Brandon Routh. It is a tall order, but I like it. I like being able to put my all into a single image, and I love the challenge of somehow distilling the ultimate, inclusive version of Superman for this moment in history.

MANDEL: Based on the images I have seen from the new movie—very well endowed.

MYK-EL: If you had written the Earth-One Superman's last adventure instead of Alan Moore (the Imaginary Tale "Whatever Happened to the Man of Tomorrow?" in *Superman* #423 and *Action* #583, Sept. 1986), how would you have concluded Superman's story?

THOMAS: Didn't read it.

JURGENS: There's no way I can adequately answer that question.

LOEB: Follow Alan? C'mon! *Pass!* [*laughs*]

MANDEL: Poorly. Alan Moore said it all.

WAID: That's like asking me, "If you'd written *Citizen Kane*, what would you have done differently?" Alan did it perfectly.

SIMONE: Or like asking, "If you were commissioned to paint the Mona Lisa, how would you have improved it?" Moore's story is one of my favorites, and I can't imagine doing it as well.

KESEL: I can tell you how I would have concluded it: *badly.* Alan Moore's story is fantastic. How did he put it? "This is an Imaginary Story ... but then, aren't they all?" Brilliant! And that's how he *starts* the story, that's how most people would *end* theirs! An amazing work.

Superman's pal Bibbo in Metropolis' Suicide Slum, illustrated by Jackson Guice for Universal Forces' 1998 *DC OverPower Expansion Tradingcard set*

"Turnaround" models for a Golden Age Superman sculpture, drawn by Jon Bogdanove in a Shuster-esque style.
TM & © DC Comics. Art courtesy of Jon and Judy Bogdanove.

ROSS: I kind of *have* put my own version of the last great Superman adventure out there. That's what I started out with, with *Kingdom Come*. I read Alan's story years after it was originally published, and I appreciated it, but it doesn't have emotional resonance with me. What's more important is that it was the instrument that existed for Curt Swan to draw, so that after so many years of patronage he could get a chance to do that last story as *his* last story—but, for me, not the one, true, end-all/be-all way to end that drama.

CARLIN: Not sure. Alan did it right. I would definitely have gone for the "wink" at the end, as well!

The *Marvels* team of painter Alex Ross and writer Kurt Busiek.
Photo courtesy of Alex Ross.　　　　Photo courtesy of Kurt Busiek.

GUICE: Pretty much like the tale Superman stumbles into in *Action* #696 (Feb. 1994).

ORDWAY: I would have done something more akin to what we all did on our "Death of Superman" storyline, having him make the ultimate sacrifice for humanity, by saving the galaxy from an entity like Galactus or something. Something where his legend would live on, and what he fought for.

BUSIEK: I think *Superman* is essentially a positive, upbeat series, so I'd have him win big. Alan did a sterling Weisinger tribute, with a pageant of little-seen characters, [but] I'm not sure the right "farewell" moment for Superman is to break his oath and retire, under the pressure of a villainous onslaught he can't stop. I'd have Superman under great pressure, but I'd have him

TM & © DC Comics.

win through—I'd have him in a world where he's reformed Lex, where he's inspired Brainiac to do good things, rather than bad. I'd have him aging, losing his strength, but able to look back on a world where he took on everything and won out. And now a new wave of danger and evil is coming, and he's not young anymore, and may not be up to it, but he'll try his best—and that's when we see that a grown-up Supergirl, a Kandorian hero squad, Superman's children with Lois, Luthor's son, Brainiac 2 maybe—that a new generation of heroes, inspired by Superman, will pick up the baton and take on the Never-Ending Battle. Superman can have his golden years—perhaps watching humanity blossom, perhaps exploring new frontiers with Lois, but knowing that what he began continues through his legacy, that it doesn't end with him.

Now, I'm willing to bet Alan's would still be better received—particularly since I'd have been too intimidated to even pitch that to Julie—but that's what I see as a fitting ending. Passing the torch to those he taught, so his mission continues forever.

STERN: I wouldn't have. I don't think Superman's story should ever end.

Plus, I couldn't buy into a key plot element of that story, that Superman is forced to kill his greatest enemy, then gives up his powers because he broke his oath against killing. Despite the fact that Julie was the story's editor, it was really much more of a Weisinger Era story. I'm sorry, but "nobody has the right to kill"? Even when I was a kid, I didn't buy that sort of absolutism.

Look, Superman was in the same critical situation as a police sharpshooter facing a mass murderer who has already machine-gunned 20 people and has begun to fire on more—including the sharpshooter himself. A sharpshooter in that predicament doesn't just have the right to use deadly force, he has an *obligation* to do so.

Now, Superman—being Superman—usually has more options than the rest of us, but this particular story was structured in such a way that he didn't. In Alan's story, an essentially all-powerful enemy has already engineered over half-a-dozen deaths that we saw, and cornered Superman and Lois in the Fortress of Solitude, vowing to spend the next 2,000 years wreaking havoc on the world. And he made it very clear that his next victims were going to be Superman and Lois.

That makes what Superman did (in the story) an act of self-defense. And a champion of Truth, Justice, and the American Way would understand that. Of course, Superman would not be happy that he had been forced to end the life of a sentient being. Few people, stuck in that situation, would be. As Clint Eastwood said in *Unforgiven*, "It's a hell of a thing, killing a man..." After everything that Superman had been through in that story—the deaths of several of his closest friends and most dangerous enemies—I could see where he might be tempted to retire and let someone else do the heavy lifting for a change.

But give up his powers? Forever? No. I didn't buy it then, and after writing Superman for over ten years, I buy it even less today.

That story was expertly crafted and beautifully drawn, but it just wasn't about the Superman that Jerry Siegel and Joe Shuster created. Their Superman never gave up.

BOGDANOVE: The story I've always wanted to do along those lines is a look at Superman as he might have lived in the twentieth century, based on Siegel and Shuster's original timeline.

Landing on Earth in the late 1910s, he was in his mid-twenties when WWII broke out. That made him, and Lois, part of the "the Greatest Generation" of 20th-century Americans.

My story would follow him through the rest of the century. Aging much more slowly than his friends and family, what would happen as his generation, his world died away? How would someone like the Golden Age/Silver Age Superman deal with that, and the changing succession of eras around him?

Page 193 from the 1996 graphic novel edition of *Kingdom Come*, by Mark Waid and Alex Ross

The Superman homage *Thor* #280 (Feb. 1978), plotted by Don and Maggie Thompson and scripted by Roy Thomas. Superman's analog Hyperion was featured, and Lex Luthor's counterpart Emil Burbank was introduced. Wayne Boring pencils, Tom Palmer inks.

At this point, I'm only comfortable telling you that I don't think he'd retire to the farm and become a recluse Super-farmer like in *Kingdom Come*—or allow himself to become a fascist government tool, like in *The Dark Knight Returns*. I think he'd bear up under the losses of history and try to keep fighting a truly "Never-Ending Battle."

SIMONSON: I'd probably have killed him off, if only because I have that Norse fatalism/Ragnarok thing going on in my heritage. And I seem to revisit the theme from time to time. On the other hand, maybe I would just have had him retire to Florida.

BYRNE: The best "last episode" I've ever seen, at least in terms of an ongoing series,

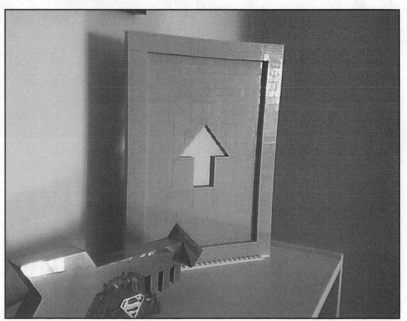

ME LIKE GAIL SIMONE, TOO!

TM & © DC Comics.

was what they did for *Cheers*, which left us knowing that tomorrow was another day. That should be the "last" Superman story, because there is no "last" Superman story.

MYK-EL: Final question: What's your Silver Age Superman guilty pleasure?

SIMONE: I love anything Superbaby. Oh, and I love Insect Queen. If I were in charge, I'd be bringing back that stuff left and right, no doubt to the embarrassment of every decent American comics reader.

GUICE: I own more issues of *Superman's Girl Friend Lois Lane* than I can comfortably justify.

BUSIEK: *Lois Lane* #60 (Oct. 1965), and particularly "The Amazing Hydro-Girl." It's little more than a succession of misogynistic plot setups in which Lois, as punishment for her feckless curiosity, is forced to humiliate herself over and over again, at one point mashing her face into Clark Kent's ink-filled fedora to stave off certain death. And in the end— ha ha!—the answer turns out to be so simple, it embarrasses her all over again. It's a story that's meant to have fun with the idea that Lois is too curious, but what it really shows us is that the universe is out to get Lois, and will arrange itself to put her in humiliating situations. But for all that, it's beautifully drawn, and however mean-spirited it is to modern eyes, it's funny. And that cover (illustrating a different story) is just the best....

THOMAS: I loved the couple of "Herko" stories drawn by Schaffenberger ... and in fact the first one inspired virtually my only letter to Mort Weisinger, which ironically probably contributed a little bit to his offering me a job in 1965. Of course, I liked Herko because he reminded me of a character in *Captain Marvel*.

BYRNE: Krypto. He pretty much sums up everything that went wrong with the mythos, but I love that mutt.

TURTLE-CARLIN: All the (fill-in-the-blanks) Olsens!

LOEB: All that lovely kryptonite. Especially gold. Always wondered how he knew that it would take away his powers forever if he never did it.

ORDWAY: Well, I guess it would be the 80-Page Giants. I love the assortments of stories, whether they were wacky, or downright stupid.

MANDEL: I loved when Superman would shrink down into Kandor. Just great and pointless.

KESEL: Oh, there are *so many* to choose from! As a concept, I just love that the Silver Age Superman obviously had crime so completely under control that he could focus most of his attention and abilities on tricking his friends and teaching

them "lessons." (Which, let's face it, is probably the way a person with super-powers would *actually* act, much more so than most of the grim-and-gritty stuff passed off as "realistic" today.) A specific guilty pleasure is "The Super-Cigars of Perry White" (*Action* #436, June 1974)—a story which is wrong on so many levels (Perry gets super-powers from SMOKING!), but that's what makes it great.

JURGENS: Kryptonite in all its forms. Man, the stories virtually write themselves at that point!

BOGDANOVE: Trying to imagine how Clark and Lori Lemaris had sex in college.

SIMONSON: Don't have one. I was kid when the Silver Age began (assuming the relaunch of *Flash* as the starting point) and as a kid, I wasn't embarrassed or guilty about reading comics. I read 'em, I loved 'em, and I didn't distinguish between brilliant and cheesy. I just devoured every comic I could afford and looked around for more.

STERN: You know, I don't have a single one. I've gotten a lot of pleasure out of reading about Superman over the years, and I don't feel at all guilty about any of it.

ROSS: I asked my wife this question and, to quote her, "I feel no guilt. I have nothing to feel guilty about." There's no part of the Superman iconography, the idea of the entertainment value of the character, or any inspiration he may hold, there's no single part of it that should be seen as a subversive kind of pastime. I'm on a very quiet mission to defame anyone who should discredit those who love any comic characters, particularly Superman, as being immature or geekish or nerdish, or to even *use* those terms. I have no patience for those who think this is an off-kilter or bizarrely indulgent thing. We've got countless people who embrace celebrities and sports figures to near-godlike worship. The enjoyment of something that is inspirational, and as purely joyful, as the idea of Superman and super-heroes—there's not a single thing to regret there.

WAID: See photo below.

Photo courtesy of Mark Waid.

ALSO FROM TWOMORROWS PUBLISHING

EISNER AWARD WINNER!

JUSTICE LEAGUE COMPANION VOL. 1

A comprehensive examination of the Silver Age JLA by **MICHAEL EURY**. It traces the JLA's development, history, imitators, and early fandom through vintage and all-new interviews with creators, an index of the JLA's 1960-1972 adventures, never-seen artwork, and more! Contributors include **DENNY O'NEIL, MURPHY ANDERSON, JOE GIELLA, MIKE FRIEDRICH, NEAL ADAMS, NICK CARDY, DICK GIORDANO, ALEX ROSS, NICK CARDY, CARMINE INFANTINO,** and others. Plus: An exclusive interview with **STAN LEE,** who answers the question, "Did the JLA really inspire the creation of Marvel's Fantastic Four?" With an all-new cover by **BRUCE TIMM** (TV's Justice League Unlimited)!

(224-page trade paperback) $29 US

HOW TO CREATE COMICS FROM SCRIPT TO PRINT

REDESIGNED and EXPANDED version of the groundbreaking WRITE NOW! #8 / DRAW! #9 crossover! **DANNY FINGEROTH** & **MIKE MANLEY** show step-by-step how to develop a new comic, from script and roughs to pencils, inks, colors, lettering—it even guides you through printing and distribution. & the finished 8-page color comic is included, so you can see their end result! PLUS: over 30 pages of ALL-NEW material, including "full" and "Marvel-style" scripts, a critique of their new character and comic from an editor's point of view, new tips on coloring, new expanded writing lessons, and more!

(108-page trade paperback) $18 US
(120-minute companion DVD) $35 US

STREETWISE
TOP ARTISTS DRAWING STORIES OF THEIR LIVES

An unprecedented assembly of talent drawing NEW autobiographical stories:

• Barry WINDSOR-SMITH • C.C. BECK
• Sergio ARAGONÉS • Walter SIMONSON
• Brent ANDERSON • Nick CARDY
• Roy THOMAS & John SEVERIN
• Paul CHADWICK • Rick VEITCH
• Murphy ANDERSON • Joe KUBERT
• Evan DORKIN • Sam GLANZMAN
• Plus Art SPIEGELMAN, Jack KIRBY, more!
Cover by RUDE • Foreword by EISNER

(160-Page Trade Paperback) $24 US

BEST OF DRAW! VOL. 1

Compiles material from the first two sold-out issues of DRAW!, the "How-To" magazine on comics and cartooning! Tutorials by, and interviews with: **DAVE GIBBONS** (layout and drawing on the computer), **BRET BLEVINS** (drawing lovely women, painting from life, and creating figures that "feel"), **JERRY ORDWAY** (detailing his working methods), **KLAUS JANSON** and **RICARDO VILLAGRAN** (inking techniques), **GENNDY TARTA-KOVSKY** (on animation and Samurai Jack), **STEVE CONLEY** (creating web comics and cartoons), **PHIL HESTER** and **ANDE PARKS** (penciling and inking), and more!

(200-page trade paperback) $26 US

BEST OF DRAW! VOL. 2

Compiles material from issues #3 and #4 of DRAW!, including tutorials by, and interviews with, **ERIK LARSEN** (savage penciling), **DICK GIORDANO** (inking techniques), **BRET BLEVINS** (drawing the figure in action, and figure composition), **KEVIN NOWLAN** (penciling and inking), **MIKE MANLEY** (how-to demo on Web Comics), **DAVE COOPER** (digital coloring tutorial), and more! Cover by **KEVIN NOWLAN!**

(156-page trade paperback) $22 US

TITANS COMPANION

A comprehensive history of the NEW TEEN TITANS, with interviews and rare art by **MARV WOLFMAN, GEORGE PÉREZ, JOSÉ LUIS GARCÍA-LÓPEZ, LEN WEIN,** & others, a Silver Age section with **NEAL ADAMS, NICK CARDY, DICK GIORDANO,** & more, plus **CHRIS CLAREMONT** and **WALTER SIMONSON** on the X-MEN/TEEN TITANS crossover, **TOM GRUMMETT, PHIL JIMENEZ** & **TERRY DODSON** on their '90s Titans work, a new cover by **JIMENEZ,** & intro by **GEOFF JOHNS!** Written by **GLEN CADIGAN**

(224-page trade paperback) $29 US

LEGION COMPANION

• A history of the Legion of Super-Heroes, with **DAVE COCKRUM, MIKE GRELL, JIM STARLIN, JAMES SHERMAN, PAUL LEVITZ, KEITH GIFFEN, STEVE LIGHTLE, MARK WAID, JIM SHOOTER, JIM MOONEY, AL PLASTINO,** and more!
• Rare and never-seen Legion art by the above, plus **GEORGE PÉREZ, NEAL ADAMS, CURT SWAN,** and others!
• Unused Cockrum character designs and pages from an UNUSED STORY!
• New cover by **DAVE COCKRUM** and **JOE RUBINSTEIN,** introduction by **JIM SHOOTER,** and more!

(224-page Trade Paperback) $29 US

BEST OF THE LEGION OUTPOST

Collects the best material from the hard-to-find LEGION OUTPOST fanzine, including rare interviews and articles from creators such as **DAVE COCKRUM, CARY BATES,** and **JIM SHOOTER,** plus never-before-seen artwork by **COCKRUM, MIKE GRELL, JIMMY JANES** and others! It also features a previously unpublished interview with **KEITH GIFFEN** originally intended for the never-published LEGION OUTPOST #11, plus other new material! And it sports a rarely-seen classic 1970s cover by Legion fan favorite artist **DAVE COCKRUM!**

(160-page trade paperback) $22 US

ALL-STAR COMPANION VOL. 1

ROY THOMAS has assembled the most thorough look ever taken at All-Star Comics:

• Covers by **MURPHY ANDERSON!**
• Issue-by-issue coverage of ALL—STAR COMICS #1—57, the original JLA—JSA teamups, & the '70s ALL—STAR REVIVAL!
• Art from an unpublished 1945 JSA story!
• Looks at FOUR "LOST" ALL—STAR issues!
• Rare art by **BURNLEY, DILLIN, KIRBY, INFANTINO, KANE, KUBERT, ORDWAY, ROSS, WOOD** and more!!

(208-page Trade Paperback) $26 US

ART OF GEORGE TUSKA

A comprehensive look at Tuska's personal and professional life, including early work with Eisner-Iger, crime comics of the 1950s, and his tenure with Marvel and DC Comics, as well as independent publishers. The book includes extensive coverage of his work on IRON MAN, X-MEN, HULK, JUSTICE LEAGUE, TEEN TITANS, BATMAN, T.H.U.N.D.E.R. AGENTS, and many more! A gallery of commission artwork and a thorough index of his work are included, plus original artwork, photos, sketches, previously unpublished art, interviews and anecdotes from his peers and fans, plus George's own words!

(128-page trade paperback) $19 US

COMIC BOOK ARTIST COLLECTION, VOL. 3

Reprinting the Eisner Award-winning COMIC BOOK ARTIST #7 and #8 ('70s Marvel and '80s independents), featuring a new **MICHAEL T. GILBERT** cover, plus interviews with **GILBERT, RUDE, GULACY, GERBER, DON SIMPSON, CHAYKIN, SCOTT McCLOUD, BUCKLER, BYRNE, DENIS KITCHEN,** plus a NEW SECTION featuring over 30 pages of previously-unseen stuff! Edited by **JON B. COOKE.**

(224-page trade paperback) $29 US

WALLY WOOD & JACK KIRBY CHECKLISTS

Each lists PUBLISHED COMICS WORK in detail, plus ILLOS, UNPUBLISHED WORK, and more. Filled with rare and unseen art!

(68/100 Pages) $8 US EACH

T.H.U.N.D.E.R. AGENTS COMPANION

The definitive book on **WALLACE WOOD'S** super-team of the 1960s, featuring interviews with Woody and other creators involved in the T-Agents over the years, plus rare and unseen art, including a rare 28-page story drawn by **PAUL GULACY,** UNPUBLISHED STORIES by GULACY, **PARIS CULLINS,** and others, and a **JERRY ORDWAY** cover. Edited by CBA's **JON B. COOKE.**

(192-page trade paperback) $29 US

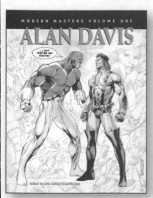

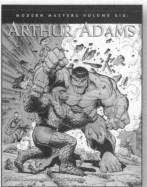

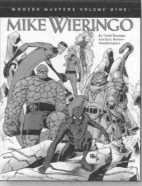

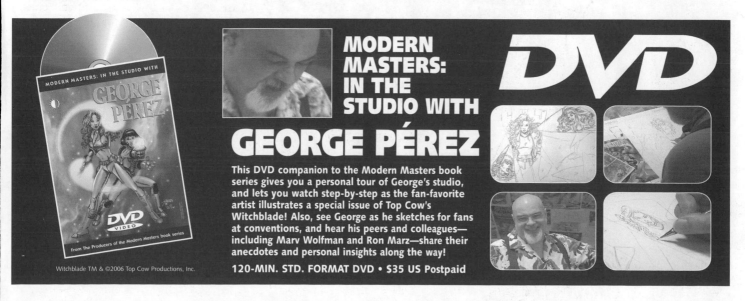

INTRODUCTION

Goodbye and welcome to *Krypton Companion*, a book all about Wonder Woman and her homeland Paradise Island. Everything you ever want to know about Wonder Woman am in this book. Why she so short and ugly? Why she always wear thick, unflattering sweaters? Why her airplane am painted bright orange and so easy to see? If you have question about Wonder Woman, just turn to front page of book and check the index. The answer am in here.

Bizarro very happy to write introduction for *Krypton Companion* because Superman himself ask Bizarro to write it. Him ask Bizarro when Bizarro kidnap Lois Lane by locking himself in trunk of her car. But that other story. Anyway, Bizarro say Superman why not write introduction yourself. You writer Clark Kent. Superman say Clark Kent am secret identity. It am big secret. Shhhhh! Bizarro tell everybody.

Everyone on Bizarro World, from man whose job is putting dog poop on streets all the way up to Bizarro President Al Gore, know that introduction is most important part of book. This book no make sense if not read this introduction first. It like watching *Star Wars* and no watch *Phantom Menace*. Must watch *Phantom Menace* first. *Phantom Menace* am favorite movie of Bizarro and bestest *Star Wars* movie ever. Bizarro say George Lucas am genius. Bizarro cannot wait for *Star Wars* TV show. It will be best *Star Wars* ever. *Indiana Jones 4* also really good idea.

You should know, this am not Bizarro's first introduction. Bizarro famous for his introductions. Him do it many, many times and everyone enjoy them. The first introduction Bizarro write am for *Presumed Innocent* by Scott Turow. Bizarro tell everyone in introduction that wife did it. Then Bizarro write introduction for *The Firm* by John Grisham. Bizarro tell people that firm evil. Last year Bizarro write introduction for *The Da Vinci Code*. Bizarro say very overrated and somewhat predictable, the novel plays fast and loose with historical facts and indulges in pedestrian Templar Knight conspiracies. Also girl am related to Jesus and cripple guy am evil.

Well, at this point, you probably want to start read *Krypton Companion*—although some of you may be listening to Bizarro read the book on 8-track tape. There am three final important facts Bizarro tell you about Krypton:

1. It am lovely place.
2. It never blow up.
7. Pieces of planet am favorite thing for Bizarro to give Superman for birthday gift.

Me hope you enjoy this book so much you steal it from library or sell it to Barnes and Noble. Bizarro also ask you not to support local comic shops—they have too much money and too many hot girls are always there buying comics. This am end of introduction. So welcome to introduction.

Hello,

BiZArro No. 1

June 32, 2006

Bizarro No. 1 am not author of The Catcher Not in the Rye, The Young Man and the Desert, *and* The Hunt for Blue October. *Him live on Bizarro World with wife Jimmy* ⬛⬛⬛⬛ *⬛⬛⬛⬛⬛ ⬛⬛⬛⬛⬛⬛ ⬛⬛ ⬛⬛⬛⬛ ⬛⬛ ⬛⬛ ⬛⬛ ⬛⬛⬛⬛⬛ ⬛⬛ ⬛⬛* Bizarro World.

(David Mandel no am write this. He also no am writer/director of *Eurotrip*, which won ten Oscars and made $100 gazillion dollars on Bizarro World.)